THE *Superego*

Books by Dr. Edmund Bergler

MONEY AND EMOTIONAL CONFLICTS

NEUROTIC COUNTERFEIT-SEX

THE WRITER AND PSYCHOANALYSIS

THE BASIC NEUROSIS

THE BATTLE OF THE CONSCIENCE

CONFLICT IN MARRIAGE

DIVORCE WON'T HELP

UNHAPPY MARRIAGE AND DIVORCE

PSYCHIC IMPOTENCE IN MEN

FRIGIDITY IN WOMEN
(in collaboration with E. Hitschmann)

TALLEYRAND-NAPOLEON-STENDHAL-GRABBE

THE # *Superego*

UNCONSCIOUS CONSCIENCE—The Key to

The Theory and Therapy of Neurosis

EDMUND BERGLER, M.D.

Every man is a suffering-machine and happiness-machine combined. . . . Sometimes a man's makeup and disposition are such that his misery-machine *is able to do nearly all the business.*
—Mark Twain

THE MYSTERIOUS STRANGER

GRUNE & STRATTON • NEW YORK • 1952

Library of Congress Card Number 52-12974

Printed and Bound in the U.S.A. (E-B)

Contents

When fiction rises pleasing to the eye,
Men will believe, because they love the lie;
But truth herself, if clouded with a frown
Must have some solemn proofs to pass her down.

—Charles Churchill
EPISTLE TO WILLIAM HOGARTH, 1763

Truly, people have finally come so far that everything
which the human mind is capable of distorting and lying
about now seems more plausible to them than truth
herself. This is so all over the world. For centuries people
have had truth lying on the table in front of them; still
they do not reach for her, but instead pursue things of
the imagination, because they consider that truth is but
a Utopian fantasy.

—F. M. Dostojewski
SOMETHING ABOUT LYING, 1873

The average person avoids the truth as diligently as he
avoids arson, regicide, or piracy on the high seas, and for the
same reason: because he believes that it is dangerous,
that no good can come of it, that it doesn't pay.

—H. L. Mencken

Foreword

IT IS MY CONTENTION THAT UNCONSCIOUS CONSCIENCE, ALTHOUGH the key to the theory and therapy of neurosis, has been grossly underestimated. To name mitigating circumstances: Conscience is a *scientific* newcomer. The popular connotation is of course age-old; it refers exclusively to a set of conscious, conventional and necessary precepts of right and wrong, specific for specific societies. *Unconscious* conscience, the *hidden but real master of the personality*, is, on the other hand, almost entirely unknown. The language does not even possess a word for it; Freud supplied the lack with the introduction of the term "superego."

The failure to differentiate between *conscious* and *unconscious* conscience not infrequently leads to a rather grotesque quid-pro-quo. Naive people, unfamiliar with the *torture principle of unconscious conscience,* are rather pleased to learn from psychoanalytically oriented psychiatrists of the existence of such an inner department. "The more conscience, the better," they claim. They mistake this inner department for a puritanical extension and reinforcement of the "long arm" of conscious conscience. Nothing of the kind. The conscious concept and the unconscious master are similar *only to the extent that they have a common claim on a badly-fitting name.*

The first steps in the study of unconscious conscience could be taken only after Freud discovered the *dynamic* unconscious, thus lifting the cloud of philosophical mysticism which had previously obscured it. His discovery transformed the unconscious into a clinically provable, dynamically effective, therapeutically accessible fact. Nevertheless, for decades afterwards psychoanalysis was focused on only one sector of the inner personality—the sector containing repressed wishes. It was only in his later years that Freud himself approached the problem of inner conscience. Few of his followers contributed substantially to these studies. Reluctance, caused perhaps by the perplexity and complexity of the problem, seemed the common denominator.

This reluctance may be observed both in investigators and spectators. Sometimes it is emotionally conditioned. It is a typical emotional reaction to shy away from unconsoling facts, which is the reason most people prefer to ignore the established and highly uncomfortable fact that *every human being harbors his worst enemy—an ogre self-created, to boot—within himself.* To get an approximate idea of the "benevolence" of inner conscience, one has only to imagine the terms of the relationship between a dictator—any dictator!—and an inmate of one of his concentration and extermination camps.

Freudian psychoanalysis began with the discovery of one specific sector of one specific part of the unconscious—libidinous id-wishes. After three decades came the discovery of the other sector of the id— repressed aggressive wishes. Still later, Freud assumed the interaction of life and death instincts as the basis, thus progressing to a quantitative variable fusion of derivatives of instincts in all human actions.

The earliest pre-stage of what later became known as the superego was the "censor," first mentioned by Freud in *The Interpretation of Dreams* (1899). Later, that part of the tripartite division of the unconscious grew in importance; it became the successor of the child's shattered Oedipus complex. A succession of statements by Freud show how he gradually became aware of the cruelty and irrationality of unconscious conscience. This is one of the most succinct of these statements:

The superego seems to have made a one-sided selection, to have chosen only the harshness and severity of the parents, their preventive and punitive function, while their loving care is not taken up and continued by it. *(New Introductory Lectures on Psychoanalysis,* pp. 89–90, 1932)

And in his work, *Civilization and Its Discontents,* Freud definitely assumed that undischarged infantile aggression accumulates in the superego:

What methods does culture use to inhibit counteracting aggression, to neutralize the latter, or even to exclude it? . . . . This can be studied in the development of the individual. What is done in order to render his lust for aggression harmless? The method is very strange, and at the same time very obvious, although we did not guess it. *The aggression becomes introjected, internalized;* finally it is returned to its place of origin, hence *directed against the individual's own ego.* There it is absorbed by one particular sector of the ego, the superego, which is counterposed to the other parts of the ego. Now, *"conscience" exhibits towards the ego that identical severe readiness to aggression which the ego would have liked to expend on an outside individual.* We call this tension between the severe superego and the subjugated ego "feeling of guilt;" it manifests itself in the need for punishment. (p. 100, German edition, my italics)

Once one accepts the fact that aggression recoils against the ego, accumulating in the superego, another inescapable result must be added: the long maturation period of the human child renders his aggression inexpressible; since it is inexpressible, it must turn against the child's ego, for drives are like rivers—if the flow in all directions forward is impeded, the river must reverse its flow. Thus, every child starts life with a negative balance, with the dice heavily loaded *against* his chances at the "happiness-machine," heavily loaded *in favor of* the "misery-machine." (Mark Twain) Inner conscience, the beneficiary of this rebounding aggression, does not ask, as the ancient gods did, for human sacrifice; as substitutes it modestly accepts "conscience money" and human suffering.

The creator of psychoanalysis, despite the statements quoted above, never undertook to correlate his newer findings on the dualism of life and death instincts with the genesis of the superego, although a few rather aphoristic approaches were attempted. Nor was there any clarification of the relationship between the early discovery, the ego ideal, and the subsequently discovered superego.

This was done nearly two decades ago in two joint studies by Dr. Ludwig Jekels (Freud's oldest living pupil and one of the most distinguished of the old guard) and myself. Our first lecture, *Transference and Love,** was read before the Vienna Psychoanalytic Society on November 8, 1933; our second, *Instinct Dualism in Dreams,†* was presented at the XIII International Psychoanalytical Convention in Lucerne, August, 1934. Later, these ideas were enlarged in my book, *The Battle of the Conscience* (1948).‡

The purpose of the present volume is not to repeat what has already been tangentially stated in *The Battle of the Conscience.* The two books deal with identical topics, but from different clinical and theoretical aspects, and each can be read independently

---

* Published in *Imago*, 20:5–31, 1934, and *The Psychoanalytic Quarterly*, 8:325–350, 1949.

† Published in *Imago*, 20:383–392, 1934, and *The Psychoanalytic Quarterly*, 9:394–414, 1940.

‡ Washington Institute of Medicine.

of the other. Some of the topics elaborated in the first volume will be summarized briefly here.

I have again taken up the problem of the superego because I came to the conclusion that any *attempt at a theory and therapy of neurosis is out of focus unless the superego, and the most important defense of the unconscious ego, created to escape the latter's tyranny—the defense of orally based psychic masochism—are put in the center.* Moreover, a series of new clinical facts has come to my attention, and other phenomena, previously described, can now be enlarged, and some misunderstandings of these phenomena clarified.

The extent of the power wielded by the Frankenstein which is the superego is still largely unrealized. Inner conscience is the master of the personality. The unconscious ego, in order to survive, must satisfy inner conscience by creating its *double sentinal of alibis. We live by, and through, these twin alibis. Man's precarious balance, dangling on the shoestring of twin alibis, is constantly endangered. At best, fifty per cent of man's psychic energy is unproductively expended in his attempts to ward off the constant avalanche of torture flowing from the superego. Man's inhumanity to man is equaled only by man's inhumanity to himself.*

EDMUND BERGLER

New York City and Dummerston Center, Vt.
April—November, 1951

I. The Superego's Power and Its Subterfuges

IN A FRIENDLY REVIEW OF MY BOOK, *The Battle of the Conscience*, a well-known professor of psychiatry recently commented: "The formulations of the author are those of orthodox psychoanalysis, *assuming there is any such thing at the present time.*" *

There is no doubt that there *is* such a thing as "orthodox psychoanalysis," even at the present time, provided one distinguishes between *fixed* and *expendable* analytic theories. There are easily visible, it is true, a host of spurious "new directions" on the fringe of psychoanalysis, which are the "new directions" of the psychotherapist who flees from the unconscious to north, south, east and west. One might erroneously conclude from these that Freud's work is now but the raw material for eclectics and simplifiers. Opposed to these pseudo-"moderns" are the "orthodox Freudians," who are ironically characterized by our foes as unable to breathe without consulting Freud's *Collected Works*.

The sober facts are slightly different. Freudian psychoanalysis is still a young science in the developmental stage. No "orthodox" Freudian has ever claimed that ours is a finished and *static* science. On the contrary, there is a dynamism in psychoanalysis which propels its students to search further and further. Freud himself modified his theories time and again in the course of his long scientific life. We, his adherents, are continuing the Freudian tradition in doing likewise. Freud had only contempt for static thinking, which disregards experience and clings to the shibboleth of conservatism.

Still, there is a decisive difference between modifying Freudian concepts, simply because *new facts* come to the fore in clinical work, and throwing basic principles of analysis overboard. It is the difference between necessary progress in science on the one hand, and—conscious or unconscious—masked flight from Freudianism on the other, with each departure flying the flag of pseudo-

---

* Prof. Karl M. Bowman, University of California, in *Quarterly Review of Psychiatry and Neurology*, Vol. 4, No. 3, 1949. Italics are mine.

modernity as it constitutes and proselytizes a new split-off group.

But Freudians themselves are not without guilt. In defending Freudianism, some colleagues have acquired a distaste for everything new. Suspiciously, they watch for possible "heresies" and deviations. Psychoanalysis is a science and not a religion. Freud's *Collected Works* contain the sum total of his ever-expanding experiences; they were never intended as a bible.

It is essential to distinguish between fixed and expendable theories in psychoanalysis if one is to avoid the dangerous dead-end of conservatism in a developing science, and the equal danger of failing to recognize that many of the new findings are tentative. The existence of the dynamic unconscious, for exemple, is obviously a "fixed" analytic theory—fixed, not because Freud said so, but because it has been confirmed by thousands of investigators in the last half-century. The discovery of a new defense mechanism is an "expendable" analytic theory, and will remain so until it is further confirmed by further research.

The same applies to genetic levels. The elaboration of specific personality traits in connection with libidinous-aggressive levels (plus "reformulation" of infantile megalomania, as some believe) is "fixed" theory. When one specific trait, miserliness, for instance, is related to the oral level rather than to the anal level where its place was previously assumed to be, this is "expendable" theory. (The theory is presented in my book, *Money and Emotional Conflicts.* *) The examples could be multiplied.

The Freudian concept of neurosis is *theoretically* characterized by the assumption that infantile repressed and repetitive conflicts constitute the core of the neurotic structure. This conception implies the existence of the dynamic unconscious. Freudian *therapy* is based on analysis of transference and resistance,† making the unconscious conscious in an affective process. The technique uses free associations, "working through," dream interpretation, and the mechanism of linking ostensible "reality" conflicts to the unconscious pattern built up in childhood. Thus, theory and practice

---

* Doubleday & Co., New York, 1951.

† Analysis of transference and resistance are the pillars of analytic therapy, not the "analytic couch" and the analytic easy chair. The couch does not make a neurotic an *analytic* patient, nor does the easy chair, inhabited by a mute listener, make an *analyst*. Some people never understand that distinction.

are interwoven, and the one is meaningless without the other. Moreover, as Freud pointed out, any separation of the two is dangerous fallacy, for without the guiding post of *clinical* experience, theory becomes mere speculation.

Psychoanalysis began and has continued as an empirical science. With empirical facts as the foundation, theories have been constructed. As new facts were uncovered, theories were necessarily modified. Since empirical-clinical facts are the substructure of analytic science, and theories the superstructure, changes in the former have led to changes in the latter. All of this required a certain amount of mental elasticity; at every new turn, scoffed at "innovators" have had to contend with the complacent attitude, "My learning days are over." The first half-century of analysis was not static; let us hope that the future will live up to the past and sterile conservatism will be avoided.

Concentrating on the specific problem of the superego, it is not difficult to detect the reason explaining the scientific obscurity of this department of the personality. An analogy is at hand in the form of a comparison with the history of the discovery of bacilli, bacteria, viruses. These minute malefactors took their toll of humanity for millions of years during which their presence was not so much as suspected. It was only three generations ago that scientific research inaugurated the difficult and complicated task of elucidating their problem.

Research on unconscious conscience is now in the stage entered upon three generations ago by the pathologists and histologists who explored the problem of bacillae. It is just beginning. Following Freud, a few scientists have approached the problem; results of their research, so far, are contradictory.*

Nobody questions the need of restrictions on conduct guaranteeing conformity with cultural yardsticks. These restrictions are communicated to the child and later embedded via identification in *conscious conscience* as well. This is Webster's definition of conscience:

* There is no necessity to repeat for psychiatric and psychoanalytic readers the well-known and important results of investigations on inner conscience, conducted by the English school around Ernest Jones and Melanie Klein, and the no less impressive earlier studies of Theodor Reik (*Gestaendniszwang und Strafbeduerfnis*), Franz Alexander (*Psychoanalyse der Gesamtpersoenlichkeit*), Karl Menninger (*Man against Himself* and *Love against Hate*), and some other authors.

Sense or consciousness of right or wrong; sense or consciousness of the moral goodness or blameworthiness of one's own conduct, intentions, or character, together with a feeling of obligation to do or be that which is recognized as good;—often with special reference to feelings of guilt or remorse for ill-doing. Hence, a faculty, power, or principle, conceived to decide as to the moral quality of one's own thoughts or acts, enjoining what is good; as the still small voice of *conscience*. (Webster's *New International Dictionary*, ed. 2, p. 567)

The unconscious conscience is quite another matter. *It is torture for torture's sake.* In the bitter-pessimistic book of his old age, *The Mysterious Stranger*, Mark Twain evidently caught a faint inkling of its aims:

Every man is a *suffering-machine* and happiness-machine combined. The two functions work together harmoniously, with a fine and delicate precision, on the give-and-take principle. For every happiness turned out in the one department, the other stands ready to modify it with sorrow or a pain—maybe a dozen. In most cases the man's life is about equally divided between happiness and unhappiness. When this is not the case the unhappiness predominates—always; never the other. Sometimes a man's makeup and disposition are such that his *misery-machine is able to do nearly all the business*. Such a man goes through life almost ignorant of what happiness is. (p. 83, my italics)

The word "machine" is not too happily chosen. Its use proves that the *language of consciousness* is entirely inadequate to express *unconscious* mechanisms, even when handled by a great writer like Mark Twain, who once said: "The difference between the right word and the nearly right word is the difference between lightning and the lightning bug." The unconscious conscience is of course an *impersonal* "department" within the personality. When a writer or scientist falls back, for lack of a more explicit term, on the use of such words as "machine," his usage should not necessarily be taken to imply a "mechanistic" approach to inner facts. Freud, for example, frequently uses the term, "the psychic apparatus." Since creation of an entirely new language—even if possible— would only serve to increase the difficulties of communication, we must make do with what we have.

Looking back at the development of analytic studies in the last two decades, one cannot claim that the study of the superego has become very popular. Analytic thinking, in this period, has been largely directed toward the study of defense mechanisms, and consequently the action of the unconscious ego. Of course, every defense mechanism carries with it the assumption that there has been a superego veto,* for otherwise there would be no reason for the establishment of inner defenses in the first place. Nevertheless, our recent literature is limited mostly to defenses.

The difficulty here relates to the problem of what has become known as *two- versus three-layer structure* in neurotic symptoms, in personality changes, even in normal structure of character in general. The heading, "two-versus three-layer structure" is in itself a simplification; to be precise, one should speak of a "three- versus five-layer structure." This is the basic question: *how many covering defensive layers must be penetrated before aborigines of an unconscious wish can reach the psychic surface, consciousness?* The older, accepted, formulation assumed that an unconscious wish (Layer I), meeting the veto of the superego (Layer II), is cloaked in a defense mechanism (Layer III) which then reaches consciousness with a rationalization. *I believe that an unconscious wish can under no circumstances find so direct a path to the surface, and emerge so thinly veiled.* In my opinion, the procedure begins when the inner wish (Layer I) is warded off by a superego reproach (Layer II), with the result that the unconscious ego institutes a defense (Layer III). So far there is agreement in numbers, though not quite in content. As I see it, this first defense, changing the wish into its opposite, and thus constituting admission of a "lesser crime," is in its turn invariably warded off once more by a *second veto from the superego* (Layer IV), necessitating the creation of a *second defense* by the unconscious ego. Having pleaded guilty to a minor charge, the unconscious ego offers *a denying alibi and accepts punishment for the lesser crime* (Layer V). Only the reverberations of this *second* defense (Layer V) become visible in the neurotic symptom, sign, personality structure.

It should be superfluous to mention that all inner defenses are *dynamic* and *not static*. They wear off after some time because the superego reinstitutes its veto, and have to be reshuffled. The

* The terms "superego veto" and "superego reproach," while grammatically not unimpeachable, can in my opinion be justified both by precedent and practicality. If "id wish" is acceptable, why not "superego reproach"? As for practicality, the advantage of this simplification is self-evident.

impression can arise, therefore, that the person has "changed;" in actuality the only change has been the installation of new defenses under inner pressure. In this procedure, the unconscious ego invariably adheres to the "itinerary of the opposites;" *libido is warded off with pesudo-aggression, pseudo-aggression with libido.*

In my recent books, *The Basic Neurosis* (1949) and *Neurotic Counterfeit-Sex* (1951) * hundreds of examples are given which clinically substantiate the existence, within the unconscious, of the *"defense against the* defense." To settle the question of the *universality* of this mechanism, Chapter V of the present volume is devoted to the analysis of *fifty* human reactions, deliberately chosen at random.

The belief or disbelief in defensively covered "Triebdurchbruch" versus "defense against the defense" is by no means a matter of theoretical hairsplitting. This seemingly small "architectonic" difference of opinion determines the health or perpetual emotional invalidism of the patient.

To take the case of a patient suffering from premature ejaculation as an instance: if we explain his repressed aggression in depriving the woman of pleasure (the aggression connected with unconscious ideas of soiling), and establish the connection with infantile images and resulting guilt, we cannot cure the patient, because his aggression is merely pseudo-aggression covering more deeply repressed masochistic submission. Thus, the orally based masochistic wish *to be refused* is the basis; the pseudo-aggression of *refusing* is the first defense and admission of the lesser crime; the denial of this spurious aggression and the mocking alibi of giving "immediately," plus shifted guilt (shifted from the masochistic layer to the pseudo-aggressive one), constitute the second defense.

Confusion between wish and multiple defense is one of the most dangerous pitfalls in therapy. Other misunderstandings, no less tragic, arise from confusion between the *real* "battle of the conscience" and the *sham* battle, for the life-long struggle of the unconscious ego is a series of decoying and delaying actions, in all of which the guilt is fastened to the secondary defense. *All of the battles fought by the unconscious ego are sham battles, fought on "foreign territory."*

---

* Both books published by Grune & Stratton, New York.

It seems to me that clarification of already described concepts pertaining to the superego, and establishment of new ones, can be subsumed under these headings:

1. Although *The Battle of the Conscience* did contain this formulation: "success or failure, happiness or depression, love or loneliness" depend on the inner conscience, which is *"the* decisive part of the personality" and leads to "decisive results for the history of the individual," the emphasis now does not seem strong enough to me. Both reviewers and individual readers seem to have gathered the impression that I believe the inner conscience is *also* involved in many human actions and reactions. Obviously, the formulation was not sufficiently emphatic. I believe that *inner conscience is all-powerful and all pervasive.* This all-powerful force requires constant appeasement, and therefore "conscience money" in the form of a double set of inner alibis and defenses must be paid daily—indeed, hourly. Since conscience rules supreme, the inner alibi rules supreme as well; *we think, feel, act, work, love, are moody, become irritated with trifles, bore or amuse ourselves, and to some extent even dream in an unconscious attempt to construct a convincing unconscious alibi and defense.* Without exaggeration, one can speak of the superego's "twenty-four hour schedule of torture."

2. All pleasant talk of "living out one's real wishes," of "doing what one really wants," is—because of the excessive "conscience money" exacted by the superego—merely a mirage. The best a human being can hope for is to erect not-too-damaging intrapsychic defenses, which will satisfy the inner conscience without reminding the victim that his "wishes" are actually substitutes, and "ersatz." To re-state this complicated phenomenon in the "short and sweet" formula constantly requested: *every human being "solves" his individual inner conflict somewhere between the ages of one and one-half and three, and spends the rest of his life supplying himself and the superego with alibis designed to prove that "it isn't so."*

3. No human being can cross the Rubicon of his inner defenses. Intrapsychically, *we all "live on a shoe-string" woven of twin alibis.* Ours is a "miserable alibi existence," to quote a bitter patient (a writer), who made this statement after arriving at an understanding of the interconnections.

4. *The subdivision of the superego into ego ideal and Daimonion,*

suggested in 1933, has been underestimated in its clinical importance.

5. The *first thoughts after awakening* and the "pre-breakfast blues" testify to the refined torture of the superego.

6. Our *daily moods,* though capable of immense variation, always fall into two types: the "punitive type" (action of conscience) or the "alibi type" (double defense offered by the unconscious ego).

7. Readers and reviewers of the previous volume failed to correlate my stress on "the defense against the defense" with the fact that the second link in the chain of defenses constitutes a part of warding off the mechanism of *"taking the blame for the lesser crime."* The reason for the misunderstanding is obvious. The term, "lesser crime," is taken from the language of consciousness, where robbery is always a "lesser crime" than murder, and smoking in the subway always a less serious infraction of the law than arson. No such immutable classifications govern the unconscious mechanism of "taking the blame for the lesser crime." *The moral codes of the external and internal lawbooks do not coincide.* Viewed in this light, it is clear that actions (and even illegalities) which in the conscious code are *greater* crimes, can be used as unconscious defense and alibi against what would consciously be classed as *"lesser* crimes." The unconscious ego, as a result, possesses a slightly paradoxical "moral code." As used here, the term, "lesser crime," pertains to *internal* and not *external* morality.

8. *Neurotic guilt* pertains exclusively to the universal *"end result of the infantile conflict," which, in my opinion is psychic masochism.* The shifting of this guilt to the pseudo-aggressive defense is merely a secondary defensive attempt on the part of the unconscious ego. Analytic diminution of neurotic aggressions, therefore, does *not* automatically decrease the amount of guilt, since the inner conscience points to the reservoir of psychic masochism. Moreover, the guilt shifted to the lesser crime of pseudo-aggression is often unconsciously *inflated and magnified* out of proportion as a means of maintaining the disguise. This in turn leads to grave therapeutic errors, for the therapist must understand that the battle of guilt for pseudo-aggression is spurious, and a sham constructed by the "inner lawyer," the unconscious ego, with intent to deceive the superego.

9. The *real prize* in the intrapsychic tug of war is the possession

of the ego ideal, a point also stressed in 1933. The practical applications of this point have been underestimated. As soon as a discrepancy between ego ideal and ego can be demonstrated by the Daimonion—that accumulation of rebounding aggression within the superego—the unconscious ego accepts the sentence of guilt. *The finality of judgment works both ways,* however. Whenever the unconscious ego can prove that it has acted according to the "mutually accepted yardstick"—the precepts of the ego ideal— Daimonion is temporarily silenced. Jekels and I proved this for a specific normal reaction, that of tender (romantic) love. One of the new developments to be presented in this volume is the fact that this *"double immobilization trick"* is of the utmost importance in *neurosis.* (See point 10.)

10. I have come to the conclusion that every neurotic uses a specific weapon in his Battle of Cannae with the superego, one which has hitherto been largely disregarded: the *quasi-moral connotation of his specific symptom.* Without exception, the secondary defense embedded within every symptom also contains *a mocking irony directed against the internalized educators.* Moral precepts actually communicated to the child during the educational process, and later also embodied in the ego ideal, are secondarily reproduced literally by the unconscious ego, where literal repetition— at the *wrong* time, in the *wrong* place, on the *wrong* occasion, out of context and with *wrong* intention—does not reflect, but rather distorts, the meaning originally intended. The result is a *reductio ad absurdum* of the meaning originally intended. This ironic technique of immobilizing Daimonion's power by speciously fulfilling the demands of the ego ideal (hence neutralizing the weapon of torture), corresponds to one of the few pseudo-aggressive retorts of the otherwise weak unconscious ego. The technique strengthens the unconscious ego's ability to create and maintain the spurious secondary defense. This pseudo-moral connotation proves to be a powerful unconscious weapon of resistance. It is exactly the strength of this defense which has so far been undervalued in its universality, although the mechanism per se has been repeatedly mentioned by different authors, including myself.

11. There are innumerable inner defenses; the No. 1 rating on their priority list goes to *psychic masochism.* The amount of confusion surrounding this problem has shown a steady rate of increase.

Since I have constantly been stressing the importance of this specific defense, I have been accused both of "simplifying" and of "complicating" the psychic apparatus unnecessarily. I have also been told that I am introducing blindfolds for every inner mechanism other than psychic masochism, and that I am blowing up a commonplace phenomenon, a Freudian precept with which everyone in science is familiar. The simplest answer to these quite contradictory objections is a bare statement of the facts. The *genetic* picture in psychic masochism is indeed a Freudian precept, comprising aggression, boomeranging because of guilt, and libidinization of the torturing guilt. My contribution has consisted of working out the *clinical* picture in psychic masochism, and its interconnection with the earliest level of development, the *oral phase*. The clinical picture is a *secondary* unconscious structure, built up because of the superego's objections to the inner pleasure embedded, and in reducing the inner tormenter to absurdity—in psychic masochism, punishment becomes alluring. To repeat my formulation: "The only pleasure one can extract from displeasure is to make this displeasure a pleasure." The clinical picture consists of the "triad of the mechanism of orality":

a. Through their behavior, or the misuse of an external situation, neurotics unconsciously provoke disappointment and refusal, identifying the outer world with the "refusing" pre-Oedipal mother.

b. Not realizing that they themselves have brought about this disappointment, they become pseudo-aggressive, acting in righteous indignation and seemingly in self-defense.

c. They then consciously indulge in self-pity, unconsciously enjoying psychic masochism: "This can happen only to me."

12. Last but not least, the hapless topic of inner conscience is haunted by a popular misconception, which has penetrated into scientific circles as well. *This is the idea that innocence of the type which pleads, "I didn't do anything wrong," guarantees guiltlessness.* Quite the opposite is true. The superego is anti-hedonistic on principle and finds its point of attack guilty or not guilty—consciously.

II. Impersonal Biology and Two Hurts in "Frustration"

GOETHE'S FAMOUS DICTUM, "WE DEPEND MOSTLY ON CREATURES WE ourselves created," refers to people we put in "the saddle," but who later turn against us. Inner conscience is not a person but an impersonal unconscious "department"—as Freud put it, a "province"—so that Goethe's idea, as a whole, is inapplicable. In one detail, however, it fits the unconscious situation, for each one of us is responsible for the creation of his individual inner conscience, and each one of us, later on, becomes the victim of his own Frankenstein.

If one wishes to be technical, one might dispute the statement that inner conscience is self-created. One might claim that credit for this dubious achievement is rightly due to rather impersonal biology. But we know that the baby is born with a store of libido, aggression and narcissism which, though undifferentiated, is at least potentially identical with that at the disposal of the adult he will become. On the other hand, the infant or baby is entirely unable to place his aggression effectively. The inner aggression is massive; its outer manifestations, in the form of crying, spitting, vomiting, occasional refusal to take nourishment, uncoordinated muscular actions, are pitifully ineffective. The result is stasis, and in the long run the unexpended aggression must turn inwards. We know from Freud that drives are like rivers; if the flow in one direction is impeded, another direction is taken. Hence, aggression is canalized against the child himself, and stored in, or rather usurped by, the superego. We also know from Freud that the tendency of a drive is primarily its own discharge, rather than the object against which it is directed.

The protracted maturation time of the human child, from which follows the stasis of undischargeable aggression and the turning of aggression inwards against the child himself, has an inescapable result. It lays the cornerstones for the subsequent establishment of the superego.

Optimists harbor the rather naive idea that, even conceding the inexpressibility of infantile aggression, one could—by "avoiding all frustration"—prevent the dormant and latent aggression from becoming operative. The fly in the ointment is the *failure to understand what the baby considers to be frustration.* Assuming that a baby wakes up, wants his milk and signals his wish. Inevitably, he will have to wait, if only a few seconds; the delay constitutes a *double* offense—*libidinous frustration and megalomaniacal frustration.* Optimists overlook the fact that the baby lives on the basis of misconceptions of reality, considering himself the center of the universe, and autarchic as well. Everything which contradicts this illusion of autarchy is a blow at the most cherished of fantasies, and produces fury. *Hence there can only be a remedy for libidinous frustration; there can be none for megalomaniacal frustration.* To apply the term, frustration, in the sense of a single wound instead of the duality of hurts which it covers means that one is dealing with fantasies of the adult, *not* with realities of the child.

Even if one hesitates to accept Freud's grandiose vision of the duality of Eros and Thanatos, a sufficient explanation for the basis of anti-libidinous inner conscience is found in the undeniable stasis of early infantile aggression, in its inevitable boomerang and accumulation in the superego.

It is of course clear that the theory of duality of instincts is merely a helpful metapsychological prop, and that no human has ever seen, met or been introduced to death- and life-instincts. Nobody has seen the death instinct promenading on the Wiener Ringstrasse in a top hat, nor riding down Fifth Avenue in a Cadillac sedan. But Freud's concept seems valid to me as the underlying reason for the readiness and celerity with which the flow of aggression is "turned against the self."

There is no point in reproducing what every student of analysis has learned from *Beyond the Pleasure Principle* and *The Ego and the Id.* The core of Freud's theory is the assumption that the human life is an unending struggle between two basic instincts: the "life instinct" (Eros) and the "death instinct" (Thanatos). Eros attempts to discharge upon objects in the outer world the tendency of Thanatos, which is originally turned inward, upon the individual himself. What becomes manifest as instinct of destruction is genetically the original Thanatos, forced by Eros to alter direction. Guided by Eros, the destructive instinct rages outward instead of inward. Its redirection toward the individual himself is unconsciously regarded by that individual as the greatest possible danger.

If we imagine two giants fighting each other, with the first trying to kill the second, while the second attempts to divert the destructive energy of the first towards a third party; if we imagine further that the two giants are operative instincts within one personality, we have in essence the Eros-Thanatos theory.

These drives never appear "unmixed." They are combined, in quantitatively varying degrees, at different times. There also exists within the personality a "neutral narcissistic energy" (Freud) which can be added to one drive or the other, thus increasing its cathexis. Neither the life or death instinct, nor even their original mixtures become visible clinically; only the derivatives of these mixtures can be seen. In this sense we can speak of libido and destrudo, assuming that each contains mixtures of both drives. Libido contains more of the derivatives of Eros, destrudo more of the derivatives of Thanatos, but both are admixtures of erotic and thanatic elements.

It is exactly against the background of this inescapable inner accumulation of "self-directed aggression" in the subsequently established superego that we must view the child's pitifully hopeless attempts to cope with *external* troubles. His first inner expedient was described by Freud as the *"ego ideal,"* and the groundwork for this inner department was laid by the child's megalomania.

In order to assess correctly the extent of infantile megalomania, one has only to listen and take *seriously* any child's boasting about what he can do and will do in the future. The adult response to this characteristic bragging is a condescending smile. The child, however, is in earnest about his braggadocio, and the consequences are tragic.

In his frantic attempt to maintain vestiges of the first and most cherished infantile fantasy—that of alleged omnipotence, megalomania, autarchy—the child (at two or two and a half) discovers an ingenious device. It consists of identification with the prohibitions handed down by the mother and father. The child thus substitutes an *inner* prohibition for the barrage of *external* prohibitions which had previously been so offensive. The effect remains the same; the message is still "Don't do it." The only change is the direction of the taboo. The child's new obedience, his acceptance of rules "of his own volition," saves face for him, saves him from punishment, even saves remnants of his illusion of omnipotence.

The ego ideal, therefore, is composed of the child's original and indestructible megalomania (later attenuated to "narcissism," and self-love), amalgamated with internalized parental prohibitions. Quantitatively, there is more of the former than the latter present. The unhomogeneous mixture, however, holds firm even under stress.

In its introjected sectors, the ego ideal is *not* a direct copy of the parents, as had been admirably worked out by our English colleagues. The precise formulation is: "parents as the child perceived them." Since the child projects a good deal of his own aggression on to the parents, their images, when incorporated into the ego ideal, have already been colored and altered by a patina consisting of the child's own projected aggression. This is drawback No. 1 to the theory of "direct copies."

Drawback No. 2 is found in the fact that besides the introjected sector, the ego ideal also contains a sector composed of the child's own narcissism. No doubt about it, the narcissistic sector is protective. But the child's braggadocio is included in it as well, and these high-pitched aims, self-created, self-advertised in childhood, later become one of the most fertile of the inner sources of self-torture.

Having established the ego ideal, the child has solved an *external* conflict. The child's *internal* conflict continues. It must continue, because of the accumulation of undischarged aggression dating from infancy. By this time, it is true, the child possesses increased control over his muscular apparatus, and is capable of placing aggression outward in games, activities, sports. Unfortunately, this ability comes too late. An inner usurper is already in position, and will not budge an inch.

The accumulation of cruelty and aggression directed inward is called "Daimonion." The forbidding term is borrowed from Socrates, who claimed that every human being harbors a "daimoniacal something" within himself.* The modern "Daimonion" bears

---

* Socrates' "daimonion" was *objectively* a malignant "spirit," although the philosopher *subjectively* mistook it for the opposite. In Plato's account (in

no connotation of demons, devils, or other spooks. It means merely an internal "something" which is each individual's worst enemy. Regardless of conscious wishes to "be happy," every human being is host to a cruel jailer, tormenter and torturer. The fact is that in the human psyche also exists an unconscious force which is adverse to happiness, success, enjoyment of life, and whose aim is misery, unhappiness, and even self-destruction.

Ego ideal and Daimonion are the two constituents of the unconscious conscience (superego). These two impersonal departments work in this way: Daimonion uses the ego ideal for its campaign of torture. By constantly holding up to the ego its self-constructed ego ideal, Diamonion asks the searching if monotonous question: "Have you achieved all the aims you promised yourself as a child?" If the answer is in the negative, the result is guilt.

The structure as a whole, therefore, is a failure as far as the ego is concerned. What happened to the "brilliant idea" which preceded the establishment of the ego ideal? The purpose of that expedient was to *protect* the ego from blows to its self-esteem. The weapon created to protect the ego is now used to attack it.

The child's idea had in fact been brilliant; its only flaw was the failure to reckon with the fact that human beings have to fight on *two* fronts: the external and internal. The ego ideal's device was designed to cope with the external conflict which arose when the child was confronted with the commands of the stronger educators. It was successful in neutralizing these conflicts. The "second front," Daimonion, remained impervious to the weapon. More than this, Daimonion cunningly capitalized on the child's narcissism, which

---

Apologia) of Socrates' speech before his judges in Athens during his trial for "corruption of youth," Socrates describes "daimonion" thus: "A godlike and daimoniacal something . . . some kind of voice that deters me from things I wish to do, but never gives positive advice." (Otto Kiefer's translation.) Socrates' extremely provocatory defense, in which every argument seems designed to make him detestable to the naive populace, his judges, contains a peculiar fallacy. This was the argument that, since his accustomed "voice" has been silent during his defense, although previously it had been heard "on the most unimportant occasions," death must be a desirable goal. Socrates was convicted, sentenced to die. He refused his consent to rescue attempts (described in Plato's *Kriton*), and drank the hemlock. Socrates wanted to die, and achieved his aim—via "daimonion."

had apparently been rescued and sustained by the ego ideal, and used that narcissism for its unsavory purposes.

The inner departments of the personality, once established, cannot of themselves be abandoned, rebuilt or modernized. The child cannot throw in the towel, like a fighter made helpless in the ring. The battle must continue, throughout life, on the original territory.

The torture, therefore, persists. Helplessly bound to the promissory note signed by the child, the individual's ego goes on suffering pain and humiliation. It would willingly recant, and withdraw the grandiose picture painted in infancy; the million-dollar fortune, the social position, the succession of beautiful women once confidently prophesied are now grist for Daimonion's mill. "You promised yourself you would be the greatest writer in the world—now look at yourself, you third-rate hack." The discrepancy between the "greatest writer in the world" and a "third-rate hack" exactly corresponds to the punishment meted out by the inner Frankenstein.

Or: "You promised yourself you would be Admiral of the Fleet. Look at your achievement—second mate on a small liner. Admit your failure, and pay the fee of depression and dissatisfaction."

Or: "You promised yourself you would live in luxury. Look at your income—hardly enough to pay your taxes. Yours is a miserable and shabby existence. Pay penance!"

In vain does the ego produce excuses. How was it to know about hard times, restricted opportunities, cutthroat competition, the individual's own intellectual limitations?

Daimonion rejects all these and dictates punishment. Punishment is the first, second and last word. And punishment it is, for Daimonion has the power to enforce its own laws.

In *Civilization and Its Discontents,* (p. 102) Freud assumes that the first traces of "bad conscience" in the child are manifested in purely "social" fear: apprehensiveness that the love of his upbringers will be lost ("Liebesverlust"). On the other hand, Freud concedes (p. 121) that feelings of guilt can be observed before any evidence of the existence of the superego becomes visible. I believe that inner guilt, which according to Freud is also a topical subdivision of anxiety (p. 119), has a much earlier origin. Its pre-stages date from the earliest oral-megalomaniacal level of development. The duality of hurts in frustration produces fury; this fury, inexpressible because of the baby's motor helplessness, ricochets and finds its target in the ego. The first expression of this ricochet is a helpless sensation that there is an absence of well-being. This is later followed by depression. These are the pre-stages of the subsequent guilt.

The Babelian confusion which surrounds the term "ego ideal" is remarkable. To my mind, these facts are clinically provable:

1. As Freud originally suggested, the ego ideal is an *unconscious* structure consisting of a compromise between, and therefore a mingling of, indestructible infantile megalomania and the introjected precepts of the images of the parents.

2. A distinction must be made between the *unconscious* ego ideal and the set of moral precepts which are fully conscious. These, too, are communicated to the child by the parents and their successive representatives.

3. The confusion is centered in the fact that the group of parental rules included under the unconscious ego ideal seems to be identical with the individual's conscious knowledge of right and wrong. How, then, can these precepts be conscious and unconscious at the same time? The apparent contradiction can be resolved, for only the *general* rules are conscious; the petty (and sometimes ridiculous) verbatim acceptance of the wording of these rules, their details, the *inflexibility* with which they are applied, the *anachronistic* circumstances under which these identifications are performed, are all *unconscious*.

Ample clinical evidence of the latter is available. A patient, a scientist, followed a set of quite reasonable precepts concerning work, and work as a duty. He observed that he was unable to read for pleasure during the daytime; even when he had an hour of leisure and wanted to read, "something" held him back. Analysis traced this inhibition back to a maternal command: "One works during the day and reads in the evening." Here was preserved the verbatim record of his mother's disciplinary remarks, when he was caught reading "for fun" instead of doing his homework.

Another patient indignantly reported her husband's comment to the effect that her preachy corrections of his table manners were intolerable ("as if you had suddenly changed into another person—a nagging termagant," he said) and entirely out of character for one with an "otherwise lovely disposition." It could be proved that, without knowing it or wanting to, she was imitating the attitude of her mother, who really was a "nagging" shrew; her husband had unconsciously chosen her because of her ability at this imitation.

Another patient, a professional woman of considerable sophistication, objected to the harmless, witty allusions to sex so common at parties. Such conversation always evoked from her the same indignant reproof: "Stop it, that's naughty." The angry voice was slightly out of place, especially since she was at the same time always eager to listen to these "naughty" stories. In both tone and gesture, she too imitated—mother.

The distinction between *conscious* moral precepts and *unconscious* ego ideal also explains why the ego ideal cannot be changed by its bearer, single-handed. The sector of the ego ideal which contains the infant's unlimited "dreams of glory" is a source of genuine tragedy. There is no way, except through clinical psychoanalysis, of lowering the high pitch of these expectations for the future so that the individual accepts himself as he really is.

In *The Basic Neurosis,* I suggested a preliminary codification of the torture methods of the superego. These "rules of torture," which are even more refined that I originally suspected, can now be enlarged:

Rule 1. *The anti-hedonistic principle is paramount.* The sentences pronounced by the superego echo those meted out to an enemy of the regime in a dictator's "court of justice."

Rule 2. Although all-powerful, the superego pronounces its judgments *in accordance with specific mock-rules of procedure.* With boring monotony, the defendant is confronted with the extravagant expectations enshrined in the ego ideal, and asked: "Is there any discrepancy between actual achievement and the achievement promised in early childhood?" When there is a gap between present reality and the bragging of the past (when no obstacles were as yet recognized by the child), penance in the form of dissatisfaction, guilt, depression is exacted.

Rule 3. The peculiar *formalism of the superego* is one of the few direct loopholes in an otherwise impervious system. This is the opening which is utilized in the most successful slave-revolt of the ego—both when normal and when neurotic. The normal ego stages the attack via tender love (see p. 53), the neurotic ego via hypocrisy (see p. 122) and the "pseudo-moral connotation of neurotic symptoms" (see pp. 257 ff.)

Rule 4. Grotesquely, the cruelest torturer known to mankind, the inner Frankenstein which is the superego, adheres to the rules of procedure in still another point: "proving" beyond the shadow of a doubt that *the forbidden wish or defense is really harbored by the culprit*. Since the superego has at its disposal direct connections to the department of repressed wishes, and the factory of inner defenses, the id and unconscious ego respectively, proof is easily adduced.

Rule 5. The most extreme travesty of justice is attained by another "simple" rule: *the equating of wish and deed*. Goethe once said that there was no crime he could not have imagined himself committing. He said "imagined." If this dictum is transferred to the unconscious, the list of punishable "wishes"—derivatives of wishes and inner defenses—becomes endless. So, too, is the torture imposed by the superego.

Rule 6. In its cavalier disregard for reality, the superego *will not accept* any of the usual *excuses,* some of which can be justifiable: hard times, limited opportunities, cutthroat competition, one's own limitations, external restrictions.

Rule 7. The superego *camouflages its cruelty by accepting the cultural standards of the specific environment*. This leads naive observers to the faulty deduction that the individual is the product and mirror of his surroundings. If we assume, for the sake of argument, that the superego's exclusive interest is in torturing the ego, the nature of the particular prohibition used as a pretext for torture certainly cannot matter. The common denominator is still a series of "don'ts." On the other hand, the acceptance of the specific taboo (which will of course be one of a group which varies in each cultural orbit) imposes an odd restriction on the superego. Anti-libidinous as the inner conscience is, it is helpless in the face of actions approved by the specific environment.

Rules 8 and 9. *Both failure and success can be converted into material for torture. Every failure*—self-provoked, purely accidental, or unavoidable—*is credited to the ego,* to the accompaniment of a reproach reading: "If you had not been such a fool, such a weakling, you would have succeeded." *But successes, too, are devaluated.* Proof of this point can be found in the existence of the widespread group of "pseudo-humbugs" and "pseudo-bluffers." * These are "correct" persons with the external signs of success; unlike the true "humbug" (the swindler), who is a psychopathic personality, the pseudo-humbug observes the accepted standards and cannot be reproached by the environment. This does not prevent the superego from accusing him of being a "fake." Frequently the pseudo-humbug has made his success in one of the professions on the fringe of creativity. He is an advertising man, a critic, a commercial artist, a designer. Even if he is a business man, however, he shares in the genetic background common to this type; he is basically a frustrated writer or artist. His real artistic productivity is blocked by voyeuristic or other inner difficulties, but productivity in *caricature* is not impaired. The superego thus reaps a triple profit. Material for torture can be found in the individual's blocked creativity; in the discrepancy, not between success and failure, but between the comparative "importance" of the career desired and the career achieved; and—most important—in the tongue-in-cheek, caricaturistic attitude which is the prerequisite for productivity in the substitute profession. This last is the basis for the painful reproach of "fakery."

Rules 10 and 11. *Immediacy of torture* and *irony in delayed, though over-severe punishment* are two rules of torture invoked at different times by the superego. In general, immediacy predominates so completely that, over a long period of time, results sometimes turn against the tormenter. For example, as pointed out in my studies on "Working Through," † *one* of the propelling reasons for producing recollections in analysis is the superego's use of analytic interpretations for the purpose of torture. To prove its

---

* See Chapter XI of *The Battle of the Conscience.*

† " 'Working Through' in Psychoanalysis," *The Psychoanalytic Review,* 32: 449–480, 1945. Partially reprinted in *The Basic Neurosis,* pp. 110–136. The decisive role of the superego in connection with the indispensable "working through" process is worked out in this study.

formalistic point (see Rule 4), the superego forces the ego to "remember" what it has conveniently repressed. This, in turn, strengthens the ego via increased confidence in and identification with the correctly decoding analyst. Thus, analytic interpretations and working through have a strange and unlooked for effect, dependent only on the *correctness of the interpretation*. Besides recollections, specific "dreams of refutation" are produced in these situations—practically a predictable mechanism. (See pp. 283 ff.)

In seeming contradiction to the rule of immediacy of torture is the *delayed-ironic cat and mouse play* in which the superego sometimes indulges. It goes so far that the torturer even allows some kind of elation (or at least optimism) in the period between the setting of the trap and the denouement—punishment.

To cite a banal example. A woman patient who neurotically hates housework (this trait is just being analyzed) "forgot" an analytic appointment by confusing the day of the week. . . . During the whole forenoon, she did her housework merrily, and to her great surprise, only to drop into a deep depression *after* realizing (hours later) that she had been fooled.

Rule 12. Like any other dictator, the superego understands but one language: *that of force*. The ego's strength, in the form of external success (how frequent can this be?) and ever-ready aggression, can best the superego. This may clearly be seen in a comparison between so-called normality and neurosis. In normality, the ego has a considerable quantity of real aggression at its disposal; the not-too-neurotic individual can therefore fight back and limit the amount of suffering it must accept from the inner tormenter. In neurosis the balance of power is completely reversed. The superego takes over the individual's store of aggression, and uses it for purposes of torture.

Even under the most favorable conditions, in normality, the ego must divert a great deal of its psychic energy—mainly aggression—to the task of warding off the superego's unjustified reproaches.

Thus the superego is not simply a necessary restrictive institution, with an aim which can readily be understood and approved. *It is the anti-hedonistic force in the personality, loaded to capacity with derivatives of the death instinct.* To see in it only a mirror of the restrictions which seemingly embody only the specific taboos

of a specific environment is to see no farther than the anti-libidinous blind set up to mask its punitive actions, which are secondarily,
as hitching posts, attached to reality restrictions. The superego's
primum movens is the formula: *no pleasure*.

All of this applies to more or less normal people. The picture
changes radically when clear-cut *neurotic reactions* are involved.

Neurosis is an anachronistic disease of the unconscious, preserving
repressed infantile wishes, defense mechanisms, guilt. These old
tendencies—in normality relinquished or at least modified—are
unconsciously perpetuated, in spite of constant countermeasures
instituted by the severe superego. But under neurotic conditions,
as is well-known, the superego is meretricious and venal. It can be
bribed, bought off and appeased. The intrapsychic currency is
that of the nursery—love and punishment, for the very young
child knows no other. The inner conscience, consequently, is partial
to punishment. The neurotic "deal" consists of the tenacity of
id-wishes, ego-defenses, superego-corruptability: the structure upon
which the neurotic compromise rests. The superego can be bought
off with consciously experienced depression, dissatisfaction, ego-
restriction; in exchange it allows innuendos of unconscious pleasure
—though these do not emerge directly—screened against repressed
wishes by a double defense mechanism. The superego exacts its full
share of punishment, while the ego receives attenuated wish-fulfill-
ments, camouflaged with double unconscious defenses, and counteracts the superego's cruelty by psychic masochism. The neurotic pays
an exorbitant price for infantile, second-hand, substitute
gratifications.

In persons who are not psychotic, three main techniques are
used in coping with the monster which is the superego: the *normal*,
the *neurotic* and *criminotic*.

The *normal* conscience confronted with an unconscious wish
automatically gives a "stop" signal—a signal which is meant to be
obeyed, and is obeyed. As a result, these wishes are driven back
into the storehouse of the unconscious, emerging as raw material
for dreams or as sublimations (after translation into socially
approved functions), or merely remaining in abeyance.

Neurotic conscience differs from the normal in that the "stop" signal is only the preamble to an inner drama of corruption and compromise. Inner wishes, modified and attenuated, are licensed for gratification in exchange for the bribe of depression, unhappiness and self-damage accepted by the superego.

The *criminotic* conscience is even more corrupt and demanding. Seeming to relent its vigilance, it allows comouflaged pseudo-aggressive defenses against masochistic wishes to enter the arena of action. It does not even impose the penalty of neurotic depression, but asks, instead, for a higher bribe. *Unconsciously, every criminal bargains for prison or the electric chair.* The reason why the strongest and most self-damaging defenses are deemed necessary by the poor ego is directly connected with the amount of inner passivity and the masochistic solution of the infantile conflict.*

From the viewpoint of reality, the inner conscience of the normal person often acts, in some sectors, as a *troubleshooter;* that of the neurotic or criminotic is always a *troublemaker.* The difference of course penetrates to deeper levels as well. The normal conscience is incorruptible, hence insisting on unconditional renunciation of the infantile; it is the force behind the normal individual's eventual rejection of infantile pleasures and the first objects of attachment. The neurotic and criminotic conscience is corrupt and meretricious. It allows innuendos of infantile pleasures—altered, it is true, by defense mechanisms—and retention of early attachments via fantasy and projection. It exacts the penalty of mental suffering from the neurotic, of imprisonment from the criminotic. It foments and abets trouble instead of fighting it. All three techniques are by no means guaranteed to succeed, as the masochistic elaboration (present in differing forms in all three subdivisions) proves.

Of course, the distinction between the trouble-shooting and the trouble-making effects of the superego in so-called emotional health and neurosis, respectively, must be taken with reservations. By keeping repressed material so tightly corked that it cannot possibly be smuggled into defenses (as in neurosis), the superego *does* prevent troubles. *But it is sometimes difficult to distinguish between punishment, and undue renunciation;* nor is the superego at all "interested" in preventing troubles for the ego.

* For theory of criminosis and review of the literature, see *The Battle of the Conscience,* Chapter XV.

Let us compare one specific trait in its normal, neurotic and criminotic elaborations.

Taking as example an undigested peeping wish (voyeurism), it will be found that the *normal* boy elaborated on it at an early age. He had, as do all children, strong desires to look at his own body and its organs. Later he became strongly interested in the bodies of his next of kin, especially his mother and sisters. He discovered that there was an obstacle to this wish: looking at matters sexual was forbidden, tabooed, declared immoral. The child countered with a double defense. First, he sublimated these (as he had found to his cost) "objectionable" desires. Instead of being interested in sexual peeping, he developed intellectual curiosity, and *exhibited* this interest. This exhibitionism, therefore ("showing off") is in itself a defense mechanism, created to camouflage the original voyeurism. This shift illustrates one of the decisive facts in the psychic apparatus: the axiom that *unconscious wishes never enter consciousness in direct form. Only the secondary defense against these wishes is permitted to appear on the surface, and even then they are disguised.*

No objections were raised to the result of the child's shift, *intellectual* peeping; on the contrary, the child was commended for his brightness. He then began on the long and trying task of convincing his inner conscience that he had completely lost his interest in his mother's and his sister's bodies. Later, when he was curious about a woman's body or a part of it, there was no reproach from conscience, for he had fully convinced his superego that he had abandoned his incestuous first deposits.

What did the man gain and lose in this procedure? He had been forced to give up a cherished and infantile wish. That was painful— for the more infantile the wish, the greater is the gratification derived from it. That debit was counterbalanced by the gain of substitute pleasures in both direct and attenuated form: the right to enjoy, as an adult, his transformed wishes via other objects (not identified with the original standard-bearers). A further gain was "sublimation" in the form of exhibiting * his intellectual curiosity, his interest in nature and in the world of reality.

---

* Freud proved that every voyeur unconsciously identifies with the exhibitionist, and vice versa. Vicariously, both pleasures are enjoyed, though strongly camouflaged.

The "normal" person thus achieved a partial victory. He paid the "price of conscience" in the form of substantial renunciations, and by changing his voyeurism into exhibitionism. In exchange, he can enjoy his now made harmless intellectual exhibitionism, because it is a substitute diet, with all of the dangerous elements removed.

The *neurotic,* confronted with the identical wish, reacts differently. He is incapable of really giving up his incestuous original objects, therefore he unconsciously retains the connotation of peeping at the infantile—incestuous—images. He, too, unconsciously tries to transform voyeurism into exhibitionism. The defense does not succeed, for it is always countered by a superego reproach which points out the connection with the infantile images. Sublimations are poorly developed, and a great part of the neurotic's psychic energy remains concentrated on the original wishes and defenses. To his surprise, the man develops a neurotic symptom, for example, street fear. Every time he wants to leave home, he is "scared to death." He has no idea of the real cause of his fear. He shifts his fear, projectively, to the alleged dangers of the street: traffic accidents, sudden heart attacks, hold-ups, "sexual attacks," or other similar perils. By "rationalizing" his fears, he tries to convince himself that he is acting rationally. Like all human beings, he is a sucker for ignorance and self-deception.

The sequence of events, for the neurotic, is this: an original peeping wish is rejected by the inner conscience because of the original incestuous connotation. The voyeuristic wish is changed (by the unconscious ego) into a defense mechanism, exhibitionism. This defense, too, is vetoed by the conscience, and a second defense is introduced: the neurotic symptom. Every time the victim even thinks of going out on the street, he feels deadly fear. Seemingly, the fear pertains to defensive exhibitionism, and with the help of a rationalization is shifted to the "dangers" of the street.

What did the man gain and lose in this precedure? He did *not,* as did his more normal confrere, renounce an early wish (peeping), although he was forced by the superego to settle for a shabby substitute (exhibitionism). He did *not,* as did his more normal confrere, renounce the original objects, and therefore could not succeed in convincing the inner Frankenstein, conscience, that he had become a good boy. His ransom was therefore higher; his payments were depression, dissatisfaction, diminution of the radius of his activities (the torturing results of street-fear are obvious). That bribe of suffering appeases conscience temporarily, an armistice which is not reflected in the misery of the victim's conscious life.

Clearly, this is a poor deal. But the victim rates his original wishes and his attenuated defense so highly that he is willing to pay the fee demanded by conscience. You cannot argue about the price of inner pleasures.

The third guinea pig, the *criminotic*, wrests an even poorer bargain from the superego. He pays the fee of social disgrace and a prison term. He enters the arena of action: he is found exhibiting before a girl's school. He lives in constant fear of arrest, or actually is arrested and finds himself on the way to jail. Once in that rather unpleasant spot, he will tell you that he acted under pressure of an "irresistible impulse," thus shifting the blame to Nature's imperfections.

What did that man gain and lose in this procedure? His so-called "irresistible impulse" reveals itself as merely another unconscious defense mechanism. What he really wanted, unconsciously, was incestuous *peeping*. What he really got in his miserable bargain with conscience was *exhibitionism* and a jail sentence. He did succeed, however, in smuggling a minimal part of his voyeuristic wishes into the defense. By identifying, unconsciously, with the involuntary viewers of his performance—(*they* peeped)—he vicariously retrieved a few crumbs of voyeurism, though only unconsciously. For these faint echoes of "pleasure," he paid the inner usurer, his conscience, the price of jail.

People without a superego do not exist, simply because every human being goes through a long maturation period, during which his inborn aggression is inexpressible and consequently rebounds against himself. *What does exist is the confusing array of manifold inner compromises with the inner ogre.* Only by confusing the *conscious* meaning of conscience with the *unconscious* structure do people arrive at the naive question, "Do you concede even to a 'crook' a conscience?" The correct counter-question is: "Do you concede even to the 'crook' an infancy?"

Certainly, the ideal state of affairs is a conscience which inhibits unacceptable actions before they can begin; unfortunately, neurotic and criminotic "consciences" work differently. Still, without being familiar with the hidden recesses of self-torture within a specific individual, the personal history of this specific individual cannot be understood.

III. Constant "Reformulation" of the Oral-Megalomaniacal Material in the "Language" of Later Stages

BEFORE FREUD, NEUROSIS WAS NOT RECOGNIZED BY ANY ACCREDITED medical associations. Neurosis existed, of course, and it is unnecessary to mention that neurotics were suffering. Without understanding the characters they were describing, novelists were writing about human "peculiarities," while in ordinary conversations comments on emotional histrionics and inhibitions were always likely to crop up. What is today called "neurosis" was then benignly viewed as "minor psychosis," or in benign ignorance interpreted as an obsession with the devil. What a wit called "the no-man's land between the sane and the insane" was not the object of scientific research. Minima non curat praetor—no time was wasted on such trifles as neurosis by medical authorities. "You are just imagining things," was the pre-Freud physician's indignant or superior response to a neurotic's complaint; "therapy," when attempted, consisted of the hope that the patient could be laughed out of his "fantasies" by the physician's reassuring bedside manner.

Time was marching on, and so was specialization. The science of psychiatry came into being, and in place of the general practitioner's contempt, the neurotic now received from the early psychiatrist—the same run-around. In fact, his medical lot deteriorated, for it is more difficult to resist a dictum when it comes from a specialist.

Nineteeth century psychiatry concerned itself with sorting out and classifying people with delusions, hallucinations, loss of reality sense. A neurotic was beneath the classifier's notice; he was considered a nuisance.

The first approach to the vast field of psychosis was, out of necessity, purely descriptive.

Psychiatrists realized, finally, that they had misjudged the preponderances, and that psychotics accounted for only a small percentage of the people suffering from emotional disturbance. On the basis of sheer quantity, neurotics took the center of the stage, for they are numbered in the millions while the candidates for Bellevue are relatively sparse.

Modern psychiatry specifically distinguishes between neurosis and psychosis. Neurosis is not a pre-stage of psychosis, nor is there an observable transition between neurosis and psychosis. What can be observed is the intrapsychic conflict and its many elaborations.

In any case, the unfortunate neurotic had to struggle to gain the medical profession's recognition of his disease. Neurosis is now fully acknowledged and seriously studied; the "nuisance" of the past has become a legitimate patient. He is even awarded the unique distinction of being offered a couch instead of a chair. It is a far cry from the demonology, disbelief, rejection or anonymous, unpitied suffering which was his destiny in the past.

The nineteenth century's recognition of neurosis as a disease was made more difficult by the very nature of medicine's approach to the patient in that period. It was preponderantly anatomic-pathologic. If a patient who apparently was healthy in body complained of "imaginary diseases," medicine was baffled. The symptoms and signs of disease were unorthodox. How, then, could a man with a healthy heart produce the symptoms of heart trouble? It was disturbing—one might even say impertinent—for the compulsive neurotic to experience his "inorganic" compulsions, for the agoraphobe to be afraid of the street. Medical helplessness found its alibi in the convenient phrase, "does not exist."

Neurotics are resilient people. Though told they "did not exist," they persisted in consulting physicians. Eventually they were elevated to medical respectability. Freud not only established an individualized therapy for them, but also restored to them one of the appurtenances of human dignity, for besides his *individual* suffering, the neurotic was conceded the *individual*—though unconsciously determined—right to be "unhappy in his own fashion" (Tolstoy) and to be cured by *individualized* treatment—if he so desires.

Individuality became trump. A comparison with the uniformity and absence of individualization characteristic of hypnotic therapy before the introduction of the cathartic method of Breuer and Freud is conclusive proof of this.

The real difficulties, for neurotics, were encountered after they were firmly established as a legitimate object of medical research. This was due, not to neuroticism per se, but to the rather accidental (although unconsciously probably meaningful) order in which the different layers of the unconscious were discovered. Freud's first descriptions were of hysterical neurotics; his first investigations, therefore, were of what later became known as phallic regression. Here the Oedipus complex is paramount. Unfortunately, as far as strata are concerned, phallic regression is also the most superficial of all neuroses. The analytic *discovery* of neurosis, therefore, did *not* follow the order of the psyche's *development,* but exactly reversed it. Analytic discoveries began at the apex of the pyramid and continued *downward,* whereas the child's development begins with the base of the pyramid and continues *upward,* to the apex. Hence the sequence of oral-anal-phallic stages does not accord with the sequence of analytic discovery, which was phallic-anal-oral. This fact made for considerable confusion in the analytic "geology."

After discovery of the superficial levels of the unconscious, Freud (and much later, his followers) was constantly confronted with the uncomfortable observation that deeper layers seemed to be lurking "beneath" and "below" those already made visible. The astonishing process of uncovering these deeper layers partially prevented investigation of the way in which one layer trespasses on the next and there finds expression, although of course attempts at such correlation were (sporadically, however) undertaken.

Besides the historical handicap of the sequence of analytic discoveries (who can prescribe to a genius the order of his visions?), there was another stumbling-block in the path of scientific explorers. Their fascinated concentration on the first great victory against the darkness of the unconscious—elucidation of libido—led scientists to postpone for a considerable period the investigation of its Siamese twin: aggression. Both partes constituentes of the id were eventually assembled, but even then (especially for some simplifying followers) the historical nexus sketched above continued to play havoc.

Today, respect for the gradual and painful achievement of discovering the different unconscious layers should not deter us from describing the psychic apparatus in its proper geological stratification. Respect for the history of discoveries can be carried too far.

It is, by the way, interesting that my recent book on impotence, frigidity and homosexuality *(Neurotic Counterfeit-sex)* is—as far as I know—the first analytic monograph to abandon the conventional order. The book starts with the description of orally regressed cases, progresses to anally regressed patients, and ends with those who are phallically regressed. But it is still not uncommon to find, in our literature, that the deeper regressions are treated in a manner equivalent to that of a society editor when reporting on people below the celebrity level. The situation is considered covered with: "Also present were . . . ." Scientifically, this amounts to a—footnote.

Still another handicap is the absence of any uniformity of opinion on the contents of the deeper layers, the oral and anal. Many colleagues still cling to the idea that oral regression denotes the parasitic wish to get, and anal regression denotes "anal sadism." In my personal opinion, the clinical contents of the two layers are different. This will be elaborated on presently.

In any case, the following sketch of the child's development contains material as I see it. It is, as explained in the preface, "expendable" theory. This is willingly and unequivocally admitted.

We know that oxygen and "nourishment" are supplied the unborn child via the blood-vessels of the mother; that in the womb hunger, cold, "air-hunger" do not exist. There is of course no way of knowing what the unborn "thinks," if it thinks at all; we can only deduce from subsequent behavior patterns that the newborn child's desire is to continue the effortless, utopian existence which was his in the womb, where all desires were satisfied magically, and apparently by "himself." We can also deduce his delusion that there has been no major change, that extra-uterine life differs from intra-uterine life in details only, and not in the essential.

The child begins life, therefore, burdened with a duality of factors: *subjective* misconception of autarchy and megalomania, and *objective,* completely passive dependence, nutritionally and otherwise, on the Giantess of the nursey, mother. The mother is by no means seen as giving and sacrificing. Quite the contrary, the infant's first impressions are of "something bad and intruding." The baby's autarchic fantasy explains this paradox, for if everything "good" is self-produced, self-given, self-bestowed, then obviously gratitude or even acknowledgment are not justified or called for. But the reality of the baby's dependence constantly contradicts his fantastic and gratuitous assumption of self-sufficiency, and this dependence is brought home in the "bad," which comes from the outside. Hence, mother becomes the standard-bearer of the "bad," since she is not only giving but "refusing," or at least dilatory in the inevitable course of events.

The double hurt which comes from every wish that is not *instantaneously* fulfilled has already been described. The wait of a few seconds or minutes for nourishment means more than caloric frustration, it is also—and above all—the graveyard of infantile megalomania. And this ineradicable infantile megalomania follows us throughout our lives like a shadow. The only concessions made are frequent "reformulations." It is as though a lawyer, questioning a witness, were instructed by the judge to withdraw a specific query. The lawyer does not give up his line of attack; he rephrases the same material, and questions the witness again.

The scars of the first weeks and months of extra-uterine existence are present in every human being. The number of scars, and the secondary elaborations on them, vary. The most powerful counteraction is the libidinous pleasure of sucking. Nevertheless, some infants are poor eaters, even when no intestinal disturbances are present to account for this fact. Dr. H. A. Bunker has recently pointed out (in a different connection) that one of the less known variations of the Narcissus myth has it that the young man, enamored of his own reflection in a pool, died of starvation—he was too absorbed in himself to eat. The megalomania of the baby does not go so far, but some babies stand with amazing stubbornness and consistency on their "Constitutional right" to stick to their megalomaniacal-autarchic "privileges."

Study of neurotic fears conclusively shows that a series of "reformulations" of infantile megalomania does take place.

The first of these is the assumption that even if "something outside of myself" does really exist (it should be noted that Freud assumed that the breast or bottle is originally conceived by the child to be a part of himself), this "something" is but an executive organ of the child's absolute power. The magical signal (Ferenczi) of crying "produces" the nourishing breast (bottle); stretching the hand out for an object "produces" the object. In short, both dependence and mother-child duality are constantly negated by the baby and infant.

In previous publications I have described *"the septet of baby fears."* This septet has one common denominator: the fantasy of the "bad," coming from the mother, is tenaciously maintained, and small concessions to reality are made in order to prolong the fantasy of megalomania.

It takes so long for the reality of the mother's loving kindness to impress itself on the child that before this point is reached the child has built up a septet of baby fears, in which the mother plays the role of a witch. These fears arise during the pre-Oedipal phase; it is in these first one and a half and two years of life, when he is beset with peculiar misconceptions about the kind of person his mother really is, that he constructs the picture of himself as the innocent victim of a witch who is capable of *starving, devouring, poisoning, choking him, chopping him to pieces, draining and castrating him.*

There are clinical proofs for this statement; they can be augmented by proofs of a different character, derived from folklore. The child's world, as it is mirrored in his very immature mind, resembles *Alice in Wonderland* or *Grimm's Fairy Tales* more than it does the adult's recognition of the world as it really is. The myth, the fairy tale, is a distorted and elaborated version of a repressed human fantasy. No other prototype is possible for "Hansel and Gretel," in which a step*mother* persuades a reluctant father to desert his two children, leaving them in the forest to die of *starvation;* in which there is a *female witch* who lures the *starving* children to her, using a chocolate house as bait, and then fattens them up so that she can *devour* them.

These fears of fantastic cruelties—starving, devouring, poisoning, choking, chopping to pieces, draining, castrating—which the child attributes to the pre-Oedipal mother have little connection with reality factors. In my opinion, the child's entire development is controlled by his constant attempts to maintain infantile megalomania and autarchy, and to ward off the blows incessantly inflicted upon his aim by reality.

The child wants, as has been noted, to continue the paradisiacal passivity of life in utero, where even the effort of breathing or eating had been unnecessary. Faced with the disadvantages of post-natal existence, so radically different from life in the womb, he counters with the illusion of omnipotence. The "new order" is thoroughly unsatisfactory; even nutrition is seen as an undesirable intrusion. Normally, this reaction is superseded by the newly dis-covered libidinous pleasure of oral intake. The "septet of baby fears" subsequently makes its dismal appearance.

Fear of starvation. The adult neurotic, simply because he is alive, proves that this fear was delusive and unwarranted. Mothers ordi-narily do not let their babies starve. The "starvation" here is an offense to the infant's megalomania, which exaggerates the hard-ship of waiting even a few seconds for breast or bottle, and resents any waiting as an insult.

Fear of being devoured. This grotesque fear has been clarified by the English school of psychoanalysis as a projection of the child's *own* aggressive designs upon the nipple (bottle). It is formulated: "I don't want to bite; mother wants to devour me."

Fear of being poisoned. Sooner or later even the child who claims that his mother is "starving" him must admit that he is being fed. He preserves the essence of his grievance by shifting around: "Mother does feed me, but the food is poisonous and harmful."

Fear of being choked. These fantasies have to do with being choked by the mother's breast or body. They are *not* set in opera-tion by the disproportion between the mother's body and the child's, nor by the clumsiness of mother or nurse, who may be too forceful in pushing the nutritional instrument into the baby's mouth.

Fear of being chopped to pieces. At the root of this fear is the baby's failure to understand the mother's harmless intentions in the routines of washing and cleaning. The baby translates these actions into a procrustean bed fantasy. Again, the evil design is imputed to mother by the child; the overforcefulness of the upbringers is not responsible.

Fear of being drained. This arises from the infant's "helplessness" against "propelling forces" in the elimination of urine and feces. The child feels that he is being forcefully "drained." He retaliates, secondarily, with megalomaniacal and aggressive ideas connected with both products.

Fear of castration. This fear is the climax of the septet. It is characterized by concessions to reality in the form of more or less rational disguises, and is most clearly visible during the Oedipal phase.

Not all children have actually been threatened with "castration"; the fact that all children manifest this fear, whether or not threats have been made, has puzzled many analytic authors. In recent analytic literature, however, it is agreed that this fear grows out of a series of non-genital precursors. The sheltered uterine existence vanished, the breast (bottle) was withdrawn, stool was "drained," later, the milk-teeth fell out. Thus, groundwork was laid for the idea that "pleasure leads to the loss of the pleasure-giving organ."

The deepest reason is more complicated. It is identical with the fact that the "septet of baby fears" is still active, although disguised by shifts to successive phases and organs. Much which is classified as "phallic castration fear" is at bottom undigested oral fear, stemming from the "septet."

It is clear that this septet of baby fears is characterized by a certain progression. Some, such as the fear of starvation, fear of being devoured, choked or chopped to pieces, preserve infantile misconceptions. Others have "reformulated" the impossible, but still cling to the projected cruelty. In this category are fears of being poisoned, drained, castrated. The fear of being poisoned at least represents a concession to the fact that the mother feeds the baby, even if it imputes sinister designs to her. The fear of being drained or castrated at least reflects an acknowledgment of the fact that only parts of the body, rather than the entire personality, are the passive aim of destruction. Nevertheless, these are but half-hearted concessions. Moreover, the "reformulations" become more outspoken in later neurotic manifestations.

In later years, for example, the reproach of starvation is modified into that of being refused, and love, kindness, gifts, attention, etc. are substituted for food. After masochistic "stabilization on the rejection level," the game, "cruel-mother-refuses-helpless-child," is made permanent. Its basis is unconsciously self-chosen and self-initiated.

The fear of being devoured becomes visible in later years through animal phobias and unconscious fantasies. Fairy tales and dreams enshrine it.

The fear of being poisoned is the ancestor of pathologic fear of impregnation, of neurotic intestinal disturbances, and hypochondriacal complaints centering about food.

Fear of confined places, from true claustrophobia to neurotic fear of elevators, can be traced back to the infantile fear of being choked. Contributaries are visible in the psychological aspects of asthma.

Remnants of the fear of being chopped to pieces are visible in those neurotics who adduce the cutting of meat, fish and fowl as proof positive that a woman is "capable of anything." In adulthood, these remnants are subsumed into fear of operations, and phallic castration fears.

One encounters the fear of being drained behind the adult's facade of miserliness in money, sex, and even words.

The distorted fantasies of the "septet of baby fears" serve to postpone, but not prevent, the child's eventual acknowledgment of the mother's generosity and kindness. Although the mother is still seen as the "great refuser" (of necessity her role in the nursery is to prevent and forbid, for the child's protection, as well as to give), there is at the same time acceptance of the concept that mother "also gives." But this recognition, which should lessen the child's conflict, only serves to increase it. His conflict is now that of ambivalence, with friendly *and* inimical feelings toward the *same* person at the *same* time doing battle within him. Obviously, this dichotomy must be extremely disturbing.

Added to this is the fact that almost all the experiences which the child has in the pre-Oedipal phase are *passive* in nature. The child is *completely dependent* on the mother; feels *passively "victimized"* even by the process of being fed (in contrast with the womb, where everything was provided "by himself," the breast or bottle system of the postnatal world is a blow at the child's autarchic fantasy); is *passively* dependent on getting milk at all; is *passively* subjected to a time schedule for his meals; and, most important, must undergo the *passively* experienced "tragedy of weaning." This is not all. A series of functions which are accepted as "natural" by the adult, such as urination, defecation, and even sleep, are viewed quite differently by the immature child. "Something irresistible drains parts of the body" ("anal castration,"

Freud) from him; "something" forces him to sleep. All these misunderstandings have to be understood against the background of
the child's only measuring rod—his alleged magic omnipotence.
The result is visible in the septet of baby fears.

It is this combination of fear and ambivalence which makes the
child's position untenable, and pushes him, at the age of one and
a half or two, into the *Oedipal phase*. Before entering it, however,
the child goes through the anal phase, which is merely a duplica-
tion of passive experiences of the oral phase, with pseudo-aggressive defenses.

The child sees himself as a victim; something more powerful
than himself, something irresistible, drains him and forces him to
expel "parts of his body." His terror is only slightly mitigated by
the accompanying "anal elimination pleasure." The similarity to
the "passive victimization" of his oral experiences is clear: the child's
mouth, too, has been "victimized" by the "undesirable intrusion
and piercing" of the nipple or bottle; this displeasure has been
only slightly mitigated by the libidinous gratification of sucking.
The perception of tragic offense to infantile megalomania via
anal victimization is sometimes co-existent with the oral experience, and also follows closely upon it. Obviously, neither the beginning of the intestinal tract nor its end (mouth and anus) are the
sites of "victories" for infantile megalomania.

The child is both optimistic and resilient, however. He tries
counter-measures, using both localities as weapons. He screams,
vomits, occasionally refuses to take nourishment (actual intestinal
disturbances are not referred to; these are "hunger-strikes" for
spite), when fighting on the oral level. On the anal level, his device
is retention. Many an "incurable" constipation in later life has
its humble but significant origin here.

These pseudo-effective countermeasures have aggressive connotations. They are strengthened, later on, by the child's realization
that anal "stubbornness" is a way of infuriating the Giantess of the
nursery, who insists on regularity and continence, on elimination
at certain set times and in certain set places. If the rules are
broken, there is conflict in the nursery.

The last stage of the megalomaniacal revolt against the "passivity"
of being anally "drained" is the institution of this defense: "I'm

not drained at all; *I* produce the feces of my own free will; I like doing it, and want to play with it." This accounts for the spectacle of children playing with the products of their own elimination, to the horror of their elders. This accounts, too, for the unconscious fantasy of an "anal penis," a substitute for the breast used for pseudo-aggressive fantasies of cruelty.

At the same time, the anal opening retains good-sized deposits of passivity. (This is also true of the oral opening.) The fantasy of being orally "pierced" by nipple or bottle has its counterpart in the passive fantasy of being "passively pierced" by the anal ("self-produced") rod of feces.

The child's progression into the Oedipal stage is to some extent due to the banal fact that he is learning to "digest" a reality situation; the more important factor, however, is his psychological situation. The father is present, and proves to be a powerful "competitor" for the mother's attention and love. Now a "new order" is set up—the triangle of mother, father and child—supplanting the Giantess-and-baby duality of the pre-Oedipal phase. In this "new order" the boy performs a magnificent *tour de force*. He manages to *demote the threatening and fear-inspiring "witch" of babyhood from her position of power*. The father is now the "big-shot," and by identifying with the father's borrowed strength, the boy converts the Giantess *into a caricature and image of his own frightened and passive self*. He now sees the mother as completely dominated by the father. He misconstrues the parents' sexual activity as a cruel act, in which the father is the conquering Giant and the mother the passive victim. Identifying with the father's "cruelty," the boy finds the once frightening Giantess of his babyhood to be completely "weak, passive, helpless," just as he had been in the past. The reversal of the roles seems complete; poetic justice has been established via the unconscious repetition compulsion.

In general, the Oedipus complex is frequently misunderstood to mean *only* that "the boy desires his mother sexually." Its prehistory, which is suffused with fright, terror, massive passivity, is entirely disregarded. The boy's identification with the father's "cruelty" has one major purpose: to counteract passivity by demoting the Giantess.

The overthrow of the "tyrant," mother—so necessary if the child's fear is to be diminished—is facilitated by the boy's discovery that the female sex has no penis. Since in earlier stages the boy has unconsciously identified breast with penis, this discovery, too, contributes to the diminution of fright. Now the boy possesses the organ, the mother does not.

The child's illusions of "poetic justice" and the penis' "power to damage" collapse after a few short years. The Oedipus complex, that triumphant retaliation designed to "end all fears," ends at about the fifth year. For by demoting the mother as fear-inspiring power, the boy achieves, not absence of fear, but the presence of another power, the father, who is not only fear-inspiring but punishment-threatening into the bargain. After the principle of "an eye for an eye, a tooth for a tooth," the boy fears that the father will retaliate upon the "criminal" organ. "Phallic castration fear" is Freud's name for the new danger. Having to decide whether to save the penis or insist on his wishes towards the mother, the boy chooses the security of his organ. His choice is also influenced by the ineffectiveness of his defensive wishes, for the mother does not take his advances seriously, and may even become angry and threatening. As a result, passivity is *again* reinforced. The misconceptions of sex embedded in the Oedipal wishes are normally renounced; in their place comes asexual filial affection. Hatred for the father, that "competitor" who is heir to the fury rooted in pre-Oedipal sources, and originally directed at the pre-Oedipal mother, is also given up, changing into "deaggressionized" comradeship.

The child's attempt to rescue himself from baby fears through the use of sex is a failure. The entire problem is then put more or less in storage. The latency period sets in (ages five to twelve), and is interrupted only by the onset of puberty. The biologically conditioned "activity-push," emanating from glands with inner secretion, unconsciously revives the old conflicts. This, the second edition of the conflicts of early infancy, confirms the final destiny of the human being. One must say "confirmed" rather than "decided," for the manner in which the individual has met his pre-Oedipal and Oedipal trials is a significant indication of his eventual lot. And how many cases are reversed by a superior court?

Even in the active Oedipal phase, the best proof of the prevalence of *passive* experiences, with weak pseudo-aggressive countermeasures designed *to demote the overpowering Giantess of the nursery, the pre-Oedipal mother,* is visible also in the passivity of the *negative* Oedipus complex.

The negative Oedipus continues the long line of enforced passivity and futile aggressive countermeasures which in my opinion characterize all phases of the child's early development. This transitory and typical stage has puzzled many observers in the past; it is still the source of a good deal of confusion. Freud declared, in 1908, that every child goes through both phases of the Oedipus conflict: "positive" and "negative." The former is classical: "The boy desires his mother sexually, and hates his father as his competitor." In the less known, perhaps because less sensational, negative Oedipus, the formula reads: "The boy hates his father and resents him as a competitor, but at the same time—in unconscious feminine identification—he wants to be loved by him, as mother is."

In this period, therefore, the fantasy of the "self-produced" fecal rod is discarded, and the father's penis is unconsciously invited to do the piercing in the child's identification with the Oedipal mother, who has by this time been demoted from her supremacy as the Giantess of the nursery.

The trait of ambivalence, in later life characteristic of anally regressed neurotics, needs additional clarification.

Ambivalence did, it is true, exist in the oral stage; as mentioned, it is one of the reasons for the transition from the pre-Oedipal to the Oedipal phase. In no other clinical entity, however, is ambivalence so predominant as in neurotics who are anally regressed.

The problem cannot be clarified if only the anal phase is investigated, and *the oral substructure of ambivalence* is overlooked. The problem has been generally neglected; few have questioned Freud's opinion that we do not know exactly why ambivalence plays so decisive a role in obsessional and compulsive neurotics, the clinical entities produced by anal regression. Equally unquestioned is Freud's resigned statement that the problem of obsessional neurosis is "unsurmountable."

In my opinion,* this pseudo-mystery can be solved through the direct question: *What is the link between the oral and anal phase?*

---

* See "Three Tributaries to Ambivalence," *The Psychoanalytic Quarterly,* 17: 173–181, 1948, and *The Basic Neurosis,* Chapter II.

Obsessional (compulsive) neurotics display, not real aggression, but *pseudo-aggression*. Male obsessional neurotics, once their symptoms and anomalies of character have been established (Layer I), are continuously reproached for their passivity by unconscious conscience (Layer II). This passivity is secondarily warded off by the unconscious ego, which offers proof of the claim: "I am not passive; on the contrary, I am extremely aggressive" (Layer III). Once more, the superego veto is made known (Layer IV) and then this defense is also warded off (Layer V). A five-layer structure is therefore observable in obsessional neurotics. This factor has decisive therapeutic consequences. The danger, in clinical analyses of obsessional neurotics, is that pointing out only their aggressiveness and the resultant feelings of guilt will inadvertently bolster up and not destroy their defense mechanism. The poor therapeutic results commonly reached with obsessional neurotics are, in my opinion, due to this failure to reckon with the five-layer structure.

The wish to be anally penetrated by the father is not merely the result of inverted Oedipal wishes and the outgrowth of castration fear. It is also a refuge from an *oral conflict, secondarily projected on to the father*. The child escapes into the normal *positive* Oedipus, but is driven back, by his passivity, into the *negative* Oedipus. Castration fear, linked to the positive Oedipus, speeds up this reversal. The Oedipal castration fear is more than ordinarily powerful in these cases, since an appetite for passivity has already been built up in oral-anal *passive* experiences. The anally-regressed child is actually expressing the old *oral fantasy of being pierced*, but on a higher (Oedipal) level.

One frequently overlooks the fact that the concept of the "anal penis" is merely an autarchic attempt to negate the child's dependence on the breast, and also on the later substitute, the paternal penis.

This does not affect the long-established fact that castration fear is an important cause of the regression. The unconscious reasoning can be expressed in this way: "It is not true that I want—in feminine identification—(negative Oedipus) to be penetrated *anally* by my father's penis (repetition of the mouth-breast conception of being pierced). The truth is that I am *autarchic*, have an anal penis myself, and want to play with 'autarchic feces'." Later the anal ("dirty") penis conception is warded off as well, leading to reactive formations.

It seems to me that the content of anal regression is the wish to play with "autarchic feces," which constitutes a defense mechanism set up to fight oral-anal passivity. The wishes of the inverted Oedipal period are merely a mask for the oral masochistic fantasy of being pierced, which was projected on to a *later developmental level* when the "autarchic defense" could no longer prevent the return of the repressed material.

This constitutes the first tributary in the stream of ambivalence. It is the *conflict between the "progressive" autarchic defense mechanism,* as expressed in the formula: "I want to play autarchically with self-produced feces; I do not want to be passively penetrated, either orally (by the maternal breast) or anally (by the paternal penis)," *and the "regressive" passive wish to be orally-anally penetrated.* Since this conflict is endless, ambivalence is perpetuated. The simple fact that the individual does not meekly surrender to oral-anal passivity, but instead puts up at least a semblance of a fight against it, in itself suggests that there is an attempt to ward off these passive tendencies, with methods that are aggressive if ineffectual. Secondarily, ambivalence is also used for passive purposes; the obsessional neurotic, for example, converts ambivalence into material for self-torture.

The second tributary to ambivalence, too, may be found in a pseudo-aggressive attempt to ward off passivity. Feces play a contradictory role in the child's world. In the first ten or fifteen months of life they are over-rated; because they are evidence of the child's nutritional well-being or lack of it, mothers and nurses are highly interested in their amount, color, odor. Throughout this period, too, the child is cajoled into "toilet training," and the attempt is made to restrict the function to specific times and places. Later on, these very same matters are placed under a taboo, and the child is told that even a mention of them is "bad manners." The obsessional child is constantly on the alert for an aggressive mask which he can use to disguise his oral-anal passivity; he finds such a camouflage in feces. He carries the high valuation assigned to feces in the earliest period over to the stage when the same products are educationally classified as "dirty" and therefore depreciated. Feces thus become a weapon against the educator, and the later internalized educator. The child constantly demonstrates the real contradiction in educational values betrayed by the changing attitude towards feces, and in this way tries to prove that the educators are inconsistent and hypocritical. In other words, the attempt at autarchy, exemplified by the manipulation of "self-produced" feces (as stressed above), complements the pseudo-aggressive defense against oral-anal surrender.

The third tributary to ambivalence consists of the obsessional neurotic's endeavor to combine *narcissistic gratification* with their pseudo-aggressive defenses against oral-anal surrender. In previous publications * I pointed out that obsessional neurotics, fighting their losing battle royal with their superegos, make use of four unconscious mechanisms.

1. *Mechanism of the inner contradiction of all "compulsive rules."*
The hopeless conflicts resulting from being handicapped by contradictory compulsive rules have the purpose of showing up the superego's demands as infeasible, since each rule promulgated contradicts another. This "fishing for contradictions" is one of the weak defenses of the battered ego.

2. *Mechanism of direct disparagement of the superego.*
By making every Tom, Dick or Harry an "authority" capable of deciding for the obsessional neurotic what he cannot decide for himself, the sick ego projects an ironic dismissal of the "glorious" superego, personified in—Tom, Dick or Harry.

3. *Mechanism of relative crudity in the compulsion.*
The mechanism of obsessionals, described by Freud (insulation, undoing, obsessional alternatives, etc.) have one feature in common: the relative crudity with which the superego is fought. The crudity is used "unconsciously on purpose." The cruder the trap into which the superego falls, the greater is the gratification of the weak ego.

4. *Mechanism of "guided miracles."*
The peculiar confirmations of their private superstitions are,

* "Notes on an Obsessional Neurosis in Ultimis: Four Mechanisms of Narcissistic Gratification in Obsessional Neurosis." *Intern. Zeitschr. f. Psychoanal.*, Vol. 2, 1936. Partial English translation in "Two Forms of Aggression in Obsessional Neurosis," *The Psychoanalytical Review*, 29:188–196, 1942. See also *Neurotic Counterfeit-Sex*, pp. 150–154.

as is well-known, self-constructed by the unconscious ego of the obsessional. The purpose of the procedure is diminution of guilt ("Fate!") *and* application of infantile megalomania, shifted outside.

All these mechanisms are a source of narcissistic pleasure. At the same time, they are part of the obsessional neurotic's chronic, truly *frantic attempts* to utilize *pseudo-aggression as a means of defense against oral-anal surrender.*

By "teasing" the superego and deriving narcissistic pleasure from this, the obsessional neurotic "proves" to himself that he is *not* passive. This spurious face-saving device is visible in ambivalence, too. "I doubt whether I should do this or that" is the unconscious phrasing in ambivalence, with the emphasis on the *"I."* In inner reality, something beyond the neurotic's control *forces* him to doubt. By converting the role of passive victim into the role of active doubter, narcissism is autarchically preserved.

Thus, ambivalence denotes a desperate inner struggle between the wish to be passively and anally pierced, and the inner denial of this wish in the form of a pseudo-aggressive pretense that autarchy is preserved. *That ambivalence is most strongly pronounced in anal regression* has its good reasons: the anal phase, being the last station before the frantic, last-ditch rescue attempt of Oedipality is made, has for the child the magic attraction of the masochistic oral-anal past. If the Oedipal rescue attempt fails, the anal-oral regression is inevitable. Thus, since anality represents the last station passed before the progression to Oedipality takes place in the boy,* plunging back means—anal regression. Only if the latter does not suffice is the result oral regression—clearcut and less camouflaged.

Anal regression is the hotbed of ambivalence, also, because unconsciously the fiction of *"not having decided yet"* (between *active* progressive autarchic defense plus Oedipality, and regressive *passive* wish to be orally-anally penetrated) *can be maintained indefinitely, although the issue has been decided in the negative.* This camouflaged dichotomy: the fiction of battle still raging and the fact that

* The psychology of the girl is too involved for a capsule description; for detailed discussion, see *Neurotic Counterfeit-Sex,* especially Chapter VII ("Differences in the Development of Female and Male Sexuality"), pp. 244–252. Half of the book's 350 pages are devoted to female development, and disturbances of the latter.

the issue of the battle is lost, reminds one of the loser who still, in fantasy, reverts to the moment before the decision!

Summarizing the child's development on all three levels (oral, anal, phallic), the conclusion reads: *

1. The child's life begins with a series of passive experiences, which he misconstrues as manifestations of the mother's cruelty; the "septet of baby fears" bears witness to these fantastic misconceptions.

2. Biological necessity forces the child into a cathexis of different organs; the model for his misunderstandings of their functions is without exception taken from passive-oral experiences.

3. These passive-oral experiences are expressed "in the language" of the successive organs; the three levels of libidinous-aggressive development are unintelligible unless the connecting links are clarified.

4. The real danger inherent in successive passive experiences is the fact that they are offenses to the child's megalomania. The invariable sequence of events is: libidinous wish, *not* instantaneously fulfilled—offense to megalomania—fury, more or less inexpressible. The latter paves the way for psychic-masochistic "elaboration."

5. Each of the three erogenous zones witnesses passive defeats and weak aggressive countermeasures.

Psychic Level	Passive Experience	Aggressive Countermeasure
Oral	Fantasy of being pierced by breast (bottle).	Grasping breast (bottle) crying, spitting, vomiting.
Anal	Fantasy of being passively pierced by feces.	Fantasy of aggressive and autarchic use of feces.
Phallic	Feminine identification (negative Oedipus).	Masculine identification (positive Oedipus).

6. Each of the three erogenous zones teaches the child new libidinous pleasures, which is the only saving grace in the defeats sustained in the spheres of megalomania and aggression. In the order of their appearance (or perception), these gratifications are:

* These sketchy outlines of the three genetic levels omits description of the scopophiliac tendencies. See pp. 24 ff and 66 ff, and Chapter V, # 19, pp. 158 ff; also pp. 266 ff.

pleasure of sucking, pleasure of eliminating, pleasure experienced
via penis (clitoris, in the girl).

7. The role played by pre-stages of inner conscience, and by
conscience when developed, is visible in all "countermeasures."
The child's fury, inexpressible because of his helplessness, is also
stifled by the externally instilled reverence felt for mother and
(later) father. Although the outside world enforces this awe by
admonition, loving (or not quite loving) persuasion, and finally
moral reproach and punishment, the real inhibitory power is
derived from conscience. The inner conscience establishes itself
gradually; once it has taken over, it translates inhibitions from
the external to the internal, not for the purpose of creating a
"good" boy or girl, but because it thus renders the child more
helpless and passive. The "triad of retribution" (punishment,
moral reproach, inner guilt) which the inner conscience eventually
sets up becomes the basis for establishment of the *"end result of
the infantile conflict"—the poison of psychic masochism.* The
next chapter will deal with this subject.

IV. The Life Blood of Neurosis— Psychic Masochism

To begin with, here are conclusions drawn from clinical observation—admittedly my own observation, admittedly evaluated in accordance with my personal convictions:

1. The end result of the infantile conflict in *every* neurosis is exclusively stabilization on the *oral* rejection level, which is the basis of psychic masochism. This means an unconscious craving for "injustice collecting." Orally based psychic masochism is *the* basic neurosis.

2. Every neurotic tries to rescue himself to higher developmental levels (anal, phallic). These "rescue stations" are incomprehensible unless their pre-history is retraced to the oral base. They remain incomprehensible when it is not acknowledged that these inter-connections are desperate defenses.*

3. The degree to which oral-masochistic remnants remain in the unconscious of the individual determines his relative health or neuroticism.

4. No neurosis can be solved or changed without thorough analysis of the oral-masochistic basis.

5. Psychic masochism is not an id-wish but an ingenious defense mechanism, created by the unconscious ego to counteract the "torture machine" of unconscious conscience. Only secondarily does the specific defense acquire the valency of an unconscious "wish"— for all practical purposes.

6. Psychic masochism consists of a genetic *and* clinical picture (see Foreword); confusion of the one with the other leads to grave therapeutic errors. Both subdivisions are schematized on the following page.

7. Exactly because psychic masochism is an artifact, it is—to an individually variable extent—changeable in analysis.

8. Analysis of psychic masochism does *not* tend to invalidate the established rules of analysis (analysis of transference, resistance, use of free associations, analysis of dreams, "working through,"

* As formulated in *The Basic Neurosis*, p. 38 et seq.

Transition, because of superego's veto, of masochistic pleasure.

GENETIC PICTURE ⟶	CLINICAL PICTURE
Libidinous wish not instantly fulfilled —double frustration (libidinous and megalomaniacal) — fury — inexpressibility of fury—boomeranging of aggression against the child himself because of the triad of retribution (punishment, moral reproach, guilt)— libidinization of guilt and punishment.	1. Provocation, through behavior or the misuses of an external situation, of disappointment and refusal. The outer world is identified with the "refusing" pre-Oedipal mother. 2. Pseudo-aggression,* seemingly in self-defense, with total unawareness of the part played in bringing about the disappointment. 3. Self-pity ("This can happen only to poor little me") accompanied by unconscious masochistic pleasure.

* The term pseudo-aggression denotes *unconsciously* mobilized *defensive* aggression, directed against the reproach of the superego, accusing the ego of psychic masochism. Objections have been made to the term; its detractors claim that it can be misunderstood as referring to conscious hypocrisy. Nothing of the kind is meant; moreover, the possible alternatives (e.g., spurious aggression, defensive aggression, etc.) are open to the same rather far-fetched objection.

connecting "actual" conflicts with the repressed past, etc.). It merely adds another component.

9. Clinical experience proves that it is not sufficient, in analysis, simply to mention that psychic masochism is "also present." When psychic masochism is left on the periphery, the interpretation is ineffective because of the patient's continuous repressions.

10. The main reason for poor therapeutic results in analysis lies in the failure to devote any time—or enough time—to working through of orally based masochism.

11. Analysis of superficial—though also unconscious layers— is no substitute for analysis of the "basic neurosis." If the deepest layers are not reached, the result is pseudo-analysis. Inner facts are

at odds with the interpretation; the two do not meet even *at* a tangent, and the whole analysis goes *off* on a tangent.

12. Psychic masochism, since it is a universal human problem, proves conclusively that the superego is the real master of the personality. If human beings must derive goodly parts of their "happiness" from consciously perceived "unhappiness," superego rules supreme.

There are three reasons for the surprising amount of resistance, evident even in scientific circles, aroused by stressing the paramount importance of the specific defense mechanism, psychic masochism.

First, the emotional element. A very powerful "something" in each of us rejects the disagreeable and terrifying fact that there is allure in "pleasure in pain, defeat, humiliation." No human being is excluded from this reaction, and as previously stated, Freud himself alluded to it:

> Another motive of "opposite wish dreams" lies so near that one easily falls into the trap * of overlooking it, *as has happened to myself over a long period of time . . . the masochistic component.*

Second, the complexity of the problem. Quite correctly, Struempel once remarked that the physician sees, in general, only what he has been taught to see. Since it is not part of the regular curriculum, psychic masochism, especially in a study of the differentiation between genetic and clinical pictures, comes under the heading of additional, voluntary, extra-curricular activity. Even then, it is rather frowned upon than otherwise.

The complexity of the problem leads to a series of objections, which have been summarized in *The Basic Neurosis* as "ten scientific and ten popular misconceptions" (pp. 8–14). Among those, one retains priority: inability to comprehend how one and the same substratum (orally based psychic masochism) can produce so different clinical pictures. The objection is based on "title reading"—it overlooks the *specific additional factor,* specifically adduced in the 27 clinical pictures, described in *The Basic Neurosis.* To

---

* The verbatim quotation (Ges. Schr. III. p. 30). "kommt in Gefahr," is idiomatic, hence untranslatable; it denotes something like "endangers oneself," "enters the danger zone."

draw upon chemistry for a parallel, it is quite true that it is difficult to imagine that one source, petroleum, is the basis for such
disparate products as synthetic rubber, alcohol, solvents, plastics,
ammonia, explosives, anaesthetics, gasoline, wax, lubricants, diesel
oil, etc. Difficult, that is, for a layman—not for the chemist. . . .
Another new-old objection misunderstands psychic masochism as
"most primary expression" of the death instinct, which of course,
has never been claimed. Finally, the complexity of psychic masochism (in its genetic and clinical pictures) is "simplified" by some
observers by simply claiming that psychic masochism is "a gross
oversimplification of human aspiration." This, in turn, is just as
naive as though someone would seriously claim that the atomic
bomb is an "oversimplification" of a child's toy.

Three, there is but one point on which honest misunderstanding
may exist. People who minimize the importance and deleterious
effects of psychic masochism make out of a boa constrictor a harmless pet; adherents of the "pet theory" of psychic masochism may
have the erroneous impression that people believing, as I do, in psychic masochism's basic importance in neurosis, advocate the neglect
of other therapeutically established and analytically commonplace
facts. Nothing of this sort was ever suggested; only an additional
element is provided.

The combination of all these points explains how so obvious a
psychic procedure as *libidinized* self-damage can be overlooked.

Of course, there are mitigating circumstances. Every human
being has gone through the Oedipal phase; when attention is
fixed on this stage, therefore, evidence of it can be found in abun-
dance in every patient. The difficulty is that while his regression
corresponds to interpretation in hysterical cases, the correspondence
is only partial in cases of anal regression, and in cases of oral regression it does not correspond at all. For in orally regressed neurotics
the Oedipal blind merely covers deeper—and usually unrecognized—masochistic tendencies. All three types, however, show the
Oedipal manifestations. Where the deeper regressions are the real
problem, pseudo-analysis, again, is the result of accepting the mask
at face value.

On the other hand, oral material is frequently analyzed. Here,
however, another rather tragic misunderstanding tends to arise.
There is no uniform opinion on the actual content of oral regres-

sion. *Historically*, in the life of the baby, orality denotes oral greed and the *wish to get*. *Clinically*—and this is the picture visible in the adult patient—we see oral wishes after they have gone through masochistic elaboration, so that they read: *"I wish to be refused."* If no differentiation is made, and the explanation given to the orally regressed masochist is that he aggressively wishes to get, the therapist is merely aiming at the wrong target. Moreover, he is playing—unwittingly, of course—into the hands of the patient's inner defenses. The therapy certifies to the patient his alleged aggression, and passes the counterfeit of pseudo-aggression as genuine aggression. That, precisely, is the purpose of the patient's secondary defense.

No less tragic is the frequent confusion between real and compensatory aggression in anally regressed cases. If one gives the obsessional patient an interpretation of anal "sadism"—without taking into account the fact that the formulation, dating from 1908, does not differentiate between sadism, aggression, and pseudo-aggression—one again, and again unwittingly, plays the game of the patient's inner defenses. Every obsessional patient is ready to admit to his inner aggression early in treatment. This is very understandable, since these aggressions cover the deeper masochistic regression. He is also quite ready to accept the guilt feeling which results from these alleged aggressions. Nevertheless, the whole business is simply a palimpsest.

In short, oral regression * and its subsequent "rescue stations" have a significance even greater than that claimed for them by the proponents of their importance.

I do not propose to repeat what I presented and substantiated in the 365 pages of *The Basic Neurosis,* in describing twenty-seven clinical entities of oral regression. I can only reiterate what I suspected long ago: *the majority of neurotics have a rendezvous with orality.*

What is the irresistible attraction of the masochistic solution of the basic infantile conflict?

First, it *makes the best of a painful situation*. The child is under continual pressure from hopeless passivity reinforced by the "triad

---

* The English school of analysis investigated this sector quite extensively. Its adherents worked out the infantile aggressions (and resulting inner guilt). They overlooked, however, the masochistic elaboration.

of retribution," and from hopeless, inexpressible fury. In this impasse, it is a truly brilliant stroke to *make pleasure out of displeasure.*

Second, the masochistic solution *preserves infantile megalomania* to an outstanding degree. Obviously, the most painful experience of babyhood and infancy—shattering of the grandiose illusion of omnipotence, autarchy, megalomania,—cannot be accepted meekly and in toto, and without some recompense. The pleasure-in-pain pattern salvages a few fragments of the original illusion, at the slight cost of some reformulation in the clinical picture. The commentary now reads: "It is not true that the bad mother punishes me; *I*, through my provocations, *make* her punish me!" In this peculiar unconscious version of logic, (metalogic, to use a term coined by Dr. G. Wilbur) the helpless child triumphs over the powerful Giantess!

Third, it seems to be a universal human tendency to *accept the painful, provided narcissistic safeguards are installed.* Freud himself elaborated ·on this point in two mechanisms: formation of "the ego ideal" and "unconscious repetition compulsion."

One should bear in mind Freud's formulation: the ego ideal was established during the educational process in order to save the child narcissistic humiliation. Instead of acknowledging repeated lesions in narcissism, the child introjects the commands of the educators, thus constructing a system in which he is no longer "forced" to obey, since he abstains of his "own" volition.

One should also remember Freud's concept of the "unconscious repetition compulsion," * which is beyond the pleasure principle, and contains the imperative urge to repeat, *actively,* experiences one has been forced to bear, *passively.* The purpose, again, is to eradicate the lesion in self-esteem (narcissism). This concept, never clinically applied by Freud, has proved to be of greater importance than originally assumed.

It was precisely an application of the "unconscious repetition compulsion" which Eidelberg and I postulated in 1933 in our joint paper, "The Breast Complex in the Male" *(Int. Zeitschr. f. Psychoanalyse).* This was the concept that the boy overcomes the trauma

---

* Not to be confused with unconscious repetitions which either serve filtered innuendos of repressed libidinous aims or are pseudo-aggressive defenses directed at the inner conscience.

of weaning by *actively* repeating what he had experienced *passively*. By identifying penis and breast, he negates the loss of the breast. The phallic penis pride has quite a massive oral substructure.

The theory is equally applicable to the psychological superstructure in (male) intercourse. Here, too, there is a reversal of the infantile situation—in which the boy was the baby, *passively* fed by the *active* Giantess (pre-Oedipal mother). The adult male *actively* pushes an oblong "object" into a *passively* recipient opening (penis = breast; vagina = mouth; sperm = urine = milk). No wonder man calls woman "baby"!

The whole concept of unconscious repetition compulsion was later applied by myself to the psychology of the "he-man." * I have given an account of the He-Man in *Divorce Won't Help* and *Conflict in Marriage.*

Moreover,—as Jekels and I assumed in "Transference and Love" (1933)—the "narcissistic unification tendency" underlies both the phenomenon of normal tender love, which is the fourth example, (see table following, and also Chapter V, pp. 193 ff.) and the superstructure of the sexual act. Psychologically speaking, there is no plausible explanation for the pronounced tendency of lovers to embrace each other as closely as possible. This is a process which goes beyond mere tactile sensations, and the proximity which is part of the sex act itself. Its importance, and its raison d'etre, become clear when it is viewed as an attempt to negate the infantile separation from the breast of the pre-Oedipal mother, which had been perceived as part of the child's own body. The lovers' closeness recreates the infantile illusion of narcissistic "unity," an illusion which cannot be created alone. Thus the normal adult is driven to the duality: man—woman.

The *clinical* picture in psychic masochism, it seems to me, is the fifth example of this tendency to accept the painful, as long as narcissistic safeguards are present. Which all goes to show that the human being has the unlimited ability to deceive himself—even unconsciously.

The following table schematizes the narcissistic safeguards and the attempts at reparation which are found in these five mechanisms.

* The havoc caused in neurotics' sex lives by undigested baby-passivity is discussed at length in *Neurotic Counterfeit-Sex.*

UNCONSCIOUS NARCISSISTIC REPAIR

In formation of ego ideal:	"Nobody has the power to force me; *I,* of my own volition, accept specific restrictions because I choose to do so."
In "unconscious repetition compulsion":	"By actively repeating an experience to which I was passively subjected, the offense to my narcissism is wiped out."
In overcoming trauma of "Breast-Complex":	"I neither lost, nor have any need for the (withdrawn) breast (bottle); I have in my own body a similar organ." (compensatory penis pride)
In tender love:	"There is no deflating discrepancy between my ego (achievement) and ego ideal (enshrined promises of achievement); by projecting my ego ideal on the beloved, I am credited in advance (without needing to offer proof) with having fulfilled all the promises made as a child."
In the *clinical* picture in psychic masochism:	"It is not the bad mother (or her successive representatives) who is punishing me; *I,* through my initial provocation, made her punish me."

Enlarging on this concept, it could be said that each additional rung on the ladder of libidinous-aggressive development represents three adjustments to the child: unavoidable cathexis of different organs; a "rescue station" from the oral danger, as previously pointed out; and in addition, a narcissistic pseudo-aggressive compromise.*

* One can observe this *reversion to autarchy after disappointment* on every level of development. To cite but one example. A patient dated his marital conflict back to a specific scene during his honeymoon. They were in Venice; he wanted sex on a specific afternoon, but his wife refused, pointing out that he would be too tired to carry out their plan to visit some curiosity in the suburbs. After pleading with her, he suddenly felt a need to retire to the bathroom. He defecated copiously, returning in a "brilliant mood." Superficially evident is the anal-aggressive countermeasure; on a deeper layer, autarchy was re-installed, for an oblong "something" penetrated his anus. Thus, by identifying rectum and vagina, penis and fecal rod, he made himself "independent" and achieved for himself a "happy mood." It is superfluous to state that his wife's refusal activated masochistic fantasies in the man, immediately evidenced in his *passive* defense (something penetrated *him!*).

Every analysis which fails to drain the life blood of neurosis by attempting to destroy (or at least diminish) *the psychic masochistic oral basis is, in my opinion, but a pseudo-analysis.* The term has no derogatory implication: it simply indicates that, in a specific case, the essentials were not perceived and therefore not worked on. Nobody is infallible; all of us, on occasion, overlook basic facts in the case of a specific patient. As Horace put it: "Quandoque bonus dormibat Homerus." Our terminology lacks a word to cover this situation; we take refuge behind such phrases as "the essentials were overlooked," "the wrong spot was attacked," etc. By and large, such oversights can be traced back to emotional problems in the analyst, which must be kept in repression. I hope that in future didactic analyses of the young analyst more attention will be paid to "orally based masochism," and that this emphasis will be reflected in the future analysts' treatment of their patients.

As matters stand now, the analyst faces two possibilities. He may get, as a patient, a genuine hysterical neurotic; in this case, the Oedipal instrumentarium is decisive and sufficient, and the patient will be cured. Or (and this is more likely), the case will be one of deeper regression, and the patient will remain uncured. There is but one exception to this rule, and this exception is neither very frequent, nor very flattering for the analyst: *"success because of unconscious fear."*

The patient projects (in the transference neurosis) his own fantasies of omnipotence upon the analyst, which makes the latter "omnipotent" and "omniscient." Hence, in the patient's unconscious fantasy, he is bound to penetrate one's deepest "secrets." Frightened by that—frequently unjustified—possibility, a symptom is given up in order to retain the basis of the neurosis.

Unfortunately, these "successes" are short-lived. They remind one of the story of the employee who was stealing money from the company he worked for, remaining undetected for some time. One morning when the young man is looking tired and dissipated, his employer makes a joking reference to his extensive night life and comments, "You look pretty pale to me." The culprit suspects that his theft has been discovered and, on the basis of this erroneous conclusion, stops stealing—for *some time* . . . . The accent is on "some time," meaning that an ad hoc constructed mechanism of temporary renunciation has no permanency.

These peculiar, short-lived, overnight "changes," bypassing the typical ups and downs of a typical and honest analytic success, are also characterized by the absence of any congruity with the material worked through in that specific phase of analysis. They are, in short, preventive mechanisms prompted by fear; afterwards, fear abates, and the symptom recurs.

Does all this mean that destruction or diminution of orally based psychic masochism is an easy or satisfying task? Not at all. One cannot escape the impression that analysis of psychic masochism is the destruction of an infantile house of cards, in which each card is a carefully guarded illusion. The amount of resistance put up by the patient cannot be overestimated. He is, in effect, a person sinking more and more deeply into quicksand, and calling frantically for help, but when you reach out to rescue him he treats you like an intruder. He does not exactly say, "Leave me alone"; he merely continues to appeal for aid, while somehow not seeing your helping hand.

Certain modifications of the technique are necessary in the initial stages of the analyses of orally regressed patients. (See p. 87f). Moreover, it is essential for the analyst to be enormously patient, thoroughly consistent, and *relatively* free of psychic masochism, at least to the degree that the patient should not intuitively feel a secret ally in the analyst's unconscious. Otherwise, even correct interpretations are ineffective.

Nobody claims that analysis is a cure-all. One should not underestimate the pleasures embedded in neurosis. In general, however, the results are very satisfactory. Even in cases where the results did not match expectations, the after-effects are surprising. As much as one or two years after the conclusion of the analysis, it becomes clear that the analysis has penetrated more deeply than early appearances indicated. Such patients were unable to give the analyst the "satisfaction" of knowing that he had helped; the old narcissistic-megalomaniacal safeguards were at work.

In cases where the patient "cannot take it," and runs away, one has at least the consolation of knowing that the battle, if lost, was at least not fought on a spurious front. Personally, I am never astonished when a patient does not "give in." I marvel, rather, at the patients who allow us to cure them.

Psychic masochism is a universal phenomenon. It is impossible, therefore, to attempt to describe the masochist externally, and purely phenomenologically. The task is as futile as any attempt to describe the infinite individual variations of the human face. There is no single characteristic of external behavior, no single specificity of surface action, which would enable even an experienced observer to spot a masochist.

Inwardly, all psychic masochists are seething volcanos, erupting "injustice collecting" instead of lava. To continue the simile, they use this *"lava"* for two purposes: *a part cools off and becomes petrified, to remain a lifelong proof of the masochist's "justification" of his endless complaints, whereas, the other part of the lava is constantly produced, for daily use only,* to be constantly exchanged.

Another attitude is equally characteristic. Psychic masochists *are painfully submissive to a "stronger" person, and as painfully brutal and arrogant towards a "weaker."* This is perhaps the most disagreeable of their traits. The naive observer who condemns them for the "cowardly" approach to human relations does not, of course, realize that psychic masochists' bullying is no more than a desperate inner alibi, designed to refute the superego's charge that they are unconsciously passive, and derive pleasure from their passivity. No human beings are more in need of the benevolence embodied in the "tout comprendre,* c'est tout pardonner" attitude than are these inner weaklings, who play the "big shot" and "kick a man when he's down." They would be entirely intolerable, if not for the saving grace of their propensity for "magic gestures," those unconscious dramatizations of the defense: "I'll show you, by my behavior, how I wanted to be treated—kindly and lovingly." †

With these necessary reservations, a few frequently encountered types can be delineated.

The Injustice Collecting Type. This is a person who at all times is potentially or actually enraged because he is the victim of some terrible wrong. He will provoke an actual—or if necessary, a potential—enemy until he succeeds in getting his badly needed dose of

---

* The French proverb exaggerates; nobody (and that includes investigators of the unconscious) can "tout comprendre." Our present knowledge is admittedly imperfect.

† See Chapter V, p. 123f.

daily—if not hourly—injustice. Between doses, he will accept as substitute a diet of impersonal, universal injustice. Since the world is what it is, the injustice collector is in no danger of remaining unsatisfied. This type is characterized by an air of hyper-excitement, hyper-touchiness, hyper-bellicosity.*

The Coldly Detached Type. Phenomenologically, he seems to represent the opposite of the injustice collector. He is an icicle personified—distant, cold, unmoved, frequently so taciturn that he is classed with the "he gives me the creeps" variety. His presence makes other people uncomfortable. His pose is that of a visitor from another planet. He pays no compliments, and is never guilty of making a moderately friendly-laudatory remark. Inwardly, of course, he is the same erupting volcano as his brother (or sister) under the skin, the clearly visible injustice collector.

The "Nice" Masochist. It is stretching the truth only sightly to call these people the only "nice" human beings. They are interested in your troubles, and eager to be helpful. They excel in "magic gestures." Under this ingratiating surface is a hopelessly entangled masochist, suffering for reasons which he cannot understand (namely, his or her construction of the unhappy situation.) In general, this type accepts his conscious unhappiness with stoicism and resignation. It is hopeless to try to help these people with common-sense advice. Their inexhaustible stock of rationalizations assures the permanence of the painful situation.

If they are women, the epitheton ornans "charming" is often applicable. In clinical analysis, these "nice" and "charming" masochists present specific difficulties: they use these qualities as a defense, the latter sometimes impenetrable. They also claim that the "mechanism of orality" does not apply to them, since they do not show the typical pseudo-aggressive defense. In inner reality, they do make use of this defense; evidence of its presence can easily be found in their dreams and conflicts. Practically speaking, this "charm" means that the analyst must perform an *additional* task; he must uncover the hidden pseudo-aggression. Once this is done—and it may take months—a secondary difficulty arises. These patients consider their newly-retrieved pseudo-aggression a "great step forward."

* For discussion of the psychic masochist's "elastic fraud corner" in money matters, see *Money and Emotional Conflicts*, p. 18.

The next step in analysis is to prove that these pseudo-aggressions are self-damaging, too. The "charming" psychic masochist's failure to built up the typical defense of pseudo-aggression has made him a "nicer" person, but no less of a masochist.

The Every-day Type. It might be more precise to designate this masochist "the unsuspected type." One meets an energetic business man, full of ideas and initiative; his private life, surprisingly enough, reveals him as the (self-created) victim of a shrewish wife. One meets a woman with the proverbial "calculating machine instead of a heart," a woman whose behavior seems to indicate that she has no "feelings" whatever; actually she tortures herself with envy, the wrong boy friends, and other injustices.

The "Heaping-Coals-of-Fire-upon-His-Head" Technique (Self-Creation of an Artificial Victim Through Silence). One of the masochistic techniques merits special attention, not because of its frequency, but because it is an example of the depth to which the inner scourge can penetrate. This is the *silence* with which some masochists prefer to meet reproaches. *Instead of defending them-* ~~mostly~~ *selves, they choose to be unjustly accused.* Allegedly, *they look forward to the malefactor's tearful acknowledgment of his injustice and cruelty.* Many of these injustices, it goes without saying, are unconsciously provoked by the victim. The procedure could be called "self-creation of an artificial victim."

One clinical, and one literary example will be adduced.

In analysis, a patient remembered a scene from his fourth or fifth year. On a bitter-cold winter day, when he was being taken to see his grandmother, his mother fastened a shawl over his cap as extra protection. Accidentally, in her haste, she passed the pin which fastened the shawl through the superficial skin layer of his chin. The boy felt intense pain, but gave no sign and made no complaint. But when the mother saw blood on his chin, and exclaimed, "Why didn't you tell me!" the boy began to cry.

In Dostojewski's little known novelette, *The Soft Woman,* the main character is a middle-aged former army captain. He had been dishonorably discharged for cowardice when he refused to challenge an officer from another regiment to a duel, to redress an alleged insult to one of the captain's comrades, and thus a reflection on the honor of the regiment. After his discharge, the captain passes through a period of degradation and poverty. Unexpectedly, he

receives a small inheritance, and settles down to semi-prosperity as
a pawnbroker. He despises his occupation, intending to continue
it only until he has saved a specified sum with which to start a
new life. A young girl of sixteen brings her few possessions to him
to be pawned, so that she will have the money to advertise for a
position as governess. She is an orphan, and is shamelessly exploited
by two aunts, who want to marry her off to a grocer. The ex-captain
marries the girl, but after the marriage he installs a regime of
"severe silence." With this method, he provokes his wife into more
or less serious flirtations, into silent fury, and finally into an
attempt to murder him in his sleep. One morning he awakens to
find his wife playing with the gun which was always left on the
table for protection against burglars. He does not indicate that he
is awake. She approaches and puts the gun to his temple. The
husband still does not move; he opens his eyes for a second, but
only to make his wife wonder whether he has seen her and understood her intention.

His purpose, in playing this fantastic masochistic game, is to
prove to her that he is not the coward she believes him to be, since
she has heard, from other sources, the story of his past. To make
it clear that he knows of her attempt at murder, the husband buys
a separate bed for his wife. This leads to some kind of hallucinatory
"nerve fever" in her, a sickness which lasts for many weeks. After her
recovery, the woman is silent and withdrawn. The "severe silence"
becomes mutual. One day she sings in his presence, as if he were an
object, not a person. This convinces the husband that his wife
"nullifies him"; his reaction is furious: a frenzy of despair, *and* love
for the rejecting wife, whose feet he kisses. He wants to restore his
marriage, and pours out his heart to his wife, but she commits
suicide.

The hyper-masochistic hero uses two techniques. The first is
senseless pseudo-aggressive provocation—the "silent treatment"—
with the connotation of revenge, for after his discharge from the
army his former friends had "cut him," and refused to speak to
him. Thus, he achieved active repetition of a passively endured
experience, although on an innocent object. More important was
this grandiose plan: "Later she will know how magnanimous I
have been, and reproach herself for having misjudged my generosity
(in choosing not to complain, and enduring in silence [transl.]).
Once this penetrates, she will value me ten times higher than she

did; she will fall on her knees, fold her hands together and adore me." Of course the plan miscarries, and what amounts to a battle of wits and inner rehabilitation takes place. His weapons are injustice (for he was misjudged), positive magic gesture (his marriage to the rejected orphan), and finally a negative magic gesture (silence). In this battle, the hero is completely defeated—that is, from the conscious viewpoint. Unconsciously, he is the victor, for he successfully shattered his plan to rehabilitate himself and achieve compensatory happiness.

One should note that the girl was by no means as "soft" as the ex-captain believed at their first meetings. Short ironic remarks, quick anger, contemptuous looks, were noted by him, but misjudged as "shyness." His subsequent disappointment was clearly planned— unconsciously. When his pseudo-aggressive provocation, in the form of silence and refusal of tenderness and luxury, is added, the scene is set for the final masochistic collapse.*

An explanation of psychic masochism, which at first glance appears rather plausible, has been promoted in private discussions for decades and recently has also appeared in our literature. This formulation holds that the aim of masochism is to win love from an otherwise unapproachable parent. When normal love cannot be achieved, the child provokes attention by his naughtiness, the consequent parental punishment substituting for the love-aim. This pattern then becomes libidinized, and takes the lead.

The idea of masochism as love-surrogate has the advantage of bypassing the painful question: how can psychic masochism pure and simple be an aim? There is another advantage in this theory; it constitutes a consoling fantasy. But the aim of science is not to

---

* An interesting sidelight is the poor motivation of the girl's suicide. Notes on suicide in Dostojewski's *Notebook of a Writer* also point in the direction of this scotoma. This is rather strange, because of Dostojewski's unusual instinctive knowledge of unconscious masochism. In *The Writer and Psychoanalysis*, I pointed out that writers express only the secondary defenses against their repressed wishes (see Chapter II of this volume). The question then arises: how could Dostojewski base many of his novels on an apotheosis of suffering, and consequently an admission of masochism? We know nothing of Dostojewski's childhood (see Freud's *Dostojewski and Patricide*); we are familiar, however, with the fact that he suffered from epilepsy (hystero-epilepsy is Freud's suspicion). It is possible that for a man who is always enacting a *rehearsal of death* in hystero-epileptic attacks, the *admission of masochism is in itself a "lesser crime."*

avoid painful facts. The best I can say for this formulation is that
I would like to see it verified. Unfortunately, the chances are slim,
if not non-existent. *For the child's development is never a faithful
reproduction of evironment plus biological endowment.* The third
and *decisive* element is always the *elaboration contributed by the
child's unconscious ego.* This is precisely the element which is
ignored when the parents are held to be the source of the child's
disturbance.

Private discussions of this theory inevitably boil down to an
alleged axion. A parent, it is claimed, never treats two children in
the same way; there are always (imperceptible) differences. This
point is adduced to disprove the star argument of the opposing
party, which contends that two brothers who have been rejected by
their neurotic mother can, when grown up, either *correct* or *perpetuate* their unhappy childhood situation: frequently one marries a loving woman, the other a shrew. Here the discussion hits an
impasse. Who can measure, or prove the presence of the
imperceptible?

I had the opportunity to analyze a young woman, one of six
children, whose mother abhorred tenderness. Even kissing was
forbidden by the mother, because it "transmitted germs." Her obsessional neurosis (which existed long before her marriage) forced
her to treat all of her six children equally. No imperceptible differences were possible. None the less, her children grew up with very
different personalities. Some were normal, some neurotic. There
was no uniformity in their neuroses, either.

As if the unconscious ego's elaboration were not enough of a
complication, it should be remembered that the child does not see
reality as it is, but only through the spectacles of his own projection. Even a lenient mother (father) can become an ogre in a child's
eyes. These projectively misconstrued images are the ones later
introjected into the ego ideal. It is virtually meaningless, therefore,
to clear ·the parents' objective record.

Finally, one should not overlook the fact that the child's aggression, always potentially present in adult strength, continues to
accumulate in the inner conscience during the years when it is
unusable.

In psychic masochists, the mechanism of "taking the blame for
the *lesser crime,*" which is always self-damaging, frequently results in

external reactions which are *semi-moronic*. If an experienced driver smashes a fender on a tree and lands in a ditch because he was unable to ward off a bee that flew into his car; if a neuropsychiatrist, just introduced to psychosomatics, overlooks obvious indications of brain tumor in one of his patients; if an acknowledged professor of English literature "forgets" that Samuel Johnson once wrote a study of Richard Savage; if a brilliant student of technology, the only one in his class to solve the theory of a complicated problem, gets no credit for his solution because he has confused the figures given in the problem—the uninitiated will marvel at such "temporary stupidity," or doubt that the driver can drive, that the physician has a license, that the professor can read or the student is familiar with the ABC of a technical problem. Actually, all these "lapses" represent the application of a *mechanism of merciless exposure of pseudo-"crimes" in substitution*. When accused of psychic masochism, the ego pleads pseudo-aggression, or even moronity. It is difficult to decide whether the ego merely exaggerates the defense, or whether the distortion is caused by the superego's injection of a few drops of irony into what a dipsomaniac woman patient called "the masochistic cocktail."

When one adds background material to the clinical incidents just cited—namely, the driver has just been involved in another accident—innocently, he claims; the neuro-psychiatrist has a neurotic wife who suffers from ulcus ventriculi, approaching perforation stage, which the "psycho-somatically" oriented husband negates; the professor has recently been forced to back down and reveal his ignorance in a discussion with a supposedly uninformed fellow, whom he had patronized; the student's father (himself a professor of technology) has been reproaching him for his unwillingness to take his finals, and discounting his claim that he is not thoroughly prepared *—the merciless exposure becomes less surprising. In their own familiar fields, these people could unerringly find a way to look thoroughly foolish. The superego is a brutal teaser, as can be seen from "anti-fallacy dreams" (see Chapter IX).

Often narcissistic safeguards are applied, seemingly as a hedge, before such ludicrous self-exposure takes place. The student of engineering, for example, was the only one in his class to solve the problem posed. Once he had proved to himself that he was a

---

* The son was unconsciously playing a self-damaging joke on the father. For details see Chapter VIII, pp. 259 ff.

"genius," he could allow himself to fail. The combination of self-provoked defeat and self-attested narcissistic self-elevation is typical for the psychic masochist.

One cannot escape the impression that specific amounts of psychic masochism, once they have been mobilized for use on a specific occasion (such as the expectation of danger), are irrevocably destined to be "spent." Depending on the makeup of the individual, this tendency manifests itself in "senseless" depression post fortuito facto, in deposition on some other point, or in other ways. It seems probable to me that much of what goes under the heading, "those who cannot take success," belongs in this group.

Let us compare the "masterpiece of neurosis"—the neurotic symptom—with the "masterpiece of health"—sublimation. The following table summarizes the theory; for elaboration and review of the literature, the reader is referred to Chapter III of *The Basic Neurosis* ("The Nine-Point Basis of Every Neurosis"), and to Chapter VIII of *The Battle of the Conscience* ("Normal Antidotes for Feeling of Guilt").

Neurotic Symptom	Sublimation
I. *Structural Basis*	I. *Structural Basis*
Every neurotic symptom has a five-layer structure, only the unconscious defense against the defense becoming visible. The sequence is: 1. unconscious wish emerges; 2. superego objects (Veto #1); 3. first defense is presented by unconscious ego; 4. superego objects once more (Veto #2); 5. second defense is presented by the unconscious ego, guilt is accepted for the lesser crime, reverberations reach the psychic surface, cloaked in rationalizations. The conflict is unconscious, of infantile origin and repetitive. The end result of the infantile conflict is always oral-masochistic. Every neurosis represents a rescue-attempt from the oral danger.	Sublimation has a five-layer structure: 1. The starting point in sublimation is not an id-wish per se, but the end result of a conflict historically originating in an id-wish. 2. The second layer represents a superego reproach directed against the solution of this conflict (Veto #1). 3. The third layer consists of the first defense of the unconscious ego. 4. The fourth layer is again a superego reproach directed against the first defense (Veto #2). 5. The fifth layer, the second defense presented by the unconscious ego, is a compromise. Only this compromise is sublimated.

Neurotic Symptom	Sublimation
Every neurotic aggression is but pseudo–aggression. The differentiation between "leading" and "misleading" unconscious identification gives the clue to the resultant neurotic personality. In every neurosis, fear is predominant. Every neurosis is regulated by the mechanism of acceptance of inner guilt for the "lesser crime." Neurosis is a progressive and not self-limiting disease.	
II. *Material* Oral, anal, phallic, according to level of regression.	II. *Material* Exclusively pre-genital.
III. *Driving Power* Tenacity of id wishes and defenses, and, more important, need to come to terms with the superego.	III. *Driving Power* Tenacity of original conflict, plus ability to get the better of the superego.
IV. *Force* Since the neurotic ego has only pseudo-aggression at its disposal, the results are meager; masochization of the personality follows, secondarily though unconsciously enjoyed.	IV. *Force* Since the more normal ego has real as well as pseudo-aggression at its disposal, the results are less meager; masochization is visible however, as watered-down substitutes are achieved instead of original aims.
V. *Pleasure Gain* Only masochistic, with *twice* filtered innuendos of original wishes and defenses.	V. *Pleasure Gain* Opposite of masochism: narcissistic pleasure at having aggressively outsmarted the superego after accepting substitution.
VI. *Social Backing* Rejection by environment; fear, external unproductivity.	VI. *Social Backing* Acceptance by environment; absence of fear; productive external advantages —money, avocations, hobbies, etc.
VII. *Stability* Constant flow of new defenses as old ones wear out (vetoed by superego).	VII. *Stability* Once established, normally no collapse.
VIII. *End Result* Victory of the superego over the ego.	VIII. *End Result* Limited victory of the ego over the superego.

To exemplify, I am choosing *stage fright* and *acting* as para-digms—a choice to some extent influenced by the fact that their underlying tendency, scopophilia, is in general a stepchild of our literature.

It is rather curious that the popular and psychoanalytic inter-pretations of the psychology of acting should coincide. One ordi-narily expects these two views to be at odds, and ordinarily they are, the discrepancy contributing largely to the popular misconcep-tion of analysis as a science of spite and sophism, concerned only with confusing the layman. In the case of acting, however, the macroscopic and microscopic assessments seem to be identical. Discarding the technicalities of analytic language and the decora-tive cliches of popular speech, it is found that both groups agree that the actor bubbles over with exhibitionism, which is allegedly the basis of his talent and the reason for his choice of a career. By unanimous consent, the actor is a "show-off" and "ham."

Is popular opinion unusually perspicacious in this case, or is the accepted analytic opinion naive? In my opinion, the accepted analytic opinion is superficial and needs revision.

To begin with, acting represents a sublimation. As noted on the preceding chart, the highly complex phenomenon of sublimation reflects, not the original repressed wish, but the result of a series of psychic detours, compromises and counter-compromises achieved in the course of the "battle of the conscience." The material of sublimation is neither the original id-wish nor the defense against the id-wish, but *the defense against the defense against a conflict originating historically in an id-wish.* In other words, sublimation is not the child, but the grandchild of the original conflict.

The five layers in sublimation are as follows: Layer I, *end result* of an infantile *pregenital and libidinized* conflict; Layer II, first superego reproach and veto; Layer III, first defense of the uncon-scious ego; Layer IV, rejection of the defense and second superego veto; Layer V, second defense of the unconscious ego, irrefutable because it is presented in the terms of the socially approved and accepted.

The power behind this victory over the superego is derived from the sublimator's *inner aggression.* The neurotic is a poor sublimator because of the unfavorable distribution of his aggression, which is almost entirely concentrated in the superego and thus used to flog the ego. In normality, or in the state of psychic health produced by successful analysis, the balance of power is different. The ego either has or acquires an adequate store of aggression, which it uses to fight the superego—often successfully—and to achieve reality aims.

This is the sequence of events in the case of the actor: * The wish which enters sublimation is *not exhibitionism at all,* but a modified end-product of the opposite tendency: *voyeurism* (peeping). In previous writings, I have repeatedly stressed the fact that one part of the scopophiliac instinct can be used as defense against the other, although (in my opinion) voyeurism alone is derived from an original drive and exhibitionism is merely a defense. After voyeurism and exhibitionism have been established, they become available as defenses.

The material entering Layer I of the actor's (or actress') sublimation is *not* the original voyeurism, which, the literature agrees, is narcissistic self-peeping. It is in the second stage that other objects are included in voyeurism. The voyeurism of Layer I ("I want to peep at mother's breast, body, and [later] father's penis") is in itself a concession to reality, since narcissistic concentration on self is forbidden (taboo of masturbation). This indicates, already said, that the material entering sublimation is not a direct id-wish.

The sublimation which takes the form of acting can be schematized as follows:

Layer I.   "I want to be a voyeur of mother, father (and later of intimacies between them)."

Layer II.   (first superego veto) "You have no right to peep at mother, father."

Layer III. (first defense of unconscious ego) "I am not a voyeur or interested in being one; I want to exhibit my body."

Layer IV.   (second superego reproach) "Transgressing educational commands by exhibiting is also forbidden."

Layer V.   (second defense of the unconscious ego) "I am not aggressive in exhibitionism, and I am not a voyeur. I want to be a good boy (or girl), be social-minded and give other people pleasure."

This fifth layer, and *only* the fifth layer, is sublimation.

The naivete of previous explanations of exhibitionism may be

* First stated in "On Acting and Stagefright," *The Psychiatric Quarterly,* 23:2, 1949.

compared with this conclusion: the actor is a "ham" and a "show-off" as a defense. Unconsciously, he is glad to attract attention to himself, even at the cost of making himself ridiculous, because exhibitionism is his inner shield against more deeply repressed voyeurism. Again unconsciously, he gladly accepts the blame for the lesser crime.

What remnants of the actor's earlier wishes are rescued? The actor wanted to be a voyeur, but instead he exhibits. His special good fortune is that, as we know from Freud, every exhibitionist enjoys double pleasure: the direct gratification of exhibitionism, and the indirect gratification of voyeurism, achieved by unconscious identification with the spectator. Through his voyeurism-via-identification, the exhibitionist peeps at himself.

One contradiction remains to be resolved. How is it possible for this particular sublimation to include remnants of the original wish, *narcissistic self-voyeurism,* which antedates even Layer I? Since no direct traces of the original wish typically appear in sublimation, this apparently places acting in a unique position. The key to the contradiction, however, may be found in the fact that the actor, identifying with the spectator, peeps at himself *as the character he personifies.* Thus his peeping at himself, via the avenue of the audience, only seems to be self-voyeurism; in actuality, he is peeping at someone else.

This ties in with the genetic aspects of the problem. One specific situation was common to the childhoods of all the male and female actors (a round dozen) I have analyzed. The evidence, although too limited for generalization, justifies the suspicion that the similarity is a pattern and not an accident. The common situation involved peeping at some sexual scene. In all cases, the children were so guilty, so bewildered, that to diminish their guilt they concluded that it was all "not real, but a play." Instead of escaping into depersonalization, they escaped into active repetition of the passively-experienced "unreal." *The unreal—the guilt-diminishing alibi—became the guiding pattern.* And since that was not enough, the alibi was reinforced by exhibitionism, which took the place of the earlier voyeurism directed at others.

This explains the usual "unproductivity" of actors. They merely act, instead of creating, the characters in their plays, thus presenting the alibi: "I'm not guilty, the author is." The actor's productivity is manifested only when he re-creates a character, and there can be considerable originality in such a reinterpretation. The re-creation, too, is fitted with a built-in alibi: "Others did it, too."

There is irony in the statement that "for the actor the world of make-believe is real." For this "game" is a facade behind which cowers a child who rescued himself from an *"unbelievable"* terror, experienced in peeping, by devaluating the experience as *"unreal,"* as a play. In my opinion, no actor suffering from stage fright can be completely analyzed, beyond any danger of later relapse, unless that infantile voyeuristic terror has been worked out. This means that at least the cover-memories must be retrieved.

Here is an instance. At the age of three and one-half, an actress had been caught by her mother peeping through a keyhole at the intimacies of a couple who were guests in the house. The mother scolded the child severely. The child shrank back at first, but then asked: "What's wrong? I just wanted to see how *they* played— don't you watch me playing with my blocks?" Of course, a secondary cover-memory is revealed here; the original voyeuristic scenes occurred during the oral stage, and could be reconstructed only from oral fears.

In general, we are not often in a position to declare *specifically* that a *specific* situation is responsible for forcing individuals into the choice of a *specific* profession or occupation. I suspect that this is precisely what we can do in the case of the actor. Specific experiences and their appropriate elaborations are encountered. Increased scopophilia, in the child confronted with voyeuristic experiences, has a traumatic effect. As counteraction, the observed scene is devaluated as "unreal." That "unreality," which has been passively experienced, is later actively repeated. The little peeper thus is transformed into a big exhibitionist, with the inner alibi: "I am not guilty."

Every actor suffers considerable stage fright. Superficially, the fear pertains to exhibitionism, to forgetting lines, being "stuck," looking ridiculous. Deeper analysis proves that this is a mirage and a defense.

Experience with all types of sufferers from fear has convinced me that neurotic fear pertains exclusively to *psychic masochism.** Under pressure of a superego veto, the unconscious ego resorts to what might be called a legal trick, in order to help his "client in distress."

* For elaboration, see *The Basic Neurosis,* Chapter 3 and Chapter 7.

Guilt is accepted, but for the *lesser* crime, *pseudo-aggression,* and
the scene of the crime is shifted to the outside. The neurotic sufferer
from fear, therefore, behaves as if he were guilty of "aggression,"
and his fear seems to pertain to outside dangers. All these shifts,
of course, are made without his conscious knowledge.

The neurotic suffering from stage fright appears to dread exhibitionistic dangers; basically, he fears to *exhibit* defeat by forgetting
his lines, making a fool of himself, etc. In the table of sublimations
given on pp. 64–65, it may be seen that exhibitionism in acting
corresponds to Layer III, the first aggressive defense. In neurosis,
the superego retaliates against this defense; it is quite appropriate,
therefore, that the ego should attempt to fight this battle, not in
the inner fortress, but on the outer walls, choosing the remotest
line of defense. This is what actually happens.

In other words, the main danger, the *mortal* danger, which is
the need to account for *psychic masochism,* is avoided by *taking the
blame for pseudo-aggression.*

At the bottom of this masochistic terror lies the whole "septet
of baby fears." All of these—fear of being starved, devoured,
poisoned, choked, chopped to pieces, drained, castrated—can be
mobilized.

I once analyzed an inhibited radio actor who was afraid to face
the microphone. He had given up his profession, and was working
at an underpaid job in a different field when indirectly forced by
his wife to enter analysis. His flight from the microphone, he
revealed, had been preceded by the flight from the stage. He had
switched from the stage to the radio for neurotic, and not realistic
reasons. He had entered radio, where parts can be read, when he
developed pathological stage fright and fear of forgetting his lines.
He dreaded the advent of television, which would wipe out the
"advantage" radio offered him.

Besides his obvious scopophilia, many elements in this patient's ·
neurosis pointed in the direction of oral regression. These cannot
be mentioned for reasons of discretion. For present purposes, two
of the patient's statements are important. The first was a recollection dating back to the onset of his stage fright. More accurately,
it was an "impression" (the patient's term) rather than a recollec-

tion, though still important enough to be repressed. This was his description: "It occurred to me one night, while on stage waiting for my cue, that if you look at the two galleries in the dark, they remind you of an open mouth ready to 'swallow you up.'" The other statement, this time not repressed, came during a stage in the analysis when the patient was able to take up his radio career once more. The patient said, "While studying my part I had the impression that someone wants to force something down into my throat, and I resist violently." The patient did not connect that observation with the fact that "digesting" his part was his "bread and butter," *forced* upon him by the "cruel" analyst in the transference repetition.

The shaky basis of the actor's sublimation explains why *every* actor and actress suffers from at least traces of stage fright. The actor of either sex is one of the most inwardly terrified persons to be found in any profession. Even his defensive exhibitionism is performed incognito. He has never fully recovered from his infantile terror, and is *never sure that his inner conscience will accept the defensive hoax.* Actors are often scorned for "having no personality," for being "empty bags" which can be molded into any shape via hysterical identification. This attitude is wholly unjustified. Actors hide behind someone else's "personality" because that is their main inner defense. Their ability to derive reassurance from "incognito exhibitionism" is a rather heroic example of whistling in the dark, or, more precisely, in the dimmed lights of the stage. Their defense is a series of reversals, even to the re-enactment of the peeping situations, for now the spectators are in the dark, just as the peeping child was. This, too, shifts the guilt: "Others peep, I do not."

Acting and stage fright, in my opinion, have been incorrectly interpreted from the standpoint of exhibitionism and Oedipal castration. Equally faulty, I believe, are the interpretations of three typical situations, visible in the lives of some actors of both sexes: homosexuality, masochistic marriages, and psychopathic trends. All three are orally conditioned.

The most grotesque of these aberrations is the constant flight into divorces and "affairs." As with all psychic masochists who live in the public eye, the masochistic actor or actress finds that this

tendency is a greater source of pain and difficulty than the stage
fright which is his or her "private hell."

Is there any way of determining the quantity of psychic masochistic components in a specific personality? Only observation can
gauge the quantity of libidinized self-damage present:

(a) *Actual Self-damage: Amount and Deposition.* One must distinguish between damage in private life, and damage in professional
life. If a man marries a shrew and passively accepts her torture
and exploitation,—though covering up with pseudo-aggression—
but still remains active in his profession, his deposition of masochism
is localized. It is concentrated on a point which, objectively speaking, is harmless, since it does not affect the visible balance of his
personality as a whole. His personal point of view will naturally
not agree with this judgment. In another type, the masochistic
tendency becomes generalized, spreading to include work, love,
hobbies, social contacts, moods, etc.

(b) *Relation to work.* Here one must distinguish between self-
chosen occupations, and occupations forced on the individual in
one way or another. Without this distinction, any evaluation must
reach a dead end.* There is quite a difference between a man who
enters his father's business, without enthusiasm and merely because
it "makes sense," and one who has "always" wanted to become a
mechanical engineer, and who works his way through school,
making sacrifices in order to achieve his goal.

Every neurosis absorbs psychic energy otherwise located at normal
depositories. The typical sequence of events is that hobbies, previously enjoyed, become meaningless; the general mood deteriorates;
depression, dissatisfaction and inner insecurity become visible. The
center of emotional life is a series of emotional disturbances. Various
symptoms, including lack of sexual interest, are evidenced. However, the mechanical ability to work is preserved. Only in rare
cases does the acute stage of neurosis begin with the inability to
work. Pleasure in one's occupation, and the originality of one's
ideas are of course impaired at the high point of a neurosis, but
the ability to continue working is usually not affected until a later

---

* First stated in "Work—the 'Last Bastion' Engulfed in Neurosis," *Diseases of
the Nervous System,* 8:317–319, 1947.

period. Work is the last fortress taken over by neurosis. Why does the situation occur typically, and how can one explain the exceptions to that sequence of events?

The person in a self-chosen profession is satisfying, in sublimated form, unconscious defense mechanisms covering deep inner desires. This accounts for the greater pleasure derived from a self-chosen occupation.

For the majority of people work represents drudgery, essential because it is essential to earn a livelihood. There are not many people for whom work is also "fun." Most people view work as a necessary evil, like taxes.

Work plays a decisive role in the psychic economy; it is the normal depository of inner guilt. The typical not-too-neurotic person evens his account with the inner conscience by paying ransom in the form of work. The punitive quality inherent in work makes it a necessity. The connotation of work as punishment is analytically well-known; it has been intuitively known to mankind from time immemorial. Adam and Eve, expelled from Paradise, were required to work as punishment for their disobedience.

A strange incongruity is visible when working ability deteriorates neurotically. *The more pleasurable work has been during "normal" times, the more quickly it is absorbed into the neurotic process. The ability to work at an indifferent job is maintained for a longer period, because the punitive element is more marked.*

There may be a further reason for the preservation of working ability in neurosis. Paradoxically, one could say that the unconscious is well aware of the fact that neurotic pleasures imbedded in neurosis have the quality of a game. A game is, after all, limited in scope. A comparison of two cases may help to clarify these points.

Mr. A., a writer of distinction, developed a writing block at the age of 39. He had previously published numerous books, and his last book—which he himself did not like—had reached the best-seller lists. After the initial elation of success, he became moody. He no longer enjoyed transitory affairs with women of his acquaintance. Everything seemed boring. He attempted a new novel, but made little headway. He took a long trip, and discovered to his dismay that he could no longer write. He became despondent, and thought seriously of drowning himself. Finally, he entered analysis.

Mr. B., a lawyer of 45, entered analysis because of a marital conflict. He was not interested in his wife, and his girl friend was pressing him to marry her. In his indecision, he seized upon what he considered to be an excellent alibi. By entering analysis, he "immobilized" his girl friend; analysis, he told her, required suspension of vital decisions until the unconscious reasons were clarified. His real reason for entering treatment had nothing to do with the girl friend. The man was a gambler; cards were his major interest. He had never been interested in law; he had entered the profession at the urging of his family and was immediately given a share of his uncle's flourishing practice. He did his work mechanically, was "neither good nor bad," as he put it, in his profession. For years he had been living in a state of "strange excitement." His day really began in the evening, when he sat down at the card table. He was able, however, to carry out his professional duties. In the weeks before he entered analysis, he had been depressed. This state of mind he attributed to the conflicts caused by "the women," and to his continuous losses at poker. The gambling addiction did not seem pathologic to him. Like all gamblers, he was certain that what he needed was more money and more luck, not a psychiatrist. One day, in court, he rose to make a motion on behalf of his client, and stopped himself at the last moment, realizing that his projected move was too dangerous. Said the patient: "At that moment I really became frightened. I discovered that I was transplanting my gambling instincts to my profession."

Case A is an example of a freely-chosen profession; Case B of an enforced occupation. Working ability collapsed quickly in the case of the writer, and at a very late stage in the case of the lawyer, thus constituting clinical proof of the statement, made earlier, that the speed with which working ability collapses in neurosis bears a direct relation to the amount of pleasure derived from the work in "quiet" times. In his vocation, the writer used unconscious defense mechanisms, while the lawyer used his work only for the purpose of making a living. It was at quite a late stage in the game that the lawyer began to project his neurotic conflict into his profession.

Intrapsychically, the writer had to contend with his deep passive-masochistic wish to be mistreated, rejected, humiliated. That tendency, corresponding to the end result of his specific infantile conflict, was alibied with a claim of pseudo-aggression. In his novels, he always placed a he-man at the center of the action. He overdid his defensive efforts; reviewers would criticise his characters as "lifeless" and "unreal." In his last novel, the best-seller, he had made his hero more human, but he paid for that slackening in his defense with a severe inner reproach. One step further, and the defensive cover would hardly conceal the real unconscious situation. Interestingly enough, that inner danger was so great that even his external success was not accepted as alibi by the superego. In previous books, he had offered his pseudo-aggressive heroes as "proof" that he was not "weak" and masochistic. This defense had now collapsed, and the inner conscience rejected the old alibi. The result was his writing block. In the successful book, he had not repeated the formula which represented his unconscious defense. The sequence of events in his working process was, first, fight against inner conflicts, and second, the rational aim of making money.

The lawyer-gambler had quite another approach to his work. He did not work to solve inner conflicts. Work was, originally, only a way of earning his living. His inner conflicts were deposited in his gambling. His real profession, one could say, was that of a gambler. It was at the card table that he fought his never-ending battle to preserve infantile megalomania, under masochistic conditions. For in all gamblers the ineffective conscious wish to win is counteracted by the powerful unconscious wish to lose. (See # 29, Chapter V.)

This was the sequence of events in the disposition of the gambler-lawyer's inner conflicts. Work, at first, was a rational act for the purpose of making money. It was more or less free of neurotic admixtures. The entire mass of inner conflicts was deposited in his gambling. Late in life, when his growing neurosis (every neurosis, if not attacked by analysis, increases with age) encroached upon previously untouched sectors, his working ability was drawn into the sphere of inner conflict.

On the conscious level, work satisfies rational factors; unconsciously, it satisfies reverberations of the triad of aggressive, libidinous and narcissistic tendencies. (Freud) The number of emotional elements involved is not the same in freely chosen occupations as it is in occupations forced on the individual; emotional elements dominate in freely chosen professions, while they are for a long period negligible where merely "jobs" are concerned. Punitive unconscious elements, however, are present in both types. Under neurotic stress, work in freely chosen occupations collapses early, because of the emotional involvement always present. In indifferent occupations, the collapse of working ability takes place in a late stage of neurosis. The punitive substratum present in work renders it less attractive as a target for the reproaches of the superego, and at the same time makes it more resistant to the superego's attacks when they are forthcoming.

(c) *"Game Quality," or "Meaning Business."* In not too severe cases, psychic masochism has rather the connotation of an unconscious game, to be played *up to* but *not including* the point of real danger. Opposed to this type are the neurotics who "really mean business"—the business of seeing to it that they go down the drain.

(d) *Hypochondria and Worries.* Strangely enough, both hypochondria and worries—in spite of the fact that they are depositories of masochism—have a stabilizing effect upon the progression of the illness. The ever-changing surface details of their "contents" are so variegated, so easily exchangeable, that *these symptoms, provided they are not pre-psychotic,* serve to keep the individual on an even keel. They supply the "necessary" dose of self-torture. Of course, these neurotic symptoms should be treated; we are referring here to untreated neuroses.

(e) *General Impression of Future Masochistic Potentialities.* This point is frankly guesswork. It is usually safe to say that one cannot be too pessimistic as far as future development is concerned. Obviously, masochistic potentialities are unlimited. Sometimes—but seldom enough—the completely pessimistic prediction (better held in suppression) is not fulfilled in a specific case. But the optimistic outlook is so frequently proved wrong by later developments that *cautious pessimism is in order.* If deterioration sets in, its progress is frighteningly swift, devouring more and more of the personality. A comparison with metastases in cancer is applicable; in exceptional cases these patients outlive, by months and years, the expectations of authorities in the field. These patients, however, are not typical. This gloomy picture describes cases in which analytic therapy is not instituted. (For chances within therapy, see Chapter XII.)

Depression and fear accompany every neurosis. To a lesser degree, they are present in normality as well. Both are products of the unconscious ego, created as defense against the superego's accusation.

I have nothing to add to my assumption of genesis of fear, presented at length in *The Basic Neurosis* (pp. 87–97) and *Neurotic Counterfeit-Sex* (pp. 73–76). My assumption is that fear pertains exclusively to repressed psychic masochism, secondarily shifted outside via the pseudo-aggressive defense. It consists of a "triad of anxiety":

1. Stage of libidinized inner passivity, and offense to infantile megalomania.

2. Stage of pseudo-aggressive defense and narcissistic restitution, using: (a) change of contents; by accepting the punishment of the superego, but for the lesser crime (illusion of aggression), thus sidetracking the guilt and "restoring" by "activity" the lesion in narcissism; (b) change of locality; an inner fear is projected outwards.*

3. Stage of "hostages." The superego, since it is exclusively interested in torturing the ego, accepts the pseudo-aggression "hostage," especially since the ego artificially increases its guilt in order to "keep the inner tormenter occupied." The ego, having overdone its own defensive pseudo-aggressive efforts, becomes frightened at the spectacle of its own courage, and preventively gives the anxiety signal.

Fear thus seems to pertain, not to the real "crime," but to the inner defense. This formulation also claims that the amount of fear does *not* correspond to the amount of repressed wishes to be discharged. It is increased out of proportion, artificially, to delude

---

* In phobic and paranoic cases; in hypochondria an organ is chosen as malefactor, and treated as if it were the "gift" of an outside person (mother), fraudulently planted in one's own body. Superfluous to state that in this section I am talking exclusively about the *psychological* problem of fear. According to newer findings of psychosomatic medicine, the *somatic* symptoms accompanying an anxiety attack are an expression of the same phenomenon which subjectively is experienced as anxiety.

the inner conscience, and is attached to the defense. The whole "battle of anxiety" is fought on a spurious front, and the ego's triumph is a pyrrhic victory.

Anxiety, in my opinion, is an auxiliary defense of the unconscious ego, used in situations in which:

1. A dramatic demonstration is required to convince the superego of "good intentions." Hence short-lived depression precedes anxiety, even in cases where it is claimed that the attack of anxiety came "out of the blue." Anxiety is produced only if depression proves insufficient as proof.

2. The amount of narcissism (or the narcissistic "type" of the personality) renders intolerable the passivity of constant reproach from the superego and constant propulsion by masochistic-passive aims. Hence *active* repetition of the *passive* situation is installed by admitting to an "aggressive" aim (application of "unconscious repetition compulsion").

3. The defensive pseudo-aggression to which the unconscious ego admits as "lesser crime" passes the safety limit. The ego is caught between the horns of a dilemma; it is required to produce defensive pseudo-aggression, and at the same time to maintain the desired "low pressure" (Freud). In such an impossible situation, the older mechanism of maintaining low tension seemingly wins out, and the nearly automatic signal of anxiety is given.

This fear and anxiety production can be compared with the automatic whistling device found on boilers. The whistle sounds whenever the tension passes a specific point. The warning whistle sounded in consciously perceived fear and anxiety confirms Freud's assumption of the "mediation role" of the unconscious ego.

Unlike the problem of fear, my previous assumption on the genesis of depression requires some amplification. In "Working Through" (*The Psychoanalytic Review*, 32:449–480, 1945), I listed seven types of depression. I now see that depressions, basically, can be traced to three major sources:

1. *Punitive Action of the Daimonion* when a discrepancy between ego and ego ideal has been proved. The ego accepts guilt, and pays penance in the form of self-produced depression.

2. *Alibi Production of the Unconscious Ego.* The unconscious ego, which creates the depression, uses it for its own purposes, also.

Guilt and depression are magnified and inflated, so that they will be eligible as substitute offenses in the mechanism of "taking the blame for the lesser crime." (See Chapter VI.) This goes so far that frequently depression is experienced *in anticipation* of the super-ego's next attack. The procedure is designed to prove to the inner tormenter that the poor fellow is suffering, and therefore cannot be experiencing pleasure, as the indictment claims.

3. *Dissatisfaction of the Unconscious Ego,* because of its inability to cope with its hopeless task. At times the demands of the id are so pressing that the unconscious ego is unable to twist them into inner defenses acceptable to the superego; at times the superego's punishment is so severe that it cannot be converted into psychic masochism; at times the lifelong task of achieving compromises and creating subterfuges becomes too "strenuous" for the ego; at times the succession of external adversities—which will inevitably be misused by the superego for purposes of torture—becomes too crushing for the inner mediator, and these circumstances, separately or together, can bring about a situation of inner hopelessness. The outer manifestation of this inner despair is a depression, sometimes so deep that it approaches the point known to the layman as a "nervous breakdown."

Some colleagues, even when they accept the pre-Oedipal Grand Guignol, seem to assume that the severity of the superego relaxes towards the end of the Oedipal phase. I believe that the introjection of the Oedipal father at that time is but an attempt to diminish the "septet of baby fears," which pertain to the pre-Oedipal mother. At bottom, the "septet" may be found lurking behind *all* Oedipal rescue attempts.

The superego's severity, however, does seem to diminish at one specific point e.g., the fear of being devoured, the fantasy of *total* annihilation stemming from early infancy, does progess to a fear of *partial* annihilation (genital castration).

Of course, the ego—having discovered that the ego ideal can be intrapsychically used as a tool of torture—strives desperately to reduce the demands of the ego ideal. In normality, the ego uses a variety of devices for this purpose (as pointed out in "Transference and Love"): irony, hypocrisy, wit, cynicism, etc. These attempts are all more or less futile. The ego has no access to the torture chamber; it can convince itself, but cannot influence Daimonion. The same futile campaign is waged in neurosis, with the addition of a neurotic weapon: the "pseudo-moral connotation of neurotic symptoms." (See Chapter VIII.) In manic psychosis, as Freud proved, there is an endeavor to cast off the torturer altogether. But the price (psychosis!) is too high, and the cover thus obtained is too thin to protect the individual from deep depression. (H. Deutsch, Schilder.)

As a literary example of the way in which the ego fights the ego ideal by revealing the hypocrisy of the introjected images, I am adducing Stendhal's *Lamiel*.

Lamiel, a precocious and highly intelligent young girl, discovers the delights of the romantic "penny dreadful," glorifying scoundrels, in which for the first time she reads about adventures rather than virtues. One evening she is naive enough to mention one of her new heroes to her uncle. He is horrified, and at the evening prayers both uncle and aunt plead that their niece be brought back to the right path, in which admiration is reserved exclusively for saints, not wasted on "literary" characters. In bed, Lamiel thinks things over. She compares her uncle with the heroes in her books, and finds him sadly wanting: no spectacular self-sacrifices, no magnificent gestures. The next day she smuggles an old Latin book from the house and sells it to the grocer for another forbidden romance.

To show the complexity, and the wide range of the problems included in oral-masochistic regression, I am adducing a purely technical problem: handling of the patient's alleged "suffering" during analysis (first clarified in my study on the topic in *Samiksa,* 1951). It can be taken as paradigm of the degree to which overlooking the *masochistic* basis of every neurosis contributes to scotomas, and how much wider the vision becomes—including elimination of the danger of being misled by unrecognized resistances—when one condescends to take psychic masochism into consideration.

Common gossip, among prospective analytic patients, has it that psychoanalysis is an "extremely painful procedure." This widespread impression is bolstered by people who have had several analysts, and who retrospectively claim they suffered "intensely." What are the sober facts? The subjective feeling of suffering is not an invention. To be sure, the ex-patient's claim is later inflated by the prospective patient, who thus acquires a new argument against entering analysis. But this is another story. What must be questioned is the presence of the suffering in the first place. Is this an intrinsic part of the analytic procedure?

In my private opinion, the patient's *"suffering"* in analysis is in the majority of cases concomitant with *a technical mistake on the part of the analyst.*

Scrutinizing the instances of alleged torture, three situations stand out most typically mentioned by patients: positive transference, which—since it is not reciprocated—is painful; the discrepancy between illusions (rationalizations) which everyone builds up around himself, and analytic explanation of the underlying reasons for these illusions; and finally, "waiting for free associations" which "refuse to come."

What is most surprising in the list enumerated by patients is the absence of another element: the narcissistic elation which comes from self-understanding. Even "analytic sufferers" cannot deny that the understanding one gradually acquires of oneself in analysis has two results: narcissistic aggrandizement, and the acquistion of a new weapon for the strengthened ego to use against unconscious onslaughts. Why are these factors (not to mention the eventual cure), ignored, while the suffering is tenaciously retained in the memory, and exaggerated into the bargain?

This point alone is sufficient to arouse scepticism when confronted with the fiction and the myth of an analytic torture chamber. In searching for the genesis of the myth, however, one should always consider the possibility that it is rooted in the patient's misunderstanding of a correctly recorded fact. Since only affective, and not intellectual, understanding is therapeutically effective, some patients misconstrue affective understanding as—"suffering."

I. *"Suffering" in Transferences*

Unrequited feelings, unconsciously shifted from enshrined images on to the chance figure of the physician, are disagreeable. That is granted. This is so, however, only as long as they are not understood. Analysis of the positive transference (which, by the way, takes up much less room in analysis than is generally assumed by the laity, who confuse the positive transference with "love" and disregard the negative transference altogether) serves to remove the sting after a short time. In some cases, however, this does not occur, and it is at exactly this point that the analyst's technical error is responsible.

The truly Oedipal case is a relative rarity, although many patients give the superficial impression that they belong in this category. As I have repeatedly stressed, I believe that *the majority of neurotics have a "rendezvous with orality."* Since this is the case, the orally regressed neurotic will, in the analytic transference, unconsciously resort to the identical defensive rescue-station: Oedipality. It is the analyst's job to see through this unconscious camouflage, and explain the defensive cover. If this is done, the mirage evaporates, and the dynamically decisive oral-masochistic substructure can be analyzed. Very soon, instead of the Oedipal palimpsest, one is scrutinizing a typical "injustice collector."

If, however, the analyst does not debunk the Oedipal disguise, the analysis, having taken the wrong turning, becomes bogged down in the endless morass of an unresolvable transference and pseudo-dependence, which the patient interprets as "real love."

There is one very pronounced warning sign, which is present even if the pre-Oedipal masochistic structure is not analyzed. If the analyst observes correctly, he cannot miss the patient's masochistic misuse of the situation. Nevertheless, the state of affairs is commonly misjudged.

Thus, the patient's "suffering" is but a disguise, behind which are smuggled in exactly the masochistic repetitions which the analyst overlooked. If the analyst is taken in, he has behaved like the proverbial innocent detective, who invariably falls for the clues which the criminal has planted to divert suspicion. Obviously not the ideal situation.

On the other hand, when the analyst does not fall for the unconscious ruse, the artificially inflated mirage of positive transference in deeper regressions collapses, and one is confronted with the real masochistic self of the neurotic.

This does not imply, of course, that the task is easy. But at least one is fighting, not a windwill, but the genuine thing, and there is a chance of success. If the analyst is misled by the patient's unconscious disguise, he has failed, although a few years will pass before he gives up—even then without understanding what made the specific analysis of that specific patient—a flop.

It cannot be stated too succinctly: under every possible disguise, the patient will unconsciously accept the "blame for the lesser crime" only for the sake of hiding his "real crime," the unsolved masochistic pattern.

The same point applies to *pseudo-aggressions*, which (in the negative transference) are too frequently misjudged as real aggression, denoting repetitions of the infantile fury against the "disappointing" educators and upbringers. Here the confusion lies in a tragic oversight. These feelings, originally quite genuine, have subsequently been masochistically elaborated. Hence, if the analyst allows pseudo-aggression (covering more deeply repressed masochistic attachment) to pass for real aggression, he—involuntarily— strengthens the patient's neurotic defense. It is difficult to convince our generation of analysts that the *neurotic sector* of the patient harbors *would-be aggression exclusively*. This does not exclude the possibility that some other—undiseased—parts of the neurotic's ego may have normal aggression at their disposal. The differentiation between normal aggression and pseudo-aggression is still misunderstood.

II. *"Suffering" While Rationalizations Are Being Debunked*

When people refer to the "suffering" experienced in analysis, they generally mean the unrequited transference. The two other sources of alleged pain are less important in the pseudo-argument. Still, they should be dealt with.

It is true that being a "professional truth-teller" is an unrewarding occupation. It is not by chance that perceptive observers of surface reverberations have issued innumerable warnings that people abstain from unpleasant truth-telling—even on the conscious level:

No normal being wants to hear the truth. It is the passion of a small and aberrant minority of men, most of them pathological. They are hated for telling it while they live, and when they die they are swiftly forgotten. . . . H. L. Mencken.

These and similar warnings pertain to consciously concealed facts, disclosed by people who have a "passion for truth," and in this way fight against the hypocritical consensus.

The analyst's business is different. He is less a "professional truth-teller" than a translator of what the patient projects upon the living movie-screen. His "crime," therefore, is even more serious; every patient claims that his inner self has been "incorrectly" translated, and "hates" the decoder—officially.

In nearly twenty-five years of practice, it has been my experience that analytic decoding of unconscious motivations is by no means as "painful" for the patient as the popular saga has it. It is true that patients are frequently angry with the "translator," and wish him in hell or other remote localities. But accompanying this consoling anger are two other redeeming factors, which make it easier for the "sufferer" to "grieve down" (Coleridge) the debunking of a rationalization. These are the unconscious feelings that, despite all his protests, the inner truth has been revealed, and the narcissistic pleasure he derives from realizing that, once the real facts are brought to the surface, he will be to some extent released from the influence of the unconscious. One should not underestimate the fact that the all-prevailing psychic masochism of the neurotic is inwardly accepted only by the diseased sector of the total personality. At the very same time, the more normal sector seeks relief and reinforcement, which are supplied when the correct interpretation is given in the transference repetition.

Psychic masochism has a Janus face in these situations. On the one side, masochism inwardly greets the disagreeable interpretation, simply because it is disagreeable; on the other side, the inner forces opposing the dangerous poison of psychic masochism welcome every argument against it.

In well-conducted analyses, the upshot is that the counter-forces against psychic masochism, strengthened by narcissistic recompenses, predominate.

Once more, the analyst's inability to cope with the state of affairs is due to his own technical error. The mistake consists mainly in taking the patient's pseudo-aggression at face value, without revealing the masochistic substructure.

III. *"Suffering" While "Free Associations" Are Lacking*

Every student of analysis is familiar with the fact that the part played by free associations has undergone considerable change in the course of the science's development. Originally, free associations had the power of an absolute monarch who ruled supreme; no constitutional reservations or restrictions existed. After Freud's discovery that free associations can be misused for resistance, the situation altered, and a few "Constitutional" safeguards were imposed. Since then, the primacy of interpretation of resistance and transference has prevailed in every Freudian analysis. This of course has not lessened the importance of free associations; on the contrary, the change enhanced their importance by eliminating the "ersatz" type of pseudo-association created by the patient's unconscious motivations of resistance. In short, free associations are used in situations where their relative "purity" is assured.

To exemplify:

At the beginning of our first interview, a patient, a Shakespearian scholar, informed me that besides suffering from a disease which his surgeons "had wrongly diagnosed as hypochondria," he was also "the victim of the second Shakespearian milk period." I answered: "Isn't that slightly unfair—taking advantage of your specialized knowledge? By chance I suspect that I understand the allusion; *Romeo and Juliet,* 'Adversity's sweet milk—philosophy.' That happens to be one of my favorite quotations. The baby is fed on milk, the unhappy adult on milk-surrogate—consolation. Still, you can learn the *Familiar Quotations* by heart, and surprise even educated and well-read people with innuendos."

Having thus been slightly deflated in his technique of pseudo-superiority, the patient continued: "Never mind that, better cure me of *my* adversity—my fear of cancer."

I asked whether he had a specific "love" in psychosomatics. He replied: "It's rather that my rectum has an unhappy love affair with me." After informing me of the external events of his life, and after a few more appointments during which he was given a short introduction to analytic procedure and aims, the patient was asked to give free associations. He demurred, first by saying he

didn't know what I was talking about, later by referring to experi-
ments in free associations which he had conducted upon himself,
with negative results. I insisted, stating that free associations are still
the best we have to sell. The patient shrugged his broad shoulders,
and with the pose and facial expression of a martyr dealing with
an idiot more powerful than himself, started: "On the left side of
your bookshelves I see eleven red books. I assume they are
Shakespeare."

What followed was a five-minute lecture on Shakespeare. I then
interrupted, telling him that this was a lecture, not free associations.
The patient indignantly objected. His associations, he declared,
were "OK, only your method stinks." His irritation, and the
gutter-language, which was unusual for him, were clear proof that
something had hit him, and therefore I suggested analyzing his
resistance.

I told him: "Unconsciously, you obviously misunderstood the
situation. Instead of taking analysis as a cooperative endeavor on
the part of two people—one offering one hundred per cent, the
other only the nominal part of his whole personality, namely his
consciousness (and even that with strings attached)—you take it to
be a pupil-teacher relationship. Didn't you tell me that the relatively happiest part of your life was while you were teaching at a
Midwestern university? You were socially isolated, had no girls or
friends, but still you were happy. Obviously, the admiration of
your students bolstered your weak ego. *Since your bogey seems to
be inner passivity,* you immediately reversed the roles in analysis:
you delivered a lecture on Shakespeare, pushing *me* into the pupil's
position. There is no doubt that you know more about Shakespeare
than I do. It is quite clear that you misconstrued my knowledge
of the theory of analysis, and my clinical experience, as something
which pushes you into the passive situation."

If an analyst honestly evaluates the patient's—*any* patient's—
association, he is reminded of the analytic axiom: the value of free
associations is comparable to the results obtained through primitive methods of digging gold. In analysis of free association, as in
primitive placer mining, tons of worthless material pass through
the sieve; with luck, a valuable nugget is turned up now and then.
Nowadays, modern and less time-consuming methods are used for

digging gold; a comparison of these methods with the analysis of resistance is to the point.

Nevertheless, there are limitations even to this rule. A specific group of neurotics, at the beginning of analysis, is quite incapable of using free associations. These are orally regressed neurotics. For patients of this sort, the classical analytic technique has to be modified *—the analyst must talk. Twenty years ago I suggested this modification, as a preparatory period before "normal" analysis can start for orally regressed neurotics for this reason: orally regressed neurotics ward off their deep masochistic attachment with the defense of pseudo-aggression. When asked to *give* words, in free associations, they *refuse*. Adherence to the classical technique on the part of the analyst, therefore, brings these patients into a premature and hopeless conflict, and at the same time gives them the opportunity to project the image of the bad, cruel, demanding, draining Giantess of the nursery upon the innocent analyst in the transference repetition.

This cannot and should not be avoided. It *cannot,* because the image of the cruel Giantess is automatically projected inside and outside of analysis by these severe neurotics; it *should not* be avoided because these affective repetitions are constantly contrasted with the harmless reality of analysis, whose chance representative, the physician, obviously wants to help. That is all true, but for the discerning grasp of this series of unconscious repetitions two people are required—patient and physician. As Thoreau put it: "For telling the truth, two people are required, one who speaks the truth, the other who listens."

These patients, however, are present only in infinitesimal proportions; the part of the ego willing or able to "cooperate" is highly restricted.

Consequently, my technical innovation with these cases consists of first *circumventing* the full impact of the patient's projection of the "cruel Giantess" by making that unavoidable projection a difficult procedure. By *giving* words (the analyst has to talk for long periods) one does not of course avoid the transference-projec-

* That preparatory phase, in my opinion, is essential in all orally regressed cases. See *The Basic Neurosis,* Chapter VII, "Differential Diagnosis; Technique of Treatment, Specific Resistances in Orally Regressed Neurotics." First stated in 1932 in "Problems of Pseudo-Imbecility," *Int. Zeitschrift f. Psychoanalyse.*

tion of the "bad mother." But, and this is decisive, one offers oneself
as model for a specific inner defense on the part of the patient.
Inwardly, these neurotics are stabilized on the rejection level, and
unconsciously they want refusal. Two defenses are encountered:
pseudo-aggression, and the alleged wish to be kindly treated. By
giving words, the analyst temporarily becomes the standard-bearer
of the patient's defense: "If some one is kind and giving to me, I
can be too." (Of course, this unconscious defense is very superficial,
and is used only to refute the inner reproach of enjoyment of
psychic masochism.) It amounts, paradoxically, to a temporary
strengthening of the patient's "basic fallacy" *—"It's not that I'm
masochistic, I'm an innocent victim of mother's cruelty. If my
mother had been different, I would have reacted differently, too."
Later, of course, the analyst has to resolve the "basic fallacy."
This defense of "kindness if treated kindly" which the patient
unconsciously produces is still strong enough to mitigate the enormous amount of pseudo-hostility, suspicion, anger, accusations of
"unjust treatment," which these patients otherwise produce.

In any case, waiting for free associations which "just don't show
up" is frequently misused as a masochistic tool by patients. This
tool can—partly—be eliminated from the picture by analyzing the
resistance *plus* the masochistic misuse.

A good deal of the "suffering" of this type, therefore, reduces
itself once more to a technical mistake on the part of the analyst:
that of failing to recognize the basic structure of the orally regressed
neurotic.

At bottom, "suffering" in analysis is the patient's untouched
psychic masochism; to leave psychic masochism untouched in the
patient is a grave technical error on the part of the analyst. Analysis
does not have the purpose of giving our psychic masochistic patients
a new and "legitimate" excuse for masochistic fiestas—without the
analyst's counteraction. The analyst is not a wailing companion,
nor should he be naively taken in by his patient's masochistic
misuse of the analytic situation.

* See "The Danger Neurotics Dread Most: Loss of the Basic Fallacy,"
Psychoanalyt. Review, 33:2, 1946. See also reference to contents on pp. 286 ff.

A well-known writer, entering analysis because of writer's block, asked at the end of his first appointment:

"Do I have to discontinue sex during analysis?"

"Who gave you that idea? Didn't you tell me that your sex life is normal?"

"Yes. But I thought one has to suffer during analysis."

"You remind me of the old joke of the patient who consults a physician because he feels under par. The practitioner starts the examination by inspecting the man's throat. 'Well, here's the reason why you are feeling so poorly—you have a typical smoker's throat. Discontinue smoking immediately.'—'But Doc, I don't smoke at all.'—'Never mind,' the unperturbed doctor answers, 'we'll forbid you something else.'"

V. The Slightly Paradoxical Moral Code of the Unconscious Ego and the Mechanism of Taking the Blame for the Lesser Crime

THE UNCONSCIOUS TUG OF WAR IS ALWAYS EVIDENCE OF THE INNER defenses, never evidence of the original wish. What is popularly called an alibi is in scientific terminology an "unconscious defense mechanism." This view of the mechanism of the unconscious is unquestioned; controversy sets in when there is discussion of the number of inner defenses. According to accepted opinion, *one* defense overlies the unconscious wish. In my opinion, *two* defenses are in operation. (See Foreword.)

In studying the emergence of any neurotic symptom or personality trait, we find that any unconscious wish, upon approaching the unconscious ego, is vetoed by the superego. (There is no direct connection, as we have learned from Freud, between the id and the outer world.) The inner lawyer, the unconscious ego, tries to help his client in distress. He presents a series of pleas to the superego. The first is a simple denial that the wish exists at all; on a caricaturistic level, this plea could be expressed as: "Your Honor, my client is not guilty of the offense as charged." Since the first step, *Simple Denial*, is always ineffective, the inner lawyer resorts to a more cunning expedient. He explains that his client harbors, not the wish detailed in the original indictment, but *its exact opposite*. On behalf of his client, the lawyer then pleads guilty to this fabricated substitute wish. This constitutes *Defense Mechanism No. I*. The superego is still veto-minded, and the inner lawyer plays his trump card, partly using once more the technique of denial, partly pledging that his penitent client will pay penance for the substitute crime, which he represents as the real one. This, and this only, represents *Defense Mechanism No. II*; this, and this only is visible on the psychic surface. In clinical practice, therefore, we never deal with "unconscious wishes covered by a defense." We deal only with the *Defense Against the Defense*.

This legalistic legerdemain has its approximate counterpart in our criminal courts, where the accused sometimes succeeds in "copping a plea"—that is, amending the indictment so that he stands trial for a crime less serious than that with which he was originally charged—as a reward for information given, or because he consents to plead "guilty" to the lesser crime instead of "not guilty" to the greater. Accused of murder, the defendant's lawyer enters a plea of "not guilty," but admits to the misdemeanor of carrying a gun without permit, hence pleads "guilty" to that.*

Within the unconscious, there is always a direct and immediate connection between the crime stated in the indictment, and the proposed substitute. The lesser crime is by no means picked at random, and it corresponds to the inner conflicts of the person involved. But it is a crime which is *not* dynamically decisive at that *specific* moment. It is the difference between, "This has been worrying me too," and "My *main* trouble is. . . ."

As a result, we find that in neurotic reactions we are dealing with frantic attempts on the part of the ego to disprove a surrogate crime, which has *not* been committed. The agoraphobe's real wish, for example, is peeping; the substitute lesser crime is exhibitionism. It is precisely the defenses against alleged exhibitionism which are enshrined in the symptom, where fear of the street covers and wards off alleged exhibitionistic tendencies.

It is difficult to escape the impression that the inner lawyer operates its defenses in very much the way that a ventriloquist manages his puppets. Continuing the simile, the inner ventriloquist has *two* puppets on the string. They are twins but with adroit costuming and clever dialogue, the puppet-master manages to make them appear unlike.

A malicious patient took up this comparison and claimed that the twin defenses manipulated by the inner lawyer reminded him of ventriloquist Edgar Bergen and his two marionettes: the clever Charlie and the dopy country yokel. The elaboration, though malicious and distorted, contains a grain of truth.

It is amazing to note the monotony with which neurotics are filled with undigested pre-Oedipal libidinious wishes, *and* aggressive

* The example clarifies the inner situation, though technically unallowable in court procedure—to ask for immediate sentence for the substitute crime.

wishes as well. The interconnection is more complex than the historical origin of dualism of instincts leads us to suspect. *The great crime in the unconscious is the elaboration of an unsolved and undigested aggressive conflict* dating back to earliest infancy—*psychic masochism.* This "crime" in itself is genetically complex—inexpressible aggression, boomeranging of aggression because of motoric helplessness and the triad of retribution (punishment, moral reproach, later guilt), finally libidinization of guilt. We can take a cue from this procedure: an originally aggressive conflict is solved by libidinous means—self-aggression becomes libidinous allure resulting in the pleasure-in-displeasure pattern. The paradigmatic result is: libido as savior of an unbearable aggressive conflict. On the other hand, since the superego's reproaches continue, defenses continue too. We see later, in the *clinical* picture, that the libidinous secondary aim in psychic masochism becomes the target of the superego's attacks, so that spurious pseudo-aggression against the (unconsciously provoked) adversary comes into play. Here, pseudo-aggression is used as defense against a libidinous conflict.

Thus, the *lesser* crime in neurosis is libidinous guilt, warded off with pseudo-aggressive secondary defenses.

To complicate matters further, inner defenses end only with the grave: continuously libido is staved off with pseudo-aggression, pseudo-aggression warded off with libido,—ad infinitum.

All this is made easier by the interconnections between libido and aggression. As already stated, if my assumption—neurosis denotes stabilization on the oral rejection level with desperate attempts at rescue to higher levels of development—is correct, it is only logical that the defensive aggression (in actuality pseudo-aggression) should be predominant over other defensive techniques in neurosis. *Neurotic malice* is the outward expression of this sorry fact.

It also explains why the expedient of pseudo-aggression is so stubbornly maintained. Accused of the *capital crime* of masochism, the unconscious ego defends its client by admitting to the *misdemeanor* of spurious aggression. More, the defense in itself becomes a moral alibi—wasn't the child told that it is detestable and shameful to be a "sissy"? This "taking the blame for the lesser crime" is predominant in neurosis.

The neurotic's mass of guilt, which pertains to the real crime, is thus "fraudulently" shifted to the defense. As a result, every neurosis offers the spectacle of conveyor-belt production of alleged inner aggression and hyper-guilt.

Graphically (and crudely), this is the inner situation:

Facts as they are:

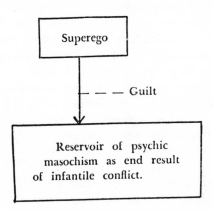

Facts as they appear after the unconscious ego's intervention:

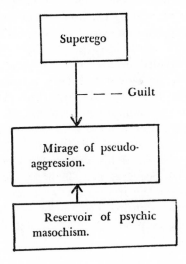

Why should the omniscient superego fall for, and acquiesce to, the ruse?

The answer is to be found in the anti-hedonistic structure of the inner conscience. Its only wish is to torture the victim. It is as if a sadistic jailer were saving his time and energy by tempting his prisoners to torture themselves.

From the point of view of the "prisoner," however, the mechanism of taking the blame for the lesser crime seems an excellent way of avoiding too severe punishment. The drawback is grave: the crime is "lesser" according to the laws of *inner* justice only. Within the unconscious, the defendant avoids sentence for the capital crime of psychic masochism by admitting to spurious pseudo-aggression. But he must then execute his spurious defense by acting out his pseudo-aggression, or defense against it, in external reality. *Externally,* his difficulties are multiplied by his inner device.

There is a marked difference, as far as internalized and externalized aggression are concerned, between the superego code and the code of external reality. (For elaboration see Chapter VI.) In the *inner* lawbook, the greatest crime—rating capital punishment— is *libidinized inner self-aggression* (psychic masochism). In the *external* lawbook, that crime is not even mentioned; whether or not you are a glutton for self-created internal punishment is entirely your own affair. But externalized aggression (whether defensive or not), e.g., murder, is *the* crime of crimes.

I observed an interesting example of "taking the blame for the lesser crime" in an inhibited writer. While reading, he would habitually count off the words in each paragraph, in groups of four. If the paragraph divided evenly, and his count was "four" as the paragraph ended, he would feel deep satisfaction. If it divided unevenly, he would be slightly disturbed. There was a simple explanation for his compulsive counting. His family, including himself, numbered four people. Unconsciously, he was reassuring himself that they were all well, all alive. Still, this man (who became successful after analysis of his writer's block) was orally regressed, as are all writers. (See #2, this Chapter.) He constantly warded off his oral-masochistic attachment with pseudo-aggression. This disposition of his counting compulsion—exclusively while reading—offered another proof of this. He had become a voracious reader after early "disappointments;" in this way he proved to himself that he could "get" as much as he wanted ("*intake* of knowledge"). His avid reading was therefore a defense to begin with. This, too, could be clinically established. Frequently, and for no apparent reason, the patient would produce a peculiar moaning sigh. When asked for an explanation, he was first unaware of his quite audible moans; later he remembered a family anecdote, often repeated by his mother. The patient, a breastfed baby, had been weaned at the age of twelve months. During the six months or so after weaning, the baby had turned his head away from his mother every time she approached. This gesture would be followed by "some kind of moaning" and then by a crying spell. The child's reaction had been so violent that for some months the father took over all of the mother's duties.

The patient's wish to get (reading matter) was therefore a defense against the masochistic elaboration of his relation to his mother. It was clear, from the man's inability to write *original* matter, that the inner conscience did not accept the "autarchic" substitution. Of course, voyeuristic inhibitions (imagination) were also involved.

To indicate the extent to which the mechanisms of "defense against defense" and "taking the blame for the lesser crime" can increase our understanding of psychic phenomena, I am adducing a literary example. This example (which will be followed by clinical cases) has puzzled literary critics for precisely one century. It is the decline and fall of Herman Melville.*

After a long period of virtual obscurity, Melville is now rated by some competent observers as the greatest writer this country has ever produced. His major work, *Moby Dick,* was a failure when published by Harper in 1851; critics dismissed it as an "extravaganza." Melville's earlier books—*Typee, Omoo, White Jacket,* and even *Mardi*—had been successes; *Moby Dick* was a rank failure, and Melville was never again a "popular" author.

Two provocative points in the Melville story have never been clarified. What is the meaning of the *Moby Dick* epic? What prompted Melville to write *Pierre,* the novel about incest which

* Condensed from "A Note on Melville" *The American Imago,* 1952.

immediately followed *Moby Dick,* and marked the end of his fruitful creative period?

In Lewis Mumford's biography of Melville, a study which is interesting but out of focus on decisive points, the most frequently offered "interpretations" of the White Whale are reproduced. This includes the assumption that the White Whale symbolizes evil. Mumford's own theory is that the story is at bottom an allegory on the mystery of evil and on the universe's accidental malice. Moby Dick represents the unending force of destruction. Captain Ahab fights the evil but in doing so—without love—he becomes evil's image; he has fought for humanity but in the process has lost his own humanity. In Moby Dick, according to Mumford, Melville himself fights and conquers evil, consciously, for art—in the broad sense—is man's best and noblest weapon against the malice of the universe.

Melville was indeed conscious of his use of the white whale as symbol of evil. Captain Ahab has two "grievances" against the whale: first the loss of his leg, bitten off by the whale years before; second, the whale's development into the embodiment of universal malice. Mumford points out that Ahab transfers this concept of evil to the figure of the whale, and then pits himself against the double enemy.

Since Melville was fully aware of the whale's "significance," this interpretation must be ruled out as his unconscious motive for writing *Moby Dick*—provided one does not deny that the unconscious in any way determines artistic creativity. As pointed out in *The Writer and Psychoanalysis* (see also pp. 112 ff. of the present volume), the writer is a defendant standing trial before his inner conscience; his double defense constitutes his alibi. We must therefore search for a deeper reason, one which Melville was *not* partly conscious of.

More than a hypothesis cannot be offered. Moby Dick, living in the ocean (". . . the sea is life whose waters of deep woe are brackish with the salt of human tears"—Melville) symbolizes the infant's fantasy of the cruel, pre-Oedipal mother of earliest infancy. The child becomes masochistically attached to the pre-Oedipal mother; when the attachment is attacked and vetoed by the super-ego, a pseudo-aggressive defense is instituted. Melville quite obviously sympathizes with Ahab's hatred. This first defense, too, is vetoed, and guilt for the pseudo-aggression is either counterposed, rationalized, or fully negated. Thus Melville must present both the query of the reasonable Starbuck, "Vengeance on a dumb brute?" and the sense of impending doom which surrounds Ahab from his first entrance to his final destruction.

Melville's formulation—"sea . . . salt of human *tears*"—is especially revealing. Projected upon the infant's situation, it means that fluid is not given by another, but *autarchically* produced by the infant, who lives on his own woes and "tears" (fluid!).

The hypothesis, Moby Dick = monster of pre-Oedipal mother, as imagined by the child, finds two confirming factors, one in *Moby Dick,* and the other in Melville's own history. The endless descriptions of whales and whaling in *Moby Dick,* of the habits, appearances, and of matters only remotely pertaining to them, are an expression of infantile voyeurism. In Melville's four months of captivity in the South Seas (described in *Typee*), he was in constant danger of being eaten by his cannibal captors, which undoubtedly revived the infantile fear of being devoured by the pre-Oedipal mother. Still another factor may be provided by Moby Dick's color: the *white* whale is reminiscent of the *white* skin of the mother.

The argument which convinces me, personally, that the above deduction is a probability comes, again, from Melville's personal history. He was in a state of hyper-excitement after finishing *Moby Dick;* nevertheless, he almost immediately began work on *Pierre*—an *incestuous* story.* Why? Unless one takes *Pierre* as Melville's obliging answer to Mumford and other critics of the future, who deplore the omission of women from Melville's books on the sea, or assumes that he naively believed a book about incest would bring him much-needed royalties†—in the America of the 1850's!—there can be only one answer to this question. Melville wrote *Pierre* out of inner necessity. The defect deplored by the biographers should not, by the way, disturb them: the "cruel sea" is the unconsciously

---

* The incestuous motif, used as a futile defense in *Pierre,* was echoed in an incident from Melville's actual life. When filling out the birth-certificate for his second child, he "absent-mindedly" put his mother's name where his wife's name should have been.

† Melville's whole life—personal and literary—was a series of sought-after injustices, and weak pseudo-aggressive counteractions. One could reach this conclusion even without the clinical experiences reproduced in *The Writer and Psychoanalysis.*

distorted fantasy of the "cruel" mother of babyhood. Even in *Moby Dick*, therefore, a woman is represented as central figure.

Pierre takes its name from its hero, a young patrician who lives in too close neurotic contact with his domineering, jealous mother. He calls her "sister"; she calls him "brother." Pierre is about to be married to Lucy, a young and beautiful girl. He calls for his mother at a village sewing-bee; Isabel, a girl whom he has never seen before, and who has never seen him before, faints at his entrance. In a secret interview with him later on, Isabel reveals that she is his illegitimate half-sister. To "protect" Isabel, Pierre decides to marry her; they will live together as brother and sister. Isabel and Pierre go to New York, taking with them Delly Ulver, who has been cast out by her family because she is going to have an illegitimate child. Bourgeois tragedy follows. Pierre is disinherited by his mother (she dies of grief shortly afterwards); his relatives turn the cold shoulder to him; he and the two women under his protection live on in poverty and near starvation. Worst of all, Pierre is a failure as a writer. At this point, the unhappy trio becomes a quartet. Lucy, Pierre's exfiancee, joins the "over-womaned" household. In the meantime, Pierre's noble program for the salvation of his illegitimate sister, with all its magic gestures, has also proved a failure. The relationship has become more openly incestuous. To "defend his honor," Pierre kills an accusing relative. At the last, Pierre and Isabel, in prison, swallow poison and die. A few minor tragedies precede this climax.

"I write to please myself," said Melville in one passage in *Pierre*. A comforting self-delusion. The writer, without knowing it, writes to furnish inner alibis to his inner conscience. Obviously Melville considered inner admission of incestuous sister-love a lesser crime than avowal of masochistic submission. He did, in fact, have several sisters. In *Pierre,* he comments: "How much that goes to make up the deliciousness of a wife already lies in the sister."

In *Moby Dick*, it seems to me, Melville rescued himself from masochistic submission by denying it via identification with the fanatic and openly aggressive captain. That defense later became too weak, and admission of incest was substituted, in *Pierre*. (Thus the Oedipal level was used as "rescue-station" against more deeply

repressed oral-masochistic dangers.*) Later, and especially after
the popular and critical failure of both books, Melville's ability to
write creatively came to a virtual end. The sublimation was rejected
by the inner conscience, and consequently collapsed. When Melville died in 1891, forty-one years after the publication of *Moby
Dick,* he was so nearly forgotten in literary circles that New York's
leading literary publication *The Critic,* did not know who he was.

Melville's writing block took a specific form. After *Pierre,* he
wrote by transposing material supplied by others, as in *Israel Potter*
and *Benito Cereno.* These were not plagiarisms, but acceptable
representations. He also published a series of narrative sketches
under the pseudonym of "Salvator R. Tarnmoor" in 1854. By and
large, however, it seemed as if the creative imagination had left
home. He did not stop writing; he later turned out a mass of poetry
of dubious value and some years earlier a few short stories. One of
these was the interesting but little-appreciated short story, "Bartleby
the Scrivener," which is about a man who remains stubbornly silent
and obstinate in the face of any— (selfcreated!)—crisis, countermand-
ing suggestions of any kind with an unvarying, "I would prefer not
to," and who finally dies of starvation in prison. Another was an
unfinished satire, *The Confidence Man,* full of bitterness against
all bourgeois values. Both of these works ironically depict or very
obviously attack Melville's own situation, or reply to inner
reproaches against it. There was, finally, the novel which is not

---

* The Oedipal palimpsest served Melville well, even after his death. Lewis
Mumford, for instance, writing in 1929, equates Melville and Shakespeare as
Oedipal victims, with equal lack of justification. *(Herman Melville* [l. c.], pp.
234 ff.) Ludwig Lewisohn, in *The Story of American Literature* (The Modern
Library, 1939), does likewise, ascribing Melville's difficulties to his strong attachment to his mother, made stronger when he was orphaned at thirteen by his
father's death. According to Lewisohn, the boy reacted to his mother's coldness
with hatred, not merely for her, but for the whole world.

Frequent allusions made to Melville's unconscious homosexuality seem to me
baseless, as is the rumor of insanity. The main argument, his one-sided friendship with Hawthorne, is superficial; this attachment was not homosexual but
masochistic, since Hawthorne's "silences" took care of that. The auxiliary argument offers *Billy Budd* (see p. 104 for description) as testimony. This seems to
me completely out of focus; here masochistic acceptance is confused with homosexuality.

really a novel called *Billy Budd*, written three years before Melville's death. Mumford, although he acknowledges this as a prose work of importance, disparages it because it is not a creative work, in his opinion, but is limited to assertions and observations.

The writing block—which refers not to the mechanics of putting works down on paper, but to creativity—was so obvious that, after twenty years of attempting to earn his living by writing, Melville was forced to accept the position of customs inspector at the port of New York. This very post, which he held from 1866 until a few years before his death, had previously been described by him, in *Redburn,* as "a most inglorious one; indeed, worse than driving geese to water." *Pierre* had been written at the age of 33; Melville died at 72 without having made a literary comeback. Except for *The Confidence Man* and *Billy Budd,* Melville never even attempted to write another novel; he turned completely away from the only literary form he had truly mastered, the form in which he had achieved his greatest successes, and his most profound defeats. It is of course true that both critics and readers misunderstood and sneered at the genius who wrote of man's innermost trouble while the majority of his contemporaries presented a front of unbroken, naive optimism. But public opinion, unaccompanied by writing block, has never prevented a misunderstood writer from writing for the "future generations" which would finally understand him.

Stendhal is a case in point. His *De L'Amour* had sold exactly seventeen copies eleven years after its original publication. His critics and reviewers were what might charitably be called "the usual misunderstanding type." Nevertheless, he went right on producing.

The desire of the writer or innovator to be published, accepted, acknowledged, admired, honored by his contemporaies is a psychological problem in itself. Obvious reasons aside, the desire has deep unconscious connotations. The writer's exhibitionism, his wish for public acceptance, is part and parcel of his inner defense. Vision (voyeurism) is converted into exhibitionism, the lesser crime. The lesser crime is further lightened of guilt by the outer world's approval. Rejection and adverse criticism, therefore, cannot be cited as primum movens of an ensuing literary block. The critic and reviewer is always—past, present, future—the lowest common

denominator of the average reader. This is so out of inner necessity.* Whatever the field, the writer and innovator has only two
choices. He can confirm what the reader (and therefore the critic)
already knows—"The public does not need any new ideas; it is
best served with the ideas it already has," pronounces a "conservative" in Ibsen's *Enemy of the People*—or he can offer original
material, and accept ridicule, ostracism, and disparagement.

Melville's bitterness over the critical reception of his work was
justified enough, if naive. *Mardi* was stigmatized with such adjectives as "melancholy," "deplorable" and "humiliating" by the
Dublin University Magazine, and compared with an amateur
painter's daub by the *Democratic Review. Moby Dick* did quite as
well. The *Dublin University Press* gave it equal marks with *Mardi*
for eccentricity and monstrous extravagance, but called it "valuable" because it contained such a mass of information about the
whale. The *Athanaeum* warned Melville that he had only himself
to thank if the general reader discarded his "horrors and heroics"
as so much trash. And the *New Monthly Magazine* called its style
"maniacal." As for *Pierre,* both style and plot were vehemently
condemned. *Putnam's Monthly* warned Melville that he was risk-
ing all his fame with such products, called the language of the
book "drunken" and the thought "poisoned." Other publications
leaned heavily on such adjectives as "unhealthy," and the *Literary
World* fell back on the familiar judgment of eccentricity.

The pronouncement that *Moby Dick* was valuable for its body
of information about the whale is memorable for its absurdity. To
jump only fifty years to 1899, and from literature to science, is it
any more idiotic than the "killing" review which strangled Freud's
Interpretation of Dreams? In Freud's own words, recently retrieved
by the posthumous publication of his letters to W. Fliess:†

(Jan. 8, 1900) . . . The new century, of which the most interesting fact
for us may be that it will include our death dates, did not bring me anything but an idiotic ("bloed") review in *Zeit,* written by the ex-director of
the Imperial Theatre, Burckhard. It is by no means flattering, extremely
lacking in understanding, and—that's the worst—promises to be con-

---

* See *The Writer and Psychoanalysis* (l. c.) and "Literary Critics Who Can
Spell But Not Read," *Imago,* 1951.
† *Aus den Anfaengen der Psychoanalyse.* (l. c.)

tinued in the next issue. I do not count on acknowledgment—at least during my lifetime. . . . (The editors of the Collection add this explanation: "The review by Max Burckhard appeared in the Vienna daily, *Die Zeit,* on January 6th and 13th, 1900, under the title 'A Modern Dreambook'; it was a malicious representation of Freud's ideas, distorted and satirized with journalistic skill.") (p. 328)

On April 4th, 1900, Freud wrote:

. . . The review in *Zeit,* which with all its stupidity killed the book in Vienna . . . (p. 338)

And on May 16th, 1900:

. . . . The publisher (Freud says "bookseller") complains that *The Interpretation of Dreams* is selling poorly . . . (p. 342)

Whether or not Melville accepted the masochistic inner elaboration of his unchanging infantile conflict remains unclear.* Nothing is known of customs-inspector Melville's feelings in middle and old age. The reasons for Melville's masochistic fixation (and the desperate pseudo-aggressive countermeasures instituted against it) are only remotely linked with reality factors. It is true that his mother came from a wealthy family, was proud, "aristocratic," and detached towards the boy; true that the father died when Melville was thirteen, leaving the family poorly provided for, so that they were the poor branch of an otherwise wealthy family; true that his early experiences were colored by half-poverty and full dependence, which impeded his formal education. But all this was more or less accidental, and could have been elaborated, intrapsychically, in quite a different direction. Not everybody undergoing unpleasant real experiences emerges as a chronic complaint expert and injustice collector.

Too often, reality factors are triumphantly produced by biographers as the "real reason" for the peculiarities of their subjects, or as proof that their subjects were not peculiar at all, when the

---

* It is interesting that Lewisohn (l. c.) with good intuition should have diagnosed Melville as a weak man afraid of himself and of life, and not the strong defiant person he tried to appear. (p. 189) On the other hand, Lewisohn objects to *Moby Dick* because it embodies the refusal to come to terms with life; Lewisohn does not see that it was Melville's deep passive-masochistic fixation that forced him into his over-furious attack, as defense!

answer lies, not in external details, but in their use and misuse within the unconscious of that individual.

Melville, who was professionaly unequipped for any trade, turned to the sea at the age of seventeen. His first books dealt with the Eden-like South Seas. Obviously, they embodied an autarchic defense. *Typee* and *Omoo*, the vehicles of his initial literary alibi, were successes; the reading public was hungry for adventure, and they filled the bill. But Melville is proof that masochistic bitterness can feed on success as well as on failure. He was a popular author at twenty-five, when he had only one book to his credit. Nevertheless, his inner uneasiness continued, growing until it required the titanic outlet of *Moby Dick*. Thus came the period of increased internal conflict; the first inner defense having collapsed, a stronger defense instituted, and in *Moby Dick* masochism is fought, not with autarchy, but through identification with Captain Ahab, who carries on a furious and unrelenting battle against the devouring "white" whale, symbolizing the "bad" mother. The substitute defense also proves too weak, and is followed by the "rescue attempt" via Oedipal admission presented in *Pierre*. Finally, (aided by the misuse of critical and popular rejection) everything collapses; the literary escape is "out," and camouflaged writing block sets in, to last until Melville's death.

One example testifying to Melville's severe masochism may be found in *Typee*, where he describes an instance of almost unbelievably provocative behavior on his own part. His cannibal captors had the usual set of strict taboos, and one of the most rigid of these forbade any woman of the tribe ever to set foot in, or even touch, a canoe. Knowing that he was always in danger of being eaten instead of entertained by his cannibal hosts, Melville took the risk of asking the chief of the tribe to break this sacred taboo so that Melville could go ahead with his plan for a canoe-ride in the company of Fayaway, a girl of the tribe. In Melville's own words:

Although the "taboo" was a ticklish thing to meddle with, I determined to test its capabilities of resisting an attack . . . . It was high time the islanders should be taught a little gallantry . . . Ridiculous, indeed, that the lovely creatures (the women of the tribe) should be obliged to paddle about in the water, like so many ducks, while a parcel of great strapping fellows skimmed over its surface in their canoes. (p. 140)

Melville (as previously stated) made no attempt at the novel form from the time he wrote *The Confidence Man* (1856) to three years before his death (1891), when he wrote his last book, *Billy Budd*. He was at that time seventy years old. *Billy Budd seems* to summarize acceptance of masochistic submission. Once more we have an innocently tortured youth, innocently condemned to death, and hanged. But in the moment before he dies, he turns to face the officers on the quarter-deck and cries, "God bless Captain Vere!" It was Vere who had condemned him to death. He dies happily and becomes the hero of legends and ballads cherished by sailors.

Final acceptance of masochistic submission is thus wisdom's last word in Melville. A stanza written in old age seems to point in the same direction:

> Healed of my hurt, I laud the inhuman Sea—
> Yes, bless the Angels Four that there convene;
> For healed I am ever by their pitiless breath
> Distilled in wholesome dew named rosmarine.

And the testimony of a contemporary reveals that in 1885 (six years before Melville's death), the writer by no means gave the impression of his old "Timonism."

Mr. Melville bore nothing of the appearance of a man disappointed in life, but rather had an air of perfect contentment, and his conversation had much of his jovial, let-the-world-go-as-it-will spirit.

In short, acceptance of masochism has its compensations, too.

Since psychic masochism, the "end result of the infantile conflict," is predominant, its typical defense is predominant as well. Evidence of pseudo-aggression, therefore, is more than ample: its external vestige is human malice.

Human malice—always present, always available for use at split-second notice, always operative—is more than a subject for sermons by moralists. It corresponds to a deep psychological inner necessity, and is virtually ineradicable. Its basis is inborn aggression, neurotically manipulated.

But the mere presence of human aggression in the average person does not explain its incessant use, or the occasions when it is smuggled on to the scene with the help of hairsplitting and prevarication. Why is the poison of human malice so indiscriminately disseminated?

Again, the answer is to be found in the human being's unending need to disprove superego's accusation of inner masochistic passivity. "How can I be accused of that—don't you see how malicious I really am?" runs the unconscious alibi.

On all levels, from the commonplace to the highly elevated, human malice is all-pervasive. This is obvious; it is equally obvious that *neurotic* malice is quite different, in its manifestations, from unavoidable self-defense.

The malice of the inner defense increases in proportion to the increasing violence of superego's blows at the hidden recesses of individual masochism. People who doubt the universality of masochism will perhaps be more willing to acknowledge its defensive reverberation—malice. Even then, however, they are likely to claim that an "original trait" is emerging *directly,* having forgotten the rule that repressed material is always covered by inner defenses. On the other hand, people frequently class as malice what is in reality but a refutation of their own impudence. Moreover, the widespread inability to see oneself objectively leads to labelling every rejection as malice. Strictly speaking, malice consists of one fellow kicking another *without* reason. Thus both self-defense and refutation are excluded.

The seemingly inexhaustible store of human malice—accurately reflecting the inexhaustible underlying masochism—is also converted into a secondary alibi by masochists. They claim they are not masochistic, they are merely defending themselves against malicious outsiders. A pertinent literary example is Dostojewski's attitude towards a protracted whispering campaign against him. The gossip had it that Dostojewski's satire, *The Crocodile,* contained a derisive portait of N. G. Tschernyschewski, a critic and sociologist who had been summarily deported to Siberia by the Tsar. In Dostojewski's *Diary of a Writer* we find his version of the incident under the heading, "Something Personal." * The entry begins with a meeting between Dostojewski and N. A. Nekrassow, influential

* First published in *Graschdarin* No. 3, 1873. Quoted from the *Diary,* Vol. I, pp. 41 ff.

editor of the monthly publication *Sowremennik*. Nekrassow tells him that *Crime and Punishment* will be panned in his publication, explaining quite frankly, "That one is for Tschernyschewski."

The diary continues:

I was quite petrified with surprise.

"M.N., who wrote the review," the editor continued, "told me: 'His novel is good; since he, however, in the novelette which appeared two years ago, wasn't ashamed to upbraid an unhappy deportee, and even to caricature him, I shall pan his new novel.' "

"Is this still the stupid gossip concerning *The Crocodile?*" I exclaimed. "Do you too believe in it? Did you ever read my novelette *The Crocodile?*"

"No, I did not."

"All this is gossip of the lowest kind, which can happen to anyone. One must be equipped with the mentality and poetic imagination of a Bulgarian (famous provocateur of the Tsarist Secret Police) to read all this into my story: a bourgeois allegory, and one directed at Tscherny-schewski at that, read into a story that was just meant to amuse! If you only knew how stupid and farfetched all this is! *I shall, by the way, never forgive myself for not protesting this dirty calumny two years ago, when it was just launched!*"

This discussion with the editor of the defunct journal took place approximately *seven* years ago. Still, I have never protested against this "calumny." At times, the whole thing did not seem important enough, at other times I had "no time." Nevertheless, this underhanded trick, supposedly perpetrated by myself, remained as fact in the recollection of some people; it was disseminated in literary circles, reached the public, and made for many irritations. Now * it is time for me to say a few words about it, and though bereft of proofs, to refute the calumny which, too, is without proof. *By my long silence and negligence I seem to have helped the calumny so far.* (My italics.)

Dostojewski goes on to recount the details of his relationship— a distant but friendly one—with Tschernyschewski, and to outline the contents of the disputed story. In this allegedly harmless satire, a crocodile is exhibited in St. Petersburg. Accompanied by his wife and a friend, an unsuccessful government official comes to see the show. To make up for the mistreatments he must swallow in his work, the official mistreats his friend, who in turn swallows the nonsense because he likes the official's wife. During the show, the

* After *nine* years!

official teases the crocodile, which promptly swallows him. Swallows, but does not kill him; from the inner depths the official's voice can be heard, stubbornly maintaining that he feels fine. To free the man, one would have to cut up the crocodile; its owner refuses to do so and sacrifice the earning possibilities of an animal who is also a high Russian official. He bargains: the crocodile in exchange for an exorbitant payment and the honorary title of Colonel. The bureaucracy, however, is unable to act. No precedent for the crisis can be found in the archives, moreover, the possibility must be considered that the official entered the crocodile because of some forbidden liberal tendencies. . . . In the meantime, the official's wife finds her near-widowhood quite pleasant. The official, too, enjoys his stay within the crocodile, which has brought him the general attention he always had coveted. He demands that his wife give a party for him; he, and the crocodile, will attend in a wooden crate. The higher bureaucracy will attend en masse, he is sure, and at long last he will be able to preach to them and teach them. His wife asks, ironically, what will happen if he is eventually digested, to become an "unexpected product." To this the great man replies that he has already devoted time and thought to this problem: he will file his protest. . . .

The Crocodile remained unfinished; nevertheless, it furnished the basis for the calumny. Detailed proofs were read into it; the alleged lover of the unfaithful wife identified, and the crocodile explained as a symbol of Siberia. . . .

Of course this question remains unanswered: why did Dostojewski write the dubious satire, and especially why did he accept the calumny silently for nine years? One could suspect that he himself used a masochistic technique, later described by him in *The Soft Woman*. (See pp. 59 ff.)

When Freud published *The Interpretation of Dreams*, one of the multitude of objections raised took a peculiar form. The objector wanted to know how many children Freud had. When Freud replied that he had six, he was told that the size of his family explained his ideas: how else but by concocting unusual ideas could he earn enough to support them all?

Less elevated examples of malice distort ordinary, decent actions. If, for example, a widow turns for a last look at the grave of a beloved husband, someone is likely to observe that she wanted to make sure that he was really dead. If you attend the funeral of a friend your motive is misinterpreted: you are there to triumph over the friend, since he is dead and you are still alive. If you make a donation to a worthy cause, you are just a show-off; if you attend a party, it is for the sake of the free drinks; if you don't attend, you are a snob. And so on.

Relieving this bleak picture is the undoubted fact that *human decency,* the counterpart of malice, is not a fantasy. The problem is complex; my book on writers contains an extended chapter on that subject.

To prove my contention that we are dealing exclusively with a defense against a defense in surface reverberations of unconscious wishes, I have—in *The Basic Neurosis* and *Neurotic Counterfeit-Sex*—adduced extensive clinical material from the psychopathology of neuroses. To prove the universality of the mechanism of dual defense, I am here presenting fifty human reactions, *selected at random.* Some of these are considered normal; some are sublimations; some are character traits of differing valency; some constitute neurotic techniques. This presentation—*deliberately a melange*—was prompted simply by topics which came to my attention in the course of clinical work. A number of the topics have been repeatedly treated in our literature; some of them have not. To avoid lengthy quotations, the original publications are listed at the end of the chapter. These previous publications of mine include a review of the literature.

It should also be understood that the "group of 50" to follow is merely a collection of skeleton sketches, bare of either details or deductions. These, too, can be found in the original publications. A minimum of examples will be adduced in illustration of the specific defenses; a fuller sampling of examples is to be found in the original studies.

As headings for these sub-chapters, I have used typical objections raised by people observing these specific traits. These objections are almost invariably reported by those on the receiving end; the reaction varies from wonder or indignation to flattered approval.

It will be noted that in the secondary defenses there are always two mechanisms stressed:

First: *part payment* (installment payment) of "internal *conscience money*", referring to self-imposed penalties for the substitute offense ("taking the blame for the lesser crime"). Stressing of "part payment" is necessary, because the total amount of "conscience money" is greater than can be seen in conscious suffering and self-damage: the original wishes are short-changed into substitutes.

Second: *temporary checkmating of Daimonion by hypocritically and spuriously fulfilling demands of the ego ideal.* (Ironic lip-service conformity with ego ideal precepts.) Educational precepts, actually communicated to the child in the course of the educational process, are twisted in a manner which hits the enshrined images of educators with their own stick. *This ironic pseudo-acceptance of ego ideal precepts* (by taking actual commands verbatim and applying them at the wrong time and place) has the advantage of temporarily wresting the most powerful weapon from Daimonion, which typically executes its torture by showing up the discrepancy between ego ideal and ego. The defensive-ironic technique of the unconscious ego is also a pseudo-aggressive retort on the part of the otherwise masochistically beaten-down sector of the personality. (For elaboration, see Foreword xiv, and Chapter 8, "The Pseudo-Moral Connotation of Neurotic Symptoms.")

1. *So you run around with the feeling of being wronged?*

No one seems to be entirely free of the conviction that he is unjustly treated. The feeling is produced in such generous quantities that one can only conclude that a good deal of bogus-injustice is in circulation. The bogus currency of injustice outnumbers the genuine by approximately ten to one.

This still leaves humanity with a generous stock of real injustice to contend with. What do neurotic contemporaries do with it?

Injustices can be divided into two types: the *unavoidable,* and the neurotically, unconsciously, self-created, which are *avoidable*. A further subdivision is necessary: unavoidable injustices can either be *neutralized,* or neurotically *misused*.

To clarify the issue: relative normality means the automatic absorption of unavoidable injustices, which are consciously and unconsciously rejected. This neutralizing attitude, in which one "makes the best of it," does not lead to slave-like submission. One fights for one's rights at the exact moment when the struggle makes sense, and has a chance of success. Neurosis means exactly the opposite. It is an automatic procurer, promotor and pursuer of avoidable injustices. It is also an inveterate misuser of unavoidable injustices, elevating them to tragedies instead of demoting them to nuisances. Both types of injustice are unconsciously welcomed and sought out by neurotics. The external rejection, which is also present, is not intended to eliminate the injustice; it is an ineffective, pseudo-aggressive expedient, designed to supply an alibi for the benefit of conscience. The transparent technique fails, however, and conscience must be further placated with alibis and pseudo-suffering. In pseudo-aggression, therefore, the choice of weapons, the timing, or the technique of the fight is always ineffective. The result is to kindle the flame instead of putting it out.

Our old acquaintance, the psychic masochist, specializes in the search for a "daily dose of injustice." His technique of being an injustice collector is simple. Unconsciously, he provokes a refusal or misuses reality to simulate one. Unaware that he has engineered his own defeat, he uses righteous indignation and ineffective pseudo-aggression to fight back against the blow he has invited. He remains on the receiving end; when his quota of kicks is filled he retires to the "whining corner," where he bitterly complains that "this can happen only to poor little me," and thus helps himself to a second dose of masochism. Fortunately for his conscious peace of mind, he remains oblivious to the fact that all this was unconsciously *self-provoked, self-constructed, self-perpetuated.*

This whole procedure, it is clear, is constructed of unconscious alibis and defenses. Psychic masochists live mainly on the defensive level of pseudo-aggression. Their outward aspect is one of hyper-belligerency. They play the permanent role of provocateur; their shoulders are loaded with chips. The impression of hyper-belligerency is misleading. The pseudo-aggression they display is merely the alibi offered to the inner conscience, allegedly to disprove the masochistic aim. At the same time, it is a technique for provoking attack, and thus *achieving* the hidden masochistic aim.

The psychic masochist is *the* expert at self-delusion. He himself, along with his environment, accepts his pseudo-aggression at face value. In inner reality, the show is put into operation as a disclaimer of the superego's justified charge that the ego enjoys secret masochistic pleasure.

If one considers the fact that *every* human being carries a quantitatively different but nonetheless heavy burden of psychic masochism, and that everyone, at bottom, is a more or less assiduous injustice collector;* if one remembers that psychic masochism is the neurotic "difficulty" most frequently met with in neurotics *and* so-called normal people (the differences between the two groups are quantitative only); one can deduce the degree to which humans live on the "shoestring of twin alibis."

PSYCHIC MICROSCOPY OF THE *CLINICAL* PICTURE IN PSYCHIC MASOCHISM

Layer I.   End result of the infantile conflict; stabilization on the rejection level (genetic picture).

Layer II.   First veto of superego, because of pleasure gain involved.

Layer III.   First defense of the unconscious ego: disclaimer (alibi) in the form of an "objective fact"—the (promptly provoked) outer world's injustice.

Layer IV.   Second veto of superego.

Layer V.   Second defense of the unconscious ego: to prove the opposite, the victim fights with desperate pseudo-aggression and seemingly in self-defense; after his inevitable defeat, he commiserates himself for his dreary fate.—"Conscience money" paid in the form of suffering and self-damage.—"Ironic lip-service conform-

* The neologism, "injustice collector," was first used by myself while analyzing a neurotic professor of English literature. Among his other difficulties, the man was constantly irritated, to the point of "bursting a blood vessel" (ipsissima verba) by the "wrong usage of words." He thus collected hundreds of bitter disappointments daily, at the same time that he proved his "aggression" to himself. I told him: "When you start with the modest capital of the one and one half million words in the English language, you can hardly go bankrupt. Why, you can even achieve the status of an 'injustice collector.'" . . . . "Don't use that word—it's simply impossible!" . . . . "But why? Doesn't the language include the words tax collector, stamp collector, and garbage collector?" . . . . The professor's excitement was so impressive that what started as a joke ended as a neologism. To my surprise, the term has since achieved literary status: Mr. Louis Auchincloss used it as the title of his collection of short stories (published by Houghton Mifflin, 1950), acknowledging my linguistic priority in his preface.

ity with ego ideal precepts": use of pseudo-aggression at wrong
time and place. ("Didn't you teach me to fight back when
attacked?")
SUMMARY: Psychic masochism is a defense against a defense.

2. *Do you have a message for the ages?*

In a poll recently taken in Louisville, Kentucky, 2.1 per cent of
those questioned confessed that they "want to write." On the basis
of this poll, a statistician calculated that no less than 2,377,132
people in the United States, or 2.1 per cent of the "voting population" (the original poll was a canvass of voters) are potential
writers.* These are people who are willing to admit their "inclination"†; one does not dare speculate on the percentage if the
reticent could be persuaded to join the ranks of the outspoken.

Every writer's opinion, admitted or not, is that he has a message
for the ages. Is this way of communicating one's "ideas," therefore,
a reliable road to discovery of the inner thoughts, undiluted by
alibis, of at least 2.1 per cent of the voting population?

Unfortunately for seekers of the "real self" in the other fellow,
this road is a dead end. Clinical analysis of more than forty writers
has convinced me that the creative writer's work is not an expression of his conscious wishes, nor even of his unconscious wishes and
fantasies. His work represents only the unconscious *secondary*
defenses against these wishes and fantasies. Instead of continuing
a theoretical discussion, which I have dealt with at length elsewhere,‡ I am presenting excerpts from a clinical case.

A woman came into analysis with me some years after having
written and published a devastating satire on the neurotic behavior
of a man who found himself out of a job because of the stock-
market crash. This satire, which was consciouly patterned on the
patient's husband, was a success, and important critics encouraged

* The New York *Times,* February 13, 1949.
† This "inclination" towards writing is more than balanced by a widespread
disinclination towards reading: one American out of two is a non-reader of books.
At the highpoint of the Korean crisis, on August 18th, 1950, this item made the
front page of the New York *Times:* "STUDY INDICATES HALF OF U. S.
SHUNS BOOKS. . . ANN ARBOR, Mich., July 17 . . . Nearly half of all Ameri-
cans do not read books, a University of Michigan survey indicated today.—More
than half of all adults live within a mile of a public library, but only one-tenth
average as much as a visit a month, the survey showed."
‡ *The Writer and Psychoanalysis,* 1. c.

her to continue in that type of writing. This had been her first satire, and was her last for many years; she shifted to the production of idyllic short stories all of which were failures.

The patient had a typical masochistic attachment to the pre-Oedipal mother, and was an industrious injustice collector. Consciously, she was unhappy over her husband's unemployment; unconsciously, she welcomed this very real denial by the mother-image. Reproached by the superego for her masochistic pleasure, she defended herself by declaring that she was furious with her husband, and ridiculed him as neurotic and incapable. Since this aggression was a defense against the more deeply rooted masochistic wishes, she was able to write the successful satire, secondarily filtered by inner guilt and external approval. Naturally, she "reacted to her own courage with anxiety," thus necessitating a new defense. This took the form of the idyllic short stories, none of which were successful. She then gave up writing altogether, and became furious if her attempts were even mentioned.

In my opinion, the writer is a perpetual defendant before the high tribunal of his severe inner conscience. His is a "self-curative alibi sickness," secondarily made palatable by social usefulness. These formulas cover the various unconscious alibis employed: "I am not guilty of being a masochistic glutton for punishment"— "If I am guilty at all, at worst I am guilty of a crime other than that charged in the indictment"—"I'm not guilty because the whole of humanity is my accomplice"—"I am not guilty of being a peeping Tom; I do admit to the lesser crime of exhibitionism."

In short, the writer is engaged in a desperate fight against an unsolved and repressed psychic masochistic attachment to the pre-Oedipal mother. Unlike other psychic masochists, who need two people in order to re-enact the repressed infantile situation, the artist establishes an "autarchy" in which the mother-child duality is reduced to a single unit. The artist denies his masochistic attachment by denying the very existence of the disappointing mother. His alibi reads: "I, myself, out of myself, give myself beautiful words and ideas." Playing both the "corrected," giving mother *and* the recipient child, the artist manufactures an alibi which accords with the basic judicial principle, "no corpse, no crime."

Following the establishment of his autarchic fiction, the artist's next defense consists of a series of "admissions of the lesser crime."

He will admit to pseudo-aggression as defense against more deeply repressed psychic masochism, and to exhibitionism as defense against more deeply repressed voyeurism. This accounts for the prevalence of books attacking mores, prejudices, institutions, injustices. This also accounts for the fact that the writer writes by developing a plot (product of imagination, which is inner voyeurism), and then putting it down on paper (exhibitionism before the reader).

The often-heard objection—"What should a writer do but write?"—entirely ignores the fact that the impulse to write cannot be taken for granted. It must be explained. One can imagine a person's conceiving a plot without wanting to elaborate on it and commit it to paper. Writing, for the writer, is an inner necessity first; only secondly is it an attempt—mostly unsuccessful—to make a living.

PSYCHIC MICROSCOPY

Layer I. Masochistic attachment to the pre-Oedipal mother, plus voyeuristic wishes.

Layer II. First superego reproach, prompted by dual pleasure gain.

Layer III. First defense of the unconscious ego: by disclaimer (alibi) in form of pseudo-aggression against the outer world, while inwardly masochistic attachment is denied by establishing an autarchy which negates existence of the mother; by making voyeurism harmless ("imagination"); finally by change of voyeurism into exhibitionism; these defenses visible on the surface in the writer's habitual attacks on mores, prejudices, injustices, and in the fact that by writing he exhibits before the reader.

Layer IV. Second veto of the superego.

Layer V. Second defense of the unconscious ego—productivity; "ironic lip-service conformity with ego ideal precepts" in the form of social usefulness and "message for the ages"; payment of "conscience money" in the form of excessive self-torture during productivity, and unconsciously foreseen relative lack of success.

SUMMARY: Creative writing is a defense against a defense.

3. Are you an admirer of exquisite "literary style"?

"Style," as a literary shibboleth, undoubtedly antedates Buffon; since 1753, when the French writer declared that "le style est

l'homme même" in the course of an address to the Academie
Francaise, this famous aphorism has been used as a seal of approval
for the almost unanimous belief that style is *the* criterion by which
one may judge a "real" writer. But neither writers nor literary
critics have ever been able to agree on a definition of the term. It
is only in the exceptional case that a writer is conceded to have
"style." The mention of "style," in the majority of cases, is followed
by a condemning and not an approving comment. And, aside from
public statements, every writer privately harbors contempt for the
manner in which the "other fellow" puts his sentences together.
No pros or cons enter the picture; the rival is automatically devas-
tated with an ironic: "Some style!"

Obviously, judgment on "style" is left to the "feelings." A writer-
patient, when asked his opinion of another writer's work, replied:
"Don't ask me why, but the man has no style." And here the matter
rests. Even if one penetrates beyond the "I just feel it," which is
the traditional refuge of the writer, one is met by a barrage of circumlocution, serving mainly to cloud the issue with elegant literary
phrases borrowed from the literary personages of the past. Coleridge's now famous definition, "Prose—words in their best order;
poetry, the best words in their best order," marches side by side
with Goethe's statement: "Modern poets mix too much water with
their ink." Nor is Carlyle's definition forgotten: "Poetry, therefore,
we call musical thoughts."

This barrage can be countered by a few opposed quotations
from one's own storehouse, but without effect on the writer's convictions. In his opinion, sacrilege has been committed, and for
no purpose. If one asks, further, whether style is more important
than content, quoting, perhaps, Thornton Wilder ("Style is but
the faintly contemptible vessel in which the bitter liquid is recommended to the world"), it is regretfully admitted that "unfortunately" there must be content, because the "stupid reader" (never
forget the bag of quotations) is, as Andre Gide put it, "greedy for
sweets and trifles."

This stalemate is reached in any argument with a worshipper of
style, regardless of his IQ. His reasoning ability is not responsible;
his unconscious evaluation of the importance of *expression* as
opposed to idea, is. Why is the expression of thoughts, or even lack

of thoughts, so highly overrated? If style is "the dress of thoughts," (Earl of Chesterfield) what lies beneath the dress?

The writer's superabundance of inner guilt is the clue. Since his work expresses only the secondary defenses against his original desires, his inner guilt (which always pertains to the basic oral-masochistic conflict) is secondarily shifted to various points. One of these deposits is the *expression* per se.

It is well-known, phenomenologically, that every writer creates his private hell plastered with perfect words. The search for the "right" word seems to be of prime importance. Viewed analytically, the writer's overestimation of stylistic and verbal artistry is merely a byproduct of his lifelong battle of the conscience. Characteristically, the writer devotes himself to the pursuit of the elusive "exact" word; characteristically, he carries a burden of guilt because the word, when found, still does not express the inexpressible; characteristically, he feels exaggerated pride in his search and his partial successes, and boasts of them immoderately. At bottom, an unconscious mechanism of shifted guilt is at work: *guilt pertaining to the defense against the repressed masochistic problem is shifted to the technicality of expressing the defense.* The inner difficulty is thus magnificently camouflaged, and even more magnificently rationalized, for who can cavil at verbal artistry? Mark Twain's remark, already quoted, that "the difference between the right word and the almost right word is the difference between lightning and the lightning bug," is an indication of the degree to which the writer inflates the importance of the shifted defense.

Words, therefore, absorb a great deal of the inner guilt which actually pertains to the warded-off problem of psychic masochism. The substitution, of course, is only partially successful. Despite his shift, the writer tortures himself with his verbal substitute. But his conflict is now on the reality level, and this is a considerable compensation. At least something palpable is used as the instrument of his daily and hourly torture.

V. S. Pritchett, the British writer and critic, was once told by one of his readers that he had exposed a flagrant injustice in one of his stories. The author was rather surprised:

> I had undoubtedly exposed an evil but I had no idea when I wrote that I was doing so . . . I recall that *all my labor and indeed all my conscience was in the choice of the best words* . . . .

The words, "all my conscience," are precisely correct; they point directly to the writer's unconscious motivation.

The irony of the situation is unparalleled. Unconsciously, style has nothing to do with style. Unfortunately, the deification of style has tragicomic consequences—a statement easily proved by even a cursory survey of the falsification of life in literature.

In *The Writer and Psychoanalysis* I described, among other facets of the subject, the vicious circle of misrepresentation of life in belles lettres. The reader is short-changed again and again. Objectivity in literature is a myth, and must be a myth, because of six highly personal and unreliable "filtration" processes.

The writer, to begin with, is not an objective observer of reality. He uses reality factors, but only as they fit into his own defensive pattern. For purposes of inner survival, he must furnish an alibi to his unconscious conscience. And he does, by hook or by crook.

To cite but one example. Suppose a homosexual writer describes a group of people arguing whether or not happy marriages do exist. The discussion is dramatized by the example of a newly-wed couple in the neighborhood; ideal love blossoms there, a baby is dearly loved. But gossip has it that these newly-weds, a middle-aged couple, had waited many years to marry, hoping the man would achieve financial success. Actually, their background was less romantic. The wife had been companion to a wealthy old woman, and the husband had been the old lady's physician. Because the wife had been mentioned in the old lady's will, the two conspired to shorten their wait by means of an overdose of sleeping pills. Both were then charged with murder, but acquitted, mainly because a gynecological scrutiny had proved the companion-nurse to be a virgin. The puritanic conscience had forbidden pre-marital sex, but not murder. Does this ironic story, written to disprove the homosexual writer's inner guilt, (e.g., at missing marital bliss), prove that marriage is a farce? Or is the story "true to life"? Or, to go to the opposite extreme, are the nymphomaniacs and promiscuous wolves so prominent in current novels proof that all modern women and men are neurotics? Or, is idealization of romantic love (presented after the principle of the neurotic writer's defense: "I am not incapable of love, love is too small for me")— an idealization accepted as authoritative model by millions of boys and girls everywhere—a precise mirror of reality?

Second, the editor, the publisher's executive lieutenant, is not an objective evaluator of reality, either. By and large he is an inhibited and frustrated writer himself; when called upon to judge the products of his less inhibited competitors, his preferences turn to trash, simply because trash offers a convenient alibi for his own incapacity. "True, the other fellow writes, but he produces only trash." Added to this is the personal danger of endorsing any writer who travels an unbeaten path, for a few financially unrewarding recommendations can cost the editor his position.

The third factor is the publisher of novels, who is a gambler speculating on the reader's market instead of the Stock Exchange. He, too, prefers trash: "It sells better." And nobody can claim that trash depicts reality as it is. The "reality" of the publisher is the lowest common denominator of his distorted fantasy of what a reader really is.

Fourth is the literary critic, the least reliable "filter" of all. The critic, not unlike the editor, is usually an inhibited writer himself, unconsciously brimming with undigested anger against the productive writer. His anger is generally camouflaged by very, very high "literary standards"—which standards, by the way, change with every critic. It is no secret that the less productive the critic is as a writer, the more destructive are his reviews. More, today's average critic, who is set up as a judge of unconscious mechanisms, is completely without psychiatric-psychoanalytic knowledge. The cloak of omniscience is thus thrown over the shoulders of a frequently malicious amateur.

The highly misleading product of this four-point filtration program is then submitted to the final judge—the poor reader. He is, so to speak the fifth dupe in falsification of reality, though but an innocent accessory. His falsification is made inevitable by the traditional respect for the printed word, by reverent attention to the dicta of the professional critics, and finally by his own rather naive wish for imported emotions, to be enjoyed in identification. Respect for the printed word is based on schoolbooks, handed down by the authorities of the nursery and later the classroom. The four-year-old's respect is successor to an even earlier uncanny respect—before the child learns to read, the adult's exclusive prerogative of understanding the printed page seems additional evidence of the upbringer's power. Even nonsense, once it has achieved print, receives the stamp of authority, impressing both the meek and the rebellious. The same authority is vested in the fourth link, the critic. The spinelessness with which the critic's biased opinions are accepted at face value is not even funny any more. "I am ashamed to admit," an intelligent man once told me in all serious- ness, "that I could not agree with the critics praising this book. It must be my ignorance, I guess. . . ."

The power of cold print and critical pronouncements deprives the reader of all independence: he is actually afraid to be on his own. What he really wants is to import emotions which correspond to his own inner defenses.

The sixth link in the falsifying process is the deification of style. The reader has no direct access to the writer—a book can reach him only when accepted and issued by a publisher. And one of the silly and distorting yardsticks determining the acceptance or rejection of a manuscript is the legend of "good" and "bad" style.

Mencken's definition of style, "It must be said with a certain grace," is closest to the facts. Thoughts, situations, characterizations, must be expressed in some readable fashion. The simpler the style, the better. Obviously, style must not impede the narrative; in other words, it must be pleasantly unobtrusive. But out of this means of communication neurotics have constructed a half-god, worshipped for the sake of "style"—whatever the word may mean for them.

In unconscious reality, "style" is one of the landmarks in the battle of the conscience which ravages the unconscious of every writer. Guilt is shifted from the real problem to the technical expres- sion of the defense. The uninitiated is not aware of this, consciously; inwardly, however, the editor, the publisher and the critic know exactly what the situation is. Therefore, when editor, publisher or critic go into their routine about the "style" of a particular writer, they are in effect accusing him of having temporarily solved his conflict with his inner conscience. If the writer's style is "good," unconscious envy comes to the fore: "Who are you to be victorious in a battle we have lost?" If they condemn the style as "bad," they are unconsciously gloating: "You, too, have lost." In projecting their own defeats, they indict the writer's style.

This minor fracas in the unending battle of the conscience is by no means without realistic importance. It is the reason some good books are turned down by publishing houses, thus never reaching the public.*

Buffon was mistaken in believing that style is the person proper. Style is not even the distant cousin of "l'homme meme"—it is, rather, a part of the conscience money paid to the superego.

PSYCHIC MICROSCOPY OF "PRODUCERS" OF LITERARY STYLE

Layer I.   Masochistic solution of the infantile conflict, plus voyeurism.
Layer II. First superego reproach.
Layer III. First defense of the unconscious ego: disclaimers (alibis) in the form of pseudo-aggression, of voyeurism rendered harmless (imagination) and exhibitionism.
Layer IV. Second superego reproach.
Layer V. Second defense of the unconscious ego: social usefulness, ("ironic lip-service conformity with ego ideal precepts"); "conscience money" paid in self-torture via search for the "right expression."
SUMMARY: Defense against a defense.

4. *So you are a cynic?*

The cynic's performance is designed to convey the impression that he, unlike the man in the street, can see through accepted institutions, mores, morals, cherished beliefs. The cynic, he avers, is the man who knows what the score really is. And that score, in his considered opinion, can be translated as "everything stinks."

Under this surface, however, hides a frightened child transfixed on the horns of his specific dilemma. The cynic's inner problem is masochistically tinged ambivalence; unconsciously, he harbors *two* contradictory feelings toward the *same* person at the *same* time. Intrapsychically, he solves his conflict with the accusing inner conscience by looking for allies who will strengthen his defense. This expedient is familiar enough, but the method by which the cynic

---

* The starting point of deliberations leading to these conclusions was my unsuccessful attempt to recommend a young writer's valuable novel to a few "experts." The book, psychologically, was first-rate; the alleged dubious style was the impediment. The amount of nonsense I heard on this occasion from professionals convinced me that the current misuse of the term "style" is worth investigating.

enlists his allies is unique. Openly expressing irreverent and even blasphemous opinions, the cynic directs this unconscious invitation to the listener: "Don't be a coward! Admit that you share my opinions!" In other words, the cynic addresses himself to the hidden ambivalence of the listener, offering himself as living proof that the red badge of courage can be earned—if you only dare.

Thus, having *consciously* reassured himself that he is aggressive, active, heroic, smart, and witty as well, the cynic is contented to rest on his laurels. These laurels are but double inner defenses. Everyone but the cynic himself is by this time aware that he "knows the price of everything and the value of nothing." (Oscar Wilde) And he is too busy with the organization of his inner defense to ask himself why he singles out only the darker side of human nature:

> The cynic is one who never sees a good quality in a man, and never fails to see a bad one. He is the human owl, vigilant in darkness, and blind to light, mousing for vermin and never seeing noble game. The cynic puts all human actions into two classes: openly bad and seemingly bad. (Henry Ward Beecher)

The assiduous "debunker" does not see that he is not a free agent, but a mere pawn in the grip of an inner conflict with conscience. Nor does he observe that his environment rejects him, for he is protected from that revelation by his conviction that "they" are naive fools who shrink from the truth—the sole trumpeter of truth, of course, being the cynic himself. Finally, he is impervious to the disadvantage—unconsciously perceived and masochistically elaborated—of never being taken seriously.

PSYCHIC MICROSCOPY

Layer I.   Masochistic ambivalence.

Layer II. First veto of superego.

Layer III. First defense of the unconscious ego: stressing the opposite (aggression in attacking).

Layer IV. Second veto of superego.

Layer V.   Second defense of the unconscious ego: "Everybody secretly agrees with these forbidden views. Anyway, I'm only joking, and besides, shouldn't one always tell the truth?" ("Ironic lip-service conformity with ego ideal precepts"). "Conscience money" is paid in the form of rejection by the outer world.

SUMMARY: Cynicism is a defense against the defense.

5. *So they call you a hypocrite?*

Hypocrisy is an unconscious technique used in the battle of the conscience. Its basis is faked submission to the dictates of the inner torturer. The paradigm is permanent misuse of the transitory childhood situation in which a stern and opinionated educator (or one whom the child considers to be stern and opinionated; see Chapter XI) insists upon *lip-service* and gives no thought to *inner acceptance.* The helpless child's conflict is later internalized. The hypocrite's smiling pseudo-submission, which is his modus vivendi, is an ironic portrayal in caricature of the now internalized educator.

At first glance, the hypocrite's ego seems to have won a victory over the inner conscience. In reality, however, the hypocrite pays for this Pyrrhic victory by incurring the contempt and distrust of his environment. He is universally distrusted because the inner mechanism is once more externalized: the hypocrite uses against real people the identical technique with which he fights the superego.

Once again, we have an example of a type in which the "real self" is not reflected in actions and words. Beneath the veneer of pseudo-flattery, the hypocrite's remarks and actions are both aggressive and contemptuous. The frightened child who is the hypocrite, like the frightened child who is the cynic, has been forced into defensive pseudo-aggression by his inner fears, masochistically tinged.

The triad is by now familiar: masochistic submission as the end result of the infantile conflict; pseudo-aggressive defense; pseudo-submission as a substitute method of warding off the original reproach.

PSYCHIC MICROSCOPY

Layer I. Masochistic submission as end result of the infantile conflict.

Layer II. First veto of superego.

Layer III. First defense mechanism of the unconscious ego: pseudo-aggression.

Layer IV. Second veto of superego, because of liaison with infantile images. ("You have no right to be aggressive towards your upbringers, either.")

Layer V. Second defense of the unconscious ego: ironic pseudo-servility and pseudo-submission ("lip service"); "conscience money" paid in form of the outer world's rejection and distrust.

SUMMARY: Hypocrisy is a defense against the defense.

6. *Addicted to "Magic Gestures"?*

A "magic gesture" unconsciously denotes a masochist's whimpering, disguised by consciously inexplicable kindness towards a beneficiary of no importance. In such situations, a peculiar metamorphosis takes place in the benefactor: if indifferent, he becomes solicitous; if a miser, he opens his purse; if malicious, he unexpectedly overflows with the milk of human kindness. Such a benefactor's propelling need is sometimes so strong that he is able to accept, with a superior smile, the malicious speculation his conduct can arouse in his environment. At these periods, he is fully armored against hints of illicit affairs, homosexuality, precocious senility, and what not.

The "magic gesture" is another of the innumerable episodes in the battle of the conscience. Its structure is as follows:

Layer I.   Masochistic submission as end result of the infantile conflict.

Layer II. First veto of the inner conscience.

Layer III. First defense of the unconscious ego: "I am not guilty of psychic masochism, as the indictment claims. On the contrary, I *hate* my upbringers, because I have so many justified grievances against them." (Pseudo-aggression)

Layer IV. Second veto of inner conscience.

Layer V. Second defense of the unconscious ego: "All I want is to be loved. In my behavior, I will *dramatize* how I wanted to be treated in childhood—*kindly and lovingly.*"—"Ironic lip-service conformity with ego ideal precepts": "What's wrong with being kind and the wish to be loved?"—"Conscience money" is paid in the form of the outer world's suspicion, and the foreseen ingratitude of the beneficiary.

The inner structure of the magic gesture explains:

1. Why *unimportant* people are chosen as beneficiaries: "You, bad mother, did not care for your own child. I, however, care even for strangers." The more remote the benefactor's responsibility towards the beneficiary, the more forceful is the accusation against the enshrined upbringers.

2. Why heretofore unknown individuals, animals, or even inanimate objects, can be used as vehicles of magic gestures.

3. Why the benefactor can—abruptly—become an enemy, shifting to the *negative magic gesture.* The object of a magic gesture can never feel secure; his position as protege is always temporary,

and subject to cancellation without notice. The turnabout is the result of a protest by the benefactor's inner conscience, which thus forces him to present a new alibi. To furnish the needed defense, the benefactor reverses his role. He now denies his inner masochistic tendencies by impersonating the "cruel" parent, casting the ex-beneficiary in the role of his own mistreated self. Thus a *positive* magic gesture becomes *negative,* and demonstrates, in caricature, the cruelty of the educators.

The magic gesture sometimes appears—and very effectively—in literature. Dostojewski's use of it, in *Crime and Punishment,* is memorable. Raskolnikow has just received a letter from his mother, containing the news that his sister has consented to marry a man she does not love, for the sake of the money he would contribute to her brother's support. In a park, he sees an obviously wealthy man pursuing a drunken girl. He calls upon a policeman for aid and rescues the girl, although it means that he must lay out money, which he needs for food, to pay for a cab which will take her home. The reader clearly understands that Raskolnikow identifies the girl with his sister, especially in view of another item in his mother's letter: the news that Swidrigailow, the man in whose house his sister is employed as a governess, has been pursuing her sexually. During the scene in the park, Raskolnikow calls the unknown man who is pursuing the unknown girl "Swidrigailow." Dostojewski cautiously explains even the policeman's interest in the girl, via Raskolnikow's thought that perhaps the policeman "had daughters" of about the girl's age. Dostojewski also shows the senseless shift from positive to negative characteristic of the magic gesture: in the end Raskolnikow suddenly flies into a fury and turns against the poor girl.

PSYCHIC MICROSCOPY

Layers I to V. See above enumeration.

SUMMARY: "Magic gestures" constitute a defense against a defense; the procedure, if exaggerated, is encountered only in orally regressed psychic masochists.

7. *Do you pay your debts of gratitude in "Guilt Denomination"?*

Some people use a peculiar technique in repaying debts of gratitude. In spite of pangs of conscience, they make no attempt, in external reality, to pay their debt. Instead, they expect the victim to accept as full payment their subjective suffering in solving an intrapsychic conflict. In short, they refuse to return favor for favor, suffering from intense reproaches of conscience because of their refusal. The end result remains the refusing action, although the refuser feels that his books have been balanced, and his debt cleared, by his inner discomfort. In other words, an external debt (the moral obligation) is paid off in the currency of inner guilt. The refuser's self-vindication does not, of course, help the refused person. Nor does it help that the refuser frequently informs him of the "facts of the case," meaning his inner conflict on this point.

This mechanism, in which debts of gratitude are paid in "guilt denomination," is at first glance reminiscent of the kind of *external* "conscience money" sent anonymously to the United States Treasury. Here a good deed is executed exclusively because of conscious guilt.* On closer observation, one detects decided differences. The two mechanisms are in many ways exact opposites. External conscience money helps the victim; payment in guilt denomination (or no external payment) damages the victim. Conscience money is paid in an externally visible action; payment in guilt denomination is an unconscious deal which the refuser makes with himself, and is characterized by the absence of external action.

I first observed this mechanism at work in an acquaintance who, in his own estimation, owed me a debt of gratitude: "more than you have the slightest realization of." The acquaintance was a highly cultured, extremely correct person. The rather protracted series of acts which evoked his gratitude were of benefit to him alone. (Their nature is immaterial to the case in point.) I had asked for nothing in return, except once (late in the game) for one small favor, which was not of a personal nature and was largely dictated by our interest in a common cause. The gentleman's reaction to the request was first to promise, then to procrastinate, then to lapse into complete inactivity. In the meantime, he continued to accept my favors. Several months after I had made the request, he wrote to inform me that Providence had delivered him from the "insoluble conflict;" he had just heard that it was too late to comply with my modest request. To quote from his letter: "Well, in the upshot, I am, I

* This external conscience money is not to be confused with the *internal* "conscience money" constantly alluded to in these pages.

have to confess, more than a little relieved. For the quite serious conflict was this: on the one hand I not at all want to . . . (accede to the request), although well aware that I ought to want to. . . . On the other hand, I could not possibly refuse . . ., if you wanted me to do it—seeing that I owe you more than you have the slightest realization of. So, from this all but insoluble conflict I am delivered—and I hope that you will not misunderstand my joy thereat—by . . . that Providence that shapes our ends, rough-hew them how we may." Although the writer acknowledges in the deleted passages that he has done considerable damage, not only to me, but to our common cause as well, he goes on to write several additional pages in which he asks for the continuation of my favors, which he neither paid for nor returned.

The letter seems to present an amazing mixture of hypocrisy and cynicism; since I know the writer, I know that it does not reflect his character accurately. He was entirely in earnest in his revelation of his prolonged inner conflict, and in his feeling that he was now "square" because of the suffering his conflict caused him. He was not aware, however, of his unconscious masochistic provocation, for ordinarily a preamble of this type leads unerringly to a kick in the jaw. Except for this unawareness, he was quite honestly convinced that, according to his strange psychic mathematics, he had paid all he owed me by having fought his inner battle.

The naivete displayed in the letter arouses decided curiosity. What is the purpose behind the self-revelation? There is more to it than the evident unconscious provocation. It also embodies a plea for absolution. This can only mean that a small part of the guilt remains unresolved. The decisive part, however, is absorbed, having been paid for in guilt denomination.

It was my conviction that, subjectively, my acquaintance did not feel guilt; it was this that prompted the tenor of my reply. As tactfully as I knew how, and refraining from pressing the point as I otherwise would have, I reminded him that in addition to Providence, perhaps the mechanism of "guided miracles—guided by procrastination" had also entered the picture; my request had been made months before the arrival of the welcome moment when it became "too late."

The discrepancy between the *large* debt of gratitude, and the *small* favor refused as payment, is also curious. The refusal of the "small favor" possesses a case history in itself. The request provokes, within the donor who refuses to give, an inner conflict which is only secondarily rationalized. (I stopped short of this deduction in the case of my acquaintance simply because he had not been analyzed; everything found as reason, therefore, would be merely speculation, and worthless.)

In analyzed cases, we are in a position to find these reasons and to analyze them. Unfortunately, the explanation in each case is a long drawn out affair; one representative example will have to suffice. A young homosexual writer, Mr. C., who was blocked in his productivity, was recommended to me by his friend, Mr. D., then in analysis with me, because of the identical perversion and the identical writer's block. (Mr. D. was a writer of factual stories for magazines.) D. was eventually cured; after analysis he achieved moderate success in the limited field of magazine articles, married (he had changed his homosexuality) and was quite content. He began to write a novel, although his main field was journalistic in scope. He was very grateful to analysis and later freely admitted to whom and to what he owed his renewed productivity. D. was well into his analysis when C., in a suicidal mood, revealed that his productivity had failed. D. then admitted, for the first time, that he was being treated, and sent C. to me.

It should be stressed that D.'s frank avowal at that time was a great "sacrifice" on his part; originally, he had wanted to keep his analysis secret. He told C. of it, he claimed, only because of his friend's suicidal manner. C. reacted with deep appreciation to D.'s admission of his secret.

During C.'s analysis, he wrote a book, which was quite a success. C. became well known, one might say half-famous, and in an outburst of gratitude thanked D. for having shown him "the living example of the efficacy of analysis," claiming "that this example, and this alone, pushed me into analysis." (Excerpts from a letter.)

Some time after this, D. finished his own novel, and asked the now-famous C. for a comment which could be used as an advertising "blurb." The unexpected happened: the deeply grateful C. hemmed and hawed, and told D. that he would have to think it over and let him know.

In analysis it became clear that C. was being tormented by two contradictory considerations: the gratitude he owed D., and the "express wish" to refuse the few friendly lines requested by D. This introduction was deserved, in C.'s objective opinion, because he liked D.'s work; subjectively, it was even more deserved, because of C.'s gratitude to D. But, C. reasoned, D. had "made the mistake" of being open about his analysis instead of keeping it a secret, while C. intended never to admit to his. And by writing the blurb he would be linking his name with D.'s in the public mind and before the critical world as well, thus, perhaps, arousing the suspicion that he too owed his productivity to analysis.

C. tortured himself thoroughly with this conflict. During analytic discussion of this problem, C. went to D. and told him quite frankly why he did not want to give him the lines requested. Whereupon D. told C., also quite frankly, that he considered him an "ungrateful dog," and then, very appropriately, threw him out. A few moments later, D. called him back and apologized, saying that a neurotic conflict was obviously involved in the ungrateful attitude. He suggested that C. analyze the incident with me.

Amazingly, C. had the strange conviction that "it was unfair (on D.'s part) to have brought him into that conflict in the first place." He also felt that his refusal was quite justified, and constantly stressed the qualms of conscience he had experienced in the last two weeks of his indecision. He casually dismissed his peculiar action in going to D. and explaining his plight; he did things "the open way," was his comment.

I pointed out the element of masochistic provocation in C.'s behavior, quoting a line from Heine which fitted the situation: "Gruess mich nicht unter den Linden." In his case, I told him, the line might be loosely interpreted to mean: "I don't want to know you in public, only in private." His lack of gratitude pertained in part to general neurotic ingratitude, which has a complicated substructure. (See pp. 146 ff.)

Two facts emerged from analysis of C.'s unexpected confession to D. First (and he was not fully conscious of this point), C.'s reluctance to be associated with D. sprang from his fear of the homosexual connotation; the avowed fear that he would be forced to admit that analysis had renewed his productivity was merely a blind. C. was afraid, too, that his own past could be indirectly divulged. At about that time another ex-patient of mine freely admitted, in an interview in *The New York Times,* that he owed his renewed productivity to Freudian analysis. I contrasted C.'s behavior with that of the interviewed writer, pointing out that deeper motives must have dictated his own reticence.

These deeper, and therefore infantile, motives could be found in a recollection dating back to C.'s fourth year. They constituted the second reason for his ungrateful behavior. His mother had caught the child in mutual masturbation with a younger brother. At the mother's approach, C. at once began to preach to his brother that it was "naughty" to do such a thing. His idea was to give the impression that he had not participated in the "game." His mother, wise to the trick, punished the boy severely. The child took the punishment, and yet persisted in preaching to the younger brother for weeks after, always pretending that he himself had been innocent.

After working out the masochistic substructure, the projection of his own guilt, hypocrisy, etc., C. apologized to D., and wrote a few enthusiastic introductory sentences which were later used to advertise D.'s book.

The aim of out-distancing one's own guilt, so obvious in the case of my acquaintance, and in the case of Mr. C., shows that payment in guilt denomination is one of the hundreds of inner defense mechanisms used by the unconscious ego in its attempts to make the life of its "client" easier. Furthermore, the mechanism shows that in the conflict "big debt of gratitude—refusal of a small favor," infantile elements invariably enter the picture. This has been observed in a series of cases.

PSYCHIC MICROSCOPY

Layer I.   Masochistic submissiveness as end result of infantile conflict.

Layer II. First veto of the superego.

Layer III. First defense of the unconscious ego: pseudo-aggression, "I don't owe the alleged benefactor anything."

Layer IV. Second veto of the superego: reproach of ingratitude.

Layer V.   Second defense of the unconscious ego: "I am neither masochistic nor aggressive; I am simply quits with the benefactor— haven't I suffered enough?"—"Ironic lip-service conformity with ego ideal precepts" by using the nursery standard of punishment

as complete restitution.—"Conscience money" paid in the form
of the indignant benefactor's retaliation.

SUMMARY: The mechanism of "payment of debts in guilt denomination"
corresponds to a defense against a defense within the framework
of masochistic life-technique.

8-9-10. *Is pessimism your slogan? Or is optimism your motto? Or are you hybrid "pessimo-optimist"?*

A pessimist, according to one patient, is a person who recognizes
the existence of the sun from the shadow cast by objects in sunlight.
To continue the simile, an optimist is the contemporary who denies
the mere existence of the shadow itself. Finally, a "pessimo-optimist"
has as his proud philosophy: "I'm always optimistic about myself,
always gloomy about the future of the other fellow."

The best approach to the triad—optimist, pessimist, pessimo-
optimist—is achieved by starting with the most paradoxical type,
that of the pessimo-optimist.

What is the genetic background of this strange personality?

The pessimo-optimist presents a series of contradictions. His is
the unlikely combination of gloating pleasure at the misfortunes of
one's fellows ("Schadenfreude") with optimistic self-confidence. It
is logical enough that aggression, mobilized against other people
and materialized in the pessimo-optimist's gloomy prediction, should
satisfy the individual's malice. But the formula should be completed
with guilt in the form of self-aggression, and it is not. One could
suspect that previously endured unhappiness serves to eliminate the
element of guilt from the pessimo-optimist's feeling that he is subjectively justified in his aggressions. One could wonder whether the
optimistic half of the pessimo-optimist is built on a solid basis, or
on quicksand. One could speculate, too, on whether the gloomy prediction made for the other person's future is not merely a projection
of the pessimo-optimist's inner pessimism, in which case he would be
merely a pessimist in disguise.

These and other suppositions are all possibilities, but their pursuit is fruitless. Clinical experience gives us the following picture.

*Neither pessimism nor optimism has any direct connection with
real life experience. Each corresponds to an individual elaboration
of infantile megalomania.*

As previously stated, every child lives, for a long time, on the basis of magic misconceptions of reality (Freud, Ferenczi). The child's acceptance of reality is gradual, and is accompanied by a complicated process of adaptation. Many children fail in the task of adaptation. Libidinous and aggressive frustrations are unavoidable; the problem is how these are perceived and worked out. In some cases, small and unimportant refusals are perceived as "terrible injustices;" in some cases, the child solves his problems triumphantly in spite of parents who are objectively difficult. These conflicts may be worked out in hundreds of ways. One of the remnants is the optimistic and pessimistic "Weltanschauung," or general outlook on life. *Optimism reflects the shabby remnants of infantile megalomania;* it is a sustained inner slave revolt directed against the victorious "reality principle" which is a perpetual reminder of the child's dependence on others.

Pessimism is a face-saving device, used by individuals who have masochistically elaborated the collapse of infantile megalomania. The original megalomania has been completely crushed; what is left becomes visible only in the satisfaction derived from outwitting the reality principle and the inner conscience by transforming external (or unconscious) punishment into internal pleasure. Normally, the conflict between punishment in reality and infantile insistence on megalomania is solved by gracefully bowing to the inevitable. The masochistic child, however, persists in his "naughtiness"—which is the parents' word for the manifestation of infantile "stubbornness" emanating from the arsenal of the child's megalomania. Punishment, moral reproach, and later on guilt, are the results. The masochistic child is confronted with the need to reconcile punishment (at first external, later internal) with his megalomaniacal pleasure fantasies. The masochistic solution is admirable: punishment is "libidinized." To repeat the formula: the only pleasure one can derive from displeasure is to make displeasure a pleasure. The psychic masochist provokes punishment and enjoys it unconsciously, thus "maintaining" megalomania in caricature.

Nevertheless, even the masochistic pessimist is unable to endure his own self-constructed misery *unless* he cushions his defeats with a face-saving pessimistic prediction. Even he, the Job of Jobs, insists on this relic of megalomania.

Other elements are of course involved. The old reproach of passivity, leveled by the inner conscience, must also be fought. This the
pessimist does: by *"active"* anticipatory prediction, he defends himself against the *passive* wish to be overwhelmed. His predictions, he
recognizes, always "happen to be" gloomy, but he has a rationalization to cover that: he has learned from "life" to see clearly. This
rationalization is of course secondary; his Cassandra-like pronouncements are an inner necessity and not the result of conscious
deliberations.

There are many connecting links between neurotic pessimism
and optimism. By overlooking reality factors, for instance, optimism
can be used for pessimistic, self-damaging purposes. One should
always be suspicious when the habitual pessimist develops an optimistic attitude in a specific situation; he is unconsciously bargaining
for a juicy defeat, seemingly to reduce to absurdity the world which
rejects his warnings.

On the other hand, it is undeniable that optimism, more often
than not, is a propelling force, while pessimism is a retarding one.
Mark Twain summed it up neatly: "All you need in life is ignorance
and confidence, and then success is sure."

That hybrid mixture, the pessimo-optimist, is, if analyzed, recog-
nizable as one elaboration of the oral personality structure. This,
in my opinion, is true of all pessimists. As is typical in pessimists,
the pessimo-optimist dwells on pessimistic predictions, using them
preventively. *He thus safeguards his narcissism,* for nothing can
surprise him. It is the professional pessimist who will most often be
heard saying, triumphantly, "I told you so." The pessimo-optimist
shares with the typical neurotic pessimist the predilection towards
gloomy prophecies about other people.

But—and this exception is important—he is obscurely aware that
his masochistically self-provoked defeats are some kind of a game.
That, too, is a face-saving device: "I'm not the victim of masochism,
I just go in for that kind of game." As the poet A. Hebbel wrote of
dreams:

> Denn jeden Traum begleitet
> Ein heimliches Gefuehl,
> Dass alles nichts bedeutet
> Und sie es noch so schwuel.

(Loosely translated: "Underneath every dream is the feeling that these terrifying events are meaningless, no matter how menacing they look.")

The apparent optimism of the pessimo-optimist has a complicated structure. It is, to begin with, only a surface optimism; basically, he too employs typical preventive pessimism, directing it at himself. He, too, unconsciously enjoys his self-created defeats and is furious with his enemies, repressing his own provocations. He is a typical adherent of the "mechanism of orality," with its tragic triad. (See Foreword.) He is, therefore, an injustice collector, a connoisseur of defeats and "bad experiences." With the help of his own provocation, the pessimist can always prove his predictions correct.

The pessimo-optimist's "optimism," therefore, must be taken with a grain of salt, although in one sense he is justified in calling himself an optimist. For, despite all his defeats, he retains his conviction that one day he is certain to achieve success. He is like the nursery toy that cannot be knocked over, for its inner construction assures that it will always return to the upright position.

While the neurotic pessimist frequently gives up the fight, the pessimo-optimist is perpetually resilient. More, he is laborious, enduring, energetic. His "optimism" pertains, in part, to the game-quality of his brand of psychic masochism, and in part to his always renewed unconscious expectation of defeat. In his pronouncements of doom for all his acquaintances, he partly projects his own pessimism, partly proves his "aggression." This pseudo-aggression arises from his inner defense against the superego's justified reproach of passivity.

The borderline between clear-cut neurotic reactions and "normal" ones is slim. If we ask in which group the pessimo-optimist belongs, we best solve the problem by the Solomonic judgment: he is a half-neurotic.

PSYCHIC MICROSCOPY

Layer	Pessimist	Optimist	Pessimo-Optimist
I.	Masochistic elaboration of the oral conflict.	Masochistic elaboration of the oral conflict.	Masochistic elaboration of the oral conflict.
II.	First superego veto.	First superego veto.	First superego veto.
III.	First defense of the	First defense of the	First defense of the

	unconscious ego: "I'm justified in expecting the worst, reality bears me out. And everybody dislikes and rejects me." (Provocative technique)	unconscious ego: "I am the most cheerful person in the world; I don't even admit that things can go against me."	unconscious ego: "I expect the best—I'm just pessimistic about other people." (Projection)
IV.	Superego sees through blind; pronounces second veto.	Superego sees through blind; pronounces second veto.	Superego sees through blind; pronounces second veto.
V.	Second defense of unconscious ego: "My gloom is harmless; besides, it's just a face-saving game;" (*Active* anticipatory prediction of evil, refuting the *passive* wish to be overwhelmed.) "Ironic lip-service conformity with ego ideal precepts": "Should one not take what Fate sends as punishment?"— "Conscience money": defeat and gloom at any cost.	Second defense of unconscious ego: complacency, living in the pseudo-expectation of love ("Ironic lip-service conformity with ego ideal precepts.")—"Conscience money": *unexpected* kicks, which, though negated, are real enough, plus lack of foresight (psychic masochism).	Second defense of unconscious ego: Mechanism of orality (clinical picture of psychic masochism) with projective safeguards and great energy in working towards next kick. ("Conscience money.") — "Ironic lip-service conformity with ego ideal precepts" by using the techniques of both the optimist and pessimist.

SUMMARY: All three techniques operate on the basis of a defense against a defense.

11. *Do you pride yourself on being a wit?*

A wit is a person with a particular forte: the ability to present facts or ideas in a way that provokes laughter. The very same material, formulated differently, would be taken as either a statement of fact or a distortion of it. The "witty" formulation, however, evokes laughter, accompanied by intense though transitory pleasure.

This definition can be tested on any joke. The laughter-provoking element will evaporate as soon as the specific witty formulation is eliminated. As an instance, there is Fred Schwed, Jr.'s joke about the naive tourist in old New York. He is shown around Wall Street, and then is taken to the East River piers where the bankers and brokers moor their yachts. He then asks: "Where are the customers' yachts?" * If the witticism is restated, perhaps as: "The bankers and brokers on Wall Street are still finding suckers; they get a luxurious living out of the market, but the suckers just lose their money," what remains is tragedy rather than comedy.

But what is the specific witty formulation? There are innumerable theories, all of which purport to dissect and explain. None of them, however, can hold their own against Freud's explanation of the unconscious basis of wit *(Wit and Its Relation to the Unconscious, 1905).* Freud assumes that in the unconscious of every human is a storehouse of repressed tendencies. To hold this "cathexis" in repression, a specific amount of psychic energy ("counter-cathexis") is needed. When a witticism touches one of these repressed drives, in the form of an innuendo, the counter-cathexis becomes superfluous for a split second, since the wit and not the listener assumes responsibility, and the released counter-cathexis changes into laughter.

The subtle innuendo form of witticism explains why shared laughter indicates a high degree of inner affinity, as well as identity of cultural level, in the people affected by the same jokes.† Jokes are by no means universally appreciated. The joke is a source of narcissistic satisfaction, which is also to be explained by its innuendo form. As far as guilt and responsibility are concerned, the listener is merely a kibitzer; nevertheless, he performs some psychic work in following the joke and "getting the point," and can thus pride himself on being as smart as the wit.

At bottom, every witticism has—at least superficially—an *aggressive* connotation.‡ This holds true even of jokes which apparently express the opposite—those which have a disguised sexual meaning. In analyzing any "dirty" joke or "off-color" story it will be found

* Mr. Schwed used this tag line as the title of his delightful satire on Wall Street, published some years ago.

† The development from "slapstick" to "psychological" jokes marks the inner development from simple to complicated defenses.

‡ Witticisms are to be distinguished from *Self Derision* and *Grim humor.* The *former* serves as preventive technique: to forestall the expected attack of the malicious listener.—The *latter* is a negative hallucination a narcissistic negation of a pitifully-tragic situation—in the person producing "grim humor"; in the listener it amounts to a humorous reaction based on Freud's principle of saving expenditure of pity. See bibliography.

that the aggression is directed at the people who originally prohibited these "transgressions into the forbidden"—in early
childhood.

Since this is the case, the next question is no less puzzling. Are
jokes and witticisms merely proof that the unconscious contains
a superabundance of repressed aggressive material? How does this
tally with our main thesis, that psychic masochism is *the* troublemaker in the human personality?

The answer is to be found in the theory of double defense
mechanisms. Personally, I doubt that the pleasure derived from wit
is based on repressed aggression, pure and simple. I believe that
witticism plays its important role in life because it enables everyone
to attest to himself—via the alibi inherent in the aggressive joke—
his high degree of *spurious* (hence defensive) aggression. Thus wit
becomes an inner alibi: "How can I be accused of psychic masochism—don't you see how aggressive I am?" In other words, the statement Freud originally made in 1905 still holds true, provided one
understands that a deeper masochistic layer is involved, and is
warded off with pseudo-aggression.

In my opinion, the witticism is an outlet for pseudo-aggression,
exclusively. Six reasons, all based on clinical facts, support this
assumption.

First, the joke itself exists, for the individual, only after he has
solved the half-riddle which makes it into a witticism instead of a
statement of fact, true or false. Any joke, if dissected, will be found
to consist of allusion, a play on words, elliptic condensation, shift,
unification, substitution, and displacement, etc., as Freud originally
pointed out. These unconscious mechanisms are always present,
though always in disguise. It is the listener's job to fill in the
blank spaces, which—as stated above—requires some form of psychic
work, and is taken as proof of "activity."

Second, the child in the listener accepts the half-riddle technique
of the joke as proof that he is being taken into the half-confidence
of adults. The situation, common to childhood, in which a question
is asked and the answer is evaded with "You will learn all that when
you grow up," has long been consciously forgotten; it is activated,
however, by the deliberate lacunae which are inherent in a witticism. It is true that the missing pieces can now be supplied by the
listener; the fact that he must supply them is a reminder that he

must still outmaneuver the adult (later superego), who continues to leave for forbidden *half*-forbidden.

Third, the amount of information needed in order to solve the riddle of a joke serves as proof to the child in the adult that he has mastered all sexual riddles—actively. This need for a broad background of knowledge is usually taken for granted; it should not be. The amount of information, conscious and unconscious, which is referred to in penetrating the meaning of a witticism is surprisingly broad. We can take as example the sentence previously quoted: "Where are the customers' yachts?" A reader who was unaware of the price of yachts, the methods of trading on the stock exchange, the ins and outs of speculation in general, could not understand the joke. In understanding every elaborate joke where the fine points of human behavior enter, the breadth of one's automatically available information must of course be large.

Fourth, the appreciative listener behaves as though his penetration of the half-riddle, his acceptance into the half-confidence of adults, his encyclopedic knowledge of "forbidden" topics, all constituted defiance of the educators' prohibitions. Since these educators are enshrined in the unconscious conscience, the explosive laughter which greets a witticism is actually aimed at the superego.

The attack against the superego, embedded in every witticism, was first stated by Jekels and myself in our joint paper, "Transference and Love," *Imago* XX, 1934, p. 14.*

Clinical observation offers further proof of this deduction. When listening to a joke, the child in the adults plays the voyeuristic, passive, peeping Tom. At the same time, he identifies with the aggressive exhibitionism of the joke-teller, which enables him, by proxy, to assume the role of aggressor. This evidence of aggression is accepted as "lesser crime" by the inner conscience, which is thus reduced to absurdity.

* A side-show concerning scopophilia has been adduced. In continuation of the Bergler-Eidelberg study on depersonalization ("The Mechanism of Depersonalization," *Int. Zeitschrift fuer Psychoanalyse*, 1935), in which we proved that exhibitionism can be used as defense against voyeurism, Eidelberg applied this idea to the psychology of wit ("A Contribution to the Study of Wit," *The Psychoanalytic Review*, 32:1, 1945). In listening to a joke, the child in the listener is playing the voyeur; via identification with the narrator, voyeurism is

Every joke, in short, has as its butt the inner conscience. The laughter evoked by a witticism is the defensive triumph of the masochistic part of the personality, through the use of pseudo-aggressive props.

Fifth, the child in the adult shivers behind his mask of pseudo-aggression while he is listening to a "forbidden" joke. The evidence of his fear lies in the fact that he listens, but shifts his responsibility for the joke to the jokester. His alibi is: "I did nothing wrong; I just listened. *He* did it." Freud clarified this element of shifted responsibility in his original formulation, which was later enlarged by Reik. This shift also explains why jokes, once heard, tend to be repeated: the inclusion of another listener distributes the guilt even more widely.

Sixth, the circumstances leading to the production of a joke are in themselves proof that pseudo-aggression, not real aggression, is involved. By and large, these circumstances are of two types. Either the individual is accused of fear by the inner conscience, or the superego indicts him for tolerating a consciously painful situation for the sake of the masochistic pleasure he derives from it. In either case, since the reproach is that of passivity, pseudo-aggression is offered as alibi. The resulting jokes take two forms: *"jokes out of fear,"* or *"jokes out of being allegedly fed up."*

In "jokes out of fear," the unconscious ego is offering this defense: "My client is not passively frightened, but actively above the situation." In the second form of witticism, the defense reads: "My client is not passive-masochistic. He is fed up with the situation, and even bored with it." In both instances, the basic theme of the argument seems to be that a joker, or a bored person, is *active*.

---

transformed into exhibitionism. But this change is made under pressure of conscience, from which Eidelberg draws the conclusion that "deception of the superego is the condition sine qua non." Otherwise, our approaches to the psychology of wit differ both in conclusions, and in the reasoning leading to our conclusions. This is most marked in consideration of the defense against repressed psychic masochism: the point which in my opinion is the decisive one, namely, taking the blame for the lesser crime (pseudo-aggression), is missing from Eidelberg's formulations. Eidelberg concludes that "exhibitionistic and aggressive pleasure from the satisfaction of aggressive and infantile instincts in laughter" is the motor of wit enjoyment.

Jokes "out of fear" and jokes "out of being fed up," therefore, are both alibis presented to the inner conscience, the frightened child in the adult acting according to the familiar precept, "the best defense is attack."

People, in general, assume, without giving the matter thought, that they laugh because they "feel" gay; it never occurs to them that they are manufacturing, in the form of jokes, weapons to be used against an inner torturer. And if they are told that every human being expends at least half of his psychic energy on the task of preparing alibis and defenses for presentation to the unconscious conscience, their reaction is very likely to be, "You are just trying to pull my leg."

The reaction is very much the same if they are asked to explain why they are laughing at a specific joke. The initial astonishment that one could question the self-evident is followed by a reply which is no reply: "Because it's funny." This is as far as polite questioning can take us in this direction. If another tack is taken, and it is pointed out that there must be some way of accounting for the fact that someone always says, after a joke is told, "I don't think that's funny," they will explain that "the fellow who doesn't laugh at the jokes I consider funny just has no sense of humor."

People do not know why they laugh, because the joke has a complicated unconscious structure. Some severe masochists, however, do on occasion get an inkling of the meaning of "jokes out of fear." Heinrich Heine confessed:

> In jenen Naechten hat Langeweil' ergriffen
> Mich oft, auch Fuercht—nur Narren fuerchten nichts—
> Sie zu verscheuchen hab' ich dann gepfiffen
> Die frechen Reime eines Spottgedichts.
> (*Romanzero, II, Lamentationen,* "Enfant perdu")

("In these nights, boredom gripped me, and so did fear—only fools fear nothing—; to counteract fear I whistled the impudent stanzas of a satiric verse.")

Here is an example of a defensive witticism, produced "out of fear." It was told me by a well-known writer, who at one time had worked on a newspaper. On one assignment, he went up to Sing Sing to cover an electrocution. The condemned murderer, sitting in the chair, watched the executioner's rather flurried handling of wires and electrodes, and remarked: "What's the matter with you, are *you* nervous?"

Obviously, the situations which lead up to the production of witticisms are not always dangerous and forbidding. But where the situation is comparatively harmless, *inner* fear substitutes for the external danger. The difference is, however, that the sufferer from inner fear is completely unconscious of it.

The joke produced by the alibi "I'm fed up" presupposes a prolonged period of pain and humiliation, misused by the superego for the purpose of torture. The defense is: "The situation does not give me any masochistic pleasure; it bores me—I even joke about it."

For decades, an old man endured his wife's liaison with her lover: the triangle seemed as permanent as the marriage. As the affair became common knowledge, people got into the habit of asking, ironically, "How is X. (the lover) getting along?" On one occasion the husband replied: "I haven't seen him for a long time; I am in touch with him only through the newspapers."—"How so?"—"Well, I check the obituary column every day to see if he is dead."

PSYCHIC MICROSCOPY

Layer I.   Masochistic storehouse, stemming from end result of the infantile conflict.

Layer II.   First veto of the superego.

Layer III. First defense of the unconscious ego: "I'm so full of aggression that I make fun of everything and everybody."

Layer IV. Second veto of superego.

Layer V.   Second defense of unconscious ego: "The other fellow (the narrator) has the responsibility; I'm just listening." (In joke producers: "I am but a commentator on other people's foolishness—besides, I evoke the laughter, hence half-approval, of the environment.") "And besides, I solved the riddle, so I'm active; besides, my upbringers doublecrossed me—they didn't tell me everything; besides, I figured out all those sexual riddles for myself—another proof that I'm active; besides, I'm listening against my educators' wishes—isn't that aggressive?"—"Ironic lip-service conformity with ego ideal precepts" in activity, smartness, etc.—"Conscience money"—a chronic jokester is not taken too seriously; he is always flirting with the danger of telling the wrong joke in the wrong environment; added to this is the danger of having his joke fall flat.

SUMMARY: Witticism is a defense against the defense.

12. *Do you dislike satire at length, and do you get "bored" in the middle of a satiric novel?*

Hilaire Belloc said of satire:

The modern reader does not only fail to understand satire, but withdraws from it as from an unpleasant experience. He is not only bewildered by it; he actually dislikes it.

One might conclude that Belloc wrote this comment after a survey of publishers' balance sheets. Satiric books do not sell. The rather highbrow explanation usually offered is that the typical reader "does not understand satire." But the typical "man in the street," as everyone knows, is given to one or another abbreviated form of satire. He goes in for "kidding;" he listens to comedians for an hour at a time, even including the commercials; he buys full-length comics; he turns to the "funnies" in his newspaper after or before reading the sports. Why, then, is he unable to comprehend satire when it is presented at full length in book form? Why, if he does comprehend it, is a satiric novel an almost certain loss to its publisher?

To complicate matters further, a book written without touches of humor, irony and satire is almost invariably castigated as "pompous" and "boring."

In order to resolve these contradictions, it is necessary to consider the theory of wit and satire, the quantitative element in satire, and the unconscious meaning, for the reader, of the printed book.

The theory of wit and satire has already been surveyed in the discussion immediately preceding: "Do you pride yourself on being a wit?" The conclusion was that jokes have an inner connection with passivity; they are pseudo-aggressive alibis attempting to answer the accusations of the inner conscience in a specific form.

Four additional unconscious meanings are to be found in the quantitative factor in satire.

The psychic work necessary in order to grasp the meaning of the

ironic, satiric or witty utterance accounts for both the deep satisfaction of the listener, and his limited ability to solve the "riddles"
—if they are presented en masse. The listener (or reader) can take
only a limited amount; beyond this, he "gets tired." Jokes, satire,
derision, can therefore be taken only in small doses.

This in itself counteracts the effect of satire, when it is made the
sole basis for an entire book. Looking through successful satiric
books, one finds that their authors have intuitively taken this factor
into account, and made use of two technical devices in order to get
around the barrier of quantitative limitation. The successful sati-
rist will either limit himself to a single theme, and fill his book
with elaborations on it (e.g., *Gulliver's Travels,* or more specifically, *A Voyage to Lilliput,* the only section of the book to become
a "familiar" classic), or mingle his satire with enough love-interest,
or other non-satiric elements, to divert the reader (e.g., Frederic
Wakeman's description of the soap magnate in *The Hucksters*).
The juxtaposition of Swift and Wakeman is also to the point,
because Swift—a master—shows how it should be done, whereas,
if we take Wakeman's inept love story into consideration, his book
becomes an example of how full-length satire should *not* be done.

The most brilliant modern example of bitter satire which was
piled too high and therefore failed to achieve popular success is
Charles Yale Harrison's *Meet Me on the Barricades.*

Satire, therefore, is "internal medicine" which the reader can
swallow in homeopathic doses only. As soon as the allopathic dose
is presented, it is rejected by the reader's unconscious.

However, these quantitative limitations also have other tributaries. If the basic assumption is correct, and satire and derision
are a frightened unconscious slave-rebellion by the fear-laden child
in the adult, then the old fear of retaliation must be present, too.
It is. The small dose represents a furtive glance, rather than a long
look, at the forbidden. Quantitative limitation of satire, therefore,
is also some form of captatio benevolenciae, an alibi in itself.

So far, three results of the quantitative factor have been mentioned: deep satisfaction, psychic work under strong pressure of
guilt, and "the furtive glance" mechanism. The fourth link in this
chain of *active half-daring and three-quarters passive scaring* is the
alleged stupidity of the reader "who doesn't understand satire."

The inability to understand satire is not a problem of low IQ but of—fear. It is true that satire exists on different levels, the lowest being represented by the "funnies;" the highest—allegedly— by *The New Yorker*. Aside from the fact that any individual will be blank to a specific joke which does not touch upon his inner conflict, or is too obviously outside his intellectual range, "lack of humor" in general is a neurotic phenomenon based on infantile fear which has not been overcome. The person who "doesn't understand" satire and wit is inwardly a child so frightened that he does not even allow himself the "furtive glance" at the forbidden.

The unconscious meaning of the printed book to the reader is the next element contributing to the general dislike of satire at length. As previously pointed out, the respect which the average person feels (admittedly or not) for the *printed* word, stems from the undigested fact that books are handed down to the child by people in authority. Moreover, for the first four to six years of the child's life printed matter is an "adult mystery," which automatically renders it awesome.

The typical reader of books (virtually an anachronism today, if one is to believe publishers aggrieved at television, radio and magazines) wants to be "entertained," thus leading some writers to the conclusion that the purpose of art is "to please." (Somerset Maugham) This applies to the hack writer, and not to the creative writer, who writes because of the inner need to get rid of an unconscious conflict via the sublimatory medium of writing. ("Self-curative alibi-sickness," to quote the definition of creative writing I offered in *The Writer and Psychoanalysis*.) The quid-pro-quo leads to frequent grotesque misunderstandings between writer and reader. In any case, the reader wants—by means of conscious and unconscious identification, although he is not aware of the latter—to enjoy his unfulfilled narcissistic, libidinous, aggressive hopes, and his all-too-real, though unconscious, masochistic suffering, or to find his badly needed alibis. Whatever the case may be, he wants to be taken seriously. But satire does exactly the opposite. The strange thing is that "reader's identification"— the essential prerequisite for "interest" in a book—counteracts appreciation of satire: the reader (once more without awareness) identifies *also* with the butt of the irony, and, to quote Belloc again, "is bewildered and actually dislikes it." Again, masochism victorious!

All these factors, taken together, explain why satire *in book form* cannot achieve popular appeal—it never did. Satire has been and will be confined to the short-short: to the satiric sketch and the satiric poem. For most people, satire is a dish causing mental indigestion (fear!) if consumed in more than minimum quantities.

PSYCHIC MICROSCOPY

Layer I.   Masochistic end-result of the infantile conflict.

Layer II.   First veto of the superego.

Layer III. First defense of the unconscious ego: "I'm so full of aggression that I make fun of everybody and everything."

Layer IV.   Second veto of the superego.

Layer V.   Second defense of the unconscious ego: "I didn't write it, I just read it—I'm not responsible. Besides, I didn't really look at the forbidden, I just gave it a furtive glance." "Ironic lip-service conformity with ego ideal precepts" by proving alleged activity and being "a good boy" by renunciation. The latter corresponds also to part payment of "conscience money."

SUMMARY: A defense against a defense.

13-14. *Is patience your forte, or are you "impatient"?*

A wit once described the universal "human itch:" everybody wants to reach his goal fast, but doesn't want to pay the fare. Reality teaches the long, hard and rather circuitous routes which lead to—one-tenth of the result aimed for. Inner conscience, and obstacles provided by external reality, take care of the remaining nine-tenths.

Patience is an artifact, which the child must learn to accept and use. The ability to wait is in clear-cut contradiction to infantile megalomania, in which the world is believed to respond instantaneously, fulfilling without delay the wish taken from the storehouse of the infant's omnipotence fantasy.

Even the so-called normal person, therefore, does not contain himself without some struggle, when forced to wait some time for expected results. To console himself, he uses one of several mechanisms:

(a) Holding fast to the aim, or displacing his interest upon another aim without pathological reaction.
(b) Half-hypocritical denial of the aim.
(c) Bitterness and contempt for mankind.
(d) Deprecation of the aim (the sour-grapes mechanism).
(e) Reveling in fantasies of revenge.
(f) Doubt of the rightness of his own ideas.
(g) Consoling himself with the idea that he is in advance of his generation.
(h) Resignation.
(i) Tearful fantasies of rehabilitation, "one hundred years hence," etc.

Some of these mechanisms (as well as others not mentioned) contain appreciable neurotic admixtures. Fantasies of revenge, for example, often used for consolation, are a defense against the superego's reproach of passivity. Doubting the rightness of one's own ideas is in itself the result of unfriendly doubts cast by the inner conscience. Psychic masochism is embedded in resignation. (The examples could be continued.) It is not surprising that the inner torturer should seize this opportunity to attack the victim, without considering whether the waiting period is self-inflicted, or externally caused.

Neurotic impatience presents an entirely different picture. Here the individual's understandable eagerness to reach his goal is merely a *palimpsest* covering the *urgent need to furnish*—and quickly, for that matter—*the defense so badly needed to withstand the accusing inner conscience.*

The distinction can be clarified by comparing two situations. A famous gynecologist living in an anti-Semitic country was passed over when he should have been promoted to the position of chief of his department in the University. He consoled himself by explaining: "First they said I was too young; later they said I was too old; in between I was a Jew."

An obsessional patient, bursting with undigested passivity, became extremely jumpy whenever there was a break in his routine of nearly daily intercourse—with different girls. The disguise of hypersex concealed his need to furnish a daily alibi to conscience: "How can I be accused of passivity—I'm a conquering he-man."

The joker in the pack was the fact that he also suffered from hypochondriacal symptoms and signs, which he "traced back," as he believed, to "too much sex."

PSYCHIC MICROSCOPY

Layer	Patience	Impatience
I.	Difficulty in adapting to realization that infantile megalomania doesn't regulate life.	Masochistic solution of infantile conflict.
II.	First superego veto.	First superego veto.
III.	First defense of unconscious ego: "I *can* wait; I learned my lesson."	First defense of unconscious ego: pseudo-agression.
IV.	Ironic doubt voiced by superego.	Second superego veto.
V.	Use of different disguises (see above). The longer the waiting period, the greater the admixture of neurotic elements.—"Ironic lip-service conformity with ego ideal precepts" by accepting the precept of ability to wait.—"Conscience money" paid in ill-feeling.	Undue haste, allegedly pertaining to reaching the given goal, in inner reality covering the need for wanted alibi. "Ironic lip-service conformity with ego ideal precepts" by using the precept "no procrastination." — "Conscience money" paid in depression.

SUMMARY: Patience and impatience are each a defense against a defense.

15. *Are you the proverbial victim of human "ingratitude"?*

Ingratitude is one of the most familiar of the complaints leveled against that catch-all criminal, human nature. The perfunctory outer form of gratitude—the "thank-you," the "you are very good," etc.—is built into the culture and encountered frequently enough, but it deceives nobody. True gratitude, in the shape of a good turn spontaneously performed to balance a favor received, is comparatively rare.

Few people go beyond complaints to wonder whether gratitude does not surpass human capacity, or to speculate on the psychological reasons for gratitude or its absence. There are such reasons, for gratitude has a genetic record.

The baby's yardstick—and to a lesser extent the young child's—

is his own megalomania. The distinction between his own body and the outer world, and therefore between the gifts he makes to himself and those which come from other people, is learned very slowly. In his concept, only the "bad," the refusal, comes from the outside. Everything "good" is taken for granted; everything "bad"— which includes refusals necessitated by his own welfare—is seen as a terrible injustice. A bad start for gratitude.

Parents can imbue the child with a feeling of gratitude by making it a moral dictum. If the child is comparatively normal, he can, in identifying with his parents, learn to translate his original megalomaniacal reaction into a feeling of appreciation. His ability to do so is a measure of the success with which he has overcome early misconceptions, and a gauge of his adaptation to reality.

We know that restriction is one of the necessary weapons of education. The more neurotic the child, the more likely he is to interpret this restriction as malice, and the more likely it is that he will feel justified in using any means of retaliation against the "aggressor." All educational limitations concerned with libidinous and aggressive wishes lead first to frustration, and then to hatred in the child. Aside from identification with the educator and internalizing of the educational precepts, which is the normal solution, the child has only one way out of the dilemma, and it is the neurotic way: he pays the price of suffering for the privilege of continuing his old slave revolt in disguised form.

It is the neurotic child in the adult who is incapable of gratitude, who prompts the direct acts of meanness and aggression with which some people repay their benefactors. Clinical experience proves that it is really dangerous to be nice to some neurotics. The kindness done them rouses them from indifference to the perpetration of some mean trick. The explanation of this seeming enigma is that the benefactor, in performing his kindness, enters the magic circle of the individual's neurotic repetition compulsion. The neurotic then projects upon him the injustices allegedly experienced in childhood, and at this late date takes his "revenge." True, the benefactor is not identical with the early disappointer, nor is he guilty of the remembered crime, but this does not matter. The unconscious identification of the benefactor with the early disappointer is all that is needed to start the mechanism going.

Two other factors enter into the inner aggression shown by some individuals towards their benefactors. First is the limitlessness of the child's desire for love and exclusive attention. When the benefactor enters the neurotic circle of the beneficiary's past, the standards of reality cease to apply. The act of kindness is measured against the insufficiency of love, attention and kindness allegedly supplied to the beneficiary in his childhood. These arrears are projected upon the benefactor, and his deed thus becomes an infinitestimal part payment of an old debt. Thus the neurotic transforms a deed of kindness into a negligible installment on an unpaid billion-dollar obligation.

The second factor is the quantitatively different degree to which unconscious self-damaging tendencies are present in a specific neurotic. The psychic masochist, who (as previously mentioned) is typically submissive to the stronger person, typically aggressive toward the weaker, will unconsciously classify the benefactor as "weak" and attack him with all the aggression at his disposal. Previous to the good deed, the neurotic had no "data," and therefore his atitude towards the benefactor was either respectful or indifferent. The reaction to the good deed, demoting the benefactor to "weakness," is not gratitude, but its antithesis, aggression.

The theory is often put forward that gratitude is rare because individuals dislike being reminded of their own beginnings, when they needed help from others. This deduction is faulty. People forget their previous dependence, and their bill of gratitude, because they live unconsciously on the basis of the autarchic fantasy, which negates all worthwhile things coming from the outside. Once more, this is a remnant of infantile megalomania.

There are times when gratitude is unexpectedly displayed on an irrational basis. Simple people sometimes show gratitude because they feel that kindness on the part of a person presumably "above" them socially brings them, psychologically, into the orbit of a higher social stratum. Via identification, their gratitude in a tribute to—themselves. And sometimes exactly the opposite attitude is seen: the kindness of a benefactor on a higher social level is made worthless by the beneficiary's inner brooding on the injustice he experiences in not being on the same social or economic level.

A very special type of ingratitude is reserved for people with new ideas: scientists, inventors, poets, innovators in general. Biography and observation alike prove that almost every great man with ideas or techniques in advance of his generation is ridiculed—if not ostracized—during his lifetime. Gratitude comes to him only posthumously.

PSYCHIC MICROSCOPY

Layer I. Grudging solution of one's own infantile conflict, one-half to three-quarters masochistic; partial acknowledgment of debt to upbringers.

Layer II. First superego veto, demanding full acknowledgment.

Layer III. First defense of the unconscious ego: "Not only do I act decently, but I even go so far that I expect it from others—shouldn't everybody reciprocate?"

Layer IV. Second veto of superego, which ironically points out the individual's own history of ingratitude (pseudo-aggression).

Layer V. The debacle of the other fellow's ingratitude; followed by great indignation on the part of the benefactor. Gratuitously overlooked are both the fact that there was no reason to expect gratitude, to begin with, and the deliberate choice of a beneficiary so selfish that he could *not* respond with appreciation. "Ironic lip-service conformity with ego ideal precepts"—act nicely and the other fellow will be nice too.—"Conscience money"—paid by choosing beneficiaries who will inevitably react with ingratitude.

SUMMARY: Victims of "ingratitude" are operating a defense against a defense.

16-17. *Are you habitually silent? Or hyper-talkative?*

In his interesting study, "The Psychological Meaning of Silence," * Theodor Reik drew attention to the fact that silence has a double meaning: it can be a sign either of hatred *or* of love.

We can keep silence with another when we two understand each other especially well, or when understanding is impossible. To be able to be silent with someone may be a sign of great mental accord or a sign of great mental discord, or a sign of complete strangeness.

* In Reik's *Wie Man Psychologe Wird, Int. Psychoan. Verlag,* Vienna, 1927.

In spite of this antithetical double meaning—which may be traced back to an original unity—there lies hidden behind the fear of silence, the fear of death (castration); expressed in another form, the unconscious fear of loss of love. The fact that speech itself often becomes the expression of enmity and hatred does not contradict this, in Reik's opinion: speech is the beginning of affective mastery of the instinctual urges. The results of psychoanalysis have shown that the expression and putting into words of hate and enmity is the first step toward making an end of it psychically.—In his study of the latent meaning of silence Reik came to the conclusion that silence is a sign of the effectivity of the death instincts, and speech is an attempt to master them with the assistance of the erotic instincts. "The expression to hush up is really a pleonasm." *

Here are two literary examples of these correctly observed antithetical meanings of silence.

Silence as the sign of hatred. In Anatole France's cycle of novels about Professor Bergeret, Bergeret surprises his wife in the act of cohabitation with his favorite scholar. After long deliberation, the betrayed husband decides on a course of action. Instead of reproaching his wife, he simply wiped her out of his existence. He did not look at her; he treated her as if she were a stranger when they happened to meet at the dinner table, or in another room of the house. If she spoke, he did not hear her. Madame Bergeret's suffering was intense. She felt dispossessed and entirely without standing in her family and her house. She would have preferred her husband to attack her violently; if he had, her terror would have been mixed with relief. But the torture of being ignored was so terrible that there were times when she could hardly keep herself from sobbing aloud.

Silence as the token of love. From "Qui tacet, consentire videtur," there are many transitions to silence as the sign of affective sympathy. Heinrich Heine, in his poem, "To Mouche," describes two lovers who sit without speaking, but understand each other's thoughts; speech is bold and brazen, he observes, but silence is love's shy flower. John Donne, in "The Extasie," wrote:

---

* Literally translated from the German, this would read: "The expression, to kill with silence. . ." There is no equivalent for this German idiom.

> Where, like a pillow on a bed,
> A Pregnant bank swel'd up, to rest
> The violets reclining head,
> Sat we too, one another's best . . . .
> And whilst our soules negotiate there,
> Wee like sepulchral statues lay;
> All day the same our postures were,
> And wee said nothing, all the day.

Similarly, Schiller in "Maria Stuart" (II, 5), where Elizabeth says:

> Silence is the deity of
> The happy—tenuous are the bonds
> That hold the strongest—secrecy, the weaver.

How does silence attain this positive role? Apparently, the basis is the extensive identification of lovers with one another, the fact that love is a projection of one's own ego ideal onto the object, with subsequent partial reintrojection, and finally, the impossibility of expressing the feelings on which love is founded. Talking to oneself about something dimly felt, which one cannot express—this is the cause of the contemplative silence of happy lovers, and the explanation of the foolish things "that lovers say to each other." *

Silence is therefore not uniform, and Reik, in discussing its antithetical double meaning, points out that we may discern several types of silence. "We speak of silence as painful, icy, depressing, or as reassuring, stubborn, mortifying, disapproving or approving, or apologetic." But all these types can be reduced to the two opposites: agreement or disagreement.

Still, Reik is of the opinion that "despite the double meaning of silence we always know what the other expresses, what he would like 'to say' with his silence." The latter statement is open to doubt; an exception which comes immediately to mind is silence of the type "heap coals of fire upon his head" (see pp. 59 and 60 ff.), and which was so tragically misunderstood by Dostojewski's heroine in *The Soft Woman*.

Our literature has treated silence only from the technical

* S. Popper Lynkeus' short story of the same name in *Phantasien Eines Realisten*.

aspect visible in clinical psychoanalysis. In a paper published in 1938 ("On the Resistance Situation—The Patient is Silent"), I recorded the summary of a discussion which arose during a technical seminar of the Vienna Psychoanalytical Society in 1928, in connection with a case I presented. In 1928, our distinguished late colleague, Dr. Fritz Wittels, wished to publish the findings of that discussion. Unfortunately, this project never materialized. Seven years later, Miss Anna Freud suggested that the subject be reopened at a round table discussion (in March, 1935) and I undertook to contribute the opening paper (later published*).

Since silence takes on different meanings in different regressions, I am concentrating, here, only on the most typical form: that of orally regressed cases, as observable in analysis. The previously stated conclusion bears repetition:

The orally regressed patient, if left to his own devices in analysis, will lapse into silence, and upbraid himself later for his silence. For patients of this sort, the classic analytical technique has to be modified: in my opinion, the analyst has to talk. Years ago I suggested this modification as a preparatory period before "normal" analysis can start. Since orally regressed neurotics ward off their deep masochistic attachment with the defense of pseudo-aggression, they can but *refuse* when asked to *give* words (free association technique). Adherence to the classic technique, therefore, brings these patients into a premature and hopeless conflict. At the same time it enables them, in the transference repetition, to project the image of the bad, cruel, demanding, draining Giantess of the nursery upon the innocent analyst.

This cannot and should not be avoided. It cannot, because the image of the cruel Giantess is automatically projected inside and outside of analysis by these severe neurotics. It should not be avoided, because these affective repetitions are constantly contrasted with the harmless reality of analysis, whose chance representative, the physician, obviously wants to help. But it is by no means an easy matter to lead the patient to a discerning grasp of this unconscious repetitiveness; in orally regressed cases the part of the ego able to, or willing to "cooperate" is highly restricted.

* The paper is still valid in many respects, although two points are antiquated: the meaning of silence in orally regressed cases is not properly centered, and I did not understand, at that time, that aggression, in obsessional cases, is defensive. (See Chapter II.)

Consequently, my technical innovation with these cases consists of first *circumventing* the full impact of the patient's projection of the "cruel Giantess" by making that unavoidable projection a difficult procedure. By *giving* words (the analyst has to talk for long periods) one does not of course avoid the transference-projection of the "bad mother." But—and this is decisive—one offers oneself as a model for a specific inner defense on the part of the patient. Inwardly, these neurotics are stabilized on the rejection level; unconsciously, they want refusal. Their defenses are pseudo-aggression, and the superficial defensive wish to be kindly treated. By giving words, the analyst temporarily becomes the standard-bearer of the patient's defense: "If someone is kind and generous to me, I can be too." (Of course, this unconscious defense is extremely superficial, and is used only to refute the inner reproach of enjoyment of psychic masochism.) Paradoxically, this serves to reinforce, temporarily, the patient's "basic fallacy": "It's not that I'm masochistic; I'm just an innocent victim of mother's cruelty. If my mother had been different, I would have reacted differently, too." In later stages of the analysis, this basic fallacy must also be resolved. The rationalization of "kindness if treated kindly," which the patient unconsciously produces, is still strong enough to mitigate the enormous amount of pseudo-hostility, suspicion, anger, accusations of being "unjustly treated," otherwise created by these patients.

Conclusions can be drawn from these clinical experiences, and applied to people who have the reputation of being "the silent type." If analyzed, these people all too frequently prove to belong to the "killjoy" classification (see #35, this chapter) or to excel in "negative magic gestures" (see p. 123 f.). Both techniques are defensive; they are layers of pseudo-aggression covering deep masochistic regression.

The *logorrhoic type,* treated at length in *The Basic Neurosis* (pp. 284–291), is characterized by a torrent of meaningless verbiage. These words contain an aggressive element, which manifests itself in:

(a) Incessant talking;

(b) Inconsistent talking: the need for transition is not recognized by even a second's pause between subjects, and no visible connections are offered;

(c) Preponderance of unimportant details, chosen aggressively without perception of the problem as a whole;

(d) Complete failure to realize how much the logorrhea irritates the listener.

The problem is further complicated by a scopophiliac sideshow. If the assumption that the two parts of the scopophiliac instinct—voyeurism and exhibition—can be used against each other, as defenses, is applied to the specific problem of logorrhea, we see at once that the garrulous person does not merely exhibit. Garrulity also transforms the listener into a voyeur, through whom the exhibiting chatterer can look at himself (self-voyeurism via identification). Furthermore, garrulity is an invitation to the listener to reciprocate with matching verbal exhibitionism, thus exchanging confidence for confidence. It is an opening, therefore, for the satisfaction of the listener's voyeurism, also. The problem becomes clearer if attention is focussed on the element of curiosity. Garrulous persons collect material about other people's lives, discuss them endlessly, and are always attempting to penetrate their secrets. They are in a sense Peeping Toms.

Uncovering the first of his unconscious layers, the logorrhoic becomes visible as a child in adult clothing, whose masquerade entitles him to talk as much as he pleases. In deeper layers, he is seen to ridicule the adult nonsense he heard as a child, when he was to be "seen and not heard."

There are logorrhoics on all genetic levels; they are most prevalent among the orally regressed neurotics. The aggressive connotation in garrulity is in reality but pseudo-aggression, which is the "lesser crime" for which "conscience money" is paid in the form of the environment's impatience and rejection, and frequently by the judgment of "stupidity." The pseudo-crime, as usual, covers more deeply repressed psychic masochism.

PSYCHIC MICROSCOPY

Layers
I to V
Both over-taciturn and over-garrulous people operate on the typical five-layer structure of psychic masochists, using words as tools; the superficially visible pseudo-aggression is defensive. Pseudo-guilt is accepted for the latter only. "Ironic lip-service conformity with ego ideal precepts"—verbatim use of admonitions like "children should be seen and not heard" (in the silent variety) and ironic comments of elders about

acquaintances: "They talk only nonsense" (in the logorrhoeic variety). "Conscience money"—rejection of both traits by people in the environment who feel irritated by both attitudes. SUMMARY: Both types work on the level of the defense against the defense.

18. Do your enemies call you a "confused person"?

The popular designation, a "confused person," describes the individual whose ideas spill over from one "mental compartment" to another, without his even realizing that they should be kept apart.

Purely descriptively, the "confusionist" (my neologism, since no scientific term exists to describe this well-known and observable type) is an amazing fellow. He translates the simplest theme into bewildering complexity; the most complicated theory into a straight-forward statement, which again is bewildering because the simplification utterly lacks logic. He can create about him an air of confusion by infusing the conversation with totally unrelated ideas. In doing so, he may use a variety of techniques.

He may specialize in misunderstanding, always misinterpreting the opponent's argument (the presentation, he will without exception claim, was faulty) and substituting either additional misinterpretations or the same error differently worded when his mistake is pointed out. He may ride his hobby-horse—a set topic which reflects his inner conflict—into any discussion, using the other person's remarks as an opening wedge for his own pet theory. As, for example, the zoologist whose passionate interest was flies. One of his pupils, a perceptive fellow, was asked to describe an elephant. He said: "An elephant is a big animal, so big that flies frequently gather on his back. Flies are in general subdivided as follows . . . ."

He may be a quotation-specialist, supporting his original aim, which may be logical enough, with a muddled argument and a series of quotations entirely irrelevant to the issue. He may be bewildered by his own deduction, starting with circumlocution, progressing to digressions, and finally reaching a point where he does not know what he is saying. For example, if this type begins by explaining how to mash potatoes, he will find himself outlining the agricultural history of the potato, which leads him to the Irish famine of 1845, and finally to a point where he does not know what he is saying. As Andre Maurois said, "The difficult part in argument is not to defend one's own opinion, but rather to know it."

He may be the type with rigid and ready-made ideas, who does not need to listen to the opponent's argument because his reactions have been prepared far in advance. This type is frequently represented in the "speakers from the floor" when the subject of a lecture has been announced in advance. The confusionist with preconceived notions prepares himself for his "question" as soon as he reads the announcement. He does not listen to the speaker, whom he views as merely a nuisance, forcing him to wait for his big moment. Lecture and "discussion," therefore, are not even indirectly related.

He may use the technique of shifting the periphery to the center, as the heroine does in James T. Farrell's "A Misunderstanding": *
When her husband comes home from the office in the evening, and greets her affectionately, asking how she is, she answers with a remark about the kind of soap she has been using, or informs him that there was no mail that day. If he persists, and she finally realizes that she has not been answering his question, her reply is a revealing, "Oh!"

He may confound different layers of conscious "reasons," with the inevitable result that his answers become confused as well. One's motives for any action are not only the "good reason and the real reason" (as J. Pierpont Morgan once said) but also the *unconscious* reason. The danger of getting one's own excuses confounded (because of inner guilt) is as great as the danger of getting mixed up in the wrong daydream, as Charles Yale Harrison put it in *Meet Me on the Barricades*.

He may specialize in simplifying and negating the unconscious, basing his technique on overlooking, being unfamiliar with, or negating unconscious motivations. He may be a victim of *pseudo*-mental deficiency. He may be addicted to incorrect analogies, uncritically applying past events to present circumstances, without taking external or internal changes into consideration.

He may use the "humorous" approach, viewing a joke—any joke—as a permanent pass to the ranks of the elite. In practice, his method usually bars him, since he frequently directs his irony

* From *An American Dream Girl*, Vanguard, 1950.

at an unimportant or related detail instead of the point which is really at stake.

Or he may create confusion consciously and artificially, for the sake of evading the issue. The classic example is the lady who arrives at the theatre half an hour late, and stifles her husband's reproaches by telling him: "You can't talk that way to a lady."

All these varied types of confusionist share two basic unconscious mechanisms, upon which may be superimposed additional, more superficial, mechanisms.

They all tend to reduce educational authorities (who have been incompletely assimilated into the inner conscience) to absurdity; they all display pseudo-aggression, as a more superficial—though also repressed—defense against the more deeply repressed psychic masochistic solutions of the early infantile conflict.

The neurotic confusionist converts the intellectual sphere into a weapon in his "battle with the conscience." He appears to be a simpleton; in reality he is offering a pseudo-aggressive alibi of stupidity as defense against the superego's charge of psychic masochism.

This explains the confusionist's tendency to make a fool of himself in public. Exhibitionistically, he is displaying what he wishes to ward off—his craving for defeat, humiliation, rejection. More superficially, of course, pseudo-aggression is used. Since the aggression is unconsciously simulated and the underlying psychic masochism quite genuine, the result is inevitably self-damaging.

The pseudo-aggressive argument, therefore, is designed for easy refutation. The incorrect, quickly confounded argument is not presented because the confusionist cannot find a better one; it is chosen "unconsciously on purpose," *because* of its weakness. Defeat, humiliation, and "pleasure in pain" are the confusionist's inner aims.

PSYCHIC MICROSCOPY

Layer I.   Masochistic solution of the infantile conflict.
Layer II. First superego veto.
Layer III. First defense of the unconscious ego: "I'm not masochistic; I'm aggressively outspoken."
Layer IV. Second superego veto.

Layer V.   Second defense of the unconscious ego: neither masochism
           nor pseudo-aggression appear in consciousness of the person
           operating the "mechanism of confusion"—he pours out his
           flood of words quite oblivious to the "conscience money" he
           pays by making a fool of himself.—"Ironic lip-service conformity
           with ego ideal precepts": "I'm just showing these conceited
           adults what fools they are—*they* mix everything up and talk
           nonsense themselves." (Copy of parental admonition once
           given to the child.)
SUMMARY: The "confusionist" operates on the basis of a defense against
         a defense.

19. *Are you shy at public appearance?*

Everyone is familiar with persons who execute self-display in
absentia, who shyly "hide behind their work," as the saying goes,
using their work—artistic, scientific, architectonic or technical—
as a screen for their own personalities.

In such cases, one simply says that the exhibitionism is shifted
from the person to the product—a very sympathetic attitude. But
these people are really publicity-shy: they *prefer* to demonstrate
the products of their labors rather than themselves. There are
other individuals, however, who are entirely *unable* to accept the
limelight, unless they are under pressure of specific inner camouflaging conditions. I have called these people "incognito exhibi-
tionists." The difference between these two types, between those
who "prefer not to," and those who "cannot," is more than merely
quantitative; it is qualitative as well.

The type I have in mind is by no means identical with the blusher
(erythrophobe). These neurotics have a different structure. (See
bibliography.)

The genetic basis of incognito exhibitionism covers four completely dissimilar phenomenologic types:

(a) The function (any direct display of oneself) is fully impaired;
(b) The function, though not quite impaired, can be performed
    only under penalty of severest fear;
(c) The function is seemingly unimpaired, but is performed
    under "peculiar" inner prerequisites, manifested in bizarre
    external conditions;
(d) The function is not only not impaired, but seemingly exagger-

ated; it contains, however, specific restrictions on other parts of the ego, e.g., inability to do anything but work in a highly restricted field.

To adduce clinical examples of these four types:

I. *Self Display Fully Inhibited*

A once famous, now deceased, French photographer (fractionally analyzed many years ago in Vienna—he had to interrupt treatment repeatedly—) went into a state of panic every time he had to attend a gathering or party, or deliver a speech or lecture of an informal nature about his specific field of endeavor. His explanation that "he had absolutely nothing to say" was easily reduced to absurdity; when it was pointed out that he was obviously better informed on his own subject than his listeners were, he had to admit that he "simply couldn't do it." He practically lived in fear of testimonial dinners, lectures and the like, and even of social gatherings.

His analysis brought to the fore a massive layer of exhibitionism, which he could show only in *substitution*: in his work, in his choice of strikingly attractive women, in the splendor of his studio. Personally, he was extremely shy, as if apologizing for his mere existence.

He was an inveterate experimentalist, never satisfied with what had already been achieved, always on the lookout for a new slant. This attitude, advantageous for his professional career, made for constant and severe personal unhappiness. It was this self-torture, combined with masochistically self-constructed "woman troubles," that pushed him into sporadic treatment.

It has been my experience, as mentioned before, that exhibitionism is *not* the direct counterpart—with equal rights—of voyeurism, but merely a defense mechanism. In my opinion, the presence of massive exhibitionism in a patient imposes the obligation to search for more deeply repressed voyeurism, whereas voyeurism itself is a direct drive, a subdivision of orality (the latter first suspected by Simmel). The two ingredients of scopophilia are used as defenses against each other only *after* the end solution of the individual infantile conflict has been established. One must guard, therefore, against confusion between the *genetic* and the *clinical* pictures.

When this particular patient had to deliver a speech, or even appear in public, his exhibitionism was forced into the open, and could no longer be hidden behind a model ("*she* exhibits"), a photograph or a situation. In short, bereft of his defensive cover, this patient was helpless.

Undoubtedly, a good deal of his voyeurism was sublimated in his work. How had he been able to convince the inner conscience that infantile peeping was no longer involved, aside from the obvious argument—the deliverance included in social approval (sublimation)?

First of all, what he found most offensive in infantile peeping at others (mother) was the element of passive dependence: whether or not anything would be displayed was another's decision and not his own. In his work, he acted out the *active* reversal: he transformed his models into his *creations*.

Second, one could also say that in looking at his artistically "arranged" models, he was making use of a subterfuge, and actually looking at—*himself,* his work! Thus, in a roundabout way, he half re-established the infantile narcissistic position which precedes peeping at others.

Third, the very nature of his work provided a constant and unfailing unconscious excuse: "I am not peeping; the model is exhibiting and therefore forcing me to peep!"

These three subterfuges, added to the guilt-resolving sublimation, made it possible for that man to be "all eye." Superimposed on this was the exhibitionistic defense. Here, however, he was confronted with difficulties, for he could exhibit in substitution only. In spite of its superficiality, it was to the exhibitionistic defense that he had fastened his inner guilt. In the usual way, he was fighting his inner battle on a spurious front. He had made the rescue attempt typical for every boy in the sphere of scopophilia— "I don't want to peep, I want to display myself"—a denial prompted by the mother's ban on sexual peeping at her. It worked poorly in his case, an outcome which can be explained by his *oral regression.* It seems that the prerequisite for the success of this scopophiliac defense mechanism is the *boy's acceptance of his penis as full narcissistic restitution for the breast envy. If the shift is not accepted,* or is only partially accepted, the child becomes masochistically attached to the enshrined mother image, and his pattern becomes that of masochistic injustice collecting. As the typical defense, pseudo-aggressive mechanisms are brought into play.

In the case of the photographer, a series of such mechanisms could be detected. In his work, he treated women contemptuously; as a rule, he made them into caricatures. For example, he would "deprive" them of their breasts by shooting pictures at an angle which concealed all contours. One of his recollections was particularly revealing. At the age of three and one-half, when at the beach with his mother, he came out of their cabin stark naked. His mother reprimanded him, telling him to cover himself. The boy obeyed by fastening a towel around his—neck. Here we still see his attempts at compensatory penis exhibitionism, later brought to nothing.

The decisive proof that he was still running away from the disappointing *living* subject for peeping—mother—was found in his poorly developed ability to photograph mass scenes. A "mass" scene, for him, meant one including more than two people. In photographs of this kind, he had to deal with *real* people, whom he could not manipulate at will as he did his models. His elaborate inner hoax, therefore, could not be used to hoodwink conscience, and his work consequently suffered. This was also a clue to his compulsion to "experiment." Hidden behind rational factors was the old reproach: *"Mother* didn't *show* every part of her body, *everything* there is to look at." This was shifted to: *"I* didn't create anything new!"

With only slight exaggeration, one could say that the photographer, although he worked with *living* people, treated his models as if they were *inanimate objects.* ("Petrification tendency" *) Besides its fear-diminishing effect, amounting almost to negation of mother's very existence, this expedient also served to correct another childhood disappointment: instead of infantile *furtive glances,* he could now impose on others the *"hold still"* attitude.

* According to Webster, "petrification" has two meanings: to change into stone, and fix in silent fear. The patient changed his living subjects into "stone" (immobility), and did so in order to overcome his own horror of the female subject (originally mother). Hence the word fits—he *actively* petrified, in order not to be *passively* overcome by—petrification. A good example of Freud's "unconscious repetition compulsion."

It was this amazing string of compensatory narcissistic and pseudo-aggressive recompenses which made the man a great photographer.

Curiously enough, there were rare occasions when he did not mind exhibiting—when he would play the witty clown, and tell of an amusing experience. Here the defense would run: "I'm only joking; don't take me seriously."

II. *Self-Display Partially Inhibited Performed under Severest Fear*

The mechanisms here are identical with those of Type I, with a slight quantitative lessening of tension. This means that the function of self-display can still be performed, but is paid for with extensive production of fear.

In my opinion, fear pertains exclusively to psychic masochism. Two subterfuges are used. Inner fear of conscience is shifted outside; the fear sufferer is seemingly afraid of an external danger. Second, the guilt which belongs, re vera, to psychic masochism is fastened to pseudo-aggression, which takes the form of overstepping educational commands. This shift to the outside, plus the trick of "taking the blame for the lesser crime" of pseudo-aggression, constitute the maximum assistance which can be provided by the unconscious ego in the fight against the inner conscience.

Sometimes a peculiar compromise is inwardly reached. The function is performed, but instead of emotions, coldness and detachment appear on the surface. The performer "freezes up," and his "act" is lifeless.

I once analyzed a man of this type *—a politician, amusingly enough. His friends objected to the coldness of his speeches, and suggested that he use more "oomph," and more gestures. As a practising lawyer in his pre-political days he had used a specific gesture: he would spread the second and third fingers of his raised right hand apart, the space between the fingers pointing at the imaginary enemy. In analysis it became clear that in this gesture he identified with a mathematics teacher he had studied with as a child. This teacher's reputation had been rather shady: he had been tried for fraud and acquitted because of insufficient evidence—a mercy sentence. The second finger of the teacher's right hand had

* The case is described in *The Battle of the Conscience.*

been amputated as the result of an accident. The patient was able to recall the occasion on which, to his amazement, he had for the first time made use of this gesture: when he had feared, despite his innocence, that he was going to be accused of embezzling a client's funds. The gesture, therefore, signified both half-admission *and* defense—for the teacher had been acquitted. There was a further complication since the gesture had an inner connotation of masturbation: "Look, I'm using my hands for gestures, not for masturbation." Though defensive in scope, the gesture also included a good deal of self-indictment and self-punishment (the empty space between the fingers also signified castration), and consequently became too compromising for use. Bereft of his gesture, the man became even more completely prey to his own fears.

He had no idea, of course, of the reasons for his original impulse to use the gesture, or for his subsequent feeling that he ought to drop it. The complexity of the problem could be reconstructed only during his analytic treatment.

Patients of this type are never free from the inner fear that conscience will see through and unmask their disguise of defensive exhibitionism. This fear is shifted to the spectator or the audience. Superficially, these patients seem to be suffering from castration fear; underneath lies the whole pandemonium of the orally based "breast complex" with its "septet of baby fears."

III. *Self-Display Made Possible by Adherence to Specific "Impossible" Conditions*

Paradigmatic for this category was a patient in whom I first observed "incognito coitus." This man would request the girl to recount to him, *during coitus,* the detailed story of her sexual performance with another man, including the pair's exact behavior, the phrases they used, her own sensations, etc. All this was to be described in "popular terms"—meaning in obscene language. If the girl did not agree, the man was either altogether impotent, or unable to achieve ejaculation. He would perform the sex act incognito, therefore; on the occasions when he attempted to do so without this crutch, when he performed "in person," so to speak, he would fail completely.

Only one phase of this symptom is of interest here. The patient was rather shy, and could exhibit (he could not even undress in the girl's presence) only on condition that he slipped into someone else's "skin." Via Oedipal identification (both positive and negative parts of the Oedipus complex), he seemingly repeated a sex act which he had observed his parents performing; even at puberty this scene had been the conscious content of his masturbatory fantasy. The question arose: why was all this retained in his conscious memory and not repressed? The explanation was that the memory served as a defense against more deeply repressed oral components. These oral components were visible in his attitude towards his sperm, and in the injustice collecting pattern of his professional and personal life, and of his personality in general. He would scrutinize his sperm closely after every ejaculation, originally he had believed that masturbation caused bleeding. More deeply repressed was the fantasy that he had "fed" the girl with his heart's blood, so that she was bleeding him to death. When his real and not his fictitious personality was involved, he would refuse sperm: when attempting intercourse without the "incognito," he suffered from "psychogenic aspermia."

This peculiar prerequisite for sex pointed to strong voyeuristic components; the defensive exhibitionism was poorly developed. (See Type I) The patient also had highly moralistic notions regarding exhibitionism: one of the reasons, for example, for his constant quarrels with his fiancee was his recurrent accusation that *she* exhibited by giving friends and acquaintances chance but generous glimpses of various parts of her body. He could exhibit, therefore, only via feminine identification. In his other personality traits, he was a typical injustice collector.*

* The amazing subterfuges used in "incognito exhibitionism" prove that more attention should be paid, and more study devoted, to the so far neglected sector of scopophilia. A series of clinical pictures connected with scopophilia has already been described; some of them have been generally acknowledged, some have not. Among the former are agoraphobia and erythrophobia; among the latter are depersonalization, boredom (alysosis), and certain types of "writer's block," as well as acting. But even where the generally acknowledged and long established neurotic entities based on scopophilia are concerned, there are differences of opinion.

In any case, one specific element has been consistently overlooked: penis *exhibitionism* plays an important part in overcoming the breast complex in the man (see Type I, pp. 159 ff.) The problem warrants further investigation,

IV. *Hyperexhibitionism as Defense*

The paradigm for this type is the actor, or professional "exhibitionist," whose case is discussed at length in a previous chapter (pp. 66 ff.)

PSYCHIC MICROSCOPY

Layer I.   Masochistic end result of infantile and voyeuristic conflict.

Layer II. First superego veto.

Layer III. First defense of the unconscious ego: "I do not torture myself by trying to peep at what I do not have: I exhibit what I do have."

Layer IV. Second superego veto.

Layer V.   Second defense of the unconscious ego: "It is not I who exhibit—they do." (Ironic, verbatim acceptance of ego ideal precepts of modesty regulations, and approved exhibitionistic display of the harmless.) "Conscience money" paid in external fear of display.

SUMMARY: "Incognito exhibitionism" is a defense against a defense.

20. *Always indecisive?*

Indecision—if chronic and applied to every harmless routine—is a neurotic symptom and sign, with two underlying causes:

(a) The *superimposed* type: the harmless problem at hand has been reinforced by unconscious material which penetrates to a weak spot in the individual's infantile past;

(b) The *anti-decision* type: the problem at hand is, per se, less important than the fact that the decision, per se—any decision!—is dreaded.

---

perhaps preponderantly directed at *how* penis exhibitionism has been actually inhibited by mother. This much is already clear: penis exhibitionism in the boy is also an attempt to negate, autarchically, the loss of the maternal breast, the child having found a "substitute" on his own body. On the other hand, the culture must—and of necessity—inhibit penis exhibitionism. But some children take this unavoidable prohibition, not as part of the culture's set of decency regulations, but as a deprecation of their private "substitution"—breast equals penis. If this happens, the masochistic solution is only too frequently chosen. The educational dilemma, while hopeless, is by no means responsible for the neurotic or non-neurotic outcome for the child. It is the mysterious elaboration of the *unconscious* ego which decides the issue.

Examples of the first type are individualized; * those of the second type belong to what is called in our literature "obsessional ambivalence." (See Chapter III.)

PSYCHIC MICROSCOPY OF AMBIVALENCE (TYPE b)

Layer I.   Masochistic solution of infantile conflict.
Layer II. First superego reproach and veto.
Layer III. First defense of the unconscious ego: pseudo-aggression.
Layer IV. Second superego reproach, forbidding the defense as well.
Layer V.   Second defense of the unconscious ego: "I'm neither masochistic nor aggressive; I simply cannot decide." Built into the resulting indecision are: mirage of activity ("*I* cannot decide" whereas in inner reality something within the person makes him the passive victim); "Ironic lip-service conformity with ego ideal precepts:" "Take your time, think before deciding, avoid hasty judgment," etc.—"Conscience money" paid in suffering from indecision and its external disadvantages.
Summary: Ambivalence is a defense against a defense.

21. *Are you the classical "misunderstood" contemporary?*

Human malice exists: sometimes the attempt to avoid it is a hopeless task. But if you provoke this malice, and provide it with a convenient justification, you are sure to be always on the receiving end.

The individual who is "constantly misunderstood" is of two types. He is either an innovator, or a masochistic provocateur. If he is an innovator in any field, he must be prepared for rejection: his naivete, if he is surprised by rejection, merely covers the identical psychic masochism which is the driving force behind his bloodbrother, the unconscious provocateur.

In my opinion, the overabundance of human malice is due less to the necessity of discharging aggression than to its effectiveness as

* I described, for example, a man who could not divorce his wife because his Oedipal defense, in early childhood, was built around the excuse: "Father wants to leave Mother." This prop would have been withdrawn if he had left his wife. He was a deeply masochistic personality, preferring to fight his "battle of the conscience" on the spurious front of pseudo-aggression—"to leave or not to leave his wife" (admission of the lesser crime) rather than on the real battlefield of psychic masochism.

an alibi presented to the accusing inner conscience. The superego is incessantly using the storehouse of psychic masochistic defenses as a source of reproaches; overt malice, therefore, serves as a convenient rejoinder. Which, after all, is the great inner need of all human beings, even though they don't know it.

It is not exactly necessary to believe in natural human benevolence (quite the contrary!) in order to identify unprovoked malice as neurotic behavior. There is simply no resemblance between the normal aggression mobilized in self-defense, and the neurotic malice used a priori to appease the superego. The accurate observation that Mr. X or Mrs. Y is malicious is thus equivalent to a diagnosis of masochistic passivity, which has been warded off with pseudo-aggression in the form of malice. The normal person just does not kick another human being without reason, simply because he "likes to kick."

PSYCHIC MICROSCOPY

Layer I.   Masochistic solution of the infantile conflict.
Layer II.   First superego veto.
Layer III. First defense of the unconscious ego: pseudo-aggression.
Layer IV.   Second superego veto.
Layer V.   Second defense of the unconscious ego: ideological, "moral," political, "racial," or any other rationalization.—"Ironic lip-service conformity with ego ideal precepts" by applying verbatim the rule that truth-telling brings increasing returns, whereas only the rule of diminishing returns can be expected to prevail if the static element in the human psyche is challenged.—"Conscience money" paid in self-damage or poor reputation, or guilt shifted to the "lesser crime."
Summary: Neurotic malice works on the level of a defense against a defense.

22. Are you the victim of "one-inch-from-victory" disappointment?

Some neurotics can "take" everything except one specific type of disappointment: the defeat which suddenly materializes when victory was seemingly "in the palm of my hand."

One patient, a young writer, explained:

"I don't mind accepting defeats and disappointments according to the law of averages. I am accustomed to disappointments in the ratio of one success to ten defeats. I am not naive enough to believe that a more favorable ratio can be achieved. What gets me, though, is a specific type of failure: where all preliminary agreements have been concluded, success is in sight, everything is settled, but—at the last minute—some senseless obstacle throws a monkey wrench into the whole deal. I cannot help thinking of the words I put into the mouth of one of my characters:

" 'Life consists of defeats and moderate successes. The most painful defeats are those which come to us at the last second, at a time when success seems already certain. You have a pearl necklace in your hands, the chain breaks, one pearl is lost. You look for the missing gem on your knees. Finally you are caught kneeling by a malicious onlooker, the missing pearl is not to be found, and, in your humiliation, you throw the other pearls before swine.' "

In analyzing these last-second defeats, one must distinguish among three types of obstacle:

(a) Those unconsciously self-provoked.
(b) Those produced by the neurotic tendencies of the second party in the deal.
(c) Those produced by unfavorable external circumstances.

To cite clinical examples:

The above-mentioned writer submitted a book, through his agent, to a publishing house. The book contained an idea which was later stolen by an older, more established author. My patient had created a character in a previous book, and the present work was a continuation of the same theme. The fact that the first book had been poorly received by both public and critics had not deterred the older author from his plagiarism. "By chance" the presumptive publisher of the second book was the same man who had published the competitor's books, and advertised them at great expense. The publisher, who was not too discerning, was interested in my patient's book until the "similarity" between it and the book written by the older author was pointed out to him by the staff. Then, of course, the book was promptly rejected, with some righteous excuse, to hide the fear of a plagiarism suit. My patient was furious, indulging in orgies of hatred and self-pity at the injustice of "being both plagiarized and penalized." It did not even occur to him that his defeat could have been prevented by avoiding that particular publisher. He claimed that his agent submitted the book on his own, reporting to him after the event. When asked why he had not then reclaimed his book, he answered that he had toyed with the idea for a few seconds.

Eventually, my patient damaged himself even more than he had through this lost opportunity. The publisher started a whispering campaign. He had obviously checked the implication of plagiarism and had it confirmed. My patient refused to sue because he said he did not want to increase the number of "crackpots of paranoiac coloration" who constantly claim that their ideas have been stolen. To increase his troubles, his agent became suspicious—for who wants to get involved in claims and counter-claims of plagiarism?

In contrast to this example of unconsciously self-constructed disappointment is a case in which the sufferer was actually an innocent victim. Remembering that "two people" frequently means "two neurotic people," let us hear the patient's description:

"I invented and patented a new device useful in a specific industry and am looking for a manufacturer and distributor. I cannot overcome the feeling of frustration I get from the preliminary discussions. The majority of the manufacturers I have contacted behaved as though their enthusiasm for my gadget's financial possibilities would result immediately in a life-long contract. But this never happened. In a number of instances we were only a few seconds from signing the contract. It is as if these people were teasing me. The letdown is terrific. All this could be avoided by a more cautious attitude on their part."

Analysis of this man proved that he could not become inured to these last-second disappointments, even though he understood that they were caused by neurotic indecision of his partners. Since he could not develop a "thick skin" to protect him from the pain of these "last-ditch resistances," he too was neurotically involved. With great skill, he proved that in no case was he responsible for the other party's indecision. He proved, further, that he had no part in choosing or rejecting these people as prospective co-workers. He would confer with any person who showed interest in his invention. All of this, though true, was beside the point. It did not explain why he felt the letdowns so intensely, or was so strongly affected by a disappointment coming after a period when the whole problem seemed definitely settled in his favor.

In the third type of last-second disappointment, external events only are responsible; i.e., war, scarcity of materials, shortages, etc.

Aside from these one-inch-from-victory defeats, one must of course make allowances for a certain percentage of disappointment in daily life and in one's work. The two patients quoted specifically stressed the timing of their defeats as the source of their greatest pain, coming as they did when success seemed to be achieved. Adult people take such possibilities into consideration; they do not pin their hopes to enthusiastic assurances. A certain amount of skepticism is normally developed as a cushion against last-second disappointments.

But neurotic optimism is a favorite technique of the psychic masochist. Inwardly, such a neurotic has a rather pessimistic approach to reality, expecting defeat and even unconsciously enjoying it. Superficial optimism is this neurotic's way of increasing the masochistic stakes. The greater the discrepancy between the high-pitched hope and the final disappointment, the greater the pain and depression. (See fuller discussion of optimism on pp. 130 ff.)

PSYCHIC MICROSCOPY

Layer I.   Masochistic solution of infantile conflict.
Layer II.   First superego veto.
Layer III. First defense of unconscious ego: pseudo-aggression, leading to biting pessimism.
Layer IV.   Second superego veto.
Layer V.   Second defense of unconscious ego: "As ordered, I'm highly optimistic, but how can I help being hurt by actual defeats?" (Choice of masochistically self-constructed defeats, badly-chosen partners, inability to accept ups and downs of fortune, are gratuitously overlooked.) "Ironic lip-service conformity with ego ideal precepts" by using over-optimism as yardstick. "Conscience money" paid in depression and defeat.
SUMMARY: Sufferers from "one-inch-from-victory" disappointments work on the basis of a defense against a defense.

23. A Raconteur?

A raconteur is inwardly an infantile peeping Tom. He denies this wish only to admit to the lesser crime of exhibitionism. Because of the specificity of scopophiliac tendencies, they may attach themselves to different levels. In the case of the raconteur, the ability at "story-telling" which he finally develops (and his inner necessity to tell them) is either Oedipally deposited, or exists as a "hysterical island" entirely surrounded by deeper, oral, regression.

In general, the raconteur possesses a stock of stories and tales invented by *others*. These stories he genially communicates at gatherings. Here, he *must* be the center. Superficially, he gives the impression of a little boy who seizes the limelight in order to compensate for his shadow existence as a child. This is what motivates the guest who is "the life of the party."

By far the majority of the stories told by raconteur are "funny." This is a relic of the period when the child tried to attract attention by being "funny." This type of infantile humor is later shifted to a higher level in the raconteur, and becomes witty presentation. The sexual connotation in these stories is pseudo-aggressive, and comes from the "spite department"—it is aimed at the parents.

The superficial compensatory exhibitionism of the raconteur is frequently connected with the problem of the "ugly duckling," to quote a patient. It is remarkable that so many raconteurs should be, or consider themselves to be, ugly, homely, unattractive. Their bodily defect (real or imaginary, always unconsciously considered "castration") is compensated for intellectually. It is as if the raconteur were pleading: "Don't look at me as a castrated person: concentrate on my words."

The raconteur, therefore, has rescued himself to the Oedipal level, and displays his word-penis. The defensive nature of his exhibitionism is visible in his usual sterility: he is an imitator and secondhand echo of other people's witty productions (inhibition of *imagination* = voyeurism).

A great deal of confusion has involuntarily been introduced into the problem by those specialists in the usage of words—literary critics. Habitually, they refer to writers as "story tellers" although the story *writer* is radically different from the story *teller* in inner psychological set-up. The very critics who concentrate on words, nearly to the exclusion of content, are in this specific case the creators of the existing confusion. To quote Coleridge:

I know nothing that surpasses the vileness of deciding on the merits of a poet or painter,—(not by characteristic defects; for where there is genius, these always point to his characteristic beauties, but)—by *accidental failure* and *faulty passages;* except the impudence of defending it, as the proper duty, and most instructive part, of criticism. *(Biographia Literaria,* Chapter 3).

PSYCHIC MICROSCOPY

Layer I.   Masochistic solution of the infantile conflict, with an appendage of voyeuristic wishes.

Layer II.   First veto of superego.

Layer III. First defense of unconscious ego: Oedipal "rescue station," denial of voyeurism, admission of exhibitionism as lesser crime, plus pseudo-aggression in transgressing educational commands of decency.

Layer IV. Second veto of superego.

Layer V.   Second defense of unconscious ego: pseudo-aggression mitigated by humorous terminology; aggression shifted to originator of jokes and stories, which are always repeated, never created; further attenuation: "I just make people laugh at social gatherings."—"Ironic lip-service conformity with ego ideal precepts": "Don't just sit around like a bump on a log; be alive, get *into* things!—"Conscience money" paid in the environment's refusal to take the raconteur too seriously, and in depression when out of the limelight.

SUMMARY: The raconteur works on the level of a defense against a defense.

24-25 *Are you the victim of "bad influence" and of not having received enough "good advice"?*

"Bad influence," so often pointed out as the cause of misconduct, is, in inner reality, but one of the episodes in the battle of the conscience. Unconscious identification is more than inner imitation (an accurate but superficial description); it is also a mechanism with a genetic background. In the specific case of a "bad influence," it is a technique of hiding behind somebody else's broad shoulders. Just as a schoolboy may come home with a poor report card, and say, when handing it over, "Johnny flunked too," the schoolboy within the unconscious may resort to the same excuse, with one addendum: the desire to show up the hypocrisy of adults. It is well-known that some people are addicted to the childish formula of showing others up by exposing their "vote dry and live wet" attitudes; the exposure becomes a weapon against the severity of the inner conscience. If, in a situation of inner conflict, a "bad influence" is at hand, the inner identification with that "bad influence" serves as an alibi. The "temptation" of the bad example is used as protection against superego reproaches, and not as a release of repressed wishes.

This also explains why a "bad example" may be "fought against" at one time and "yielded to" at another. The "bad example" is followed only on the occasions when it is needed as an unconscious prop.

What is the psychologic situation of a person when presented with either a good or bad example? In the first place, the example per se hasn't the slightest influence on the psychic apparatus. What can happen, however, is the coincidence of two factors. For unconscious reasons, completely unrelated to actual events leading to the good or bad example, a specific person can be ready for an unconscious identification. Then and then only the example has effect and is followed by what the man on the street erroneously calls imitation. Hence the problem reduces itself to the psychology of unconscious identification.

A patient, orphaned and left without fortune at one and one-half, was brought up with his wealthy cousin. Both boys were strongly attached to the mother of the rich boy, but lived in constant fear of the father, a rigid, cold individual who was always preaching. At the age of five, the patient came under the "bad influence," as the family put it, of a male servant, imitating him in theft and swindling. A strong identification with the servant was discernible. Analysis could prove that preceding this identification the boy had developed a strong Oedipus complex and had been driven out of this libidinous position through "fear of castration" (Freud) by the potential threat of the punishing uncle. The boy had then identified ("negative Oedipus") with his aunt, a kind, submissive woman. He could later remember that at the age of four he had been teased because of his shyness and "girlishness." A few months later his behavior had changed once more; he had become provocative, a miniature truant and a delinquent. His family attributed this change to the influence of the servant, and dismissed the man. However, the boy continued to cheat and steal until late in life. We see in his case both the "good example" (represented by the hypermoral uncle) and the "bad example" (the servant). From the descriptive viewpoint it is not understandable why the boy finally chose the "bad example" with which to identify. Theoretically, both possibilities for identification were present at the same time. From the genetic viewpoint his choice is understandable. Instead of giving up his incestuous wishes and identifying himself with the uncle (the process leading to normality) the boy identified with the woman, thus accepting alleged "castration" as a punishment. This identification was counteracted by a strong inner feeling of guilt, so that a new alibi-identification had to be established proving his "aggression." Therefore he identified with the pseudo-aggressive servant. However, his passivity was smuggled into the defense. Through stealing and swindling he came into deeper conflicts.

Another example: The son of a well-known historian devoted his life to proving that all history is based on fallacy, thus belittling his father's life work. There were constant "scientific" conflicts between father and son. The son gleefully quoted statements disparaging the accuracy of historians. His favorite quotations were: "History is a fable agreed upon." (Napoleon). "On the breast of that huge Mississippi of falsehood called history." (Matthew Arnold) "History is bunk." (Henry Ford) The father was furious when his son quoted, first in conversations, later in his writings, the witty sentence of an "Anonymous": "History is something that never happened, written by a man who wasn't there." It was obvious, in analysis, that the son's spiteful approach to his father's profession had as its basis not an intellectual but an affective conflict. The young man was inwardly deeply submissive toward his father ("negative Oedipus"). He warded off this attachment with pseudo-aggression: "I'm not submissive toward my father; quite the contrary, I hate and ridicule him." This accounts for the irony against his father's profession. Here, too, two possible objects of identification could be discerned: the father and a cousin, an inhibited writer who constantly made "cracks" at the expense of his more successful relative. The sequence of events in this case was: neurotic solution of an inner conflict; use of an identification with a "bad influence" as a prop ("Other people don't believe father, either").

If, therefore, a "bad influence" is at hand in such a situation of inner conflict, an inner identification can take place as an episode in the fight with the inner conscience. The "temptation" of the bad example is thus used as an intrapsychic weapon against the severe inner conscience and not, as is naively assumed, just as a release of repressed wishes.

The unconscious setting in getting "good advice" is no less imbued with psychological meaning. Good advice is always met with mistrust, particularly by neurotics. For these people have never overcome the feeling that their parents were hypocritical, in forbidding sex to their children, for instance, while themselves indulging in it. More than that, good advice is bound to be ineffective in most instances because it conflicts with the infantile megalomania so deeply embedded in every individual. Very few people are free from the unconscious conviction that they are "exceptions," to whom human experience does not apply. The advice they receive never seems to have anything to do with "their case."

PSYCHIC MICROSCOPY

Layer	"Bad Influence"	"Good Advice"
I.	Masochistic end result of the infantile conflict.	Masochistic end result of the infantile conflict.
II.	First superego veto.	First superego veto.
III.	First defense of the unconscious ego: pseudo-aggression.	First defense of the unconscious ego: pseudo-aggression.
IV.	Second superego veto.	Second superego veto.
V.	Second defense of unconscious ego: hiding behind someone else's "broad shoulders," plus	Second defense of unconscious ego: "Is that what you would do yourself? Anyhow,

exposing hypocrisy of ego ideal sectors of superego. ("Ironic lip-service conformity with ego ideal precepts.")—"Conscience money": actual self-damage. it doesn't apply to me—I'm different." ("Ironic lip-service conformity with ego ideal precepts.")—"Conscience money": actual self-damage.

SUMMARY: Each is a defense against a defense.

26-27. Are you one of the mothers who go into tantrums because your child is a "feeding problem" or a nail-biter?

In a series of analyses of neurotic women in whom conflicts with their children were predominant, one specific situation arose again and again: the mother's "uncontrollable" fury when confronted with a "hunger-strike" on the part of a daughter who was a poor eater. These mothers were quite familiar with, and approved, the more recent principles of child-pedagogy, in which the abolition of forceful, punitive measures is advocated. Nevertheless, they reacted with outbursts of anger, hitting, threats. Moreover, their fury was observable exclusively with girls: the identical mothers reacted with much more leniency when their sons were guilty of the same offense.

Analysis of this fury promoted the assumption that a reversal of the woman's own infantile situation was involved. These mothers were acting out a "negative magic gesture" (more fully described on p. 123 f), an *unconscious* dramatization of how badly *their* mothers had treated *them* when they were children. This is not a direct repetition, but an *ironic exaggeration and caricature,* since it is not rooted in objective observation but in the child's distorted misconceptions of reality.

This being the case, unconsciously the grandchild of the original "malefactrix" is being used as scapegoat for an unresolved inner conflict. In *external* reality, a mother and daughter are on the stage; they are the *second* generation. In *internal* reality, the mistreated child represents the mother herself *as a child,* and the neurotic mother represents the grandmother: the *first* generation recreated. All the fury belongs to the grandmother, who is represented as a repellent caricature: "Look—this is how I did *not* want to be treated! You are mean!"

It was also interesting to observe that the original reproach directed against the mother was in itself an elaboration (unconscious, to be sure) of an even earlier reproach leveled by these neurotic women. In the earliest formulation, the reproach read; "Mother wants to starve me." Later it was reformulated: "Even if mother gives food, she does it ungraciously, and only because it is her duty." The reformulation was necessitated by the untenability of the original "objection"—mothers do not starve their children. Instead of accepting the real situation, in which the mother is generous and providing, the old anger—which covers the masochistic "solution"—is maintained. As a result, the masochistic child feels victimized: *he (she) really eats his (her) cake and has his (her) grievance, too.*

Thus a sacrificial act on the part of the mother is intra-psychically transformed into malice: bad mother forces the unwilling child. Sometimes this attitude is combined with slightly paranoiac ideas: the food is rejected as spoiled, unattractive, or at the very least tasteless. Many food idiosyncrasies, and hypochondriacal ideas connected with food, have their affective bases as this point.

In the previously described "mix-up of generations" (daughter-child—grandmother-daughter), the old infantile fantasy of the victimized child is frantically maintained. This is an attitude which cannot change of itself, because of its derivation. Accused by inner conscience of having accepted the masochistic "solution," there is a desperate attempt to avoid paying penance for the real "crime," and the victim pleads guilty to the pseudo-aggressive act. There is an additional advantage to this procedure: it is possible, in this way, to demonstrate how "bad" mother really was. The "basic fallacy" that one is only an innocent victim is again strengthened.

There are three tentative explanations for the fact that the situation, as described, is especially pronounced where daughters are involved. First, there is the seemingly irresistible allure of specific repetition (dramatis personae being identical in sex); second, the unconscious mitigating connotations of a boy (as described by Freud) are absent with a girl. Third, I have gathered the impression from some cases that the disappointment of having a girl and not a boy activated, in the mother, old injustice-collecting fantasies connected with her own mother, thus paving the way for the "negative magic gesture."

The reaction of mothers to nail-biting did not vary from aggrava-
tion to leniency in strict accordance with the sex of the child. Here,
blank fury was prevalent in neurotic mothers. As though they
understood the meaning behind their children's attitudes, these
mothers fought their losing battle with determination.

In general these mothers were *consciously* naive, and considered
the "habit" an outgrowth of babyish thumb-sucking. There was one
case, however, in which I heard a really intuitive explanation:
"The boy acts as if I would starve him."

The mother hit the nail on the head. Nail-biting, so frequently
described in analytic literature as a phallic castration symbol, has
a deeper layer: It denotes the child's accusation that the mother
starves him, so that it is "necessary" for him to eat himself.

At the same time, it unconsciously represents both an autarchic
attempt to be independent of the mother, and a masochistic-exhibi-
tionistic demonstration of mother's "cruelty."

PSYCHIC MICROSCOPY

Layer	Mothers of "Feeding Problems"	Mothers of "Nail-Biters"
I.	Masochistic end-result of infan-tile conflict.	Masochistic end-result of infan-tile conflict.
II.	First superego veto.	First superego veto.
III.	First defense of unconscious ego: pseudo-aggression.	First defense of unconscious ego: pseudo-aggression.
IV.	Second superego veto.	Second superego veto.
V.	Second defense of uncon-scious ego: "All I want is to be loved—don't you see how I *don't* want to be treated?" (Negative magic gesture and mockery of ego ideal.)	Second defense of unconscious ego: "All I want is to be loved; I am generous and giving, as I wanted my mother to be to me, and my child *must* believe me." ("Ironic lip-service conformity with ego ideal precepts.")

SUMMARY: Conscience money paid in conscious unhappiness. Each reaction
is a defense against a defense.

28. *Do your enemies call you a "success-hunter"?*

I suggested the term "success-hunter" (promptly translated by a witty reviewer into "ulcer-ridden captain of industry") to describe an individual characterized by these symptoms and signs:

(a) Contempt for moderate earnings, high-pitched ambitions, and exaggerated ideas of success, combined with a drive to overwork.

(b) Constant inner tension, stemming from inner *passivity*, regardless of the importance of the stakes.

(c) A propelling impetus toward more and more success.

(d) Dissatisfaction and boredom if deprived of new business excitement and resulting opportunities to show off.

(e) Cynical outlook, hypersensitivity, and hypersuspiciousness.

(f) Contempt for and ruthlessness toward the unsuccessful.

(g) Onesided and opinionated I-know-better attitude in general.

(h) Hypochondriacal worries; doubts concerning continuous flow of ideas and luck.

(i) Inability to enjoy the simple pleasures of life.

(j) Hidden depression, warded off with tempered megalomania and extensive air of importance.

Clinical analysis proves that this type of person lives above his emotional means, and is driven to his "ambition" by an inner conflict of truly over-dimensional masochistic passivity. To ward off the latter, a suitably over-dimensional defense is used—hyperwork. It is also interesting that the usual "brilliant" idea most often emerges at the deepest low of the recurring depression caused by the superego's reproach of relative failure. (The normal business man, it goes without saying, is by no means identical with the neurotic success-hunter.)

An anecdote from Napoleon's time offers an illuminating example of how despair can engender unexpected brilliance. Napoleon once summoned all his generals to a council of war in order to disentangle a knotty problem of strategy. No solution could be found, and the council continued for hours. In the meantime, one of the least talented tacticians present found himself confronted with a painful dilemma. He was suffering from prostate trouble, and needed immediate relief. It was unthinkable that any one present could leave the council chamber before Napoleon's formal dismissal of them all; it was quite clear that there would be no dismissal until the problem was solved satisfactorily. In this desperate emergency, the sufferer—who had never before been known to offer any constructive opinion on anything—came up with a brilliant solution, and the council was triumphantly dissolved. Substitute for prostate troubles "pangs of conscience" and the comparison fits.

Not infrequently potency is disturbed, as is, typically, the department of "tender love." To give but one example from the extensive material presented in *Money and Emotional Conflicts*:

I was consulted by a New York business man, one of the most successful in his field, who complained of constant tension and worry over his ability to finish the amount of work he daily prescribed for himself. This self-enforced overcrowded schedule entailed not only extensive business dealings but also working for a number of cultural and humanitarian institutions. "I worry day and night," he said. "For years I've managed to do every bit of the work I set myself, but that knowledge doesn't help. I know I could curtail my killing schedule—I promise myself constantly to work less—but I can't seem to do it. I just keep on overworking—and worrying about it. It's fantastic."

I explained that he lived beyond his emotional means. This suggestion was accepted immediately, but countered with the argument that if analysis were to change his neurotic tension he couldn't work at all.

The man's story was supplemented by his wife with several details which he had left out, e.g., symptoms of impotence, pathological stinginess, and irrational rage. However, he decided not to enter treatment—because he could not afford the fee. (See "The Miser," #45 of this chapter.)

Happy people, a rare species anywhere, are not to be found even among success hunters. More inner misery obtains there than in any other group of money neurotics.

PSYCHIC MICROSCOPY

Layer I.   Masochistic solution of infantile conflict.
Layer II.   First superego veto.
Layer III. First defense of unconscious ego: pseudo-aggression.

Layer IV. Second superego veto.

Layer V. Blame taken for pseudo-aggression mitigated by rationalization of success, general admiration of success. Irony directed at ego ideal precepts: "Shouldn't one work?"—"Conscience money" paid in inner dissatisfaction, hypochondria, vulnerability to psychosomatic diseases.

SUMMARY: The success-hunter is driven by a defense against a defense.

29. Do they offend you by calling you a "gambler"?

A chronic tongue-hanging-out gambler is one of the most desperate of the adherents to the oral-masochistic wish to be refused. He is, at the same time, a confirmed and frenzied addict to infantile megalomania. Both aims are unconscious, and are cloaked in pseudo-rational purposes characteristic of all "money-neurotics." This neurotic gambles *"to win,"* though unconsciously he means *to lose.* His pseudo-rational aim to win, although it is ineffective, nevertheless is a useful alibi to present to people in general and to inner conscience. There is a "good" reason, therefore, for his refusal to be deterred by such condensations of experience as the popular adages: "Horseplayers always die poor," and "The gambler is a sucker," or even by the joke he ironically tells on himself, "I hope I break even today, I need the money."

What are the gambler's signs and symptoms?

(a) The gambler *habitually* takes chances.

(b) The game precludes all other interests.

(c) The gambler is full of optimism and never learns from defeat.

(d) The gambler never stops when winning.

(e) Despite initial caution, the gambler eventually risks sums which he cannot afford to lose.

(f) "Pleasurable-painful tension" (thrill) is experienced between the time the gambler places his bet and the outcome of the game.

The moment the gambler has played his stake, the outcome of the game is beyond his control. This is the simple *objective* fact. *Subjectively* the gambler feels that he can control the outcome: he hopes to influence it by wishing, and behaves as if it were possible for certain acts of his own to bring about the desired result—as witness the gambler's numerous superstitions. He uses a shabby and torn wallet because once, when it was new, he won while carrying it. Or he avoids certain dates and numbers because they are unlucky for him. He will abstain from, or perform, certain magic little actions because he knows from experience that they carry specific meanings. Sometimes the more intelligent gambler will laugh at his superstitions—and continue to obey them. A patient once admitted that while at the television set, watching a race on which he was betting, he kept crossing and recrossing his legs in a certain way—meaningful actions performed for the purpose of influencing the jockey.

Behind this admission lies the whole extent of the gambler's infantile megalomania. Infantile megalomania (as has been pointed out) conflicted with the reality principles communicated to the child by mother, and later by father. The child's resultant fury was either handled or neurotically mishandled by the child. If mishandled, guilt caused the aggression to turn against the child himself, and the aggression was secondarily libidinized, leading invariably to psychic masochism.

Hence an adult promoting infantile megalomania in a decisive life situation automatically puts the masochistic elaboration into operation. This is the self-imposed *penalty* for unrelinquished infantile pleasures, only secondarily *made pleasurable*.

The psychic masochist who is a gambler unconsciously deludes himself twice: first, consciously, in believing that he wants to win money *(the battle of dollars)*; and second, in unconsciously believing that he is acting aggressively against the educational commands which aimed to destroy his stubborn infant belief that he could do whatever he pleased—the substratum of infantile megalomania *(the battle of alibis)*. Unknowingly, the gambler is still, as an adult, fighting the educational rules with pseudo-aggressive weapons. Inwardly he delivers a soliloquy, directed at his upbringers, which might be phrased somewhat as follows: "All your talk about normal conduct was pretty hypocritical, wasn't it? Look around you. 'Work leads to success?' 'Logic and consistency are reliable guide-posts?' Well, at the gambling table, at the race track, and on the stock exchange millions of dollars change hands every day—the people get rich without work. Chance is the important thing. I've got no use for your ridiculous normal rules of conduct!"

It is exactly this rebellion against educational commands which made Dostojewski intuitively put into the mouth of his gambler the words: "It was the wish to give Fate a punch in the nose and show her my tongue." The gesture and the language used to express it are relics of the nursery—where the trouble started.

Having unconsciouly provided himself with the necessary excuses, the gambler proceeds to his *real* wish: to be masochistically refused. This wish is unconscious: under no conditions could it occur consciously to the gambler himself.

The real and dynamically decisive factor in gambling—the happiness-in-unhappiness pattern—manifests itself twice in the course of play. First, it provides that mysterious thrill, which, as honest gamblers admit, is even more exciting than the hope of winning. That thrill, according to the same honest gamblers, is difficult to describe. One patient called it *"pleasurable-painful* tension." I subsequently submitted this formulation to a series of patients who were addicted to gambling and found that most of them confirmed its accuracy. It was interesting to observe, in this connection, the mixture of surprise and hesitation with which these patients reacted to the request that they check on their feelings. Though all of them were familiar with the "thrill," none of them had ever attempted to define it, and some acted as if it were sacrilege, in a way, to mention it at all. "Let sleeping dogs lie," said one. "But they are not sleeping at all," was my reply. "They are very much awake."

The reason for this reluctance is plain: understanding the thrill means stripping it of mystery, thus leaving the masochistic substructure in clear view. This is a development the gambler wants to avoid at all costs. Under pressure, one patient finally responded, telling me that the nearest he could come was a comparison with a particular situation he remembered from elementary school days. He had come home with a poor report card, to find his mother out, and had waited an hour for her to return. "That hour of waiting, knowing I was going to get the usual spanking, produced in me a feeling of terror—and some kind of elation."

This recollection contains an elaboration of the "elation in terror" experienced in the gambler's thrill. The elation corresponds in more superficial, though also unconscious, layers to the lesser crime of pseudo-aggression: the gambler oversteps educational commands. It is shifted to that point as an admission of the *lesser* crime, though genetically it belongs to the *real* crime of masochistic pleasure.

The case of the gambler may be stated as follows: having become "stabilized on the rejection level" as the end result of his specific infantile conflict, he re-enacts in his gambling the whole rigmarole of his wishes and defense. The unconscious wish, "I want to be refused," is counteracted by severe inner guilt. To assuage the latter, the mechanical gambling device and its animated substitutes become unconsciously identified with the infantile prototypes. These must, by their unjust and refusing behavior, feed the alibi: "I am just the innocent victim." Losses provide the necessary proof of the alibi.

Hence my conviction that the gambler—unconsciously—wants to lose. In the long run he always loses.

To formulate it in another way: the gambler risks good money for the bogus coin of his inner wishes and defenses. Since no exchange rate exists to bridge the gap between inner and outer reality, he takes monetary losses as part payment for his happiness-in-unhappiness.

These losses, and the depression which follows, provide the second installment of the gambler's masochistic pleasure. The depression has a complicated defensive structure. Seemingly, it pertains to mourning over being unloved (originally, by the first upbringer). In reality the despair and depression are a form of appeasement: "conscience money" paid for the proof that the gambler does not enjoy his psychic masochism—as the inner indictment justifiably claims he does. Being a psychic masochist, he cannot lose—at least intrapsychically: by misusing his depression secondarily, as well, for the purpose of extracting masochistic pleasure. In fact, in this way he adds to his masochistic bank account. The unavoidable consequence is that his *actual* bank account dwindles.

Hence the three R's (remorse, regret, repentance) reported by one gambling patient as the remedy recommended by his father, are of necessity ineffective. They can only add fuel to the battle of alibis and secondary masochistic pleasure.

There is no genetic or psychological difference between pure games of chance, and the "intellectual" games like chess or bridge, which combine chance and "reasoning." The difference lies only in the number of concessions to reality which are made by the individual who is pursuing remnants of his lost omnipotence.

PSYCHIC MICROSCOPY

Layer I.   Masochistic solution of the oral conflict, with specificity on megalomania.

Layer II. First superego veto.

Layer III. First defense of unconscious ego: pseudo-aggression against educational precepts with strong irony aginst their applicability.

Layer IV. Second veto of superego.

Layer V. Second defense of unconscious ego: gambling to win; the masochistic tension rationalized as waiting for outcome and wish to be ahead of the game, winning allegedly equated with being loved by Fate (parents); unconscious wish to lose paradoxically becomes moral alibi—proof that the gambler is not masochistic, Fate is merely cruel to him. The latter alibi creates a vicious circle. Guilt is accepted for the lesser crime—pseudo-aggression in overstepping educational and social precepts, plus a secondary ironic rationalization hitting at the ego ideal: "Life itself is a gamble—one has to take chance." "Conscience money" paid in losses, insecurity, social half-ostracism.

SUMMARY: Gambling constitutes a defense against a defense.

30. Do you take a drink or does the drink take you?

A chronic alcoholic is a victim of oral regression; he used "fluid" means to fight his unfinished battle with the image of the pre-Oedipal mother. The pharmacodynamic effects of alcohol are the substructure; upon it rests this psychological superstructure:

Layer I.   Masochistic attachment to the pre-Oedipal mother, as end result of the infantile conflict: "I wish to be refused."

Layer II. First veto of superego.

Layer III. First defense of the unconscious ego: pseudo-aggression.

Layer IV. Second superego veto.

Layer V. Second defense of the unconscious ego: "I'm independent of mother—who needs her ugly 'udder' anyway—I am self-sufficient (liquor bottle) and can get as much as I want myself. Besides, I drink only as diversion, or because of real trouble, or out of boredom, just as everyone else does." "Ironic lip-service conformity with ego ideal precepts", autarchically costumed: "Shouldn't one be self-sufficient?" "Conscience money" paid in the form of self-damage through drinking, plus the whole gamut of the sequels to injustice collecting.

Even popular observation divides a protracted drinking bout into four distinct phases: jocose, morose, bellicose, comatose.

If this assumption is correct, and the alcoholic unconsciously is repeating the situation of the bad mother refusing and frustrating him, orally, why does he allow himself to be served drinks? Why is there not a direct repetition of the situation of scarcity and refusal? Two factors explain his reasoning. First, drinking in itself begins as an attempt at self-cure and reparation—"Mother refused me, now I will give myself everything she refused. I am independent and autarchic"—which accounts for the initial happiness when drinking. (Jocose phase.) Drinking is at first a triumph over the refusing mother. The second factor is the drinker's inner identification with his mother, whom he fills with poison.* A compulsive drinker, years before he entered analysis with me, had had a violent conflict with his mother, whom he accused of responsibility for the unfair (to him) distribution of his father's estate. His mother defended herself against these unjustified accusations. During their argument the man drank one brandy after another. His mother asked reproachfully: "Why do you drink so heavily?" His retort was: "What's that to you?" She replied with the sober and rather melancholy statement: "Everything which harms you harms me, too." The patient responded by taking *two* brandies at once. In evaluating this scene, we have to assume that the man, in identification with his mother, wanted to harm *her*. He was, figuratively speaking, filling her with poison. Actually he harmed himself: his over-drinking gave expression to his self-damaging or psychic masochistic tendencies.

The jocose phase also reflects irony achieved through ridiculing authority in general, while the attitude towards the environment is

* A similar conclusion has been reached by British analysts, although through a different line of reasoning.

that of kindness. This mood of the drinker is familiar: "You are my friend; everyone is my friend." This mood shows the ambivalence of the conflict: pseudo-aggression against the intrapsychic mother-image, coupled with the denial of loss of love. It also advertises the drinker's own kindness, based on the theme: "You see how good I am, even though mother was so bad to me."

The "morose" stage which succeeds the initial geniality of the drinker is de facto the stage of depression. The first attempt at reparation and denial of dependence on mother, via pseudo-aggression, seemingly exhausts itself. According to a woman patient: "Whenever I drink, I am happy *at first*. Then I feel a deep depression coming on. I keep on drinking in order to recapture my initial happiness. Unfortunately, in vain." Her experience seems to indicate that the defensive power of the unconscious ego is limited; once it is used up the original depression re-emerges and must again be warded off. This stage of depression is characterized either by morose silence or by pessimistic remarks about the senselessness of life. Additional drinks only deepen the depression: the technique which was so successful in the first, jocose, phase, fails in its repetition.

The third phase in the course of a drinking spree is not hilarity but bellicosity. Verbal or physical attacks on either persons or objects are not rare, and quarrelsomeness is frequent, although the single instance is easily forgotten. This is the stage in which various sexual acts take place. The relation between alcohol and genital sexuality is interesting. According to the testimony of the alcoholic himself, alcohol is sexually stimulating up to a certain point, then becomes sexually debilitating. The explanation lies in the fact that the alcoholic, an orally regressed neurotic, uses genital sex as a rescue station and "moral alibi" for the dangerous pseudo-aggression. It should not be forgotten that the basis for neurotic oral pseudo-aggression is bitter revenge, which in turn is a defense against more deeply repressed psychic masochism. Even in pathological conditions (with the exception of "lust-murder"), genitality requires an affirmative and let-live attitude towards the object. This attitude, therefore, is assumed as a disguise, in the alcoholic's attempt to save himself from defensive oral fantasies of cruelty on the one hand and from self-destructive masochism on the other.

These aggressive fantasies, however, are in themselves a desperate inner defense against the masochistic attachment. This explains why alcohol, at first seeming to enhance genital sexuality, actually serves to reduce it. It provokes oral revenge fantasies in oral neu-rotics, or rather murderous fantasies directed against the mother or her surrogate, as a primary defense against psychic masochism. Genitality is produced as a secondary defense, and as a life-affirm-ing mechanism. It is a familiar fact that this mechanism works poorly—the coitus of these people is permeated with aggression and often, in the later stages of drunkenness, fails entirely.

There is little to say about the fourth, the "comatose" stage. It is the stage of sleep, and later on, of the hangover. As far as can be ascertained from patients, the dreams which follow drinking excesses seem to deal habitually with situations of being refused. The hangover, psychologically speaking, is a period of guilt-feeling, and the setting for solemn resolutions of "never again,"—resolutions which are always "forgotten."

PSYCHIC MICROSCOPY

Layers I to V. See above.

SUMMARY: The alcoholic is unconsciously driven by a defense against a defense.

31. *Chain Smokers?*

Chain smokers share with drinkers, overeaters, overtalkers, incessant gum-chewers, the honor of constituting the star argument for those who believe that orally regressed people are "greedy" and "wish to get." As usual, externals are deceptive, and all these star witnesses are flops in cross-examination. Under analytical scrutiny, the original and undisputed *infantile* wish to "get" is by no means identical with that of the *adult* neurotic. What lies between is the individual's masochistic elaboration, which, in the clinical picture, leads to the admittedly astounding fact that oral neurotics uncon-sciously use the "wish to get" as inner defense against the superego reproach: "You wish, masochistically, to be refused."

This became clear in the analyses of a long series of chain smokers; it was first apparent in the analysis of a pathological gambler whose wish to lose could be analytically established. He described his chain smoking thus: "Every time I guess wrong at poker, when I am outbluffed or lose, I light up a cigar. It helps for a moment." I asked whether he also felt an impulse to light a fresh cigar every time *he* outsmarted his opponents. He replied: "Definitely not. Smoking means that I have lost. When I have a winning period, I smoke only two cigars in all the time I am playing—one at the beginning of the session, when I can't tell whether I will win or lose, and the other at the end. I call that one my 'cigar of triumph.'" In other words, this gambler would smoke two cigars in three to four hours while winning; when losing, he would consume fifteen to twenty cigars in the same length of time. In terms of his inner defenses, therefore, he could only dispense with his pacifier while supplying proof (in the form of his winnings) of his alibi to the inner conscience: the assertion that he did not want to be refused, but to get (winning). It is interesting to note that he always began the evening with a cigar—clear proof that inwardly he expected to lose.

The conclusions reached in all cases scrutinized read as follows:

Oversmokers all have a similar neurotic substructure. They represent a specific type of psychic masochist who unconsciously wants constantly to be refused. To counteract the superego's reproach, they "prove" that their "real" wish is "to get." The cigarette or cigar, besides its value as an external symbol of their defensive wish to "get," serves as an oral pacifier, reminding the individual of the first reassurance he received in infancy.

PSYCHIC MICROSCOPY

Layer I.   Masochistic solution of the infantile conflict, stabilized on "I wish to be refused."

Layer II.   First superego veto.

Layer III. First defense of unconscious ego: pseudo-aggressive transgression of educational commands.

Layer IV. Second superego veto.

Layer V.   Second defense of unconscious ego: "I don't want to be refused, I just want to get. Besides, I'm only doing something socially accepted—what's wrong with smoking? Don't all adults smoke?" (Ironic lip-service conformity with ego ideal precepts.)—"Conscience money": expectation and fear of organic consequences.

SUMMARY: Oversmoking represents a defense against a defense.

32–33. *Are you a woman-hater or a victim of "cruel women"?*

A very successful industrialist, noted for his original ideas, was hopelessly attached to a schizoid girl. She casually accepted his extravagant gifts, and in return bestowed upon him reproaches which were equally extravagant. To put it figuratively: if a stone fell from a house in China, he—in New York—was held responsible. Despite the outward hopelessness of the situation, the man clung to this "impossible" girl for years. One day, after the most fantastic and humiliating of their scenes (she wanted the industrialist, now her ex-lover, to take her new boy friend into his business), the patient decided to do something drastic: he would remove the life-sized portrait of this girl from his library. "How much can a man take?" he asked me indignantly. I answered: "There is no limit to what a masochist can take. As far as the picture goes, better leave it where it hangs—for the time being; otherwise you will have to tell your handyman to put it up again tomorrow."

In spite of all this, the man cherished the conscious conviction that he hated aggressive women, and that he was their victim. What he really wanted, he was sure, was love, kindness, understanding.

This declaration of good intentions was quite serious. Unfortunately, it was also but a covering cloak for the wish to be mistreated. The whole tragic rigmarole of the wish to be kicked around was in operation. When asked why he had chosen *this* girl, he answered helplessly: "How was I to know?" Well, he knew inwardly.

The case is paradigmatic for the masochist of the success-hunting variety (see #28, this chapter). It also proves how little one knows of people when unfamiliar with *all* the facets of their lives. None of the tycoon's business associates would have suspected that this strong man was but putty in the hands of a "cruel" woman, and that at the end of every scene in his private drama, the curtain came down on the pie in the face.

The other subdivision—the "woman-hater"—is but a few degrees more emotional in denying his masochism (provided no homosexual perversion is involved, see #40, this chapter). In any acutely "humiliating" situation, every "victim of cruel women" is also a "woman-hater," although he reverts to his habitual mechanism sooner or later.

PSYCHIC MICROSCOPY

Layers I to V. The usual five-layer structure is present, beginning with masochistic regression, progressing to pseudo-aggression, and ending with rationalizations and extensive ransom in the form of "conscience money."—"Ironic lip-service conformity with ego ideal precepts"—in the victim type: "Shouldn't one be good to women?"—in the woman-hater: "Shouldn't one protect oneself against danger?"

SUMMARY: Each is a defense against a defense.

34. "Insanely jealous?"

Scrutinizing the centuries for what poets, writers and philosophers have reported of the opinions on jealousy held by "simpleton sages and reasoning fools" (Thomas More), one finds with surprise that the psychological value of this accumulation is exactly nil. There are but three exceptions to this mournful judgment. One of these is Shakespeare's penetrating observation in *Othello* (III, 4):

> But jealous souls will not be answered so;
> They are not even jealous for a cause,
> But jealous for they are jealous: 'tis a monster
> Begot upon itself, born on itself.

Another is La Rochefoucauld's opinion that there is more self-love than love in jealousy. Finally, there is Schleiermacher's dictum: "Jealousy is an emotional hurricane searching with thoroughness for self-torture." *

Psychoanalytically, we know little about this emotion, except for Freud's description of three types of jealousy, which have been confirmed and tested time and again. Almost exclusively, the effect of the considerable literature on the topic is simply that of "repeating backwards and forwards" (Voltaire) that which had already been discovered and subdivided by Freud. His divisions are as follows:

Type I corresponds superficially to the popular notion of wounded

---

* The original authorship of the quotation is unknown and it is usually ascribed to Schleiermacher. In German it reads: "Eifersucht ist eine Leidenschaft, die mit Eifer sucht, was Leiden schafft." Since the original is a pun, this statement of the pastor and philosopher is untranslatable.

pride and self-esteem. The deeper connotation is the revival of the
Oedipal triangle. The jealous man wants to keep out the disturbing
third party—the father of the nursery.

Type II corresponds to a projection of the jealous man's own
desire to be unfaithful. He "feels" that his wife wants to be unfaithful and leave him; in reality he himself (without knowing it consciously) wants to leave her. This explains why the objective innocence of the partner cannot soothe the jealous husband.

Type III has reference to the *negative* Oedipus. The unconsciously passive-feminine man identifies with his wife, and wants
to be seduced by her lover. This unconscious fact is warded off, and
officially the man is furiously jealous.

These types do not, of course, cover all the psychological problems involved in jealousy. For example:

Why is the emotion of jealousy subjectively so much more painful
than the narcissistic injury seemingly warrants?

Why does jealousy, in the majority of cases, imply a "visual
imperative," which forces the afflicted person to imagine the unfaithful partner in a love scene with the rival?

What is the determining factor for the direction of ideas of
revenge: in some cases against the rival, in others against the
unfaithful partner?

What is the aim of jealousy: regaining the beloved, restoring the
lesion in narcissism, or the emotion, per se?

Can the type of jealousy displayed be used as a definite indication
of the type of underlying love?

Does the jealous person want to hide his emotion or display it?

How many unconscious layers are involved? Is jealousy a reaction
to an inner wish, an inner defense mechanism from the start, or
the defense against the defense?

How can one explain cases of suicide, apparently in reaction to
jealousy?

What is the inner connection between jealousy and self-torture?

Why are the "logical deductions," on which the jealous person
bases his case, so flimsy?

Is jealousy "the injured lover's hell" (Milton) or the "jaundice
of the soul" (Dryden), or "cruel as the grave" (the Song of Solomon)?

It is impossible to understand the problem of jealousy without having a clear conception of the unconscious reasons for love. If we are to believe the jealous person, jealousy is but a reaction to love.

Tender (romantic) love consists of an emotion based on *projection of one's own ego ideal on to the beloved*. The beloved has to fulfill two emotional aims. The beloved must correspond to the lover's "type" (infantile repetitions or defenses), thus satisfying infantile wishes, and at the same time serve as an alibi which will aid the lover to immobilize his torturing Daimonion. Daimonion constantly points out to the victim his self-created ego ideal, posing the painful question: "Have you achieved the aims you set for yourself?" By projecting the ego ideal and getting constant confirmation (the beloved sees in the lover the embodiment of all virtues, mostly bestowed on credit), the Daimonion is deprived of his weapon. No discrepancy between ego ideal and ego can now be proved, which accounts for the idyllic state of *guiltlessness* and *megalomania* which characterizes romantic love, especially in its first stages.

This type of love (the *submissive* type) results in the lover's psychic dependence on the beloved. It explains the ridiculous overvaluation of the beloved, and the exclusion of the critical function. In this way, the lover can exorcise his greatest enemies— guilt and depression.

There exists, however, another type of love, in which the lover appears to behave quite differently. Here he plays the role of protective grand seigneur, the beloved becoming a child in need of constant protection. The lover does not look up to the beloved; he makes her dependent on him. He chaperones, cares for, and protects "his baby." This second type, which may be called the *protective* variety of love, has its psychic origin in the same mechanism of projection, with one modification—here the lover projects his *ego* on to the beloved, and intrapsychically assumes the role of his own ego ideal. The roles seem reversed, but the purpose and results are indentical.

What determines the choice of the "submissive" type of love, which is predominant, and what causes the rarer form, that of "protective" love? Basically, this choice depends on the amount of narcissism and guilt resulting from passivity embodied in the act of "submissive" love. This tour de force, to be sure, exorcises the Daimonion, but in the process a submissive-passive state of dependence on the beloved is created. The superego objects to that passivity; in some cases, therefore, it can be observed that weak and narcissistic people follow a "submissive" attachment with a "protective" one. A pertinent example can be found in the life of the poet Heinrich Heine.

At an early age, Heine fell in love with the daughter of his wealthy uncle. The result of this attachment, as he put it, was "a stab in the heart." The wealthy girl took no notice of her indigent cousin. Later in life, Heine married a Parisian grisette, an uneducated and primitive girl. She was truly Heine's "creation." He sent her to school, tried to make a lady of her, and even gave her a new name, calling her Mathilde when her real name was Crescentia. Unconsciously, Heine had reversed his roles. In his first love affair, he was the poor boy shabbily treated by a "queen"; in his marriage, he was the protective grand seigneur.* But the masochistic wishes he was attemping to oust were smuggled in nevertheless: Mathilde tortured and mistreated him soundly.†

A man must be quite sure of himself to be capable of "submissive" love without suffering the penalty of superego reproaches on the score of passivity. The "protective" type of love is the inner choice of the weak man. To counteract his passivity, he must act the super he-man even in love, as a defense.

What happens when either of these types is confronted with waning love or unfaithfulness on the part of the projected ego ideal, the beloved (or the projected ego, as the case may be)?

Before the lover becomes conscious of his jealousy, the ground must be fertile for its appearance. Jealousy does *not* begin with the beloved's behavior, but with an intrapsychic battle raging in the lover's unconscious.

It is true that Daimonion has been rendered helpless by the lover's "unconscious trick" of projecting either the ego ideal or the ego, depending on the type of love. Daimonion recovers quickly,

---

* A magic gesture was involved: outwardly, he demonstrated his alleged wish to be treated kindly; inwardly, he wanted exactly the opposite—masochistic mistreatment. The magic gesture was a defense concealing psychic masochism.

† In a letter written to a friend at this period, Heine reported on the progress of his educational program for Mathilde, announcing that she no longer tortured him in the daytime, but only in his dreams.

however, and re-enters the battle by pointing out all the big and little defects of the beloved. By contrasting fantasy with reality, it tries to regain the driver's seat, temporarily lost.

In addition, the lover is constantly doubting whether his hoax has really been successful in outsmarting Daimonion. The human psyche seems to be so constituted that it cannot even trust its own slave revolt against the inner tormenter.

Putting both together—Diamonion's attempts to regain its position, and the lover's doubt that he has dethroned Daimonion in the first place—and one has in a nutshell the basis for jealousy.

Jealousy is the surface expression of the inner conflict in which Daimonion desperately attempts to regain its role of terrorizer, and the unconscious ego doubts its own ability to summon sufficient strength to maintain its slave revolt. To make matters worse, Daimonion's victory is a foregone conclusion once the unconscious ego begins to doubt its own strength. For in jealousy, the victim **is the dupe** of the counter-revolution following the ego's revolt.

This explains why the grounds for jealousy are so flimsy.

> Trifles light as air
> Are to the jealous confirmation strong
> As proofs of Holy Writ,

said Shakespeare in *Othello* (III, 323).

One gathers the impression that in jealousy—the phase of Daimonion's imminent restoration to power—Daimonion gains additional pleasure from applying a sort of poetic justice. The beloved was chosen on "flimsy grounds"—in retaliation the grounds for breaking up the slave revolt are equally flimsy. Daimonion is ironic as well as revengeful at this point.

Jealousy is so painful an emotion because it telegraphs the imminent loss of the greatest of intrapsychic battles: the victim's own narcissism, accumulated in the ego ideal, lets him down. The lover is of course not conscious that he has dug his own grave. He is equally ignorant of the fact that he is not struggling to regain his beloved but to maintain his freedom from inner guilt. By playing Daimonion's game, and believing "trifles" and "little signs" which are actually means of trapping him into jealousy, he loses that very freedom he has been fighting for.

Jealousy is the last hopeless engagement in an inner revolution, which is about to be put down. The "fifth column" operated within the lover himself, in some cases driving him to suicide.

According to the type of love—the "submissive" or the "protective"—the last convulsions of freedom, known as jealousy, will differ. In these last convulsions the lover will attack either the "unfaithful" beloved, or the intruding third party, the competitor.

The "submissive" type of lover will inevitably attack the standard-bearer of his own ego ideal, the beloved. Instead of rebelling against Daimonion, his real torturer, he attacks his potential unconscious ally, accusing it of collaboration with the enemy.

The "protective" type of lover will invariably attack, not the beloved, but the rival. He will consider the beloved the innocent victim of the rival's "seduction."

Compressed into a brief table, the formula for both sexes reads:

Subdivision of Jealousy after "type" of love	Male	Female
"Submissive" lover	Aggressive against woman.	Aggressive against man.
"Protective" lover	Aggressive against rival.	Aggressive against rival.

Either the man or woman of the "submissive" type, therefore, will be jealous of and aggressive against the person of the *opposite* sex. Vice versa, the "protective" type of either sex will be jealous of and aggressive against the person of the *same* sex.

One can, therefore, deduce the underlying *love-type* from the *type of jealousy* shown.

The technique of jealousy, in both types, presupposes two strong components: increased voyeurism and increased psychic masochism.

The voyeurism component is so apparent that its virtual absence from our literature is surprising. The simple description furnishes the clue: every jealous person, regardless of sex, admits that what tortures him most is the *visualization* of love-scenes between the beloved and the alleged rival. That "visual imperative" is something forbidden, as can be seen from the fact that the jealous person is not consciously aware that he enjoys it. On the contrary, he allows himself these fantasies only under the protection of defensive fury and self-torture.

The forbidden element in peeping arises from the infantile unconscious connotation of sexual voyeurism, *plus* the unconscious identification with the unfaithful beloved. In this way the jealous man enjoys feminine, and the jealous woman masculine repressed tendencies. The whole procedure is saturated with masochistic "gravy."

The voyeuristic component accounts for another peculiarity in jealousy: the initial tendency to hide the emotion, and the later urge to display it in a plea for sympathy and commiseration. Once more poets have misrepresented the facts. For example, Byron says in *Don Juan*:

> Yet he was jealous, although he did not know it.
> For jealousy dislikes the world to know it.

This observation pertains exclusively to the initial stages of jealousy, where voyeurism is unconsciously activated and enjoyed in the "visual imperative." Later, when guilt is mobilized because of peeping, voyeurism is transformed into exhibitionism and self-display (open discussions, pleas for pity, "spilling it all" in divorce proceedings, etc.).

Jealousy is an internal episode in the battle of the conscience. It has little to do with the beloved per se, and uses the latter as a screen upon which unconscious conflicts can be reeled off. The appearance of jealousy presupposes the existence of strong repressed masochistic and voyeuristic tendencies, and is evidence of the weakness of the individual's normal narcissism. Clinically, therefore, it is not correct to say that *every* lover is jealous, as poets and prophets claim:

> No true love there can be without
> Its dread penalty—jealousy.
> (Owen Meredith, Lucille)
> He that is not jealous is not in love.
> (St. Augustine)

So far we have dealt with the jealousy of relatively "normal" persons. The problem changes when we enter the neurotic scene. Neurotics are incapable of the "slave revolt" of love, and use transference as a vehicle. They reenact infantile conflicts, are far more masochistically tinged than so-called "normal" people, and "suffer" more extensively.

Neurotic jealousy is encountered on every level of regression, hence is possible in *every* neurosis. Every neurotic conflict is intimately bound up with psychic masochism, and jealousy is an excellent vehicle of expression for that tendency. At bottom every neurotic is an injustice collector; his booty is a series of imaginary, often unconsciously self-created, wrongs. *One* of the many possibilities of deposition is jealousy. Of course, the *general* tendency to cash in on injustices does not explain the *specific* use of jealousy as an outlet. Here a variety of individual determinants enters the picture.

PSYCHIC MICROSCOPY

Layer I.   Having temporarily won the upper hand by eliminating guilt through projection of the ego ideal (the superego's instrument of torture), the lover dwells upon his happiness, consciously and also in fantasy (voyeurism).

Layer II. First superego reproach, pointing out in petty ways the beloved's faults, as well as flimsy evidence of alleged unfaithfulness; the veto is also directed against voyeurism.

Layer III. First defense of the unconscious ego: pseudo-aggression directed against the object of love or rival, depending on type of love; voyeurism changed into *painful* observation, partly shortchanged into exhibitionism.

Layer IV. Second superego reproach; ironic disbelief, and veto also directed against scopophiliac elements.

Layer V. Second defense of unconscious ego: self-torture and humiliation; exhibitionism in the form of a search for indignant allies; "Conscience money" paid in the form of torture, and enduring the ridicule of the environment; mockery of ego ideal by clinging to the precept: "I want to be loved exclusively."

SUMMARY: Jealousy is a defense against a defense.

35. *Are you a "killjoy"?*

Webster defines the killjoy as "one given to gloomy moods; a person of sullen disposition." Popularly, however, a killjoy is a "sourpuss," who gets a gloomy pleasure out of casting a pall over another's mood exactly when he wants to enjoy himself. The German equivalent to "killjoy" comes nearer to the popular concept: "Speilverderber" means a spoiler of games.

In the first definition, the accent is on the killjoy's gloomy disposition, in the second on the pleasure he derives from spoiling other people's "fun." Webster views the killjoy as the victim of his unhappy disposition, while the popular view of him is of a pleasure-hunter of a specific type with, it is admitted, a gloomy disposition. Whether the killjoy is a misanthrope first, and extractor of his peculiar brand of pleasure second (because no other pleasures are open to him), or seeker-of-peculiar-pleasure first and misanthrope second, is not made clear.

In clinical psychoanalysis we are frequently confronted with neurotics classified as killjoys by their environment. In this diagnosis, however, the killjoy never concurs. At most, he will complain that he is depressed and cannot participate in the conventional pleasures of his friends and acquaintances. What prevents the killjoy from assessing himself correctly?

Here are a few comments from close associates of the killjoy. Mrs. E: "My husband is a chronic spoiler of harmless fun. He has a peculiar ability to freeze people. He uses two tricks: either he is silent—and I mean he goes in for 'stony' silences—when other people try to joke and have some fun, or he makes derogatory and biting remarks about the fun proposed and enjoyed by others. The strange thing is that he doesn't seem to be aware of his frigidaire attitude. If I reproach him, he answers that he was perfectly amiable."—Mrs. F: "My husband knows only one form of conversation with people—to hear himself talk. Who can stand that? Somewhere I read a humorous definition of conversation—a vocal competition in which the person who is catching his breath is called the listener. Which is very accurate—everyone wants to talk, and everyone resents having one person monopolize the floor. What makes it worse is that my husband is interested in just a few topics. For a long time it was impossible for me to convince him that he bores people, is intolerant, and a killjoy. Finally he became cynical whenever we had these arguments, and now he quotes Disraeli: 'If I want to read a book, I write one.' He claims that he can endure people only on condition that he does all the talking."—Mr. G:

"My wife is a snob who intimidates people. She doesn't know it, but she runs around with that Queen Victoria look on her face: 'We are not amused.' She misuses my social position to be arrogant, and this directly damages me. People think I'm insincere in my friendliness to my staff—they think, wrongly, that this is just a pose, or how could I have married a woman who is cold, bored, and a killjoy?"

Descriptively, here are the characteristics common to the killjoy attitude:

(a) The killjoy is not conscious of being one.
(b) He does not have the amiable sense of humor built on the principle: live and let live.
(c) He has at his command a biting irony which he directs against people who have any kind of harmless fun.
(d) Characterologically, he impresses the observer as a depressed person.
(e) The killjoy seems to derive some surreptitious pleasure from "freezing" other people either by pointing out, in a derogatory way, the low level of their fun, or by conspicuously failing to laugh at their jokes.
(f) He gives the impression of a stern and disgusted governess, confronted with a bunch of silly children.

These six descriptive signs correspond to a complicated unconscious substructure. The killjoy is actually performing a "negative magic gesture," (see #6, this chapter) on the basis of the following layers of unconscious attack and defense:

Layer I.   Confronted with "fun," experienced by other people, the neurotic of this type is painfully reminded of real or fancied disappointments reaching back to the time when he wanted to have some "fun in the nursery." That pleasure, in his opinion, was inhibited by the upbringer. Instead of compensating for infantile frustrations later in life—the technique of the "normal" person—he repeats the disappointment; secondarily, the psychic masochism acquires the validity of an unconscious wish.

Layer II.   First veto of superego.

Layer III. Under pressure of guilt, the unconscious ego installs its first defense: "I don't want to be mistreated; I hate the disappointer."

Layer IV. Second veto of superego.

Layer V. Secondary defense is installed, according to the formula: "I want to show them (the authorities of the nursery) how badly they treated me."

The fifth layer constitutes the "negative magic gesture."

This deduction explains a series of contradictions in the killjoy's behavior. For example:

The killjoy does not know he is one because his aggressive behavior corresponds to the vetoed layer III of the genetic structure. The killjoy, who tries to inject into his behavior as much aggression as he can command, must at the same time disguise his aggression, since it has been forbidden by the inner conscience. Inwardly, he emphasizes that aggression, because it disguises the more deeply repressed basic conflict: psychic masochism. Analytically that aggression is but defensive pseudo-aggression.

It also explains why the killjoy cannot be amiable, and tolerant of other people's humor. Intrapsychically, his is the role of the malicious, fun-forbidding educator—"he acts like a stern and disgusted governess"—played either "straight," or in caricature. The more humorless he is, the graver is his accusation against an infantile image.

Finally, it clarifies his obvious depression: the psychic masochist is consciously the most miserable of human beings, mostly for the purpose of furnishing an inner alibi.

The killjoy is a specific type of neurotic, the opposite of a "good sport." He is not born a killjoy, but made into one by his neurosis. The process, therefore can be therapeutically reversed. It is possible to change this bitter, hardly endurable, neurotic into a human being.

Examined with the analytic microscope, the killjoy is seen unconsciously dramatizing a complicated double inner alibi for the benefit of conscience. Once more, the "real self" is not visible, even in this disagreeable fellow.

PSYCHIC MICROSCOPY

Layers I to V. See above. "Ironic lip-service conformity with ego ideal precepts" via caricaturistic reversal of adults' attitudes towards "childish" waste of time, and also via mocking adoption of disgusted facial expressions on such occasions. "Conscience money" paid in dreariness and in rejection by environment.

SUMMARY: The killjoy dramatizes a defense against a defense.

36. Are you a chronic "Divorce-ionist"?

Divorce is considered an inalienable right by some people; deplored by others; regretted by all. Teaching, preaching, moralizing against divorce continue; the real futility of the procedure is seldom, if ever, stressed. These are the facts so consistently overlooked:

(a) Divorce is not a solution, but an involuntary admission of inability to master a psychic conflict.

(b) This psychic conflict is unconsciously self-chosen; there are no innocent victims in the marital graveyard.

(c) It takes *two* people to make a divorce: each of the participants in a sick marriage chose the other because—unconsciously— two interlocked neuroses met; one partner supplies the neurotic needs of the other.

(d) There is constant confusion between correcting a mistaken choice—which can happen to every "healthy" person—and *chronic* divorce, in which the individual neurotic pattern is repeated again and again.*

(e) Since this is the case, changing one's marriage partner does not solve the inner conflict: the mate can be divorced, but not the neurosis.

(f) The practical conclusion: before running to the nearest divorce lawyer, run to the nearest psychiatrist.

Theroretically, the most amazing feature of this entire situation is the fact that divorce is merely the technical-legal term for an alibi presented to the inner conscience.

* This confusion once led to an amusing misunderstanding. The program director of a television station invited me to participate in a panel discussion of divorce. They had already secured two people who advocated changing the New York divorce laws, and were looking for someone to defend the present laws. "What gave you the idea that I'm the man you're looking for?" I asked.—"Well, didn't you write a book, *Divorce Won't Help?*"—"You seem to be a title reader; the full meaning of the title is *Divorce Won't Help—NEUROTICS.*"

The raison d'etre of a neurotic marriage is the opportunity it offers for the fulfillment of neurotic wishes through the re-enactment of the infantile conflict. But this inner pleasure is vetoed by the superego, necessitating a defensive alibi in the form of *conscious* unhappiness. For a time, the surface impression of misery is convincing enough to serve as a denial of unconscious pleasure. When the superego renews its inevitable attack, the alibi must be reinforced, first with more intense conscious misery, and later with the last desperate argument: Reno. When the "I can't stand it any longer" stage is reached, it is a sure indication that the superego can no longer be appeased with half-measures.

One of the familiar cliches of the newly-divorced is: "Now I'm free—I can start all over." This mirrors another unconscious purpose of neurotic divorce: the opportunity to repeat the infantile conflict with a new partner. In neurosis, retention of the unconscious pattern is decisive; the individual used to re-enact the pattern is much less important.

In unconscious reality, divorce is no more than a strategic retreat, decided upon when inner tension becomes too great, and the inner alibi position untenable. The earnest confidence of the newly-divorced who declare that they are now "through" with their "mistakes" is entirely misplaced; *the inner maneuver is aimed at perpetuating, not overcoming, the neurotic pattern.* The next marriage is again a *conscious* fiasco, for experience has no effect on the unconscious feelings which govern emotional life.

On the unconscious level, divorce is resorted to when *too much unconscious masochistic pleasure* has been experienced; this brings the anti-libidinous superego out on the warpath, and the forbidden pleasures must be temporarily relinquished. Since it is a retreat and not a surrender, remarriage sees a repetition of the identical tactics: achievement of neurotic pleasure, paid for by ever-increasing conscious suffering; superego reproaches, and more and more desperate alibis.

In some not very typical cases, the second marriage is "successful," for complicated reasons. In these exceptions, the new mate represents a "change of type"; a domineering first husband is followed by a shy, weak one, a clinging-vine first wife is followed by a brisk and confident second. This is not common sense at work, but a switch in the unconscous alibi, necessitated by the intense torture of the superego. The alibi reads: "I can prove I'm innocent; I don't want what you accuse me of wanting, but exactly the opposite." Unfortunately, the alibi carries with it the penalty of conscious boredom.

It is impossible for me to reproduce in a few lines the contents of three books and numerous papers dealing with the problem.

PSYCHIC MICROSCOPY

Layer I.   Individual neurotic solution of the infantile conflict.
Layer II.   First superego veto.
Layer III. First defense of the unconscious ego: "I'm in love." Under this disguise, the specific conflict is repeated.
Layer IV. Second superego veto.
Layer V.   Second defense of the unconscious ego, presented in two installments: Part I—unhappiness; Part II—divorce, hence denial of neurotic pleasures. "Ironic lip-service conformity with ego ideal precepts": "Shouldn't one get out of an impossible situation?"—"Conscience money" paid in real emotional and financial troubles, plus suspicion (and sometimes rejection) on the part of the environment.
Summary: A chronic divorce-ionist works on the basis of a defense against a defense.

37. A "Wolf"?

The "all-conquering" wolf is an especially apt choice for demonstration of the thesis of *double* inner defenses. Superficially this roving player of "one-night stands" tries to impress his environment and himself with his superior technique of enjoying life via sex: variety is trump. Analyzed, the wolf is revealed as an exquisite *seeker of disappointment,* with a no less exquisite *method of concealing his psychic impotence.* To avoid having his impotence denounced and noised about, the wolf employs a convenient unconscious preventive defense mechanism: unconsciously he anticipates the inevitable fiasco and runs away ("leaves her") after a short time.

Thus masochism plus prevenire of impotence spells *"wolf".*

Superficially, of course, one finds masks pertaining both to the positive and negative Oedipus. (The latter is frequently confused with unconscious homosexuality; see #40, this chapter.) Deeper probing reveals the inner wish to be disappointed—promptly, every woman fulfills this wish. Considering the "material" at the wolf's disposal, it is not surprising that this proof should be so readily forthcoming, for his victims are *frigid* women who believe that the "professional" will succeed where the "amateur" failed. Once more, the cheated cheaters are drawn to one another. Nothing infuriates a wolf more than the statement that he did not "conquer" the woman, but was merely used as an aphrodisiac by her, and discarded as bad medicine. When the wolf's pseudo-aggression is not fed, the fallen wolf becomes visible, and this part of him is the opposite of heroic.

PSYCHIC MICROSCOPY

Layer I.   Masochistic stabilization on the refusal level.
Layer II. First superego veto.
Layer III. First defense of unconscious ego: pseudo-aggression, Oedipal rescue station (especially negative Oedipus).
Layer IV. Second superego veto.
Layer V.   Second defense of unconscious ego: blame for lesser crime accepted with rationalizations of pseudo-superiority; technique of preventive defense mechanism (see above). "Ironic lip-service conformity with ego ideal precepts": see mechanism of cynicism, #4, this chapter.—"Conscience money": every woman "disappoints" the wolf; he suffers from social disadvantages, slightly counterbalanced by admiration of would-be-wolves.
SUMMARY: The "wolf" is a rather grotesque product of a defense against a defense.

38. *A garconne and "she-wolf"?*

The female counterpart of the wolf, the garconne, is typically frigid, although she lives her sex life on the basis of "sex on my own terms." She promiscuously uses passive-feminine men, whom she inwardly despises, or (more frequently) falls for the wolf, who kicks her by "leaving" her, thus supplying her needed dose of masochism. Frequently, there is a race to see who "disappoints," and therefore leaves whom first.

The psychic microscopy is, mutatis mutandis, identical with that of the wolf, plus the strong wish to "castrate" the man.

SUMMARY: A defense against a defense.

39. *Are you an adherent to the finality of the phrase, "I said I'm sorry, didn't I?"*

A blocked writer, a woman of great potential abilities and high intelligence (who with the greatest regularity used her mental capacities against, not pro, herself and analysis) told me of an incident in her daughter's New York kindergarten. A girl displayed an orange which her father had picked in Florida and sent to her; a boy snatched the orange from her and ate it; when the boy brought another orange to school the next day and offered it as restitution, the injured party refused to accept the settlement. My patient concluded: "Full restitution is impossible; the sentimental value of the original is missing."

Observe your own reactions in the crowded subway when someone steps on your big toe, turns around, and says "Sorry." You are caught in a quandary. Your adult, cultured self must accept the spoken apology as full compensation. Your infantile, less cultured self is furious, and would like to kick the offender. This is only one horn of the dilemma; the other is even more disagreeable. If you dare make a disparaging remark ("Why don't you keep your big feet to yourself?"), the offender acts as if you had transgressed the most elementary rules of civilized conduct: "I said I'm sorry, didn't I?"

Here the matter rests, on the Procrustean bed of convention.

The magic formula of restitution in minor offenses ("Sorry") seems to be based on an exchange mechanism. A small amount of narcissistic humiliation, included in the formula, is offered as full payment for the injury. The formula is necessary; without it people would hit, kick, and knock one another about constantly. Acceptance of the apology may be more or less graceful (although suppressed anger is always discernible); on the other hand, one may encounter inability to accept such an apology at all. What makes for the difference?

The difference is based on the urgent inner necessity—or the absence of that propelling need—to collect injustices. In the former case, the real injustice is part and parcel of the inner personality structure, which is fed on injustices; in the latter case, the propelling need is not felt, and consequently small or unavoidable injustices are shrugged off, minimized, evaluated as nuisances. In short, the identical injustice is intrapsychically elaborated in different ways.

It follows that these injustice collectors magnify trifles, not because these trifles are important per se, but because they fit only too well into the constant inner need to prove to one's own inner conscience that one is but the "innocent victim" of some other person's "meanness."

This tendency to alibi oneself goes so far that even inanimate objects are utilized for that purpose.

A patient lived on Fifth Avenue, in the eighties. He would go from his home to my office on Central Park West (and also in the eighties) by walking in the Park for a while, and then crossing to the West side. Since the efficacy of treatment was uncertain "in his mind," as he informed me ironically, he wanted to get "something tangible" out of his visits; this certain advantage consisted of the benefit to his digestion conferred by the walk. Tactfully, I reminded the industrialist that his time was valuable, and that by walking to his appointment he was "throwing good money after bad," echoing one of his favorite phrases. In spite of his "refreshing walk," he would regularly arrive at my office in a depressed mood. One day he told me his reasons: time and again he would get to the corner of 85th Street and Central Park West (the corner opposite my office) at the moment when the green light changed, thus forcing him to wait a full minute before he could cross.

"Do you assume that there is a conspiracy of traffic lights against you?"

"I wouldn't go so far," answered the man, also ironically. "I just take it as a sign of how everything works out against me."

"A bad omen?"

"Don't be flippant. I would say, rather, a confirmation of my pessimism."

"Isn't it interesting that you are overlooking, changing, even distorting facts to suit your purpose?"

"Prove it."

"That's simple enough. First, you overlooked the fact that the light at the corner is timed for half a minute on green, and a full minute on red. There is a good reason for this: automobile traffic is heavy, pedestrian crossings are light. What you believe to be a

bad omen now reduces itself to the greater probability of arriving
at the corner while there is a red light."

The patient exclaimed with some excitement: "You are misin-
formed, it is a fifty-fifty proposition! How do you know that it isn't?"

"Because I observed the same phenomenon, and looked at my
watch."

"Don't believe it."

"Just use your watch. That was a fact you overlooked; here is one
that you changed to suit your a priori deduction. If you remember,
there is a little hill at exactly this corner of the park. To get to
the street level one must go downhill. Approximately fifty feet
before reaching the pavement, the traffic light comes into view.
By regulating one's own speed, therefore, one can 'regulate' the
arrival at the light. Is this also my fantasy?"

"Never observed it. It's true that one goes downhill. The light
should be visible."

"Now for point three: you distorted facts by omitting the first
and second observations only so that you could prove what you
were out to prove, that 'everything is against you.' Not to mention
the fact that pedestrians in New York pay little attention to lights,
and are always crossing when the light is against them. But you
stand at the corner like Lot's wife—a statue. To sum up: do you
call all these omissions the objective evaluation of facts?"

"I have to check on your facts."

This the patient did, after which he had to admit to the accuracy
of my statements. Next time, he shifted to some other "proof," more
or less on the same level. A psychic masochist can only lose, since
losing is his inner aim.

After the injustice collector has by hook or by crook (and mostly
by some mental sleight of hand) constructed the much needed
assurance that the projected "bad mother" of his infancy is mean,
the typical mood is one of self-pity. There exists but one exception:
some of these neurotics show a rather *ironic-sarcastic complacency,*
as if saying: "I knew all along that I'd be on the receiving end."

One such patient explained his mood by adducing a wornout
joke: on his deathbed, an old man describes to his sons the disappointments of his disappointing life; he concludes his recital by
saying: "I would laugh if things are no better on the other side."

In short, these people behave as if a race in prediction not in psychic masochism, were involved: although they end up behind the eight-ball, they knew it before the game started. *They seemingly accept defeat,* but only on condition that they *predicted* the defeat beforehand.

The ordinary masochistic technique is enlarged on by these neurotic pessimists (see #8-9-10, this chapter), who experience the additional, megalomaniacal pleasure of being a good prophet.

Still another subdivision of psychic masochist is the type which indulges in "preventive pessimism." Here Fate (the inner conscience) is appeased by the expression of a pessimistic prognostication which is not seriously meant.

In the case of the industrialist victimized by traffic lights we see a combination of both elements (though only in an innuendo). At first he behaved like an innocent victim, although he had skillfully created the victimization himself. At certain times (e.g., while describing the incident to me), he claimed that he took the "misfortune" as proof that everything he touched turned against him. If he had ironically told this to himself, he would have acted like a typical neurotic pessimist.

The psychology of the phrase, "I said I'm sorry, didn't I?" reduces itself to a magic pronouncement, which tells the victim: "You have to stick to your own hypocritical rules, even if you don't believe in them." At the same time, it includes *unconscious irony directed at parental authorities,* from whom the child learned the conventional rules of civilized "restitution." That the "sentimental" damage allows for no restitution is exactly the masochistic complaint of the child. It is as though the "coldness" of the adult toward the child were embalmed in the magical phrase.

PSYCHIC MICROSCOPY

Layer I.   Masochistic end result of infantile conflict.

Layer II. First superego reproach.

Layer III. First defense of unconscious ego: pseudo-aggressive transgression of educational rules.

Layer IV. Second superego veto.

Layer V.   Second defense of unconscious ego; including also "Ironic lip-service conformity with ego ideal precepts": "Well, I stuck to your rules, didn't I—if they're empty and cold and meaningless that's no fault of mine."

SUMMARY: A defense against a defense.

40. *A homosexual?*

Genetically, a male homosexual is the product of vicissitudes of his unresolved "breast complex" (oral regression), stemming from early babyhood. His sexual philosophy is a compendium of rationalizations; he believes himself a member of humanity's elite, prides himself on hating and rejecting "stupid" women, delights in being "different" and "special"—so special that the ordinary run of humanity persecutes him.

The facts are slightly different. At the crossroads of weaning time, when it was necessary to accept or not to accept the loss of the breast (bottle), the future homosexual did *not* resort to the usual way out of the universal dilemma: he did *not* disparage the feminine nutritional apparatus via "unconscious repetition compulsion." The male infant who later becomes the heterosexual adult "discovers" in his penis a substitute for the withdrawn breast, and narcissism is triumphant. Actively repeating passively endured experiences, the boy—once *passive* recipient of milk—becomes the *active* bestower of urine (later sperm); in intercourse, as an adult, he plays the role of "giving mother," reducing the woman to the passive image of himself as a baby. With reason *he* calls *her* "baby."

The future homosexual goes along for part of the way. He, too, identifies breast and penis. But his narcissistic wound is deeper, and inwardly, as a result, he dissociates himself from the disappointing sex—woman. In his adult sexual life, the homosexual pursues the "reduplication of his own defense mechanism"—man's penis (unconsciously, his own).

The frequently observable imitation of women, which leads to the no less frequent, and false, concept that the homosexual is an "effeminate man," is but "taking the blame for the lesser crime"— the homosexual's inner defense. The differences between the homosexual and the "effeminate" man can be schematized as follows:

	Perversion Homosexuality	Spurious Homosexuality
1. Level of regression.	Oral.	Hysteric (negative Oedipus).
2. Ego-reaction to homosexuality.	Conscious acceptance, with or without conscious guilt.	Conscious rejection, sometimes self-suspicion of homosexual "tendencies."

3. Unconscious identification.	Leading: either with pre-Oedipal mother (active partner), or with baby (passive partner). Misleading: either with Oedipal husband (active) or with wife (passive).	Leading: with passive mother of Oedipal period. Misleading: with hyper he-man.
4. Characterologic signs.	"Triad of orality," injustice collecting. Specific signs: unreliability, instability.	Two types: either hysterical personality with compensatory hyper he-man attitude, or weak Milquetoast-type, also hysterical. Ego: correctly functioning.
5. Relation to women.	Rejection.	Woman-chaser or shy, with alternating periods of hyperpotency, easily collapsing, or weak potency of the Milquetoast type; both often impotent.
6. Narcissism.	Megalomaniacal-compensatory.	Overcompensatory; hysterical.
7. Transition.	There is no transition between the two diseases.	
8. "Latent form."	Consciousness of perversion in early twenties, often earlier.	Lifelong.
9. Original drive or defense.	99.9 per cent of all cases neurotic. Exception: hormonal disturbance.	Exclusively defense-mechanism.
10. Curability.	Majority shun treatment. Persons who ask for treatment have favorable prognoses; specific prerequisites are indispensable. (See "Eight Pre-Requisites, etc." cited in bibliography.)	These persons ask for treatment because of potency disturbance. Prognoses are favorable.

What the homosexual is really acting out is the passive baby and the active, pre-Oedipal mother. These roles are both separated and intermingled. Without adducing the duality—masochistic oral regression *and* the mechanism of "reduplication of one's own defense"—the homosexual is incomprehensible.

Homosexuality is not a unit, and it comprises markedly different pictures, elaborated on in *Neurotic Counterfeit-Sex*.

PSYCHIC MICROSCOPY

Layer I.   Masochistic solution of the relation to the pre-Oedipal mother.

Layer II.   First superego veto.

Layer III. First defense of the unconscious ego: pseudo-aggression towards mother, disparagement of her, claim of self-sufficiency.

Layer IV.   Second veto of superego.

Layer V.   Second defense of the unconscious ego: denial of self-concentration, acceptance of the self-substitute (reduplication of one's own defense mechanism—pursuit of the partner's penis), unconscious feminine identification as Oedipal blind (taking the blame for the lesser crime); "Ironic lip-service conformity with ego ideal precepts": "Shouldn't one be self-sufficient and discontinue attachments which prove detrimental?"— "Conscience money" paid in social ostracism, danger of detection, etc., plus the whole gamut of the result of the "mechanism of orality."

SUMMARY: A male homosexual works intrapsychically on the basis of a defense against a defense.

41. *A Lesbian?*

Except for two distinguishing marks, the psychological setting of the Lesbian is unconsciously identical with that of the male homosexual:

(a) In the absence of the penis, the consoling fantasy of self-sufficiency, and the negation of nutritional dependence on the mother can be upheld only for a short time, via identification of nipple with clitoris, urine with milk.

(b) Thus being deprived of the possibility of instituting the double defense of "fleeing to another continent" (exchange of sex) and "reduplication of one's own defense mechanism" (penis of male partner, unconsciously equalling one's own reassuring penis), Lesbians achieve their tour de force by putting up with the disappointing sex—woman. To do so, they must repress both the masochistic attachment and the pseudo-aggressive defense.

Once more, the Oedipal game of husband and wife, purporting to indicate the Lesbian's masculine identification, is merely a defensive blind. It contributes as little to the clarification of the Lesbian's unconscious processes as feminine identification does in the case of the male homosexual. How does it explain the "passive" homosexual woman, or the "active" homosexual male? What is really going on behind this defensive screen is the eternal game of the passive baby and the active pre-Oedipal mother.

PSYCHIC MICROSCOPY

Layer I.   Masochistic attachment to the pre-Oedipal mother.
Layer II. First veto of the superego.
Layer III. First defense of the unconscious ego: pseudo-aggression against the mother; attempt to disparage her through very transitory claims of self-sufficiency.
Layer IV. Second veto of superego.
Layer V.   Second defense of the unconscious ego: denial of self-sufficiency (narcissism); acceptance of the image of the *mother* substitute as "love object"; in some cases masculine identification as Oedipal blind. "Ironic lip-service conformity with ego ideal precepts"—"Shouldn't one love mother at *any* cost?" "Conscience money" paid in practical disadvantages of the perversion, plus all the troubles engendered by the "mechanism of orality."

SUMMARY: A Lesbian lives, unconsciously, on the basis of a defense against a defense.

42-43. *Do men call you a "golddigger"? Do women call you a "playboy"?*

Superficially, the golddigger and her masculine version, the playboy, are emotional cripples whose looks are their stock in trade. Unconsciously, they are both orally regressed injustice collectors, desperately trying to convince their superegos and themselves of two things: that they are above "emotional nonsense" and therefore have no scruples in selling their genitals to the highest bidder in exchange for money or social position; and that they will be "perfectly happy" once they have cashed in on penthouse, mink coat and luxury, or the equivalent masculine rake-off.

The fiasco follows immediately. Having gained the objective, both playboy and golddigger discover that something is missing: they are bored, restless, and on the lookout for adventure—which will of course endanger their newlywon "security." Selling out the "commodity" sex leaves these emotionally icy people only cash or cash equivalents; they treat their generous mates with aggression and contempt. Invariably, a boy (or girl) friend is found upon whom the game can be acted out in reverse, and the golddigger-playboy becomes the masochistic victim of the "torturing" companion. In these relationships, these neurotics allow themselves to be financially exploited and emotionally mistreated. And this leads to a hopeless conscious conflict, for their opinion of themselves as "smart operators" is hopelessly shattered.

The "money neurosis," as outward expression of the oral regression, results in this dichotomy of the "two-step technique": cruelty towards the legalized (or "official") provider, and masochistic submission to the self-chosen "torturing" boy friend (or girl friend). Typically, neither golddigger nor playboy ever realize that the tables have been ironically turned—at the prompting of their superegos. They consider their conduct towards the official provider quite normal: the world owes them a luxurious living, work is for idiots, the "smart" ones know the ropes and—what's more—pull them. When the third act rolls around and the final reckoning is due (with hair down and pretenses ripped off), what remains is a deeply depressed injustice collector who cannot be appeased by any of the things he (or she) consciously yearns for: every gift is succeeded by a new demand, and so on ad infinitum.

One question has been left unanswered: the specificity of financial sponging. There are many ways of elaborating on a masochistic conflict; why does the golddigger, in addition to the turn-the-tables technique, also resort to a second elaboration—the financial exploitation of the mate?

With monotonous regularity, in dozens of analyses of golddiggers and playboys, I have found this infantile elaboration: whether justifiably or not, the child had felt unjustly treated (exaggerated demands of the child in a normally busy household have the same effect as genuine rejection of a child, since neurosis is an elaboration of infantile fantasy and not a copy of reality), and had become stabilized on the masochistic level. The same child who unconsciously accused his mother of coldness nevertheless witnessed excited quarrels connected with money. The inner conclusion drawn by the child was that his mother (father) had feelings —but only about money. Thus money became a weapon in the battle of feelings, and in later life this inference led to the formula: "I shall take away what you love most: money."

PSYCHIC MICROSCOPY

Layer I.   Masochistic stabilization on the rejection level as end result of the infantile conflict.

Layer II. First veto of the superego.

Layer III. First defense of the unconscious ego: pseudo-aggression, irony, depreciation of all feelings.

Layer IV. Second veto of superego.

Layer V. Second defense of the unconscious ego: cynical appraisal of reality maintained under "smart safeguard": "There is nothing more to it than selling what suckers want to buy" (sex), plus "The suckers like it." Typical "accidental" involvement with "mistreating" extra-marital companion, from which is derived full share of the end result of injustice collecting—"Ironic lip-service conformity with ego ideal precepts": "Didn't you say that money is important?"—"Conscience money" paid in form of dissatisfaction, depression, endangering and frequently shattering the unconscious aim by means of the "two-step technique."

SUMMARY: Golddigger and playboy alike operate on the basis of a defense against a defense.

44. *Are you a mystery fan?*

Hundreds of dissertations have been written to explain the popularity of mystery and detective stories, which began (on a large scale) with the publication of Poe's "Murders in the Rue Morgue" more than a century ago. Why this addiction to "murder for pleasure"? Diversion, the opportunity offered the people with "murder in their hearts" to play with the thought of murder, love of adventure, the exhilaration which comes from matching wits with the detective (or the author), identification with the detective's keenness, enjoyment of the ironic attitude usually shown towards the official police, have all been offered as explanations. So have the theories that reading detective stories is a means of learning about new chemical-microscopic methods of crime detection, and that through these stories one gains insight into "higher social circles." The decisive elements are not present in any of these explanations.

The element of pleasure they leave untouched hinges on the *double* identification made by the reader: *consciously,* he identifies with the hunter; *unconsciously,* with the hunted, and the uncanny-masochistic situation of uncertaintly. To complicate matters, the unconscious identification is also composed of two layers: a superficial Oedipal palimpsest (darkness, mystery, murder viewed as pseudo-sadistic parental sex), and a more deeply buried oral regression—the allure of being mistreated. Inwardly, therefore, the reader admits to pseudo-aggression (playful preoccupation with murder), while the "real crime", once more, is psychic masochism. This psychic masochism is the cornerstone of a triad whose two other elements are passive enjoyment of the uncanny, and passive voyeuristic enjoyment of the forbidden. All three partes constituentes spell masochistic passivity, which is especially pronounced in the element of the uncanny. (See studies on uncanny, which have already been summarized in *Neurotic Counterfeit-Sex,* pp. 105–111.)

The widespread interest in detective stories has been the starting point for far-fetched—and still incorrect—conclusions about the alleged presence of underlying aggression in the reader. All these conclusions, in my opinion, are erroneous—just as is the impression that nothing lies hidden beneath the Oedipal palimpsest. This problem is similar to the problem of wit (see #11, this chapter) in that the reason for the "necessity of harmless release" ("It's only a game, and I'm not serious about it") is not unplaceable aggression but unplaceable psychic masochism in the reader's unconscious.

No less erroneous, again in my private opinion, is the conclusion that interest in murder stories testifies to the "universal potential criminality" of the average person. Not everybody is a potential murderer. The prerequisite for murder is not a gun but a specific inner mechanism, which is quite foreign to the genus of mystery fans. Proof of this statement requires extensive investigation of criminal actions: the reader is referred to these studies in the index appended to this chapter.

PSYCHIC MICROSCOPY

Layer I. Universal solution of the infantile conflict with masochistic stabilization.

Layer II. First veto of the superego.

Layer III. First defense of the unconscious ego: pseudo-aggression, mostly on the level of the Oedipal palimpsest.

Layer IV. Second veto of the superego.

Layer V. Guilt accepted for the lesser crime, more or less mitigated by rationalizations (see above) and game quality. "Ironic lip-service conformity with ego ideal precepts": "Wasn't I told to play?"—"Conscience money" paid in social irony: "I never suspected that an intelligent person like you could be interested in this kind of stuff." In another layer: "Who do you think you are—Justice Holmes, who used to read one a day?"

SUMMARY: Interest in mystery stories is based on a defense against a defense.

45. A miser?

Since Freud's investigation of obsessional neurosis (1908), the miser has been considered the prime example of "anal sadistic" personality traits. No doubt, obsessional and compulsive neurotics demonstrate the Freudian triad of hyper-meticulousness, stinginess, and stubbornness.

As stated in previous chapters (see Chapter III), anal regression is but the reduplication at the end of the digestive tract of oral-passive experiences, originally fought through at its entrance. Thus, the masochistic elaboration of "I wish to be refused" is pseudo-aggressively changed into "I wish to refuse and to accumulate." In short, miserliness has an oral basis.

Oral components are expressed in the language of higher levels, without any change in the basic oral connotation.

The miser is a typical example of an orally regressed injustice collector, expressing his *infantile* emotional grievances in *adult,* money-neurotic, terms. The child has no precise concept of money during the period when his individual psyche is being formed (form the beginning of extrauterine life up to the age of five). Money has no meaning for the child until a later period. The money neurotic is an individual who secondarily shifts to money the values stemming from the nursery. If, for instance, a child of two and a half desires the exclusive possession of a doll, and struggles fiercely with a sibling for the toy—is the child thinking of the dollars-and-cents value of the doll? Again, if the child becomes furious because the mother pays more attention to a younger brother—does the child want the exclusive possession of the mother's love and attention because it thinks of the insurance "value" of the mother as expressed in dollars? The answers to both questions is of course "no." Yet this greed for exclusive possession can, after some psychic detours, be shifted to money in later life. Such a child can develop into a miser.

Does this mean that the wish to amass money is the result of an instinctual drive to possess? Not at all. Such a drive does not exist. What is clinically observable in the child is infantile megalomania and ideas of grandeur and omnipotence: he believes himself to be the center of the entire universe. This fantasy, when destroyed by reality, is succeeded by a series of shifts—first from the child's self-admiration to admiration of other individuals, and still later to over-valuation of inanimate and impersonal objects, like money. The greed for money is rooted in the child's infantile delusion of omnipotence.

The masochistic elaboration of the miser's fantasy leads to two pseudo-aggressive disclaimers: refusing to part with money, and/or accumulating money.

Every demand for money is interpreted as an accusation of passivity: "If I weren't thought of as a wishy-washy sort of person, they wouldn't dare ask me for it." The excitement of such neurotics, when confronted with a demand or request for money, activates the latent reproach and its inevitable defensive result: the hyperaggressive refusal. Everyone has witnessed cases of such hyperaggression, and to date, no one has logically explained why a simple, detached, "Sorry, I can't," is not considered sufficient. No one has explained why the neurotic's full reserve of fury is unconsciously mustered.

The reason seems to be this: to refuse money demands or money requests means, for the sufferer from money neurosis, not what he *consciously* believes (satisfaction because he has not been a sucker), but an *unconscious,* and therefore much more decisive satisfaction— that of supplying, through his aggressive refusal, an alibi for the superego's charge of masochistic passivity. This seems to be the crux of the matter.

The second unconscious pseudo-aggressive defense presented to the inner conscience is, of course: "I don't want to be refused. I want to accumulate and to get."

Both these defenses are at work at the same time in the miser. He is unwilling to spend, and frantically eager to accumulate. In doing both, he clings desperately to his pseudo-aggressive defense on the unconscious level. The real battle of stinginess, however, is not fought with dollars and cents. The real battle of money is fought intrapsychically from the reservoirs of unconscious guilt and unconscious defense mechanisms.

The differences between the normal and the neurotic approach to money can be schematized, as attempted in *Money and Emotional Conflicts:*

Normally	Neurotically
Money is a means to an end, that end the acquiring of things one desires.	Money is an end per se.
One does not allow oneself to be taken advantage of in money matters, and does one's best to avoid it.	The fear of being taken advantage of in money matters is greatly out of proportion to the threat itself.
One tries to make money, as best one can, as much as one can, but not by sacrificing health, love, hobbies, recreation or contentment.	Money becomes the center of life; everything else—health, love, hobbies, recreation, and contentment—is subordinated to the urge to possess it.
Money has no infantile strings attached to it.	Money is a blind for continuing infantile conflicts, now repressed.
The spending of money is taken for granted; it needs no surgical operation to put a dollar into circulation.	The possession and hoarding of money becomes the predominant motif.
Unjustified demands for money are warded off (out of necessity) in a matter-of-fact way.	Demands or requests for money generate fury, excitement, and indignation.
The phrase "I cannot afford it" is a simple statement of an objective fact.	The phrase "I cannot afford it" represents a defensive triump over psychic masochism.

PSYCHIC MICROSCOPY

Layer I.   Masochistic solution of the infantile conflict.
Layer II.   First veto of the superego.
Layer III. First defense of the unconscious ego: pseudo-aggression in
            two subdivisions: "I want to refuse and wish to accumulate."
            (Later shifted to money.)
Layer IV.   Second veto of superego.
Layer V.   Second defense of the unconscious ego: changing the blame
            for the lesser crime into a "necessary" defense—"Everybody
            wants to take advantage of me: what's wrong with self-protec-
            tion? Besides, everybody in *my* circle approves of it"—"Ironic
            lip-service conformity with ego ideal precepts": "Be prudent
            and cautious in money matters."—"Conscience money" paid in
            form of dissatisfaction, the constant fear of losing all that
            has been amassed, and constant excitement in warding off
            attacks of "greedy exploiters," with minor compensation from
            "victories" over these "scoundrels," and from actual possession
            of money.
SUMMARY: The miser is the product of a defense against a defense.

46. *A spendthrift?*

The spendthrift is a neurotic carved out of the same wood as
the miser. His infancy begins with the same inner conflict: masochistic attachment first to the mother and then to the father. This
produces unconscious feelings of guilt, similar to those of the
future miser. Only after these two initial steps do the paths of the
miser and spendthrift separate. The third step—the alibi, the
unconscious defense mechanism—is totally different. The miser's
defense is pseudo-aggression derived from refusing money to others,
while the spendthrift's defense is the veiled pseudo-aggression of a
magic gesture of a specific type.

As already described, a magic gesture denotes an unconscious
dramatization of the thought: "I shall show you, bad mother and
father, how I really wanted to be treated—with kindliness and
generosity." This pseudo-wish, in itself, is a defense; it does not
correspond at all to the dynamically decisive wish of the future
spendthrift, who has already been stabilized on the rejection level.
What he is really after is psychic masochism. He achieves that goal
by *depriving himself of money,* thus going one step further than
the adherent to magic gestures.

PSYCHIC MICROSCOPY

Layers I to V.   See "Addict to magic gestures," #6 of this chapter.—
            "Ironic lip-service conformity with ego ideal precepts":
            "Don't be so greedy! Share!"
SUMMARY: The spendthrift lives on the basis of a defense against
            a defense.

47. *Do you show pity on specific occasions only?*

Analytic investigations of pity have so far produced two classical
descriptions: Freud's statement that pity is based on unconscious
identification, and Jekels' contention * that the emotion of pity
arises from an unconscious demonstration, by the ego, of how it
would like to be treated by its own inner conscience, with the whole
problem then being projected upon an object in the outer world.

Both theories can be substantiated with clinical facts; both have
remained undisputed; both represent psychological bull's eyes.

There exists, however, a third variety of pity, which has strangely
enough not been described in the literature on the subject. This
type consists of an unconscious, split-second identification with a
pitiable situation (or person), an identification so terrifying that
the inner defense instituted—pity—is an attempt to outdistance
that fear. The purpose of the defense is to demonstrate to the
superego that one is not part and parcel of the unconsciously
approved masochistic and dangerous situation, but an outsider
and mere spectator whose only involvement is through the feeling
of pity.

This third type could be called "pity as attenuated terrorlike
fear." It pertains exclusively to *one* specific situation: psychic masochism of the greatest intensity. The allure of the masochistic
situation which is to be imitated is to some extent the reason for
the identification performed. The major reason is the reproach
of the inner conscience, which points to the individual and declares:
"That's you!" *To ward off the terrifying reproach of heightened
psychic masochism, materialized in the pitiful object of pity, the
unconscious defense of putting distance between them ("mechanism of out-distancing") is utilized, and conscience is told: "No\
connecting link exists: I just pity the poor man."*

* "Psychologie des Mitleids," *Imago* XVI, 1930.

The coincidence of two facts brought this type of pity to my attention. I had just been writing a psychobiographical sketch of the poet Richard Savage, using Samuel Johnson's famous sketch as source material, and at the same time had been analyzing a pathologically stingy patient, who none the less allowed "dependees" to take financial advantage of him. The two experiences crystallized, in my mind, the theory presented above.

To start with Savage: Richard Savage was a chronic "supportee" who, according to Johnson, "appeared to think himself born to be supported by others, and dispensed from all necessity of providing for himself." His claim was allegedly based on his illegitimate birth; he claimed as his mother a noblewoman who denied any responsibility for him. Although Savage finally achieved a pension, through the means of writing a blackmailing drama called *The Bastard,* he provoked conflicts with the donors of the pension, and eventually they withdrew their support. He was also the recipient of a yearly pension from the Queen; this he habitually squandered in a few days, so that for the rest of the year he would live in direst poverty. He was constantly asking his acquaintances for "small sums" which he never repaid, except to provoke his benefactors.

What is the psychology of people who—as the cliche has it— "think the world owes them a living" and therefore "never prosecute any scheme of advantage," as Johnson says of Savage?

In Savage's case, his discovery (at the age of seventeen) of the circumstances of his birth provided him with a lifelong rationalization. He used that single fact remarkably well: he convinced himself, his environment, and his biographer. It makes for a good story, but unfortunately it does not tally with the facts. *If Savage's exclusive aim had been to make up for past deprivations, he would have cultivated the benefactors who did materialize to substitute for the absent mother. He did exactly the opposite: he provoked them all, quarreled with them, alienated them, in order to achieve his unconscious masochistic aim—to be refused.* It was dangerous to help Savage, Johnson comments rather naively. "Compassionate" as Savage was "by nature and principle," Johnson acknowledges he was very easily provoked, and when offended in any way, revengeful to an extreme degree. His friendship could not be trusted; even a minor quarrel was enough to cancel both "ties of honor or gratitude." He resented his dependence on his benefactors; his excessive pride came to the surface either as insolence or as vanity.

Savage was of the opinion that he had to be supported by others, but he would not accept help unless it was offered with due ceremony. Once, Johnson reports, when he was entirely destitute, he received a message that one of his friends wished to see him. This could only be an offer of help, but Savage was disgusted at the form of the message (a specific time had been named), and rejected the kindness by refusing to visit the friend. Johnson mentions other examples of the same trait.

Savage's friends finally decided to "support him by subscription," on condition that he leave London. As usual, Savage's reaction was provocative, and as a result some of the "subscribers" withdrew from the hopeless rescue work they had undertaken. Savage died in debtor's prison, into which he had maneuvered himself; when a friend wished to pay the small sum owing, Savage refused. Even in prison he found a sucker—the Warden, who provided for him.

The problem of the dependee contains two question-marks: what kind of personality becomes a dependee, and who are his supporters?

The dependee is an orally regressed neurotic, whe regularly attains a position of dependence upon another person or group of persons, only to complain bitterly of the disappointment caused him by the "inconsiderate" attitude of the "stingy" provider. It is of no consequence to him that the provider never asked to be elevated to his present position, and now rebels against the burden of it. Inwardly, the dependee needs him for two purposes: as monetary donor, *and*—since he gives little, and that infrequently—as provider of "injustices."

The dependee's rationalizations vary. They range from the ideological, the artistic, and the cynical, to "arguments" which are slightly paranoiac. The common denominator is the motto: "Don't ask me why, the world owes me a living."

At first glance, one gathers the impression that the dependee is an infantile "gimme," repeating the child's receptive attitude. Clinical experience specifically contradicts this impression. In early childhood, the "gimme" attitude is real enough. It must be emphasized, again, that in adults the phenomenological similarity covers

a genetic difference: this wish has gone through masochistic elaboration, and covers another wish, that of being refused.

My first clinical experience with the "provider" type pertained
to a young man of considerable inherited wealth, who had rather
deprecatory ideas about the "less fortunate." Although he was
entirely incapable of earning a decent living in the field of his
specialized knowledge (his only interest was his hobby, numis-
matics), and in fact had never tried it, his attitude towards people
who *had* to work was one of contempt. He acted as if personal merit
were a prerequisite to being born with a diamond spoon in one's
mouth. His contempt covered more than the typical defensive attitude; a good deal of infantile megalomania was involved, since
he considered himself an "exception." Peculiarly enough, he did
not think of himself as a wealthy playboy, but as a "hard-working
perpetuator of family tradition." His fortune, originally amassed
by his grandfather via rather dubious land speculations, had been
deodorized by his father with judicious donations, and by the installation of a coin collection. "I am more than a coin polisher, as my
malicious friends claim," said the heir ironically, "I know what I'm
polishing." Expressed in terms of money, his earning capacity was
around $50 a week; he lived on ten times that amount.

Typically, he was rather stingy, or, as he put it, "conservative."
What it amounted to was the inability to part with a dollar—for
somebody else. Only in one way was he a "sucker," as he called it:
he could not resist dependees "of the *fat* variety." What he meant
was that human suffering in any form or fashion left him cold,
except in the case of "fat beggars." He cited an example. Once,
while seated in a Paris cafe he had observed a rather fat, middle-
aged man making the rounds of the guests, soliciting a few sous.
Nobody paid any attention to him, or gave him a contribution: if
he occasionally garnered a casual look, it was a look of indignation,
as if to say: "With all that fat, you aren't starving." Said the patient:
"A peculiar feeling of pity came over me; I thought that this might
happen to me, too. Being rather stout myself, I imagined my own
plight if I were to lose my money. To my own surprise, I gave the
man one hundred francs. I shall never forget the expression on the
man's face—grateful and surprised."

Analysis of the incident proved that behind the superficial narcissistic identification, which was fully conscious, a deeper layer was hidden. In addition to a magic gesture, the latter consisted of a reproach of conscience, which pointed to the identical inner situation—of an internal, not an external nature. In short, conscience accused him of harboring self-damaging masochistic traits identical to the beggar's—though they were concealed in him, clearly externalized in the beggar. To outdistance the reproach, the defense was instituted: "I *merely* feel pity for him."

Since this clinical experience, I have observed the variety of pity described (the third type) again and again. It accounts for the opening of purse or checkbook by people who under other circumstances are quite incapable of making this gesture on behalf of a stranger. It also accounts for the irrationality of the gift which is frequently elicited under false pretenses, e.g., with a fabricated sob-story. The money paid or donated is truly "conscience money," but of a specific kind. It is not an appeasement of simple pity; it is, so to speak, *"out-distancing" money*. In the victim of frequently self-provoked misfortune, the average human being—whose ego is more nearly intact—is confronted with a living extract of psychic masochism, naked and unabashed. The inner conscience immediately shows the prospective donor his own hidden recesses of masochism, and asks ironically, "Are you really different from this man?" To counteract that reproach, the prospective donor puts into operation a mechanism designed to place him at a distance from the incarnation of masochism. The inner alibi runs something like this: "I am different; I have only pity for so much self-destruction." The whole internal dialogue is of course unconscious, but it has an outward manifestation in the form of a gift. At bottom, the gift is contributed as proof that the donor is not identical with the victim. Pity is but the outward covering cloak with which this donor unconsciously disguises his own psychic masochism.

PSYCHIC MICROSCOPY

Layer I.   Masochistic end result of the infantile conflict.
Layer II. First reproach of the superego.
Layer III. First defense of the unconscious ego: pseudo-aggression.
Layer IV. Second veto of the superego.
Layer V.   Second defense of the unconscious ego: "It's not that I get

any pleasure out of defeat and humiliation—it just arouses my pity when I see the results in someone else."—"Ironic lip-service conformity with ego ideal precepts": "Shouldn't one commiserate with the unhappy?"—"Conscience money": hyper-emotionalism or suppression of emotion.

SUMMARY: Pity as disguise of unconscious fear is a defense against a defense.

48–49. *Truly bored? Or only bored in anticipation?*

Boredom, if typically encountered, is a complicated neurosis, for which I have suggested the distinguishing term "alysosis" (derived from the Greek equivalent for boredom, "alys").

By and large, the people who suffer from boredom do not complain about it. Its latent presence is betrayed, however, by the characteristically frantic activity in which they indulge in order to avoid it. The incessant search for "fun" observable in many people is their inner protective defense against the constant danger of boredom.

Boredom combines a feeling of emptiness and dissatisfaction with the inability to concentrate on work, or other activities which might be pleasurable. The danger of boredom is universal; susceptibility to it varies with the individual, and with the strength of the bulwarks—hobbies, sports, social or humanitarian interests are all examples—he erects against it. Any favorite activity, in addition to its function in fulfilling specific unconscious wishes and defense mechanisms, is also a protection against boredom. So is work, in the ideal cases where it is also a sublimation.

In my opinion, boredom (as a neurotic disease) is always associated with three inner disturbances: weak or shattering sublimations, inner inhibition of voyeurism, and defense against the accusation of masochistic pleasure.

To clarify these assumptions:

Weak sublimations. In all cases of inability to create sublimation, or where sublimation is weak (see previous discussion, Chapter IV, pp. 64 ff.), the individual's store of aggression becomes unavailable to the ego, and is used by the inner conscience to fight the ego. Psychic masochism—the unconscious ego's counteraction—is the result.

Where the sublimation is only weak, or unstable, boredom represents the unconscious ego's defense against the intermediary phase of the superego's attack. That attack always follows after external defeat; it shakes the very basis of sublimation. The superego seizes on external defeats for use as torture material; its attack is not powerful enough to destroy the sublimation, but is sufficiently effective to make it unworkable for some time. This interim period is visible on the surface only in the conscious boredom which is the unconscious ego's defense.

Voyeurism. Basically, there are two ways of avoiding boredom—through sublimation, and through fantasy. Fantasy, which is imagination in free flight, is a product of the scopophiliac instinct. One is, therefore, prepared to expect that in persons having a neurotic inhibition of fantasy (and therefore of voyeurism), boredom will appear more frequently than in others. This expectation is borne out by observable facts. The reason for the inhibition of voyeurism is to be found in its unconscious connection with pre-Oedipal and Oedipal fantasies.

Defense against superego reproaches of psychic masochism. There are three groups of neurotics who are, by and large, immune from boredom. These are obsessional neurotics, depersonalized individuals, and hypochondriacs. Consciously, these patients live lives of constant worry; they concentrate, according to the disease, on obsessions, disturbance of perception, or imaginary diseases. Since in each case voyeurism remains intact, these types of neurotics seldom experience boredom. Their infrequent periods of boredom come only after prolonged torture, and are then offered as unconscious defenses against the superego's reproach of masochistic pleasure. Boredom serves the same purpose in persons suffering from "alysosis," but here it is the central rather than a peripheral defense, and is of course present in a quantitatively higher degree.

Abortive reactions of the same sort are observable when one thinks too long about a problem without finding a solution. After a while one gets "bored." The inner conscience misuses this failure for masochistic purposes, and the ego defends with the formula: "I don't enjoy failure; I am bored." At the same time, the narcissistic ego denies that any feeling of defeat followed upon the unsuccessful attempt to solve the problem.

Recognition of alysosis as a distinct disease entity is based on the use of boredom by many psychic masochists as their major defense mechanism in fighting against the reproaches of the inner conscience.

To be distinguished from alysosis is another phenomenon for which I have suggested the term "pseudo-boredom."

There is a specific group of people with "vivid imaginations," who frequently complain that reality bores them. In anticipation, they claim, they are always a few steps ahead of that reality. A patient, a well-known writer, declared:

"Reality can be compared to a drama in two versions. The first is acted and debated in my own mind; that one is exciting and novel. Then comes an interval of days and weeks before the anticipated drama occurs in external reality. Since all has already been foreseen, the real event is boring and stale. To give you an example: during my last vacation, I received the editorial comments on the manuscript of my latest novel, with weighty suggestions for changes. The editor, a not too bright fellow, as usual misunderstood what I had written. He wanted to eliminate passages which seemed essential to me. My reactions were first consternation, then anger, then disgust with those human actions which are regulated by the guiding principles of stupidity, ignorance, malice. After this I began working out what my reply should be, how far I could go in my protests, the editor's probable answers, my literary agent's interference, protests sent to the chief editor, etc. In short, all possible pros and cons, all possible emotions, were covered. After the letters were written, protests and threats filed, the drama was over. When the real conferences with editors and agent started, it was all stale, like soup warmed over for the tenth time. In this way, most of life is boring."

But the writer was incorrect: he should have explained that in this way, most of life seemed to him *pseudo*-boring. One of the prerequisites for true boredom, or alysosis (as pointed out earlier in this section) is a triad of disturbances, none of which applied to him. The patient's power of imagination was not impeded, since his writing block had been successfully removed in treatment and he had just finished a novel, nor was his power of fantasy weak— it had worked overtime in defending his text against the editor. The second prerequisite is faulty sublimation: this obviously could not apply, since successful literary productivity is a classical example of sublimation. Third, treatment had reduced his psychic masochism to the "normal level," so that he had achieved love, contentment, and success in his work.

The quoted reaction came during the end phase of my patient's cure, when his emotions were regulated by relatively normal principles. He had acquired a good-sized store of aggression to ward off the reproaches of the superego, and his ego was now able to use part of this aggression in formulating defenses against the inner conscience, and the other part in achieving realistic aims.

This new balance of power, established in analysis, was temporarily endangered while the writer was under severe stress (and this happens in normality, too). His receipt of editorial commands from his publisher's second lieutenant immediately threw him back—temporarily—into the passive position, with the superego taking the lead. He counteracted with substantial aggression: fury against the proposed mutilation of his work and the people who proposed to do it. After having acted both parts of his inner drama (in his description condensed into "first consternation, then anger"), the problem was solved along reasonable and active lines: "working out what my reply should be and how far I could go in my protests." But instead of continuing in the satisfied state of mind which he had when first writing these letters, "boredom" took over shortly afterwards. Before that time, however, he had allegedly anticipated "*all* possible pros and cons."

Now, *all* possible pros and cons cannot be anticipated. Nobody can gauge coming events so precisely. Schopenhauer's dictum to the effect that reality is mostly a caricature of our expectations still hold at least partially true. Still, the clever patient must have had some good, though unconscious, reasons for emphasizing this detail so persistently.

The reason happened to be an inner defense against remnants of masochistic passivity, which is present in varying quantity in *every* human being. The patient's *pseudo-boredom represented merely an unconscious attempt on the part of his ego to prevent the inner ogre, the superego from reopening the case.* The man had met the situation with aggressive countermeasures, displayed in thought and action. The inner conscience, in turn, had insisted on the now anachronistic accusation of passivity, and later had brought forward all possible damaging potentialities. The writer skipped that part in his description, or rather alluded to it lightly in saying, "all possible emotions were included." As he later admitted, one of these was the idea of being released from his contract, should the publisher get too angry with his "difficult" author.

This barrage of masochistic-passive reproaches was also warded off with pseudo-boredom. In short, he told his accusing conscience off—intrapsychically—thus: "I solved the problem actively; don't bother me." His final "Roma locuta—causa finita" had its surface reverberations in pseudo-boredom.

Proof of this could also be found in another "angle," also not mentioned in the patient's report. For days following his initial excitement he had not been bored at all. During this time, he was chewing over and repeating to himself all the aggressive sentences he had put into his letter to the editor, and rehearsing those he was expecting to use at their forthcoming conference. These aggressive statements, too, were a shield against passivity. It was only later that the patient pushed the problem aside, and developed the theory that he was "bored."

Since having encountered the unconscious defense of pseudo-boredom in this case, I have observed a series of other persons who make use of this very defense. The mechanism is seldom presented on a platter; one has to ask for specific descriptions of how people react after situations of conflict. The mechanism per se is overlooked because of the feeling that the problem has been solved. In analytic patients, the mechanism is presented only in the undamaged part of the ego; otherwise, neurotic misuse of after-effects of conflict goes on on the masochistic conveyor belt.

Pseudo-boredom has no connection with alysosis. It represents an unconscious defense mechanism, encountered in normality and in the undiseased sectors of neurotic personalities. It denotes an inner defense against the reproaches of the superego, the latter concentrating its attack on the perpetually "ready-to-jump" psychic masochistic tendencies. The catalytic agent is an external conflict, misused by the inner conscience as material for the ironic reproach: "This can happen only to you, you passive weakling." The reproach of the inner conscience is frequently unjustified: it "can happen" to anybody.

PSYCHIC MICROSCOPY

Layer	Alysosis	Pseudo-Boredom
I.	Masochistic solution of infantile conflict.	Remnants of the universal masochistic solution of infantile conflict.
II.	First veto of superego.	First veto of superego.
III.	First defense of the unconscious ego: pseudo-aggression.	First defense of the unconscious ego: pseudo-aggression.
IV.	Second veto of superego.	Second veto of superego.
V.	Second defense of unconscious ego: emptying of all "psychic chambers," inability to imagine anything—alibi of being a "good boy." "Ironic lip-service conformity with ego ideal precepts"—"The reward for being a good boy is love and happiness." "Conscience money" paid in rejection by the environment.	Second defense of unconscious ego: "I'm neither masochistic nor aggressive; the problem is solved—I'm bored." (Fear of reopening the case.) "Ironic lip-service conformity with ego ideal precepts": "Don't be a bore, repeating the same thing endlessly."—"Conscience money" paid in self-torture.

SUMMARY: Both alysosis and pseudo-boredom constitute a defense against a defense.

50. *Do you indulge in "small deprivations"?*

A devotee of the mechanism of "small deprivations" comes in two models: the "self-depriving" or the "hoarding." The "self-depriver" waits until the very last second before replenishing the supplies which he finds absolutely necessary for his well-being, or deprives himself of accessible pleasures. The "hoarder" does exactly the opposite: he is always overstocked, and therefore always safe from the terrible danger of finding himself without one of these pleasure-minutiae. To quote such patients:

Mr. H: "I don't know why, but cigarettes give me a lot of trouble. Every time I see that there are only a few left in the package, I remind myself to buy a new one, but I always seem to forget my decision. The result is that several times every week I run out of cigarettes, exactly at the moment I need one badly."

Mr. I: "My wife tortures me with her sex-demands at the wrong time. She is frigid and basically disinterested in the whole act. Her ability to time things wrong is remarkable—she always chooses the time when I am ill-disposed or tired. Once she admitted that she asks for sex only because she is afraid she might want it in a few days and not get it. She takes in sex for hoarding purposes."

Mr. J: "I am an early riser, my wife is not. I paint my best pictures in the early morning hours. While painting, I smoke my pipe. Don't be surprised, other creative people do similar things. Do you remember that Jerome K. Jerome dedicated his book, *Idle Thoughts of an Idle Fellow,* to his best friend—his pipe? In any case, I love to smoke my pipe while I work. At this point the tragicomedy starts: all too frequently I forget to take my pipe from the bedroom. Of course, I don't want to disturb my wife again; the result is that I'm furious and work poorly—the whole morning is spoiled."

Mr. K: "I once read that one should stop eating during a meal at the very moment when the dish tastes best to you. I have no need of a medical regimen for diet, no heart or any other troubles, but still I have followed that rule for years. I call it the rule of small deprivations. The result is that I get a slight feeling of melancholy from every tasty dish. It is as if I were mourning for the part I did not eat. Sometimes, I even picture myself as an old and decrepit man whose physician has prescribed a limited diet; that makes me even more gloomy and self-pitying during meals."

Phenomenologically, the self-depriving and hoarding types seem to be opposites. Genetically, however, they have an identical source. The self-depriving type acts out his self-constructed deprivations; the over-cautious hoarding type tortures himself with the identical deprivations in *fantasy,* and acts preventively.

In both types the fantasy of being deprived and left wanting is predominant. The unconscious reasons propelling both types are secondarily rationalized.

Analysis of these patients proves that an oral regression is involved. The superficial expectation of anal elements is either not confirmed at all, or, if present, does not play an important role. These neurotics are typical psychic masochists, in the grip of the mechanism of orality.

The two types differ in the defenses they present when confronted with the superego's accusation of masochistic pleasure in being refused. The hoarder's defense is by far the stronger; his formula reads: "I want to get; I am even over-cautious against the possibility of being deprived." The self-depriver is incapable of that defense; the best he can do is allege that his bad memory led to his temporary deprivation. Both types are completely unconscious of their inner aims.

The excuse of "forgetting" is an obvious rationalization. Mr. J., the pipe-smoker, constantly blamed his wife for his unsatisfactory morning's work. The irrationality of the reproach can be understood if one takes into account the fact that the "mechanism of orality" is acquired in relation to the mother, and later repeated with the mate.

Mr. I clearly blamed his wife, forgetting the little detail that he had chosen her—unconsciously—not despite, but because of her corresponding neurosis. There are no innocent victims in marriage.

The self-depriving group is especially grotesque when the rationalizations are thin. Mr. K., for example, admitted that he had no medical reasons for his queer abstinence. When asked why he constantly imagined himself old, toothless, and afflicted with stomach troubles, instead of enjoying life while he could, he quoted Victor Hugo: "Melancholy is the pleasure of being sad." When, however, his psychic masochism was explained to him in analysis, he protested violently.

Why does the inner conscience tolerate the unconscious pleasurable game embedded in the "mechanism of small deprivations"? The inner demon is captivated by the punishment inflicted. In all neurosis, the inner conscience is corrupt: its fee is unhappiness, pain, depression, self-torture. And the neurotic pays, and pays.

PSYCHIC MICROSCOPY

Layer I.   Masochistic solution as end result of the infantile conflict.

Layer II.   First veto of superego.

Layer III. First defense of unconscious ego: pseudo-aggression against "depriving" parents.

Layer IV. Second veto of superego.

Layer V.   Second defense of unconscious-ego: In hoarding variety: "I'm neither masochistic nor aggressive, I want to get," and in self-depriving variety: "I'm independent of these silly things, I even forgot them."—"Ironic lip-service conformity with ego ideal precepts": In hoarding variety: "You should be prudent and look ahead," and in self-depriving variety: "Don't be so greedy." "Conscience money" paid in fear and preoccupation respectively.

SUMMARY: Devotees of "small deprivations" operate a defense against a defense.

In reviewing this "group of 50" one finds the monotonous basis:

   I. Masochistic end result of the infantile conflict;

   II. First veto of the superego;

  III. First pseudo-aggressive defense;

   IV. Second veto of the superego;

   V. Specific second defense, making for the difference in externally visible reactions.

What is most amazing in this entire technique is the *monotonous common basis* and the *infinite variety of elaborations* produced by the unconscious ego. The inner lawyer's weaknesses are obvious, and it is invariably inept in planning major strategy, but where details are involved, what resilience and cunning are displayed! In the end, this small power whose task it is to withstand a Giant loses out, but its resourcefulness in creating ever-new defenses compels admiration. The ego's defeat is a foregone conclusion, but its gallant delaying actions never end.

REFERENCES

The following references cover the "Group of 50"; my studies cited all contain a review of the literature on the topic (if any), and extensive clinical examples. The numbers refer to the chapter subdivisions.

1. Numerous studies, summarized in *The Battle of the Conscience*, Chapter VI, "The Injustice Collector"; also *The Basic Neurosis*, Chapter 3, "The Nine-Point Basis of Every Neurosis." Also, "Is Psychic Masochism an 'Over-Simplification'?" *The American Imago*, 9:1, 1952.

2. "A Clinical Approach to the Psychoanalysis of Writers," lecture delivered before the New York Psychoanalytic Society, January 27, 1942, published in *The Psychoanalytic Review*, 31:40–70, 1944. Also, "On a Five-Layer Structure in Sublimation," *The Psychoanalytic Quarterly*, 14:76–97, 1945; "The Danger Neurotics Dread Most: Loss of the Basic Fallacy," *The Psychoanalytic Review*,

33:148–153, 1946; "Psychopathology of Pseudo-humbugs and Pseudo-bluffers," *The Psychiatric Quarterly Supplement*, 20:14–22, 1946; "Psychoanalysis of Writers and of Literary Productivity," *Psychoanalysis and the Social Sciences*, (edited by Dr. Roheim), Vol. I, 247–296, 1947; "Further Contributions to the Psychoanalysis of Writers, I and II," *The Psychoanalytic Review*, 34:449–469 and 35:33–50, 1948; "Samuel Johnson's 'Life of the Poet Richard Savage'—A Paradigm for a Type," *The American Imago*, 4:42–63, 1947; "John Ruskin's Marital Secret and J. Millais' Picture 'The Order of Release,'" *The American Imago*, 5:182–201, 1948; "The Relation of the Artist to Society," *The American Imago*, 5:4, 1948; "This Type-writer to Hire—Psychology of the Hack Writer," *The Psychiatric Quarterly Supplement*, 22:290–299, 1948; "Story-Tellers and Story-Writers," *The American Imago*, 6:51–56, 1949; "Anxiety, 'Feet of Clay' and Comedy," *The American Imago*, 6:97–109, 1949; "Did Freud Really Advocate a 'Hands-off' Policy Toward Artistic Creativity?" *The American Imago*, 6:205–210, 1949; "A New Misconception in Literary Criticism," *The American Imago*, 6:275–279, 1949; "Does Writer's Block Exist?" *The American Imago*, 7:44–54, 1950; *The Writer and Psycho-analysis*, Doubleday, New York, 1950.

The first approach has been attempted in *Talleyrand-Napoleon-Stendhal-Grabbe*, Internationaler Psychoanalytischer Verlag, 1935.

3. "Myth, Merit and Mirage of Literary Style," *The American Imago*, 7:249–287, 1950; "Literary Critics Who Can Spell But Not Read," ibid., 8:189–218, 1951.

4. "Psychology of the Cynic," *Psychoanalytische Bewegung*, 5:19–52 and 130–166, 1933; *Talleyrand-Napoleon-Stendhal-Grabbe*, 1935; *The Battle of the Conscience*, Chapter IX, and *Money and Emotional Conflicts*, Doubleday, New York, 1951, Part 2, Section 4.

5. "On the Psychology of Hypocrites," *Int. Zeitschrift fuer Psychoanalyse*, 21:96–97, 1935; "Hypocrisy—Its Implications in Neurosis and Criminal Psycho-pathology," *Journal of Criminal Psychopathology*, 4:605–627, 1942; *The Battle of the Conscience*, Chapter IX; *Money and Emotional Conflicts*, Part 5, Section 18.

6. "The Problem of Magic Gestures," *The Psychiatric Quarterly*, 19:259–310, 1945; *The Battle of the Conscience*, Chapter VI, pp. 93 ff.: *The Basic Neurosis*, Chapter 6, # 26; *Neurotic Counterfeit-Sex*, p. 136; *Money and Emotional Conflicts*, Part 5, Section 15.

7. "Debts of Gratitude Paid in Guilt Denomination," *Journal of Clinical Psychopathology*, 11:57–62, 1950.

8-9-10. *Talleyrand-Napoleon-Stendhal-Grabbe*, Part IV; "The Problem of Oral Pessimists," *Imago*, 20:330–376, 1934; "The Pessimo-Optimist," *Samiksa*, 3:207–211, 1949.

11. "A Clinical Contribution to the Psychology of Humor," *Psychoanalytic Review*, 24:34–53, 1937; *The Battle of the Conscience*, Chapter IX, pp. 172 ff.; *The Talent for Stupidity*, Chapter VI (in press); "The Dislike for Satire at Length," *The Psychiatric Quarterly* (in press).

12. "The Dislike for Satire at Length," *The Psychiatric Quarterly* (in press).

13-14. "On the Psychoanalysis of the Ability to Wait and of Impatience," *The Psychoanalytic Review*, 26:11–32, 1939.

236 THE SUPEREGO

15. "Psychopathology of Ingratitude," *Diseases of the Nervous System*, 6:226–229, 1945; *Money and Emotional Conflicts*, Part 10.

16–17. "On the Resistance Situation: The Patient Is Silent," *The Psychoanalytic Review*, 25:170–186, 1938; "Logorrhea," *The Psychiatric Quarterly*, 18:26–42, 1944; also *The Battle of the Conscience*, p. 102.

18. "The Confusionist," *The Psychiatric Quarterly* (in press); *The Talent for Stupidity*, Chapter III (in press). "The Problem of Pseudo-Mental Deficiency," *Int. Zeitschrift fuer Psychoan.*, 18:528–38, 1932; Summary in *The Basic Neurosis*, pp. 197–201.

19. "A New Approach to the Theory of Erythrophobia," lecture delivered at the XV Int. Psychoan. Convention in Paris, France, August, 1938; published in *The Psychoanalytic Quarterly*, 13:43–59, 1944; "On the Psychoanalysis of the Ability to Wait and of Impatience," *The Psychoanalytic Review*, 26:11–32, 1939; "Some Special Varieties of Ejaculatory Disturbances Not Hitherto Described," *Int. Journal of Psychoanalysis*, 16:84–95, 1935; "On Acting and Stagefright," *The Psychiatric Quarterly Supplement*, 23:313–319, 1949. See also bibliography for Section # 2, on writers.

20. "Four Types of Neurotic Indecisiveness," *The Psychoanalytic Quarterly*, 9:481–492, 1940; also chapters on ambivalence in *The Basic Neurosis* and *Neurotic Counterfeit-Sex*.

21. *The Talent for Stupidity*, Chapter VII (in press).

22. "One-Inch-From-Victory Disappointments," *Diseases of the Nervous System*, 10:3, 1949.

23. "Story-Tellers and Story-Writers," *The American Imago*, 6:51–56, 1949.

24–25. "Psychology of 'Bad Influence' and 'Good Advice,'" *Diseases of the Nervous System*, 7:51–54, 1946.

26–27. *The Basic Neurosis*, pp. 19 ff.

28. *Money and Emotional Conflicts*, Part 2, "Some Recurrent Misconceptions Concerning Impotence," *Psychoanalytic Review*, 27:450–466, 1940; "Short Genetic Survey of Psychic Impotence, I and II," *Psychiatric Quarterly*, 19:412–437 and 19:657–676, 1945; "Newer Genetic Investigations on Impotence and Frigidity," *Bulletin of the Menninger Clinic*, 11:50–59, 1947. Summary in *Neurotic Counterfeit-Sex*.

29. "On the Psychology of Gamblers," *Imago*, 22:409–11, 1936; "The Gambler—A Misunderstood Neurotic," *Journal of Criminal Psychopathology*, 4:379–393, 1943; *The Basic Neurosis*, Chapter 6, section 15; *Money and Emotional Conflicts*, Part 3.

30. *Talleyrand-Napoleon-Stendhal-Grabbe*, Chapter 4; "The Psychological Interrelation between Alcoholism and Genital Sexuality," *Journal of Criminal Psychopathology*, 4:1–13, 1942; "Contributions to the Genesis of Alcohol Addiction," *Quarterly Journal for Studies on Alcohol*, 5:434–449, 1944; "Personality Traits of Alcohol Addicts," ibid., 7:356–359, 1946; *The Basic Neurosis*, Chapter 6, # 14.

31. "Psychopathology of Compulsive Smoking," *The Psychiatric Quarterly*, 20:297–321, 1946; *The Basic Neurosis*, Chapter 6, # 22.

32–33. *Divorce Won't Help; Conflict in Marriage,* Harper, 1948 and 1949.

34. "Psychology of Jealousy," *Int. Zeitschrift fuer Psychoan. und Imago,* 24: 384–397, 1939; "To Reject Someone—To Accept Someone," *Imago,* 23:289–303, 1937.

35. "Psychology of the Killjoy," *Medical Record,* 162:11–12, 1949; "The Problem of Magic Gestures," *The Psychiatric Quarterly,* 19:295–310, 1945.

36. Summary of various publications: *Unhappy Marriage and Divorce; Divorce Won't Help; Conflict in Marriage;* Chapter "Marriage and Divorce," in *Patterns of Modern Living,* pp. 193–237, The Delphian Society, 1949; Chapter "Marriage and Divorce," in *Elements of Psychoanalysis,* The World Pub. Co., 1950.

37. *Divorce Won't Help,* pp. 85 ff., *Neurotic Counterfeit-Sex,* pp. 101 ff.

38. See # 37.

39. Psychology of the Magical Phrase: 'I Said I'm Sorry, Didn't I–" *Diseases of the Nervous System,* 12:343–345, 1951.

40. Summary in *Neurotic Counterfeit-Sex,* pp. 184 ff.

41. "The Breast Complex in Men" (in collaboration with L. Eidelberg) *Int. Zeit. f. Psychoanal.,* Vienna, 19:547–583, 1933; "The Present Situation in the Genetic Investigation of Homosexuality," *Marriage Hygiene* (old series), 4:16–29, 1937; "Respective Importance of Reality and Fantasy in Genesis of Female Homosexuality," *Journal of Criminal Psychopathology,* 5:27–48, 1942; and *Riv. de Psicoanal.* (Buenes Aires), 3:514–542, 1946; "Eight Prerequisites for the Psychoanalytic Treatment of Homosexuality," *Psychoanalytic Review,* 31:253–286, 1944; "Psychology of Friendship," *Medical Record,* 159:101–104, 1946; "Differential Diagnosis between Spurious Homosexuality and Perversion Homosexuality," *Psychiatric Quarterly,* 21:399–409, 1947; "The Myth of a New National Disease; Homosexuality and the Kinsey Report," *Psychiatric Quarterly,* 22:66–88, 1948; "Lesbianism: Facts and Fiction," *Marriage Hygiene,* 1:197–202, 1948.

42–43. *Money and Emotional Conflicts,* Part 4; *Neurotic Counterfeit-Sex,* pp. 135, 289 ff.

44. "Mystery Fans and the Problem of 'Potential Murderers,'" *American Journal of Orthopsychiatry,* 15:309–317; *The Writer and Psychoanalysis,* Chapter VIII; "Psychology of Crime" Chapter XV of *The Battle of the Conscience.*

45. *Money and Emotional Conflicts,* Part 5, section 14.

46. *Money and Emotional Conflicts,* Part 5, section 15.

47. "Pity as Unconscious Disguise of Terror-Like Fear," *Quarterly Review of Psychiatry and Neurology,* 6:4, 1951; "Samuel Johnson's 'Life of the Poet Richard Savage'—A Paradigm for a Type," *The American Imago,* 4:42–63, 1947; *The Writer and Psychoanalysis,* Chapter III, pp. 47 ff.

48–49. "On the Disease Entity Boredom ('Alysosis') and Its Psychopathology," *The Psychiatric Quarterly,* 19:38–51; "Boredom of Anticipation (Pseudo-Boredom)," *Samiksa,* 4:19–23, 1950.

50. "The Mechanism of 'Small Deprivations,'" *The Psychoanalytic Review,* 37:341–344, 1950.

VI. Differences between External and Internal Justice

THE CORNERSTONE OF CIVILIZED SOCIETY IS THE CONCEPT THAT THE law-breaker is individually responsible for his infraction. And the cornerstone of justice is the series of safeguards set up, by the law, to prevent the individual from being held responsible for a crime he did not commit. As Jefferson put it: "It is more dangerous that even a guilty person should be punished without the forms of law than that he should escape." As a matter of principle, therefore, our conscious idea of justice puts a high value on the checks and counter-checks of the legal mechanism. The extreme requirement, according to the American Constitution, is that in cases of high treason there must be confession in open court, or the testimony of two witnesses to an overt act. For lesser crimes, the requirements are somewhat less stringent.

Civilized society considers that the greatest danger, to itself, is punishment of the innocent. Individual freedom is the ideal, and deviations are branded as jungle morality.

The precept of *collective* legal responsibility is entirely rejected; the wholesale reprisals upon innocent hostages which were part of the barbarous Nazi technique were viewed with horror and abhorrence.

The concept that person X, who has committed no crime, can be punished for a crime committed by person Z, is contrary to our sense of justice. This conviction is so strong, so nearly automatic, that public opinion is easily mobilized in cases of conspicuous injustice—in countries, of course, not crushed under the heel of a dictator.

In general, the presence of a "sense of justice" in the individual is taken for granted; it is viewed as merely another of our "cultural achievements." In reality, the existence of this conscious concept has a complicated substructure, which can be studied by examining the steps through which the idea of "fairness" is implanted in the child. The educational argument is simple and impressive: "What would you say if that happened to *you?*" Education—when it is

238

in essence cultural adjustment, and not the criminal ideology taught in all forms of dictatorship—makes the child feel a direct and personal connection with the wrong done to the innocent victim. That external identification later becomes internalized. In favorable cases, the result is part of the foundation for the adult's sense of justice.

Another tributary to the growth of the concept of justice is the necessary nursery practise of rewarding good behavior. If injustice prevailed in the nursery, and no premium were placed on self-restraint, the child would have no incentive towards "good" behavior. Sooner or later, the child does come to understand the reward-punishment practise; the reward of approval and parental love is a tempting prize.

However, there are certain contradictions, even in civilized law, which indicate that strong inner opposition must be overcome before the sense of justice can be achieved. There are inexplicable gaps in the network of safeguards. Why, for example, is it legal to convict a person of a capital crime, and send him to his death, on the basis of purely circumstantial evidence? Repeated suggestions have been made to change the criminal code so that capital punish-ment will be possible only when attested eye-witnesses testify against the accused. And even then, the possibility that there will be a miscarriage of justice cannot be fully excluded. But at least this change would preserve the possibility of reversal, restitution and rehabilitation for an innocent person convicted on circumstantial evidence, for he would still be alive.

The admissibility of circumstantial evidence at all is in fact a controversial matter; the high valuation placed on it certainly indicates that our law-makers overrate common sense as a gauge for judging evidence.

Another glimpse of the unconscious substructure which is part of the conscious sense of justice is afforded by the morbid interest in criminal cases shown by some sections of the public. There is a strong impression that some vicarious pleasure is extracted from these well-publicized crimes; the pleasure is hidden behind very thin rationalizations.

Admittedly, the human mind is rich in imperfections. Neverthe-less, the structure of law has been steadily amended through the centuries, and always in the direction of affording greater protection to the innocent, and less to the criminal. Only the cynical laugh at the law; the majority of law-abiding citizens fully agree—both consciously and unconsciously—that "crime does not pay," and that justice pays dividends.

All these—and other—contradictions in the *conscious* laws of our culture are more clearly understood when contrasted with *unconscious* law. The precepts of inner law in no way resemble the Constitution, the Code Napoleon, or the Magna Carta.

This is perhaps the fundamental difference: the "purpose" of an unconscious tendency is to find an outlet; the direction of the discharge and the identity of the "victim" thus created is of minor importance, if any. This is in direct violation of our concept of conscious justice, which holds that only the criminal *himself* can atone for the crime. Inner drives and their reverberations, however, have but one propelling tendency, and that is to be diverted, somehow, from the person himself. The victim—the other fellow—is chosen more or less indiscriminately. Freud used a telling anecdote to illustrate this characteristic:

In a small village behind the lines in the first World War, an enemy court-martial tried the village shoemaker for spying, convicted him and sentenced him to death. The mayor of the village petitioned for his release, telling the presiding officer: "We cannot do without him—he is the only shoe-maker in the village. But we have three tailors—hang one of them."

This is not the only difference. In unconscious law, the thought is equivalent to the deed—an even more extreme distortion of justice than the methods of the totalitarian secret police. This equation— thought equals deed—is clinically visible in neurotics. Nearly nine-tenths of the "crimes" for which a neurotic punishes himself have never been executed in reality. They are not even crimes he has considered committing—they are "crimes" of *unconscious* fantasy! Moreover (as pointed out in previous chapters), he punishes himself for a *substitute* crime.

In the law-courts of consciousness, communication between the prisoner and his attorney is privileged, and secret; the prisoner's defense, and perhaps his real story, are not known to the district attorney until revealed in open court. The inner district attorney, however, is in full possession of every secret of the accused. The unconscious conscience has a "microphone" in the departments of unconscious wishes and of inner defenses, and there is no hope of circumventing its omniscience. The record of the unconscious in detecting "crime" beats that of any police force in the world— even those aided by the newest methods of criminal laboratory work (not to mention the criminal's proclivity to "mistakes," based on his unconscious wish to be punished). The inner conscience's score is a round one hundred per cent.

What of that other familiar precept of our society, "making the punishment fit the crime"? In essence, this precept is adhered to, despite the variations in importance of any specific crime which follow from the variance in standards between one specific environment and another. Rustling does not exist as a crime in New York City; it is a little boy's game. But on the cattle ranges of the West it is a grave infraction of the legal code, and is severely punished. Blood vengeance, privately executed, is still part of the *unwritten* code in some societies, and tacitly recognized as excusable in their *legal* codes; it is the crime of crimes in a society in which the right to punish has been vested exclusively in the State and its freely chosen representatives.

These differences do not change the central principle that there must be a logical relation between the severity of a crime and the punishment imposed for it. Picking up and keeping a dropped purse is a lesser offense than snatching it from a woman's protesting hands; this in turn is a lesser offense than killing her in the process. In all modern societies crimes are gradated in an ascending scale from least to most damaging, and punishment is lenient or severe in accordance with that gradation.

In the unconscious code of "justice," however, punishment is disproportionate to the "crime." Penalties, because of the anti-libidinous structure of the inner conscience, are always over-dimensional; regardless of the nature of the infraction, the inner district attorney seizes the opportunity to "throw the book" at the victim. Punishment is exacted in the form of depression, dissatisfaction, self-reproach, and sometimes suicide.

The severity of the sentence is increased by another disparity between conscious and unconscious codes of justice. The principle of double jeopardy—no individual can be tried twice for the same crime—is not recognized by the inner conscience. Every trial for a new infraction means, at the same time, a retrial of a similar case which has already been tried in the past. Every sentence is punishment for the current crime, plus punishment for crimes which have already been expiated again and again. If, for example, a neurotic is accused by his superego of refusing money to his family, the indictment is padded by citation of a hundred and one instances of past "crimes," which may be completely unrelated to the neurotic's current conduct. The result is a tremendous increase in the depression which is the neurotic's punishment.

Pleas of innocence are of no value, nor are indignant demands for the right of appeal to a higher court. Intrapsychically, the judgment of conscience is final. Review by a higher court is possible only in the law-courts of external reality; intrapsychically, the first verdict is always the last.

The inner code's entire attitude towards expiation is diametrically opposed to that of external law. Modern criminal law views punishment as the debt the criminal owes to society. Punishment, at least theoretically, is the preamble to rehabilitation; the concept of the "reform school," faulty as it may prove in practice, is steadily being extended. The punishment imposed by the inner judge, however, is unlimited; paroles and "time off for good behavior" do not exist.

Every detail of the two codes, in fact, is decidedly at variance. The juries of reality are chosen from a panel picked at random, and carefully screened to exclude bias either for or against the accused. The "jury" of the unconscious parades its prejudices against you, and its appetite for cruelty; nevertheless, it cannot be challenged.

The judge, in external reality, is the judge; the jury is the jury; all the departments which work together to administer justice, though interlocked, serve their separate purposes independently. In the internal law court, the judge's code is also Lewis Carroll's: "I'll be judge, I'll be jury, said cunning old Fury; I'll try the whole cause and condemn you to death."

The lawyer for the defendant, in external reality, is independent of the judge, and—as long as he adheres to legal procedure—is fully privileged in his choice of means of achieving an acquittal. The inner lawyer, the unconscious ego, is a half-hearted protagonist from the start, because of its fear of the inner judge. The ego's prime consideration is self-protection; its function as a defender is merely secondary. This dictates the ego's unvarying plan of action, which is always a plea of "guilty," followed by an attempt to get his client off by accepting punishment for a crime less serious than that charged in the indictment. The inner lawyer always declares: "My client is guilty—but of another offense. Punish him, but for the lesser crime." In other words, the unconscious ego never dares to fight for full acquittal.

In this dark and hopeless picture, one possible advantage stands out: external justice can, and sometimes does, convict an innocent person on the basis of contradictory or spurious circumstantial evidence. This cannot occur in the court presided over by the inner conscience. The superego's omniscience ensures proof of guilt; before punishment is imposed, all doubts have been removed. This advantage is blotted out by the severity of the punishment: the detective work of the unconscious is magnificent, but the ensuing trial is a mockery.*

The final difference is that of purpose. Society's taboos and its punishments are designed to maintain civilized conduct in the framework of a specific cultural setting, and are accepted by the vast majority of individuals within that setting. Unconscious justice has but one aim: punishment and refusal of pleasure. It uses cultural standards as a blind for its anti-hedonistic purposes, thus

---

* The strange fact that elusive circumstantial evidence is admissible as legal "proof" in court is but the reflection of man's desperate fight for conscious and pseudo-rational dominance over the uncanny forces of the unconscious. The basis for acceptance of circumstantial evidence is the assumption that the "logical" mind of the average person in the jury box is capable of distinguishing between conclusive and inconclusive "evidence." The long line of unjustly convicted individuals bears witness to the fact that the conscious faculty is, to say the least, overrated. At bottom, admissibility of circumstantial evidence is merely a remnant of the inner conscience's attitude: guilty in any case. The old Roman law worked on the assumption: *in dubio pro rheo*, which means, in cases of doubt give the defendant a break. Circumstantial evidence works on the opposite principle. The widespread respect felt for circumstantial evidence is a rational camouflage of the reflection, on the conscious level, of the inner conscience's tendency to punish in any case.

deluding naive observers into the belief that inner conscience is fashioned after the cultural code. The superego's purpose is exclusively the individual's misery; its label of "forbidden" and "positively punishable" is attached both to cultural taboos and to actions accepted by the environment. Inner conscience is not concerned with the maintenance of taboos; inner conscience recognizes the taboos only for the purpose of misusing them. In every culture, therefore, people torture themselves unconsciously, regardless of the fact that the external "don'ts" are fastened to different prohibitions.

The following table * summarizes the differences between the two types of justice.

Differential Diagnosis Between Conscious and Unconscious Justice

	Conscious Justice	Unconscious Justice
Defendant	Only the wrongdoer can be held responsible and punished.	Innocent bystanders, upon whom an infantile conflict has been projected, are held responsible and can be punished.
Crime	Deeds are the only basis for prosecution.	Deeds *and* unconscious fantasies are bases for prosecution.
Concealment	Possible to a limited degree.	Impossible, because of direct "television and eavesdropping system" between inner conscience and department of repressed wishes and defenses.
Severity	"Punishment fits the crime" according to specific cultural orbit.	Disproportionate punishment.
Duplication of punishment	No defendant can be tried or punished twice for the same offense.	Constant revivals of identical accusations, leading to punishment on the conveyor belt.
Appeal to higher court	Possible.	Impossible.
Expiation	Punishment is considered debt to society; debt is cancelled by the specific and limited penalty imposed.	Unlimited punishment.

* First stated in the *Psychiatric Quarterly,* 1952.

Jury	Twelve people from all walks of life.	Inner conscience.
Technique of punishment	Detention, social disgrace, fines, and in extreme cases, capital punishment.	Depression, guilt, dissatisfaction, self-damage (failure in profession, marriage, sex, enjoyment of life), even suicide.
Constitutional safeguards	Judge, jury, prosecutor—*not* combined in one person.	Judge, jury, prosecutor, executioner combined in impersonal institution of inner conscience.
Council for defense	Hired lawyer.	Unconscious ego.
Objectivity	Defendant unknown to jurors; if suspicion of prejudice justified, can be rejected a priori by counsel for defense.	Conscience prejudiced from the start, because of its lust for cruelty. No rejection for bias possible. Bias so marked that conscience frequently lures victim (by relenting vigilance) into lamentable situation, only to extract more punishment, imposed by the same conscience.
Miscarriage	Possible in exceptional cases.	Impossible—as far as the facts of the "crime" are concerned. Severity and bias of the "jury," however, make trial a mockery.
Favorite defense	Denials, alibis, witnesses, invocation of mitigating circumstances.	Denials, alibis, acceptance of guilt for lesser crime: "I couldn't have killed the girl in Brooklyn; I was stealing a watch in Manhattan at the time." No witnesses admitted.
Corruptibility	Under normal conditions: incorruptible.	Corruptible. Bribe consists of self-imposed anticipatory depression and self-punishment, notably acceptance of guilt for lesser crime.
Court-room	External, and open to the public.	Internal and absolutely secret; the victim is not even consciously aware that he is being tried.
Purpose	Maintaining specific standards, agreed upon in a specific cultural setting.	Anti-hedonistic principle of "no pleasure," using cultural standards as blind.

VII. The Unconscious Process of Resolving Normal and Neurotic Guilt

EVERY SCIENCE IS FORCED TO WORK WITH A SPECIFIC TERMINOLOGY covering simplified abstractions; without this shortcut, communication would be impossible. The terms "normal" and "neurotic" are simplifications; like all simplifications, they have been widely misunderstood. On the one hand, an ideally normal person exists only in the fantasies of neurotics, who need this unreal comparison for purposes of self-torture. On the other hand, no neurotic is an unbroken expanse of neurosis; he has his "normal"—and therefore undiseased—areas. Long ago I suggested that a normal person be defined as one "who isn't *too* neurotic." It is indisputable that admixtures of both normality and neurosis are present in every person. The determinants are the quantitative factor, the deposition of pathogenic material (in harmless or in damaging sectors), and finally the extent to which psychic masochism drives the individual.

In the following investigation of resolution of "normal" and "neurotic" guilt, the simplifying yardstick is—nolens volens— adhered to. It is superfluous to state that in real life the divisions are less schematic, less clearcut.

Time and again, I have insisted that neurotics, in the parts of their personalities which are infused with neurosis, cannot draw upon real aggression, but only on *pseudo*-aggression. The reason is obvious. If, as I claim, the psychic masochistic solution of the infantile conflict is *the* basic fact in neurosis, then their defense can only be pseudo-aggressive appeasement of the superego. This procedure has a two-fold purpose. First, the alibi of would-be aggression is thus presented, and these sick people plead guilty to this aggression as the "lesser crime." Second, the pseudo-aggressive behavior sets the eight-ball of external retaliation rolling, automatically providing the other alibi which the psychic masochist lives by: "I am not a glutton for punishment; the bad outer world is unjust to me." The psychic masochist is of course oblivious to the fact that the eight-ball would have remained safely quiescent without his own initial provocation.

Schematized, these are the differences between normal and neurotic aggression.

Normal Aggression	*Neurotic Aggression (Pseudo-Aggression)*
1. Used only in self-defense.	Used indiscriminately when an infantile pattern is repeated with an innocent bystander.
2. Object of aggression is a "real" enemy.	Object of aggression is a product of fantasy, or artificially-created enemy.
3. No accompanying unconscious feeling of guilt.	Feeling of guilt is always present.
4. Dosis: amount of aggression discharged corresponds to provocation.	Dosis: slightest provocation, greatest aggression.
5. Aggression always used to harm enemy.	Pseudo-aggression often used to provoke "masochistic pleasure" expected from enemy's retaliation.
6. Timing: ability to wait until enemy is vulnerable.	Timing: inability to wait, since pseudo-aggression used as defense mechanism against inner reproach of psychic masochism.
7. Not easily provoked.	Easily provoked.
8. Element of infantile game absent; no combination with masochistic-sadistic feelings; the only feeling is that a necessary but disagreeable job had to be performed.*	Element of infantile game present, combined with masochistic-sadistic excitement, usually repressed.
9. Success expected.	Defeat unconsciously expected.

Since first schematizing these differences, I have observed that clinical proof of its correctness can be adduced, in the form of a minute psychic microscopy of the resolution of the two types of guilt resulting from the two types of aggression.

The following table schematized the differences in resolution of normal and neurotic guilt:

* With reference to item 8 of this table, it is my opinion that what appears as *sadism* in *adults* is but a defense against more deeply repressed masochistic tendencies. For elaboration, see *Neurotic Counterfeit-Sex,* pp. 115 ff.

Normal Guilt	*Neurotic Guilt*
1. Pertains to a specific aggressive act perpetrated in external reality.	Pertains to an inner reproach for general masochistic attitude, only secondarily shifted (in a defensive step taken by the unconscious ego) to a pseudo-aggressive, defensive thought or act, thus taking the blame for the lesser crime.
2. Direct quantitative relation between aggressive act and resulting guilt.	No direct quantitative relation between pseudo-aggression and guilt—unconsciously, the inner guilt is constantly fed by the inexhaustible reserves of psychic masochism; the assumption of an external source is a mere disguise.
3. Expiation or restitution possible.	Expiation and restitution ineffective per se, since inner conscience points to the genetic-masochistic basis; hence in desperation the defensive pseudo-aggression is constantly and artificially replenished, and magnified out of proportion.
4. Definite time limit.	Indefinite time limit.
5. Pleasure principle effective in bringing about termination.	Pleasure principle in direct form ineffective in termination, since psychic masochism is in itself an elaboration of the pleasure principle: it makes pleasure out of displeasure.
6. Self-limiting in intensity.	Self-aggravating in intensity through the misuse of unrelated material; at the same time, though secondarily, the conscious displeasure of suffering is unconsciously libidinized, thus reinforcing the vicious circle.
7. Guilt not attached to infantile images; the enemy is the real enemy.	Guilt attached to infantile images—the enemy is also (and especially) the imaginary enemy; this connection is secondarily misused for the production of infinite guilt.
8. Pain and displeasure of guilt real, hence exhaustible.	Pain and displeasure of guilt unconsciously hypocritical, since it is created

	and maintained as camouflage, and in addition masochistically misused.
9. Entire battle is fought on a realistic front.	Entire battle is fought on a spurious front.
10. Process ends with expiation.	Process does not end with expiation; even in cases which give this impression one can detect a shift to some other point of deposition.
11. Real guilt.	Sham guilt.
12. End in sight.	No end in sight, and no inner wish to terminate the conflict.

I remember the incident which made me understand the lack of direct congruity between the intensity of a neurotic guilt and the seriousness of the offense which led to it. A patient had been playing the injustice collecting game for a long time in his marriage. After working it through in his analysis for several months, he finally accepted the dreary fact that he had to carry a double load: "remnants" of his own neurosis, and the results of his wife's unconscious masochism. One Sunday, his wife imposed on him the company of a garrulous elderly woman, a friend of her "hated" mother. He went through the day with grace until the ordeal was nearly over, when he slipped and showed some signs of impatience. The next day, he awakened with the identical feeling of "enormous" guilt which had been typical for him in the past. "But my offense was minor," he said to me, "why this terrible guilt?"

"That's the point," I answered. "Your guilt did *not* pertain to the minor aggressive offense, but to the reproach of conscience concerning the impossible situation you got yourself into by your masochistic choice of a wife! Hence no congruity between the *official* offense, for which you consciously blame yourself, and the *real* intrapsychic one."

In neurosis, the superego is meretricious and venal, as F. Alexander correctly pointed out (1926). Conscience money is paid in the form of constant, self-inflicted punishment. What has not been pointed out is the fact that the crimes for which this conscience money is paid are but pseudo-crimes; this was shown in my concept of taking the blame for the lesser crime, and the consequent assumption that there is a mechanism of defense against the defense. This, however, is not all. In neurosis, there exists a strange tendency to anticipate the punishment which is to be meted out by the inner conscience. This *"anticipation tendency"* manifests itself in two ways.

First, before the superego's whip cracks down, *the prisoner starts to whip himself;* after having proclaimed his innocence of charge I, he voluntarily proclaims himself guilty of charge II ("taking the blame for the lesser crime"). The inner tormenter, being interested in punishment only, seems to accede, perhaps because the victim has relieved "him" of the task of doing his "dirty work" himself.*

The "anticipation tendency" manifests itself, second, in *"preventive depression."* This phenomenon is by no means as simple as the frequent assumption—depression is the superego's punishment—makes it. No doubt, this type of depression exists. But another type is no less common: anticipating the expected punishment, the unconscious ego produces the depression beforehand. This, of course, makes it possible for the "lesser crime" to be used as hitching post, so that—once more—the defense scores a victory over the superego.

One can hardly find a better capsule distinction between normality and neurosis than the fact that anticipatory depression is *not* observable in not-too-neurotic people. They seem to bide their time, reacting only when the inner tormenter actually strikes. Anticipatory depression is not their technique. Perhaps a naive patient of mine (a gambler) hit the nail on the head when, after coming to understand the neurotic mechanisms of his unconscious, he remarked: "The neurotic behaves like a scared and chronically beatendown gambler, who has stopped thinking of how he can win, and now thinks only of how to lose as little as possible."

No direct conclusions as to the alleged inner offense can be drawn from the depth of neurotic guilt. All too often guilt actually pertaining to psychic masochism, which has been shifted to a substitute crime, is magnified and inflated, so that the real crime of psychic masochism may remain untouched. In clinical analysis, failure to see through this ruse, failure to unearth and work through the real reason for guilt, leads to dead ends which cannot be retraced.

* Inner departments are impersonal; the metaphoric use of personal pronouns or personalizations such as "inner district attorney," etc. are merely a simplifying technique.

Therefore, I can only marvel at the emotional oversight exhibited when serious people claim that neurosis and repressed aggression can go hand in hand as causative factors. Neurosis and pseudo-aggression covering psychic masochism are interconnected, but *real* aggression simply is not present in neurosis. *Who but the severest masochist would unconsciously choose the neurotic painful "solution"?*

To prove my point that guilt, pertaining to the *painful* masochistic "solution," is inflated and shifted to alleged aggression, I am adducing a pertinent phenomenon: *the neurotic helplessness in the masochistic situation in reverse.**

I have suggested this term to describe the neurotic marital set-up in which the husband—in the pursuit of his pseudo-aggressive "rebellion"—is met with a look of martyrdom on his wife's face. Before this look he is helpless. He has feelings of futility, of half-fury, and of being "stopped by a stone wall"; the result is apology and unconditional surrender. This simple technique successfully procures for many neurotic wives anything they want from their otherwise quite abusive husbands. It is a technique that doesn't even require spoken words. A facial expression, a helpless movement of the hand, the "tearful eyes of a beaten puppy," are sufficient. The question arises: what is the meaning of this helplessness in the husband, and why is this wornout technique so effective?

As long as the type of neurotic represented by the husband gets his daily "dose of injustice," which he can counter with the unconscious alibi of fury (representing pseudo-aggression only), all goes well. On the one hand he can enact the end result of the infantile conflict, which in these cases happens to be psychic masochism; on the other hand, his conscious suffering and defensive fury serve to appease the inner conscience.

When the rules are reversed, however, complications ensue. The wife's attitudes tempt her husband to identify her, unconsciously, with the fantasy of the "mistreated" child who was himself. This leaves the real husband in the role of the "cruel" mother. Generally, in these peculiar marriages, the wife is unconsciously cast as the "cruel" mother, the allegedly victimized husband playing the role of the "mistreated" child. Exactly the opposite occurs in the "masochistic situation in reverse." The "mistreated" child is forced into

* First stated in *The Psychiatric Quarterly*, 25:418–423, 1951.

the role of tormenter. This is more than this type of neurotic can stand, more than he has bargained for. His inner conscience accuses him of playing the part he "hates" most—that of the "cruel" mother. In order to stay "in the act," the original situation has to be restored. It is—until the next incident. Hence, the masochistic situation in reverse is based on *avoidance* of the typical unconscious double identification in masochistic-sadistic relations, a fact first stressed by Freud in 1915.

To underline the irony of the state of affairs, the poor husband consciously accuses himself of being "too aggressive" towards his poor wife. His inner guilt, pertaining genetically to unsolved psychic masochism, it thus shifted to the pseudo-aggressive defense. As usual, the site of the neurotic battle is transferred to a spurious front by acceptance of "blame for the lesser crime," and on this spurious front it is fought, and lost.

From the practical aspect, the helplessness resulting from "the masochistic situation in reverse" accounts for the perpetuation of these neurotic marriages. The husband pleads that he is unable to cut the Gordian knot—the guilt engendered by his "cruelty" prevents any action on his part.

Here is a representative example, one of many observed.

Mr. L. had been married for thirty-four years. This was his description of his wife: "She was a good-looker, and the brightest girl. She had a truly photographic memory. One of those kids with the college stigma, 'most likely to succeed.' Well, she wasn't so smart in marrying me. What she really wanted from life was a penthouse, a mink coat, and real financial security. Personally, I don't care much for money; I even get bored with success. I've had my ups and downs—mostly downs, I admit. The truth is that I never offered my wife what she expected—what she got was mostly a lower middle-class existence. As a personality, she is rather contradictory. I always considered her an immature, rather childlike person. My daughter finally convinced me that my opinion was wrong—my wife could never have been the harmless weakling I thought her. My daughter's idea is that her mother has a cruel streak. As far as I can make out, my wife is an infantile person who never grew up. I don't detect much aggression in her, unless you understand the word pretty broadly to include a kind of leechlike quality, an attitude of seemingly helpless hanging-on. She is always saying reproachfully,

'Don't leave me alone.' If that's part of aggression, I can go along with my daughter's opinion, but even then I have reservations. The keynote of my wife's personality, I think, is her childlike quality. That's exactly what irritates me most: infantile bragging with learned words, holding the spoon like an adolescent girl, and trifles like that. Her infantilisms irritate me more than the fact that her interests and mine are completely different."

As usual, the facts did not coincide with the patient's perception and evaluation of them. In the course of analysis of his marital conflict, it became clear that this deeply masochistic person had married an aggressive woman, unconsciously patterned after his matriarchal mother, or more precisely, after a *caricature* of his real mother. His mother had been an aggressive domineering woman. Her intellectual aspirations had been supported by little real knowledge. The patient's wife had amassed a great deal of book knowledge, but she could not "think," the husband complained. What he meant was that his wife was unable to connect facts intelligently; she could only recite. Her actual store of knowledge, covering a variety of subjects, proved to the patient that she was "different" from his mother. This "superiority" was counteracted by his wife's inability to put her "information-please" proficiency to any intelligent use. Her store of information, therefore, represented an unconscious irony on the part of the patient, at the expense of his mother's pseudo-intellectualism.

The same technique—an alibi in the form of slight or meaningless improvement over the original, covering the continuation of masochistic attachment behind a thin layer of pseudo-aggression— was also evident in the patient's approach to his main neurotic problem, which was the wish to be aggressively treated by his mother and her later representative, his wife. Mother was "outright" aggressive; his wife—at least in her relation to him—was not. Her technique was more subtle. She displayed a "possessive" quality; she "clung" and played the martyr. These superficial improvements over the mother's character made no difference in the results.

In another layer, the wife's clinging quality represented the patient's own infantilism and "sucking-in" tendency. In unconscious identification with his wife, *he* was the martyred child; at the same time he continued to play the role of the refusing mother. In other words, there was a double identification, with the patient acting both parts in his marital pantomime. He was, unconsciously, the tantalized child and the tantalizing mother. It was a perfect set-up, masochistic and defensive at the same time. In living out the role of the mistreated child, his masochistic wishes were fulfilled. In acting the part of the "bad" mother, he gave himself proof of his alleged aggression, thus supplying an alibi. Simultaneously, he demonstrated his mother's cruelty in caricature. There was only one drawback. The unconscious narcissistic identification of his wife with himself, as the masochistically-victimized child, made it impossible for the patient to put up any resistance at all to his wife's real and unwarranted demands.

The wife's simple trick of incessant complaints invariably brought her husband to his knees. He felt "terribly guilty" when he refused anything; when, for example, he objected to her unreasonable demands on his time. "Don't leave me alone," was her magic formula; the result were as spectacular as they were for "Open, Sesame." It was easy to understand the reasons for what the patient called "his weakness." He was certain that in his childhood he had mourned his mother's coldness and detachment, and the lack of love which had left him largely to his own devices. Since he narcissistically identified himself with his wife, every refusal unconsciously meant: "You objected to your mother's refusals; what right have you to repeat them?"

This was not all. The patient had two other psychic tasks to perform. First, he had to use considerable psychic energy to hold down his masochistic enjoyment of his domestic drama. Second, he had to provide a pseudo-aggressive defensive facade; hence his angry and irritated attitude towards his wife. He managed to work himself into a really grotesque situation. Whatever he did with his wife caused him discomfort. If he wished to spend the evening away from home with friends, he was torn between the Scylla of feeling "terribly guilty" for leaving his wife alone for even a few hours, and the Charybdis of feeling irritated if he chose the path of self-sacrifice and stayed in.

Partly because of her own neurosis, partly in an intuitive understanding of her husband's inner wishes, the patient's wife isolated herself completely. She had no friends, no acquaintances. As a result, she could find some justification for her argument that her husband could not "leave her alone."

The patient learned early in life—and the hard way—that one cannot do business with the inner conscience. Although he did not consciously understand what was going on, nor what had "hit him," his inner conscience was well aware of the infantile double game he was unconsciously playing in his marriage. It was as transparent as an actor's tour de force when, in different disguises, he takes over two leading roles in the same play. To counteract the superego's chronic objection to his hidden masochistic pleasures, the patient had to mobilize pseudo-aggression. From this came his financial failure, which unconsciously enabled (and consciously forced) him to deprive his wife of the penthouse, mink coat, and financial security she coveted. He damaged himself, too, but that is precisely the inner aim of the masochist. The aim is unconscious, so that it does not prevent, but rather produces, self-accusations, complaints, and self-pity. His chronic irritation with his wife was another camouflage of his masochistic pleasure-gain in marriage.

This man's tragedy lay in his unconscious choice of a wife who would represent both a weak ironic replica of his mother's rejected personality traits, and a caricature of himself. His wife's leechlike quality and her clinging, infantile attitude mirrored his own defensive attachment to his mother: "I don't want to be rejected, I want love and attention." (In other words, it already comprised defensive elements, used after his infantile conflict was stabilized in psychic masochism.)

As the patient unconsciously used it, his wife's empty intellectualism corresponded to an ironic comment on his mother's literary aspirations.

This complicated web of neurotic wishes, defenses, alibis, pseudo-aggressions, etc., was stigmatized as "fake" by the patient's superego, a taunt which became more and more biting as years went by. In consequence, the patient's depression and dissatisfaction increased, as did his need to attest his unhappiness to himself and to pick on trifles to use as alibis.

This man's life was so thoroughly dedicated to self-abasement and self-torture that he found cause for complaint in his wife's uncritical admiration for him. This is exactly what most men want in their wives, but this patient could not stand praise because unconsciously he wanted rejection.

The ironically-tinged continuation of the mother-image in his wife, coupled with strong masochistic elements, explained why he was so helplessly drawn to and repelled by his "impossible" wife. He was obsessed with "irritating trifles" in her conduct and behavior because these trifles represented both his attitudes in condensed form.

The "masochistic situation in reverse" has considerable practical importance. Unless the analyst is familiar with this mechanism, even psychiatric-psychoanalytic treatment will not resolve some marital conflicts; the vicious circle of unconscious aggression and unconscious guilt remains, seemingly, unchangeable. It is not; the impression merely arises from confusion between the masochistic substructure and the overlying pseudo-aggression.

VIII. The Pseudo-Moral Connotation of Neurotic Symptoms

THE EGO IDEAL WAS ORIGINALLY CREATED TO SAVE THE CHILD FROM constant narcissistic defeat, and to avoid chronic conflict with the educators. (See Chapter II.) Once the ego ideal has been established, the parents, armed with their power to enforce "suggestions," need no longer tell the child what to do; the child voluntarily performs the identical act, "because he wants to do it." Within this benevolent inner structure are incorporated both parental and cultural taboos, and it is a source of happy pride to both parent and child. Its presence means, for the parent, that he has achieved an educational success; for the child, it means that he has nearly outsmarted himself, narcissistically, and has found a way of avoiding external conflicts.

So far, so good. The trouble starts with Daimonion's misuse of the ego ideal for its own purpose—which is the manufacture of torture on the conveyor belt. The ego ideal contains more than a collection of environmental taboos. It also enshrines all the grandiose ideas the child has built up in speculating about his own glorious future. All this is permanently and carefully registered so that, in the future, actual achievement can be measured against rash promises. Since a discrepancy is unavoidable, guilt is unavoidable too. What began as a blessing for the child, therefore, proves to be an instrument of torture for the adult. The ego ideal is a formidable barrier to the adult's pursuit of happiness.

Strangely enough, another facet in this complicated game, where Daimonion turns the tables on the outsmarted victim, has been overlooked so far. The internalized taboos of the environment, which are part of the ego ideal, become both yardstick and shibboleth: Daimonion metes out punishment by holding the ego ideal up to the ego. The ego learns from bitter experience the trick of turning the opponent's strength against himself, and in time it too becomes an adept at this unconscious jiu-jitsu technique. Every time a defense corresponds to one of the precepts enshrined in the ego ideal, the Daimonion is stopped cold. *Thus, strangely enough, the dicta which make up the ego ideal silence both ego and Daimonion:*

ego ideal serves as a double-edged immobilization trick. By pointing to the unachievable ego ideal, Daimonion silences the ego, which then accepts punishment for the descrepancy. On the other hand, any defense instituted by the ego which corresponds to the ego ideal's precepts will silence Daimonion; such a defense becomes "abage Satanas." This is clear in the case of romantic love, where a living person (the beloved upon whom the ego ideal is projected; see #34, Chapter V) is presented as incontestable witness.

To exemplify on two mechanisms:

Item I. When the infantile ego ideal unconsciously enshrines the big order: "I want to become the world's greatest engineer," and the actual achievement is assistant to assistants in a big concern, with twenty-two superiors, the discrepancy is obvious and the ego inwardly accepts punishment, since it cannot disclaim its own promise. The mere presentation of the comparison, and the unavoidable admission of "failure," silences the victim.

Item II. On the other hand, if a person performs a magic gesture (see #6, Chapter V), this demonstration that one allegedly wished to be treated kindly and lovingly is the final step in a long drawn out conflict. The inner Frankenstein has already rejected two antecedents: masochistic submission and an initial defense of pseudo-aggression. Confronted with the second defense, "What's wrong with kindness and love," the Daimonion is immediately, though grudgingly, silenced, for this defense is fully in accord with the cultural precepts of the ego ideal.

Still, the ego's recourse to the ego ideal as an ally against Daimonion is a weapon of merely temporary effectiveness. After a short respite, Daimonion returns to the attack, uncovering the artificial structure of the defense, and thus rendering it useless. The result is—new guilt, and a new defense.

The mechanism through which the ego allies with the ego ideal to achieve temporary immobilization of the Daimonion sector of the superego is, in my opinion, even more far-reaching than I at first supposed. The regularity with which this mechanism appears in the "Group of 50" could arouse suspicion even in skeptics.

Neurotics use this mechanism in conjunction with a technique which may be called "pseudo-moral connotation of neurotic symptoms." It works this way:

Every secondary defense (layer 5) is chosen in such a way that it coincides, if only tangentially, with some precept enshrined in the ego ideal. Without exception, this secondary defense will contain a mocking irony directed at the educators. The moral precepts communicated to the child are reproduced verbatim—a deadpan approach which results in distorting their meaning and reducing them to absurdity. Verbatim parroting of enshrined precepts strengthens the unconscious ego's ability to defend neurotic symptoms by claiming pseudo-moral connotations for them. This pseudo-moral connotation, it now seems clear, is a powerful unconscious weapon of resistance; its strength has so far been underestimated.

To adduce some clinical examples:

After hearing an explanation of this mechanism, an orally regressed woman remembered the following incident. Her father, a rigid educator, had specifically forbidden the children to pick any of the fruit from his prized apple-orchard. When harvest time came, he discovered that the apples had been left on the trees, but this girl had been climbing the trees and nibbling at the apples as they hung from their stems. The father's severe reprimand was countered with an impeccable argument: "You didn't say anything about eating. All you said was—'Don't pick!' "

Mr. M., a young man with severe masochistic personality neurosis, and inability to work, who also suffered from "psychogenic oral aspermia," * persisted for a long time in his refusal to take a specific technical examination. "Take this idiotic examination!" his infuriated father would demand. "I am not thoroughly prepared yet," was the son's constant reply. The superficial layers of his examination-fear were easily explained. His father had tried to teach him the alphabet at the age of four; dissatisfied with the child's progress, the father constantly complained that he was not "thorough" enough in his studies. Two decades later, the son executed his (by then) full-fledged masochistic neurosis (also manifested in his wish to fail the examination) via pseudo-aggression: "Well, I'll give you thoroughness—till you're blue in the face!" The fact that the student damaged himself more than he did his father is another story. . . . Once more, blame for the lesser crime (pseudo-aggression) is ac-

* The case is described at length in *Neurotic Counterfeit-Sex* (Chapter III).

cepted; once more the quasi-moral connotation of the secondary defense is obvious: "What's wrong with doing as father said, and being thorough?" Time, place and occasion are of course different, so that father's demand is reduced to absurdity—another characteristic quality of the pseudo-aggressive defense.

Miss N., a girl with severe agoraphobia, understood in analysis that her original wish had been voyeuristic; guilt had been shifted to the exhibitionistic defense, and the inner battle fought on "foreign territory." All her secondary defenses (avoidance of the street, fear of entering the street, etc.) were fastened to the shift. The tenacity of her defense was bolstered by a series of educational commands which ostensibly encouraged exhibitionism. "Show your aunt your new dress," her mother had said once. And "Why don't you play the new song you learned on the piano?" And, "Show us the little drawing that you made." In short, the unconscious ego here adduced, hypocritically, the exact statements made by educational authorities, and used them to prove that the defense (exhibitionism) was—moral.* Interestingly enough, the patient claimed that when the mother, *fully dressed,* bathes her *naked* child, she is issuing a double invitation to the child: to exhibit before the mother, and to abstain from looking at her (peeping). . . .

Miss O. suffered from a "torturing thought" of which she was deeply ashamed. In the masturbatory fantasies of this puritanically educated patient, she was always raped by a gangster. This fantasy appeared to be a banally disguised Oedipal wish, an assumption which was contradicted by the patient's life history. Her whole life was unconsciously dedicated to the provocation of her mother. Her first fiancé had been unacceptable to her religious mother because he was Chinese, her second had been unacceptable because he was an alcoholic and a ne'er-do-well.

The father had died when she was a young child, and she had been educated by English governesses whom her mother supervised.

---

* In pre-Hitler Austria, a popular joke told of a little Jewish boy in the first grade, who proudly came home from school with a small silver swastika. His father was horrified: "Do you know what this stands for?"—"Sure," was the boy's reply, "but I got it in exchange for matzos." (Matzos are flat discs of unleavened bread eaten at the Jewish holiday of Passover.) . . . Mutatis mutandis, the business deals and pseudo-narcissistic triumphs which mark the ego's attempts to outsmart the superego can be compared with the action of this boy.

The Oedipal palimpsest covered a more deeply repressed masochistic attachment to the image of the pre-Oedipal mother. What startled the patient most (and drove her into analysis) was a change in her "shameful fantasy," as she called it. In this modification, she was no longer raped by the gangster, she was now a prostitute. "We were conversing on the same level, a bad girl and a gangster were thrown together—it even went so far that I made all the advances."

Why did the fantasy change? The original masochistic fantasy (covering the desire to be mutilated by the mother: see below) was first warded off with an Oedipal shift; here the responsibility was the father's, and the child but an innocent sexual victim. But every repetition meant a greater store of reproaches of conscience; though the sex of the torturer had been shifted (first mother, then father), masochistic enjoyment remained the basis of the fantasy. The next step in the development of the fantasy was pseudo-aggressive: by stepping down the social scale (from jeune fille bien elevee, raped by a gangster, to the consenting and even seducing prostitute), fear was diminished. It is not surprising that so severe a masochist should have degraded herself to a prostitute in her fantasies.

Fear of passivity was also diminished, because a new pseudo-aggressive defense was discovered. The original fantasy was first clarified in the patient's dreams: a *female "witch"* institutes a reign of terror, cutting off arms and legs. But this, too, was a second edition; the first had been cannibalistic in nature.

In this case, the quasi-moral connotation in the symptom could be traced back to the advice the mother gave the patient, then five, after hearing that "a man had come through the window while she slept." The mother pooh-poohed her complaint, and told her "to do everything to avoid imagining such silly, frightening things." "Everything" included, obviously, any form of activity: it cannot be denied that the patient was "active" enough in the later versions of her fantasy—even to the point of seducing her favorite gangster.

Mrs. P., a severe obsessional neurotic who was afraid to touch glass in any form, tortured her family by forcing them to abide by her phobia's complicated set of rules. Her phobia was glass, but her will was iron, as her martyred family put it. With fury, irony and helplessness, her husband, her father and her mother described the difficulties of a life lived according to the patient's "simple" rule of eliminating glass. A drink of water is forbidden: the container is glass. Headaches cannot be treated: aspirin is packed in glass bottles. Electricity is taboo: the switch is mounted on a glass plate. The window mustn't be opened: it's glass. Washing is allowed, but drying is impossible: the towels hang on a glass rod. Spectacles are unusable: they are made of glass. The secondary boycott is even worse. If the father puts on his spectacles, or the mother touches the glass pane of a door, or the husband drinks a glass of water, then a state of contamination is declared, and the victims are put through a ritual of purification.

The young lady's cold reply to her family's desperate complaints was simply that she was "not responsible for her fears." Then she went on, indignantly, to declare that "with a little consideration, all these requests could easily be granted." At first, she could not be shaken in her conviction that she was the reasonable person, and that her family was highly inconsiderate. "They just don't want to remember what I tell them." She admitted, when asked, that her family's report of violent scenes was quite accurate; "Sometimes my patience is stretched too thin," she said.

According to the patient, her fear had started when her mother and father made a "terrible mistake." She had been taking a bath when she happened to notice a glass thermometer. "It was the very same one," she said, "that had been used a few weeks before to take Father's temperature *rectally,* when he had pneumonia. That frightened me terribly. Why did mother have to put *that* thermometer right in front of my eyes?" She did not mention whether or not she also blamed her father for having had pneumonia.

As usual in obsessive and compulsive neurotics, the current symptom had a long series of precursors. In my opinion, the so obvious cruelty of these neurotics is secondary, and covers a more deeply repressed masochistic substructure. In the patient's Oedipal disguise, she saw the thermometer which had been in her father's rectum as a symbol of her own repressed anal-Oedipal fantasies; in the past she had believed that sex consisted of introducing the penis into the woman's rectum. From this, later on, came the defensive abhorrence of the symbol; still later, the abhorrence was shifted to glass, the material from which the thermometer had been made.

This also explains why she imposed her glass taboos on her parents with a "clear conscience"—wasn't it their job to prevent incest?

The tendency to bolster the neurotic symptom with a pseudo-moral connotation is a powerful weapon of resistance in psychotherapy, and especially in psychoanalysis.* It represents an additional difficulty—by no means the basic one, but one which contributes to the tenacity of the neurotic balance. One has to uncover the "private moral code" of the specific unconscious ego: one must also debunk the unconscious irony which has distorted educational rules—that technique which permits the weak child to beat the powerful educator with his own stick. This infantile mockery whereby reasonable educational precepts are reduced to absurdity (by perverting their meaning though preserving their sound) proves that the weak ego uses every available pseudo-aggressive means of warding off reproaches as to the basic conflict: psychic masochism.

In all this discussion of the ego ideal one should not lose sight of the fact that the *ego ideal is exclusively an unconscious structure.* It has no connection with the compendium of moral precepts harbored by every individual, for which the term "ego ideal" is sometimes incorrectly used. This usage is misleading; as a substitute term I would suggest "conscious moral precepts."

The classical example of "pseudo-moral connotation of neurotic symptoms" can be studied in premature ejaculation. The end result of the infantile conflict here is the masochistic wish to be refused (Layer I). The veto of the superego (Layer II) leads to establishment of the first defense mechanism: "*I refuse*" (Layer III). When this, too, is vetoed (Layer IV), the final layer (V) appears (second defense): "I give, I even give *immediately*—shouldn't one give immediately, if one gives at all?"

This irony encompasses both *maintenance* of pseudo-aggression (in previous publications,† I compared the prematurist's "giving" with a Barmecide's feast), *and acceptance of blame for the lesser crime* (pseudo-aggression). The latter manifests itself in constant self-reproach for depriving the woman of pleasure—even a normal

* First stated in my study on the topic in the *Psychiatric Quarterly*, 1952.
† Summarized in *Neurotic Counterfeit-Sex* (l. c.)

woman cannot achieve orgasm when the coitus is terminated after two or four thrusts.

What additional insight into the neurotic manifestation is provided by the assumption of a five-layer structure? In my opinion, the five-layer structure clarifies the following points:

A. The unconscious ego uses a double and not a single system of sentinels: only the defense against the defense is shown in the neurotic symptom.

B. By "accepting the blame for the lesser crime," the complicated defense of a positive and punishable action is presented to the superego, instead of a simple denial. This refinement "keeps the torturer busy."

C. The choice of the "lesser crime" presented as alibi has two drawbacks for the defense. First, its alternatives are limited: since the opposite mixture of derivatives of instincts is typically used, there is a monotonous sequence of libidinous tendencies (regardless of the level of regression) warded off with pseudo-aggression, and of pseudo-aggressive defenses warded off with libidinous ones. Second, this undeviating rule of "the opposites" gives rise to the unconscious ego's slightly paradoxical moral code, in which crimes ranked as major in the external lawbook may be used as "lesser crime" internally, serving as alibis for actions which externally would not be ranked as crimes at all.

D. The wide disparity between the internal and external moral codes frequently involves the neurotic in hopeless conflicts with earthly justice. For example, a deeply masochistic-passive person may, in order to ward off the superego reproach pertaining to exactly this passivity, use the strongest possible denial of passivity, which is murder. He thus exonerates himself before the internal forum, but at what an external cost!

E. The secondary defense is, if possible, constructed after the principle of narcissistic safeguards: the passive man's admission of pseudo-aggression, for example, gratifies him by adding another detail to his self-portrait of himself as a he-man. When he adheres to this defense in psychotherapy, he is fighting for his defensive balance, and for his narcissistic-megalomaniacal illusion as well.

The weak ego is an ironic ego,* which explains why our patients are *hypersensitive to irony* directed at them. For a long time after I first made this observation, I interpreted it to mean that the infantile ego wants to be taken seriously; these patients complain that one is "making fun" of them, and cannot understand that the irony is aimed, not at them, but at the infantile "conflict solution." Nor do they understand that this irony includes an invitation to an alliance and an identification, whereby they, too, can be inwardly above the situation, and even ironic at the expense of the neurosis.

I see now that their protests arise from a much deeper source. Since irony is typically a part of the neurotic symptom or personality structure, neurotics are unconsciously wary of the danger of "wising up" the superego. From their point of view, therefore, irony should be taboo—to the analyst. Moreover, in analysis the superego seems to be attacking on two fronts, for they project parts of the superego on to the analyst. Thus, an ironic remark from the analyst means that they "are being seen through" by the superego!

Irony, therefore, is a powerful weapon in the hands of the analyst. This does not mean that one should "make fun" of the patient— quite the contrary. It does mean that *irony can be included* with profit in one's formulations and explanations.

Since, as previously noted, the unconscious ego is limited in its defenses, and the superego's veto of an aggressive unconscious wish must be warded off with a libidinous wish as admission of the "lesser crime," while a vetoed libidinous wish must be warded off with an aggressive one, the ego is forced into an automatic *itinerary of the opposites.*

Nevertheless, Freud's early investigations uncovered a superabundance of libidinous wishes, which, as experience expanded, could be traced to phallic, anal and oral sources. Especially in dreams and neurotic symptoms, infantile repressed libidinous wishes seemed to predominate over aggressive ones.

I believe that a specific reason can be found for this *over-libidinization;* namely, an *inner defense.*

1. If my assumption that the infantile conflict of every human

* To clarify: the stronger ego *can* choose irony as a weapon or reject it, while the weak ego *must* resort to irony.

being spells "psychic masochistic oral regression" is correct, then one has only to review the genesis of psychic masochism (double hurt in the form of megalomaniacal and libidinous frustration—inexpressible fury—rebounding aggression plus secondary libidinization of this aggression) to understand that here *an aggressive conflict has been solved with libidinous means*. The defensive solution remains paradigmatic: libido, in the *clinical* pictures, is seemingly predominant.

2. *Historically,* libidinous frustration (always coupled with offense to infantile megalomania) was at one time real enough; later, in the clinical picture, it is too often merely an inner defense.

3. Of course, inner defenses are not static but dynamic in the life of the individual. When a secondary libidinous defense, too, is vetoed by the superego, a new pseudo-aggressive defense is then presented.

4. The startling predominance of infantile libidinous wishes in dreams has been explained by Jekels and myself in 1934, as "mobilization of ultimate reserves." The frequency of this material is not the direct expression of the quantity of repressed id wishes, but a desperate attempt on the part of the ego to mobilize derivatives of the life instinct against the equation: sleep = death.

5. The most puzzling problem—how can orally regressed neurotics use the Oedipus complex as defense?—can be solved by taking the following facts into consideration:

(a) The Oedipus complex demotes the all-powerful Giantess of the nursery, making her a passive being (the image of the baby) completely under the dominance of the father. The Oedipus complex of the boy is a pseudo-active "rescue station" from his passive-masochistic dependence.

(b) This defense is an admission of the lesser crime—once more aggression is used as defense against more deeply repressed masochistic-passive submission.

To prove my point, I am adducing the case of a woman suffering from depersonalization.

In a lecture delivered before the Vienna Psychoanalytic Society in December, 1933, I reported on an investigation of depersonalization, made in collaboration with L. Eidelberg, and on the basis of extensive clinical material.* Our conclusion was that the depersonalized neurotic labors under the following conflict: an anal-exhibitionistic repressed wish is warded off with pleasurable self-voyeurism: when that defense, too, is prohibited by the inner conscience a secondary unconscious defense is installed: "I don't peep at myself, I just mournfully observe my sickness."

The constant self-scrutiny of the depersonalized individual is well-known; this type of neurotic, to use Theodor Reik's apt phrase, changes himself into a "psychic observatory." This characteristic is not a byproduct of the disease, as previously assumed, but an integral part of it.

But why is the starting point precisely *anal* exhibitionism? This question could not then be answered; a clinical observation was merely recorded. No answer could be found in the extensive analytic literature, either, although, as Schilder remarked, "The number of interpretations offered for this facinating picture is almost limitless."

Further experience, during the next fifteen years † convinced me first, that the *scopophiliac "exchange mechanism"* is the basis of the neurotic disease entity, depersonalization ‡; second, that the therapeutic pessimism so frequently voiced is unjustified; third, that a specific answer can be found for the typical and variety of exhibitionism predominant in depersonalization. The answer hinges on *beating fantasies;* depersonalization seems to represent *one of the many possible attenuated end results of "a child is being beaten" fantasy, insofar as it is executed with scopophiliac means.*

Here is the experience which provoked the thought—later confirmed in four other cases—that there is an interconnection between the phenomena. A Canadian woman of French extraction of thirty-six entered analysis because of severe depersonalization. The symptomatology was typical; she said she was *"constantly"* suffering from "quite severe feelings of unreality." What was subjectively

---

* "The Mechanism of Depersonalization." *Int. Zeitschr. f. Psychoan.*, XXI: 258–285, 1935.

† "Further Studies on Depersonalization," *The Psychiatric Quarterly*, 24:268–277, 1950.

‡ The disease entity "depersonalization" must be distinguished both from transitory symptoms of depersonalization, occurring frequently at the high points of all types of neuroses, and from depersonalization encountered in schizoid-schizophrenic states.

even worse, she was "constantly" frightened "to death" of a "great attack" of the unreality feeling. That "great attack" had been experienced by the patient for the first time ten years before she entered analysis. At that time, she left her husband (after five years of marriage), allegedly to visit France and other foreign countries, (attempt at sublimation of voyeurism) and to write a book. In reality, she had been unhappy in her marriage, she was frigid and recently her discontent had been aggravated by the presence of her mother-in-law, who had come for a short visit but had stayed on and on. The attack, which was a state of sheer panic—"I'm losing my mind, am completely unreal, I feel as though I had broken loose from everything, a swimming feeling"—sent her back to her husband a few days after she had left him.

A few months later, she again started out to explore foreign countries. She entered upon a friendly relationship with a ship captain whom she had met on her short-lived first trip. For no apparent reason, she returned to her husband six months later, although the attachment to the captain continued for another three years. The break came when the captain insisted that she divorce her husband and marry him.

During the following years she had felt but "mildly" depersonalized. However, one year before entering analysis, a sudden and "full-fledged" attack had set in. She had been "drinking moderately, as usual" one day while reading a dreary English novel about two unhappy spinsters. She got up to turn the radio off, and "couldn't believe in the reality of the radio." Her panic lasted half an hour, subsiding slowly only to return shortly afterward at the dinner table. Feeling unable to fight off further attacks, she underwent psychotherapy and later spent six months in a sanatorium where insulin shock and superficial psychotherapy were employed. Finally, she started psychoanalytic treatment.

The patient described her childhood situation as one in which she was completely dominated by a malicious, irrational, petty and sponging father. The mother was submissive to the father's whims. The child had but one confidante, her grandmother. The patient described her grandmother in glowing terms. Her over-enthusiasm seemed designed to demote the mother, who had nursed her for only four months, and then left her in the grandmother's care for a year while she went to the west coast to take care of the father, who had been stricken ill during a trip. The patient's intimacy with the grandmother had been interrupted when she was ten years old, because the family moved to another part of the country.

Her father's attitude towards her had been one of ridicule; at the same time, he was ambitious for her, and wanted her to stand first in her class. She disliked him intensely, heaped all her hatred upon him, and finally completely severed her relationship with the family. At twenty-two she married a young man "with whom she could talk." The husband was a "friendly, shy, reticent, understanding and forgiving person." He had been deeply attached to his wife and refused the divorce she wanted, condoning her peculiar behavior and her protracted escapade.

Characterologically, the patient presented the typical picture of an injustice collector. A series of facts in her case history pointed in the direction of *oral regression:* her *drinking,* her being an *inhibited writer,* her *injustice collecting,* and last but not least, her *blushing* and *erythrophobia.*

In the transference, she quickly projected a series of "injustices" upon the analyst. She felt "uncomfortable," and constantly looked at her watch, as if trying to escape some danger. She refused to produce associations or to use the couch. She viewed both requests as evidence of personal malice on the part of the analyst. To produce associations was "impossible;" to use the couch unwise, because there might be a "stronger feeling of unreality when in that position." Her refusals, and a dream she had during the first days of analysis, made it possible to analyze her exhibitionism. The manifest contents of the dream were: "A *cow* is bleeding from a wound in the side; I *observe* the scene, horrified, from somewhere in the *rear* until a veterinarian comes."

Attention was drawn to the fact that when on the couch she seemingly "exhibited" herself from the rear. Her refusal to associate, too, corresponded to a defense against exhibitionism ("to reveal oneself"), while in the dream she observed the cow from the rear, and the wound, also, was on the side or back. Why that superabundance of direct or defensive showing of herself, and of peeping?

The patient could contribute nothing but a conscious recollection. At the age of five she had been taken to the bathroom by her mother,

and there watched her *father* take a bath. Thus shifting to the
father, she said ironically: "Obviously, I don't want to allow you
all the pleasure." It turned out that her blind hatred of her father
had been allowed to pass in her previous treatments; all her troubles
were explained as "fixation to the father."

The patient was shown that her transference was truly a *mother*
transference, fastened to the father image later in life. She was also
told that she obviously identified herself with the "cow" in the
dream. (In another layer, since the cow was the mother, the dreamer
was watching her own sadistic-masochistic misconception of sex.)
Attention was focused on the sequence of wish and defense—anal
exhibitionism being warded off with peeping. In her refusal to
use the couch, she "prevented" the analyst—*with whom she identified herself*—from being a "voyeur." But this of course pertained
to her, and not to the physician.

Interestingly enough, the material presented "convinced" the
patient. She accepted the exhibitionistic-voyeuristic "exchange." In
a long series of "refutation dreams" (see Chapter IX) she defended
herself against exhibitionism; these dreams were patterned after
the formula: "I am on the beach, everybody is naked, I am fully
dressed." She protested against only one point: she did not want
her weak mother dragged into the "story." She maintained her opinion that the real malefactor in her life was her father, and adduced
convincing reasons to prove his malice and irrationality. All this,
however, was but a secondary shift.

The patient's psychic masochism had been warded off with extensive pseudo-aggression. She constantly took the blame for the lesser
crime, fastening her guilt to alleged aggressions against her family.
That blind guilt, too, had to be discarded, and the guilt had to
be placed where it intrapsychically belonged: to her psychic
masochism.

What was the connection between beating fantasies and depersonalization in this case? The patient had very vague recollections
of being beaten by her father. Later, the recollections became clearer;
she remembered the father using a leather strap, a *cane* or a broom.
Naturally, she recalled only the fact that she was beaten, and the
pain; the alluring pleasure was fully repressed. A small incident
convinced her. Her favorite easy chair was made of woven rattan.
She spent all her free time sitting in that chair. She could not

explain exactly how that chair (which had previously belonged to her *mother-in-law*) had escaped the frequent "clean sweeps" of old furniture she made when redecorating her apartment. During analysis she toyed with the "unexplainable word": "ratatouille." After some time she recalled that this "meaningless" word was French slang for "ragout grossier," coarse stew. She pronounced the word "ratatue," which was reminiscent of "tuer," the French for "to kill." I asked whether she could possibly have created a synthetic word from "rattan" and "tuer," and inquired if she knew the material from which her father's cane had been made. It had been rattan-bamboo. Thus the word meant: "The beating 'kills' me." In toying with the word, therefore, she was accusing her mother ("bad stew") *and* her father!

Sitting with her buttocks in the chair, she exposed herself to the hated—and loved—rattan-bamboo, and to an undercurrent of associations with Chinese torture techniques and beating methods.

The whole impact of the patient's repressed beating fantasies could be approached—paradoxically—through her erythrophobia. In two papers, published in 1938 and 1948,* I have tried to prove that an enlargement of Freud's original formulation (described in his famous paper, "A Child is Being Beaten" †) has become necessary, due to Freud's own discovery of the pre-Oedipal phase of development. This enlargement, covering the substructure, presumed first that the child's aggression was originally directed against the mother's breast, and was only secondarily shifted towards its own buttocks under pressure of guilt—later, sexualized guilt. After the "executive" has been shifted from mother to father, Freud's original tripartite scheme applies: "My father beats a child whom I hate— I am beaten by my father (repressed)—a father substitute is beating boys."

On the other hand, in erythrophobia ‡ the two cheeks unconsciously have the meaning of two breasts; that pre-Oedipal structure is later changed, in the Oedipal phase, because of the exhibitionistic

* "Preliminary Stages of Masculine Beating Fantasies," *The Psychoanalytic Quarterly*, VII:4, 1938, and "Further Studies on Beating Fantasies," *Psychiatric Quarterly*, 22:480–486, 1948.

† *Ges. Schriften V* and *Collected Papers II*.

‡ "A New Approach to the Theory and Therapy of Erythrophobia," *Psychoan. Quarterly*, XIII; 1–43, 1944. (Read before the Fifteenth International Psychoanalytic Convention in Paris, August, 1938.)

penis-connotation of the head. The sequence of inner events is:
Layer I: "I want to gaze (tear, bite) at mother's breast;" Layer II:
first superego reproach; Layer III: (first defense) "I don't want
to peep, I exhibit *my* breasts (cheeks, later fantasied penis) "; Layer
IV: second superego reproach; Layer V: (second defense) "I am
afraid of making a spectacle of myself, I blush." In blushing, however, both warded-off scopophiliac wishes are smuggled in. By
blushing the erythrophobe centers attention on himself, thus exhibiting, while in unconscious identification with the spectator, he
peeps—at himself.

This patient used both defensive techniques. She fought the
unfinished conflict (originally pertaining to breasts) with cheeks
and buttocks. To complicate matters, a scopophiliac problem entered
the picture, leading to erythrophobia and depersonalization.

The connection between *beating fantasies,* executed on the *buttocks,* and *depersonalization,* warding off *exhibitionism of the
buttocks,* appeared to be this: In both cases the masochistic battle
was fought on foreign territory, with the buttocks substituting for
the breasts. The unconscious identification of breasts and buttocks
(a well-known phenomenon repeatedly described by different
authors, especially in dream symbolism) was of major importance
to the patient because, as a child, she had exhibited her breast-
buttocks as a means of negating her lack of breasts—one of the
possessions her mother had, but she missed. The buttock-exhibi-
tionism, therefore, was in itself a *defense.* It was also used as a
masochistic invitation to be beaten.*

*In seems that in cases in which beating fantasies are combined with
extensive scopophiliac tendencies, depersonalization is used as a
typical defense mechanism.*

The combination of beating fantasies and exhibitionism also
explains why the patient so readily remembered the scene in which
she watched her father take a bath. In this convenient recollection,
the guilt was shifted: not she, but father, exhibited! She did not
peep; mother forced her to look!

We see in this patient a long series of desperate attempts to shift

---

* The preponderance of scopophilia and beating fantasies perhaps also explained why no recollection of infant masturbation could be elicited. It is
possible that her puritanic education, combined with the real satisfaction derived
from being beaten, overshadowed direct masturbation.

both the scene of the original conflict, and its dramatis personae. The scene is shifted from the breasts to the buttocks, the conflict with the mother is transferred to the father. But it was precisely her pre-Oedipal fixation which prevented the normal and full-fledged development of the Oedipus complex. In this patient's case, the latter was always imbued with pre-Oedipal connotations. In her choice of husband she proceeded on the defensive level, marrying a kind, rather passive man in order to disprove her masochistic wish to be tortured. Even normal activity in a man was feared by the patient; every activity was identified (unconsciously, of course) with being pushed into the passive-masochistic position. Therefore, she could not divorce her husband, although she was dissatisfied with him in many respects; therefore she refused to marry the captain, although their "mutual understanding" was "perfect."

In her depersonalization, she partially succeeded in escaping the too-dangerous territory of the breasts, since she denied their loss by exhibiting her buttocks. The blame was thus taken for the lesser crime—*exhibitionism* * *substituting for the masochistic wish to be beaten.* It was interesting that the external factor which presumably led up to the second "great attack" was the "unreality of the radio." As mentioned previously, she was turning the radio off when the attack set in, and made her doubt the radio's "reality." The unconscious reason was: *she* had *willfully* silenced the harmless announcer's voice; therefore action should follow. Transposed to the infantile situation: father stops shouting, and starts beating. At precisely the moment when the buttocks should be exposed, depersonalization set it.

Her first attack of depersonalization had been preceded by a similar situation. She had just escaped a *woman's* tyranny (the mother-in-law who had overstayed her welcome), but the attack of depersonalization brought her back *in four days!* The "slave rebellion" was of short duration. The allure of mistreatment and exhibitionistic substitutes proved too strong.

---

* The father's attitude fostered the idea that exhibitionism "isn't so bad." For instance, on her graduation day he remarked, "You weren't the first in your class, but at least you were the girl with the best legs!" Much earlier, he had promoted the idea that the girl become an actress. Her "shyness" (defense against exhibitionism) made this, of course, impossible. Because her pronounced exhibitionism was connected with beating fantasies, it was strongly repressed; she did not even want to take off her coat during her appointments!

All of these desperate attempts to escape the original conflict with the pre-Oedipal mother, and to disguise it by inner shifts, proved ineffective. In certain areas of the patient's personality, even the secondary shift to father did not work: in *drinking* (see #30, Chapter V), in her *writer's block,** in *injustice collecting,* and *blushing.*

The patient's drinking represented both a *pseudo-aggression* against her mother, *and* a self-damaging, masochistically tinged self-destructive attitude.

The deep *oral-passive*-masochistic attachment to the image of the pre-Oedipal mother had been unconsciously fought by the patient via two other *pseudo-aggressive* and *autarchic* means: a predilection for cooking, and attempts to write. She was an excellent and discerning cook, thus counteracting both culinary dependence on the mother, and the reproach that she had been served poor food (see her pun on uneatable stew, "ratatouille"). On that battlefront, she was both ingenious and successful. The other, the sublimated culinary battlefront—writing—was a more or less losing proposition. She had no great difficulty in imagining a plot (voyeurism). Her difficulty was with the writing, and the working out (exhibitionism). She did manage to write a few stories, in fact a whole book, for children and adolescents. Here her cherished magic gesture entered the picture defensively: "I am showing you how I wanted to be treated—kindly." (See #6, Chapter V.)

That patient's writing block related to her inability to solve her masochistic attachment to her mother. As previously stated, it is my opinion that the writer "sets up shop" autarchically, refuting his unsolved psychic masochistic attachment to the mother by denying her very existence: *he gives himself, out of himself,* beautiful words and ideas.

It was also interesting that the "fear of being drained" (the reversal of her own draining tendencies) was very pronounced. The patient rationalized her retirement from her family by pointing out that her parents would sponge on her and take money from her husband.†

---

* The oral substructure is explained in *The Writer and Psychoanalysis* (l. c.).

† This attitude was also repeated in her sex life. She was either tender, though refusing sex, or else unconsciously pushed her husband into the role of "refusing mother" via frigidity; he thus "denied her pleasure."

Finally, her fear of being *"at any moment"* and *"without warning"* subjected to an "attack of unreality" found its simple explanation in the father's unpredictability in his beating procedures!

It was of interest to me, also, that the obvious idea of connecting *anal* exhibitionism and *beating* fantasies had not occurred to me (or to anybody else, for that matter) earlier. In re-reading the case history of a patient I analyzed twenty years ago, however, I did find a passage referring to attenuated beating fantasies:

Another game instituted by father (the patient's father) consisted of acting as a "scout": approaching the patient, the latter bent over a table, then administering a "tender slap" to the girl's buttocks. It became apparent that the patient provoked that game again and again; neither the father nor the patient ever marvelled at the fact that she so frequently found herself in the rather unusual position of being bent over the table. The father could not understand how it was possible that the girl could hear his approach and at the "decisive moment" make a half-turn in his direction. . . .*

The unusual feature in this case was that the father was rather kind and never punished the child. Nevertheless, the child had developed beating fantasies; they pertained to the mother.

A piquant detail in the case history of this (the Canadian) patient should be mentioned. After the connection between anal exhibitionism and beating fantasies had been clinically established in her case, she confessed: "The moment you mentioned anal exhibitionism, I thought 'It must have some relation to father's beatings' "—"Why didn't you say so?"—"Well, this was months ago!" . . . That is paradigmatic for the "help" patients give us!

One of the typical tongue-in-cheek defenses of the unconscious ego is that of "giving" under impossible conditions—an action which, in inner reality, is tantamount to "refusing."

One patient, who suffered from premature ejaculation, was capable of intercourse lasting *three to four minutes* if one specific condition was fulfilled: intercourse had to take place immediately after he awakened, when his wife (still half-asleep) abhorred sex. Otherwise, the duration of his intercourse was three to four *seconds,* and frequently his ejaculation was ante portas.

Analysis of the patient's prematurity revealed the typical oral-

* Quoted from "The Mechanism of Depersonalization."

masochistic substructure. The defense against the dynamic masochistic *wish to be refused* is pseudo-aggressive *refusal*. Since this
defense, too, is vetoed by the superego, the secondary defense is
registered: "How can I be accused of refusing—I give *immediately*!"
But this promptness is but inner mockery: no woman can derive
pleasure from two or four thrusts and a premature ejaculation
executed by a husband who is depressed, to boot.

Now, giving under conditions of mockery is identical with refusing. My patient derived what was actually a triple unconscious
defense from his ability to have "normal" intercourse in the morning. First, he proved to himself, once more, how "unjust" his wife
was—she refused sex merely because she was half-asleep! Second,
he proved to himself—and to her—that he didn't suffer from prematurity at all. Third, this intercourse in the early morning was
still under the influence of his ever-changing "dream girl," and therefore more or less impersonal; again, this was a pseudo-aggression
against his wife.

These interconnections were explained to the patient; he
demurred. I told him that he could make an experiment: why
not try intercourse on the occasions when his wife would awaken
before him, and would be amenable to his advances? The experiment was attempted; it was a complete fiasco. The patient concluded:
"If she wants sex, I feel drained, forced, trapped." In short, he
still (unconsciously) saw in his wife the monster of his baby days.

The complexity of manifestations of defensive neurotic refusal
must be great, because defenses in general are not static. When a
defense is vetoed by the inner conscience, the trimmings and external expressions are altered, as a compromise designed to maintain
the substructure intact. Of course, phenomenologically, this results
in a confusing array of seeming contradictions.

To name a typical contradiction: sometimes, out of analysis, and
rather typically within analysis, neurotics with premature ejaculation go through a temporary period in which they suddenly find
themselves unable to ejaculate at all, despite protracted intercourse.
This change from *ejaculation praecox* to *psychogenic aspermia* is
baffling only when one is unaware that the prematurist refuses
by giving too soon, while the aspermist refuses to give at all. Both
refuse defensively; both are orally regressed psychic masochists.

The mechanisms of "giving under impossible conditions" is, however, quite apt to produce a mirage which thoroughly deludes the "giver." How frequent, for example, are marital conflicts in which the wife objects that the husband "fails to create the mood for sex," and the husband—in real or pretended naivete—replies: "You wanted sex, you got it; what are you whining about?"

The identical conflicts are carried out in the sphere of money. To name but one of the numerous types addicted to this technique: the "refusing giver" is the man who "goes wild" when his wife asks him for money; he shouts, curses, reproaches, complains, and slams angrily out of the house. When he has gone through the entire antic performance, he gives exactly the amount he was asked for in the first place. The inevitable result is that the wife cherishes in her recollection only the disagreeable scene; she disregards the fact that eventually he "forked out." Thus this neurotic fosters in his spouse the feeling that he is a refusing miser. Consciously, the man remembers that he gave his wife the money and forgets the row; while the woman remembers only the row, forgetting the money.

Unconsciously, the situation is slightly different. The husband has an easy conscience because he gave "freely," and when his wife reproaches him for his stinginess, as she invariably does, he feels terribly abused. This feeling is exactly what he was looking for, hence the opening scene of the drama. In short, the stage was set, once again, by a psychic masochist.

Some neurotic women do actually drive their husbands to desperation with exaggerated and irrational demands. We are not dealing with this situation here, however, but only with that of the neurotic type, the "refusing giver," for whom the inability to *give with grace* is typical. Whether the demand is rational or not, the identical initial refusal follows *automatically*.

A description of a psychic phenomenon can teach us little of its genesis; two symptoms which appear to be identical, on the surface, may have widely disparate genetic structures. On the other hand, identical phenomena may have disparate outward appearances. For the latter, the inner identity of "refusing" and "giving under impossible conditions," is a paradigm.

Of all the problems of psychopathology, perhaps the most difficult to comprehend is this *constant change in inner defenses. There is nothing static about them;* they wear out because they are exposed by the superego. Hence, they must be replaced and reformulated. The untrained observer tends to conclude that the person "has changed." He has not, although his defenses have—temporarily.

Equally "confusing" is the fact that the many-faceted reproach of the inner conscience is—out of inner necessity—countered by a series of seemingly haphazard defenses emanating from the unconscious ego: libido is warded off with pseudo-aggression, pseudo-aggression with libido, ad infinitum (meaning "till death do us part").

And fully as puzzling is this detail: once one has digested the complications embedded in the precept of "the defense against the defense," it is apparent that *the whole battle of the conscience, in "normal" people as well as in neurotics, is fought on a spurious front.* If one falls for the ruse, one is in the position of the military strategist who mistakes the enemy's diversionary movement for an all-out attack—defeat is inevitable.

IX. Dreams and Inner Conscience

IN A LETTER ADDRESSED TO W. FLIESS,[*] DATED JUNE 18, 1900, FREUD asked the rhetorical question:

Do you believe that on a marble slab, placed at this site, one will in the future read:

> "Here revealed itself on July 24, 1895 to
> Dr. Sigmund Freud
> the mystery of the dream"

So far the chances are slim.

Strangely enough, the world did even better: today Freud's theory of dreams is hardly questioned by serious scientists. Freud had the fate (unusual for innovators) of seeing his theories widely accepted during his own lifetime. This was not, I believe, directly and solely due to the inherent scientific truth of his writings—many other accurate discoveries in science have had to wait for a century or even longer before being acknowledged—but to a rather coincidental factor. Freud's theories were introduced at precisely the time when Victorian stuffiness and hypocrisy were beginning to give way before growing opposition.

The famous dream of "Irma's Injection" (to which Freud alludes in the quoted letter to Fliess), reproduced in *The Interpretation of Dreams,* has served generation after generation of young analysts as guiding post in their study of the famous formula: *"Dreams represent unconscious infantile wish fulfillments, couched in a symbolic language."*

The accent in the early formulation was on libidinous infantile repressed wishes. The role of the superego (at that time still undiscovered by Freud) was merely suggested in the assumption of a "censor." More than ordinary credit is due Freud for the scientific

---

[*] Quoted from Freud's *Aus den Angaengen der Psychoanalyse,* Imago Publ. Co., London, 1950, p. 344.

honesty which impelled him to reproduce nearly all the associations in his dream, though some of them do not fit the proposed formula at all. This honestly made it possible for Jekels and myself to use the dream to prove our thesis that "every dream represents both repressed wishes and *refutation of superego reproaches.*" The thesis was presented in a paper read at the XIII International Psychoanalytic Convention in Lucerne (1934).*

Before scrutinizing the dream, a few general remarks are in order.

Half a century ego, Freud proved that dreams are the preservers of sleep. The disturbances which would otherwise interrupt sleep are absorbed, in a harmless-hallucinatory manner, by dreams. Freud at first considered that these disturbances were resolved by fulfillments of repressed libidinous wishes, stemming from infancy, and also by attempts to neutralize the day-residue. In *The Interpretation of Dreams,* Freud enumerates the following group, which is also included in the day-residue:

> *Unsolved problems, harassing cares, overwhelming impressions,* continue the activity of our thoughts even during dreams. . . . It is also certain that the day-residue *may just as well have any other character as that of wishes.*†

According to Freud, the dream as unconscious wish-fulfillment uses the day-residue in three ways: as integral part of the dream mechanism ("transfer of intensity from unconscious idea to harmless preconscious idea"); as a means of absorbing the disturbance embedded in the day-residue per se; and as camouflage against the "dream-censor," i.e., the superego.

These formulations date from 1899, when Freud published his epoch-making book on dreams. Later on, he discovered that aggression is a fifty-fifty partner in repression, and he proceeded to the formulation of the eros-thanatos theory. But he never correlated his newer findings on instinct dualism with his theory on dreams. As previously stated, this correlation was attempted by Freud's oldest living pupil, Dr. Ludwig Jekels, and myself in 1933. We came to the conclusion that the formulation, *"every dream represents an unconscious wish-fulfillment"* should be enlarged to read: "every

---

* "Instinct Dualism in Dreams," *Imago,* 20:4, 1934, and *The Psychoanalytic Quarterly,* 9:3, 1940.

† *Ges. Schr. II,* p. 475/6. The italics are mine.

dream represents an unconscious wish-fulfillment *and a defense against a reproach of the superego."**

We ascribed to this reproach of conscience the same psychic value as that of the repressed infantile id wish. On the basis of clinical material, we assumed that every dream must cope with "disturbance" stemming from the superego, as well as with the "disturbance" which was clarified first, that stemming from the reservoir of repressed wishes, the id.

This formulation increased the importance of the day-residue. Use of the residue for the purpose of providing a camouflaging "package wrapping" to the "censor's" scrutiny had already been established by Freud; according to our thesis, the residue *also* represents, symbolically, the superego's reproach.†

It seems that what Freud called *"unsolved problems, harassing cares, overwhelming impressions"* (see previous quotation) *in the day-residue are seized on by the inner conscience for the purpose of torture.*

Inevitably, the ego must defend itself—even and especially in dreams—against the avalanche of reproaches emanating from conscience. The fact is that dream-content, honestly reproduced, plus dream-associations, honestly reproduced, will automatically reveal the superego involvement. As previously mentioned, Jekels and I used the "Dream of Irma's Injection" to prove this thesis in the joint paper we presented at Lucerne.

Although it is a personal dream of Freud's dealing with the specific problems which faced him in July, 1895, and with his own childhood, the dream of "Irma's Injection" has become public scientific property.

As is well-known, the actual incident which is used as the day's

---

* The theoretical and clinical reasons for this reformulation can be found in the original paper, "Instinct Dualism in Dreams" (l. c.). In this study, the well-known unconscious interconnection between sleep and death is worked out. It is even possible that many erotic dreams are less the result of repressed infantile-libidinous tendencies that heretofore thought; they may also (and perhaps predominantly) be a defense against the "death connotation" of sleep. This may explain the frequency of morning erections. (See my paper, "Morning Erections," *Int. Journal of Sexology*, 3:3, 1949.)

† The day-residue even has a third function—it is also chosen because it contains attempts at refutation of the very same reproach. See *The Battle of the Conscience*, p. 234 ff.

residue in this dream is the somewhat hesitant and half-ironic reply of "friend Otto," a physician, to Freud's inquiry about the progress of his patient, Irma: "she is better, but not well yet." Freud says:

> I realize that these words of my friend Otto's or the tone of voice in which they were spoken, annoyed me. I thought I heard a reproach in the words, perhaps to the effect that I had promised the patient too much. . . . *The disagreeable impression,* however, did not become clear to me, nor did I speak of it. The same evening I wrote the clinical history of Irma's case, in order to give it *as though to justify myself,* to Dr. M., a mutual friend who was at that time the leading personality in our circle.*

The dream consists of a long series of defenses against reproaches of conscience, which is misusing the day-residue. The dreamer, the defenses run, is not responsible for Irma's illness—Otto is, for he administered an injection with a dirty syringe; the young widow is incurable because her sexuality has been dammed up through living in abstinence; she is hopeless because she rejects analytic interpretations, etc., etc. Thus we find a series of refutations of the accusation that the dreamer has been inadequately conscientious, professionally, linked with aggression against the alleged accuser, Otto, and the invoking of the "judge," M, the representative of the ego ideal, buttressed by the opposed authority of another, sympathetic, friend. In short, the dreamer is exonerated.

The question presents itself: exonerated by whom? Obviously, by his own conscience. Freud is justified in calling his succession of arguments in this dream a "defense in court." The plea is made before the inner tribunal of conscience. It is with admiration for Freud's genius and honesty that we observe how—without being conscious of it at the time—he elaborated on the role of the super-ego. At a certain point in the interpretations of his dream associations, he says:

> Curiously enough, there are also some painful memories in this material, which confirm the blame voiced by Otto rather than my own exculpation. The material is apparently impartial. . . .

And in another place, referring to the use, in the recollection, of three cases in which his treatment or diagnosis had been followed by unfavorable results, Freud comments:

---

* *The Interpretation of Dreams,* p. 196. The italics are mine.

It seems as though I were looking for pretexts for accusing myself of inadequate professional conscientiousness.

These contradictions can be resolved by applying the Jekels-Bergler theory. The superego uses, or rather misuses, the day's experiences in accusing the dreamer's ego of inadequate professional conscientiousness, as well as for raising doubts concerning his new method of treating neurotics. Acquittal is finally achieved by means of an almost formal legal defense, in which the plaintiff's arguments are turned against himself, and use is made of refutations, alibis, qualifications, counter-accusations, derisions, citations of exonerating witnesses.

Once the inner reproaches are dealt with and dismissed, the dream of "Irma's Injection" can succeed in fulfilling its second function, hallucinatory gratification of repressed infantile wishes. There are many easily discernible aggressive, erotic (especially voyeuristic) components in the dream.

The assumption that every dream represents an attempt at wish fulfillment of repressed infantile material, *plus* refutation of reproaches of conscience, pertains, of course, only to successful dreams. All too frequently, the dream is unsuccessful, and the superego has a clear field. Without going into the details of dream types (already clarified in *The Battle of the Conscience*), a few characteristic types, not described in the literature on the subject, should be mentioned here. I have drawn attention to them in previous studies (recently summarized in *Samiksa,* 4:4, 1951).

To begin with four types of dream indicating progress in analysis:

There are specific dreams directly connected with the analytic procedure, which make it possible for both the analyst and the analysand to test whether the specific analysis is on the right track, and at the same time to check the progress of the analysis.

One of these four types is encountered at the beginning of the analysis, one at about the middle, the other two as the analysis approaches its end. All four types appear with the greatest of regularity.

TYPE I: "REFUTATION DREAM," *encountered at the beginning of analysis when the interpretations given to the patient are dynamically correct.*

The actions of the inner conscience during analysis are entirely consistent with its anti-libidinous nature. It seizes every opportunity to extract additional punishment from the victim. Paradoxically, correct analytic interpretations presented by the analyst in the transference and resistance situation constitute such opportunities. These interpretations are presented for curative purposes, but there is no way of preventing the superego from misusing them. If the interpretation given to the patient is correct—and unfortunately this is the prerequisite—the inner conscience takes it up and makes the most of it. It is remarkable that correct interpretations, only, should be singled out; the formalism of the superego explains this, and it is one of the superego's "rules of torture." (See Chapter II.)

The superego's misuse of analytic interpretations is a "predictable mechanism," * and can be utilized as such. I make use of this mechanism in the first few introductory appointments of every analysis. After a general resume of analysis, and some discussion of its meaning, I tell the patient: "You will be more than skeptical about everything you hear; that's only natural, since you are not familiar with the world of the unconscious. Analysis is an affective, and not an intellectual experience—wait and see. But you will also be able to check up on me—with analytic means. If the interpretations given you are correct, you will produce dreams to prove to me, and to your inner conscience, that I am wrong. If, however, the interpretations are incorrect, you will not have these dreams. Your 'refutation dreams' will be your unconscious alibi. Since I don't know, yet, what your conflict is, nor what interpretations I will be giving you, I am handing a powerful weapon over to you. You will be able to check on me scientifically—you will have to admit that this is more than fair."

Here is an example of a "refutation dream."

A man in his early thirties entered analysis because of his irrational fear of going into business. His wife had supported him for years so that he could finish his academic studies. With her help, he had finally achieved the higher social position they aspired to, and a higher financial potential. But then his irrational fear set

---

* First described in "On a Predictable Mechanism Enabling the Patient Even at the Beginning of Analysis to Check on the Veracity of the Interpretation." *The Psychoanalytic Review,* 30:1, 1943.

in, preventing him from attaining the financial return his wife expected. In analysis, it became clear that his conflict with his wife—his refusal to "give" her social and economic advantages—was but a pseudo-aggressive repetition of infantile grievances against his mother. Consciously, he felt deep hatred for his mother, unconsciously, he was masochistically attached to her.

In the transference repetition, the patient revealed the traits of the habitual injustice collector. Both the masochistic substructure and the pseudo-aggressive defense were interpreted. While working out these interconnections, the patient had one repetitive dream (his only dream) which he ironically dubbed "the overcoat dream." His irony pertained to the impossibility of utilizing this dream analytically, since he could not describe its contents, or produce any associations with it. He could only say that the dream "had something to do with an overcoat." He could not describe the coat, identify its owner, or supply details of any sort. He began to ridicule my insistence on his remembering dreams, and my inability to "do something" with this one. My suggestions that he wait for material which would clarify the allusion seemed silly to him.

One day, in quite another connection, the patient mentioned his disappointment with his wife's wealthy but parsimonious relatives. He claimed that these English relatives, who were cloth manufacturers, had played a "dirty trick" on him. After the war, the patient had visited their factory, and ordered an expensive coat. The miserly relatives had not only allowed him to pay for the coat, but had subsequently cheated him out of his money, since he had to leave England before the coat was finished. In order to avoid the payment of duty, it was arranged that a nephew, who was due to visit the United States shortly afterwards, would deliver the precious coat. The nephew arrived—without the coat. He claimed that it had been stolen during his journey. The money was not returned to the patient, nor a substitute coat provided.

Thus the overcoat dream had more than the obvious symbolic connotations. The overcoat-motif represented for the patient the strongest possible refutation of the two reproaches mobilized by the analytic interpretations, and then taken up anew by the super-ego: "It is not true that I am masochistically attached to mother, and, in neurotic repetition, to my wife; I am aggressive. Moreover,

I have no reason to feel guilty because of my aggression, either, because my wife's financial help was just a trick through which she could exploit me later on—just as her family did, the cheating crooks!"

In this way, the patient refuted the interpretation (and later on, the accusation leveled by the superego) that he was at bottom masochistic, and defensively pseudo-aggressive. It should also be noted that in this dream the patient tried to fight his battle of masochism on the spurious front of aggression—a typical example of taking the blame for the lesser crime.

TYPE II: "ANTI-FALLACY DREAMS," *encountered in the middle of analysis.*

Every analysis has to contend with the patient's "basic fallacy." The latter is an erroneous picture of the patient's real childhood situation, or misuse of it for an unconscious purpose. Behind this fallacy is the assumption that neurosis is the direct, and photographic, result of the environment. In short, the patient denies his own unconscious elaboration of his real experiences. He believes that dragging out the family skeleton—"Father was cruel; mother did not love me; she preferred my brother; my sister hated me; the whole family was 'half-crazy;' our neighbor's son seduced me, etc."—is quite sufficient. The neurotic-masochistic unconscious elaboration accomplished by the patient is gratuitously overlooked, the blame is shifted, and the "conditioned reflex" elevated to the role of neurosis-creator. If analysis tries to include the patient's part in this drama, the patient furiously objects. By constantly exposing the "basic fallacy," guilt is mobilized, and the crutch removed.* This conflict manifests itself in a specific variety of dream, for which I have suggested the name "anti-fallacy dreams." † Once more, the superego pounces on the analytic clue, misuses it for its own anti-libidinous purposes, and with irony and malice shows the victim that he is really deceiving himself about his real motives.

A patient who was being treated for premature ejaculation had

* "The Danger Neurotics Dread Most: Loss of the 'Basic Fallacy,'" *The Psychoanalytic Review*, 32:2, 1946.

† First stated in "Three 'Battles' During Analytic Treatment," *The Psychoanalytic Review*, 35:3, 1948.

as his specific "basic fallacy" the fantasy that he was but an innocent victim of his mother's cruelty; in actuality, he was masochistically attached to her. After the fallacy had been exposed, again and again, he had this dream: "My mother is in the hospital and wants to see my sister-in-law." The association concerned two sets of facts: the actual sickness of his mother, and the beginning of the patient's marriage. His mother was suffering from cancer and was living on borrowed time. This did not lessen the number of family quarrels, or in any way abate the enmity between the patient's wife and his mother. The patient married under peculiar circumstances. He did not inform his mother of his plans, he "just told her"—the day before his wedding—that he would be married "tomorrow." His mother was infuriated, and was not present at the ceremony. Later, there were constant quarrels between the two women, the patient's wife being the more provocative of the two.

As usual, analysis could prove that the patient's mother was in no way the direct cause of his neurosis. His own unconscious masochistic attachment was the real malefactor, an attachment which he perpetuated by constant provocation. His exclusion of his mother from his wedding plans was typical, as was his alleged inability to maintain peace between his wife and his mother. His masochistic attachment explained, also, why he had married a shrew: once more he found himself confronted with a nagging and disagreeable woman. Officially, he wanted to escape his mother's nagging and "malice;" unconsciously, he duplicated these characteristics in his choice of a wife. His marriage, therefore, was not an "escape marriage," as he believed, but a continuation of unresolved infantile trends. His whole life was built on this masochistic-provocative technique, warded off with pseudo-aggression. His orally conditioned refusal of sex was a case in point: he "gave" mockingly, in a way unconsciously calculated to deny the woman pleasure.

In his dream, which emerged after a few months of working through the material in analysis, the superego showed the victim that his comforting "basic fallacy" was pure nonsense: "Mother isn't refusing, even though you provoke her; she still wants to see your wife (represented as her sister in the dream). And besides, mother is fatally ill with cancer, and you still keep up your fake grudges!"

The fact that the patient's wife is represented by her sister in the dream denotes an especially malicious attack against the patient's "basic fallacy." The patient had always considered his mother "half-crazy." His sister-in-law was a highly neurotic person, who had recently developed paranoiac ideas, which worried the family. In the dream, the inner conscience points out that the dreamer has no right to accuse his mother of "craziness," since his wife's family is on the same level; at the same time, the identification of wife with sister-in-law hints at their inner similarity. The ironic motto of the dream seems to be: "Look who's criticizing." Only in one point does the weak ego attempt a counter-attack, and even then only on the basis of taking the blame for the lesser crime. There are hints of the patient's identification with the sick sisters, and therefore a double admission of unconscious feminine identification, and of psychic illness. The second retort also contains a pseudo-aggressive note: "If I am sick, it's mother's fault—isn't she half-crazy?"

These "anti-fallacy dreams" seem to me to be of great clinical importance; for that reason, I am adducing two additional examples.

A patient in analysis because of masochistic personality conflicts had this dream after a few months of treatment:

"Escaping from pursuers in an area mostly destroyed by bombing. Run to back of damaged house, hiding in back yard. Four children, including my little daughter, are there. An old lady (gray, ugly, toothless), the grandmother of children (or some of them?) returns to room in house. I am hiding from her. She left but returned. Finally, children run out of yard, past grandmother in kitchen. She apparently hears them. Then I run and she comes after me, apparently in pursuit, repeating, 'I thought there were only two!' I understand the meaning of her words as indication that she knew of my presence all along, but had *no* intention of exposing me."

This patient's masochistic regression had led to severe conflicts. His first wife had left him for a friend; the second was no less aggressive and constantly quarreled with him. In his two marriages, the patient unconsciously repeated his masochistic attachment to the image of the "bad" mother. The patient had two sisters; he included his two and a half year old daughter with himself and his sisters in the dream, which was an innuendo accusation ("You act like a child") as well as admission of the lesser crime (feminine identification.) The "old lady" described as "gray, ugly, toothless" represented a caricature of the dreamer's mother (detailed associations were provided by the patient); the witch was allegedly the danger, and not the "pursuers."

In this dream, the inner conscience demonstrates the fallacy in the patient's assumption that his mother was his "enemy," for the "old woman" returned, obviously sacrificing herself for her children, and had no intention of exposing the children. (The real mother had herself been persecuted in the European country of her origin). The only defense—and it is a weak one—the dreamer's ego can put forward is one of self-deprecation: It denies that the dreamer was a beloved child by making the mother say, "I thought there were only two." The implied accusation is that the patient's mother ignored his very existence, and was interested exclusively in her two daughters. The underlying defense is, "If mother wasn't my enemy, she wasn't my friend either—she didn't love me." The prevailing mood of danger in the dream (bombing, pursuit) is once more an ironic memento: the danger is outside, and not in the family, as the patient assumes. Analysis seems to be subsumed under these "dangers," too.

The third example of an "anti-fallacy dream" is that of a woman in analysis because of severe depersonalization. (Described in Chapter VIII.)

The dream reads: "I sink in peat moss."

The patient's "basic fallacy" centered around the accusation that her mother had never loved her. Her evidence consisted of the fact that her mother had left her in the care of the grandmother at the age of four months, in order to travel to the bedside of the patient's sick father, and care for him. The mother and father spent the next year away from home.

The patient used peat moss to protect her flowers from cold in the winter. Prior to the dream, she had had the disagreeable experience of seeing some of the plants in her garden die because she had covered them with too much moss. The inner conscience used the incident to point out ironically: "One can be damaged by too much love, too!" The weak repartee is the symbolic-libidinous connotation of moss, thus, admitting to sexual wishes only.

Anti-fallacy dreams in the course of analysis prove that the inner battle to expose the patient's pet fallacy is proceeding— in the right direction. Once more, the prerequisite is correct interpretation.*

TYPES III and IV: "DREAMS EMBODYING GUILT FOR NOT BEING WELL YET," and "DREAMS OF DEVALUATION OF SUCCESS ALREADY ACHIEVED," *encountered as analysis approaches its end.*

After protracted working through of resistance and transference, the superego gradually abandons its position. Unable to maintain

---

* It should not be assumed that the neurotic tendencies of the personality endure without protest the superego's attacks, as manifested, for example, in anti-fallacy dreams. Quite the contrary. The unconscious ego fight back, sometimes using a weapon which can be called the "neurotic vindication dream." For example:

A woman of forty-four, an orally regressed neurotic, dreamed (after her use of the mechanism of orality had been pointed out and explained): "My mother-in-law sends me a present for my second wedding anniversary. It is a neatly wrapped package containing horse-manure. An accompanying note explains that the manure 'blossoms' only once in a hundred years. My husband asks me seriously to thank his mother for her present, and objects to my use of the word manure in my letter. He wants me to use a more refined word."

The patient's mother-in-law is wealthy, aggressive, rather crude, cynical and purse-proud. In her neurosis, the patient makes extensive use of the older woman's aggression, and is unable to resign herself to the nuisance-value of the tactless woman. The patient also accuses her husband of taking sides with his mother against her. The husband is a pedantic person, who constantly corrects his wife, especially in her speech, which is less "elegant" than his. The "blossoming" of manure (anal conception of sex) relates to the patient's guilt about her age and myoma, and therefore her inability to bear children.

The dream starts with the ego's counter-aggression to the superego's reproach: "It is not true that I'm masochistic. My mother-in-law is really aggressive, and even has my husband's support." She is ironic about her mother-in-law's stinginess, and her husband's pedantry.

The inner conscience, however, persists in its accusation of psychic masochism —the accusation which prompted this type of dream in the first place. "Even in one hundred years you couldn't get pregnant. You are old (one hundred years old). And even if your mother-in-law is impossible, she is correct in being disappointed at your inability to have children." The ironic defense is mustered to withstand this accusation: "That old horse of a woman (the mother-in-law actually has what is usually called a 'horse-like face') cannot produce anything but sterile sons." The blame is thus shifted, and "vindication" achieved. *Those neurotic "vindication dreams"* have, however, the inner purpose of maintaining the edifice of neurosis.

its old corruptibility, it becomes a champion of health—only because health includes the renunciation of old neurotic pleasures.* The result is a series of reproaches fashioned after the formula: "Why aren't you well yet?" These reproaches enter dreams, and are responsible for a type of dream for which I suggested the identifying phrase, "dreams embodying guilt in connection with recovery." † An example follows.

"I have to visit a new hospital. A great mass of people is gathered before the hospital. I pass a store handling china wares and pots. The crowd prevents me from entering a barber shop."

The dreamer was a patient suffering from psychogenic oral aspermia. The dream came at a time when the man had given up his symptom, but was still clinging to his neurotic personality traits. This was the situation preceding the dream: the patient's father-in-law had died a few days before, and the patient had missed a few appointments. Consciously, he was not moved by the old man's death. However, "death" was the cue which activated guilt in connection with his own mother's death, though that had occurred several years previously. The mother, or rather the distorted image of her, was the focal point of the man's analysis. The day immediately preceding the dream he had almost killed an old woman in his car, although he was an experienced driver, and himself admitted that the old woman was no more (and no less) careless than the typical pedestrian. On that day, too, he had fallen on the staircase of his mother-in-law's house. The patient identified the crowd in the dream as the mass of people who attended the father-in-law's funeral. The patient had been surprised at their number; he had not been aware of the old man's popularity. The china store had connections with a commission given him by his wife; she was an artist, producing fine pottery, and had asked him to fetch a pot from the store for her. Of course he had forgotten this commission. This was his association with the barber: "I did not have time to go to the barber that day, as I wanted to."

The dream demonstrates the patient's fight against the accusation that he retained sizable remnants of his masochistic attachment

* For elaboration, see " 'Working Through' in Psychoanalysis," *The Psychoanalytic Review*, 32:449–480, 1945. Reprinted in *The Basic Neurosis* (l. c.).

† First stated in my contribution to the symposium, "Theory of Therapeutic Results," held at the XIV Int. Psychoan. Convention, Marienbad, 1936. Published in *Int. Journal of Psychoanalysis*, 18:2–3, 1937.

to the enshrined mother image, and against the guilt which came
from his persistence in these wishes. The masochistic attachment
is denied and desperately warded off with pseudo-aggression: he
nearly kills a harmless pedestrian—an old woman—in substitution
for the mother. He is callous about the death of his father-in-law,
and accepts the guilt for the lesser crime of pseudo-aggression in
order to disguise his real crime, psychic masochism. This explains
his fall down the steps. In short, he is frantically trying to demonstrate and underline his defensive aggression. In his dream, he is
the sadistic voyeur of sickness and death, indifferent to the suffering of his whole family, and intent only on the petty, disturbing
details of the funeral. He admits, too, that he is not interested in
his wife ("pot"). Altogether, he acts the "bad boy" to mask his real
role, that of the masochistic infant. His feeling of guilt at the
temporary interruption of his analysis—in unconscious reality, his
guilt for clinging to the remains of his masochism—is handled with
the excuse: "I wanted to come to my appointments; how can I be
blamed if it was my father-in-law's death that prevented me from
coming?" He removes all significance from his analytical appointment by describing it as a routine visit to the barber. The dream's
allusion to "cutting" (via the barber shop) points to castration
fantasies, but at the same time these fantasies are made harmless
by comparison with an accepted routine. More, this allusion constitutes an alibi against his dynamically decisive conflict, since it
embodies a shift from the mother to a man (father). The mere fact
that missing few appointments provoked such a barrage of aggression from the superego proved that something of greater importance
was at stake: the inner accusation that he did not want to get well.

The second type of terminal dream is one which might be called
"dream devaluating success already achieved." The superego, when
unable to prevent analytic success, denies the value of that success
as a last resort.

A patient in the process of being cured of writer's block having
already resumed his creative productivity, dreamed:

"I was at a party, quite the center of attraction, holding the
floor. Suddenly someone (or was it I?) said condescendingly, 'Not
bad for a journalist.' "

The superego's irony is directed against the patient as raconteur,

(See #23, Chapter V) an ability which he retained even during his period of complete blockage. Tellingly, the inner conscience points out: "You are—at best—a story teller; as a story writer you're merely a—journalist."

In general, it seems clear that when guilt is mobilized in force, or the store of guilt accumulated within the unconscious is great, the dominating motif of the dream tends to become the attempt to ward off superego reproaches.

X. First Thoughts on Awakening, and Our Daily Moods

IN THE EIGHTIES OF THE EIGHTEENTH CENTURY, THE PHILOSOPHER Georg C. Lichtenberg observed:

Why is it, I wonder, that *unpleasant thoughts* should worry us so much more *on first waking* in the morning than a few hours afterwards, when the day has started and we are up and about; or why then more than at midday, or at night when we go to bed? I have experienced this again and again. I have gone to bed in the evening with a perfectly easy mind as regards some affair or other, and at four the next morning have found myself so much troubled by it again as to lie awake tossing from side to side for an hour or two at a time. By nine o'clock, if not earlier, I would be indifferent again, or even hopeful.

The philosopher's observation was correct in essence, though unprecise in description. He had noticed a typical phenomenon, frequently visible in some people, and occasionally in *everybody*. What happens is that out of the muddle of vague, half-formulated thoughts, one item is seized on for the purpose of self-torture. Minutely examined, these half-formulated thoughts, including pictures of the disagreeable events and duties the day has in store, present themselves as uncathexed *"bloodless schemes," to be put into full operation only secondarily by ego-cathexis.* One gathers the impression that the ego slowly regains cathexis upon awakening (sleep also means that the conscious ego is devoid of cathexis), and honors the debt incurred to the superego (a debt which is never paid in full) by picking up one of these "bloodless schemes" and filling it with—apprehension. Since only microscopic observation reveals this process, the erroneous impression arises that the torturing idea appears immediately, as the first waking thought. But the individual does not register the thought until after it has been crystallized, and made fear-inspiring. These painful reminders are not voluntarily chosen; "I found myself thinking" is the formulation repeatedly used by those who have noticed the phenomenon.

Here is one patient's description of his first waking moments. Mr. Q. said: "I woke up without recollection of a dream; in my half-dazed state I had the impression that a few disconnected thoughts were slowly emerging. These thoughts were ephemeral and peripheral, like looking at an old, blurred print of a movie. For a second my first wife appeared. Then I thought of a boring luncheon date I had for the next day with an acquaintance—a date I tried to avoid but couldn't. Parallel with this, like a marginal thought, came this idea: My first wife, even though she has remarried, and has been out of my life for nearly ten years, is going to revenge herself on me by telling my fiancee about the scene that officially broke up our marriage—the scene when she unsuspectingly came home from the office before I expected her, and caught me in bed with a girl. Because of my fiancee's jealous nature, I knew that this silly, long-forgotten tale could influence her adversely. The peculiar thing was that all these possible interconnections were not accompanied by any feelings at first; the thoughts were automatically produced, without any emotion. Gradually, I became frightened by the dangers involved, and then all at once I got really scared. . . . It took me some time to get rid of the thought; I finally did so by figuring out the excuse I would use."

Mr. R.: "The moment of waking is peculiar. My thoughts are as disjointed as Hemingway's latest style . . . Don't you think that the state of awakening, and alcoholic intoxication (in the depressed later stages) have certain similarities? They have for me, at least; I react in the same way when I wake up in the morning as I do in the *morose* stage of intoxication. The connecting link is morose thoughts. . . . No, there is a difference; I fall into a depression immediately after I pass the initial jocose phase in drinking, but when I wake up, I am indifferent at first, even though the thoughts that come to my mind are no less gloomy. . . . What happened today was that when I woke up I was seemingly having a discussion with the editor-in-chief, who was tearing my book to pieces after having accepted it. In reality, the man can't tell one hole from another, but in that discussion he was pretty astute, and pointed out a mistake in structure that I had never worried about. I had the impression that a clever and hyper-malicious critic had tipped him off. I was horrified, and had a vision of an endless rewrite job. In despair, I jumped out of bed. The irony of the situation is that all this time I had the erection I woke up with. You told me that these morning erections are less erotic than they appear to be, and more in the nature of a final reserve force, mobilized by the life instinct fighting against the connotation, sleep equals death.* If this is so, the situation is even more grotesque: by jumping out of bed with an erection which is a fake erection, I am running away from torturing thoughts, which are real enough. Isn't that double irony?"

Mrs. S.: "It seems that immediately after waking up, all my enemies have a rendezvous in my mind, sending me a gift of frightening thoughts. I don't exactly believe in human benevolence, but the malice with which my day begins is something extraordinary. The strangest part is that these painful thoughts start off, or introduce themselves, so harmlessly—as if someone were talking in a detached, matter of fact manner, even though the message is 'murder.' It is like the familiar movie 'double-take,' when a person hears something dangerous or damaging, doesn't see that it pertains to him, and then suddenly exclaims in terror, 'He means me!' This sly way of conducting an attack is really something! If you want a specific example: I recently invested additional funds in our business. I know that my partners feel that I am the eternal sucker, just because my grandmother left me some money, so I arranged to have this loan come officially from my husband. He consented to the hoax, and before going to bed I patted myself on the back for having found such a clever solution—now my partners will be dealing with my husband, and they know he is a sharp, hard man in money matters. This was my first thought in the morning: Ann, my hypocritical partner No. I, will instigate Mary, my dopy partner No. II, to start an affair with my husband, and then I will lose my money *and* my husband! What a mess, and these are *my* thoughts. A nice beginning for the day!"

There is little to add to the excellent descriptions of these three patients—all intelligent observers. In a "sly way," painful *possibilities* are enlarged out of all proportion. The technique seems to be invariable: peripheral thoughts, only secondarily cathexed. Malice is predominant ("as if all my enemies have a rendezvous in my mind"). In short, the superego is on the warpath. And still,

* See also *Neurotic Counterfeit-Sex*, Chapter I.

the cathexis comes from the ego; the fear is produced by the "sucker." The superego merely "suggests" the painful thought.

It would be an exaggeration to claim that everybody regularly awakens with "painful thoughts." Frequently, one awakens with the memory of a dream. This seems to be an antidote to torture— the general feeling is indifferent surprise, and some curiosity about what prompted the specific dream. Unless one is a member of that infinitesimal minority which understands scientific dream interpretation, the mere recollection (provided the *manifest* part of the dream has no painful contents to be misunderstood as the essence) seems to be a force in opposition to *pre-breakfast torture*. On the other hand, this is an antidote without guarantee: frequently painful thoughts appear as associations, even to people who have no idea of the possibility of finding the *latent* meaning of a dream.

There also occur optimistic moods on awakening, when there is no recollection of a dream, but only the sheer "pleasure of being alive." It is remarkable, by the way, how frequently a disagreeable dream is remembered later on. Obviously, the allotted dose of torture had been fully administered in the dream.

Then there are two defense mechanisms, clarified in my previous studies: the *"hypnagogic hallucination,"* * and some subdivisions of what I suggested should be called "small change" of guilty feelings, in the form of "senseless" but recurring words, tunes, visual images.†

Silberer's term, "hypnagogic hallucination," ("material phenomenon") fell into discredit because of the mystical misconceptions which Silberer attached to his initially correct observation. In my opinion, this phenomenon corresponds to a blocked anxiety dream. It may be observed in situations of drowsiness upon awaking or before going to sleep. The initial thought is of a quasi-rational nature; it is followed by the flash of a dream-like picture; finally the picture is dismissed with a slight feeling of surprise, and the original thought reverted to.

* "An Enquiry into the 'Material Phenomenon,'" *The Int. Journal of Psychoanalysis,* (London) XVI:203–218, 1935.

† "'Small Change' of Guilty Feelings," *The Psychiatric Quarterly Supplement,* 23:54–62, 1949.—"On an Ubiquitous Defense Mechanism of the Unconscious Ego: 'A Senseless Word Persecutes Me,'" *Contributions to Psychoanalysis and Psycho pathology,* Psychiatric Clinic of Tohoku Univ., VI:33–49, 1937.

Here is a single example from the extensive material available. A patient reported a "dream-like picture," asking whether it should be described as a dream. He said that before going to sleep on the previous evening, he had been laughing at the methods of analytical interpretation, and had vented his sarcasm particularly on the constant emphasis placed on "so-called unconscious connections." While engaged in this diversion, he had evidently dozed off. In his half-sleep, he saw the picture of "an uncanny being, who gripped me under the arm and hovered with me over a deep abyss." When the patient awakened—he stressed the fact that only a few seconds could have elapsed—he was astonished at the "picture" he had seen, and rather surprised at his equanimity, since it had caused him no feeling of anxiety. At once, he thought of Mephistopheles, and—forgetting Faust—proceeded to draw some more ironic parallels between psychoanalysis and the subtleties of the Talmud. He continued in the trend of thought he had pursued before the "picture-experience."

I asked the patient for his associations, and after a short pause he exclaimed: "Now I know where I got the scene. In a series of reproductions of details of Luca Signorelli's frescoes of 'The Damned,' in the cathedral at Orvieto, there is a scene in which the devil is carrying a man to hell. The whole picture I reproduced is simply a satire on psychoanalysis."

It so happened that I was familiar with the Signorelli frescoes, and with the book of reproductions to which my patient alluded. By taking the book from my bookcase, and showing the patient that very picture, I was able to convince him that he had made two changes in the fresco. The figure of the "Damned" is *not a man at all but a woman,* and the devil is not gripping her under the arm, but carrying her astride his shoulder and forcing her arms down. The evidence was incontrovertible, and the patient made no attempt to dispute it. He even volunteered the connection himself, interpreting the "picture" as his unconscious, passive feminine wishes. All the anger of the patient was based on exactly that interpretation.

The situation which preceded this "flash" can be reconstructed. First, the man ridicules analysis—through which he was confronted with the contention that he harbored feminine identification. His defense is counteracted by a superego reproach confirming the interpretation. The unconscious ego changes the impact into a "senseless picture" which the patient shakes off—investing it with a slight feeling of surprise—to continue with his previous defensive technique. Without that strange and successful unconscious expedient, the patient might very well have been sleepless and depressed for hours.

The problem of "small change" of guilty feelings pertains to a familiar observation. During some rational activity (working, "logical" thinking, reading, writing, talking), the person involved has a mental picture of some locality which he cannot place, or a senseless word is repeated in his thoughts, or he hums a tune. These pictures, words or tunes have an odd, recurrent quality; they are persistent, and cannot be easily dismissed. The typical reaction is surprise mingled with some annoyance, and even that reaction appears only in cases in which the repetitions persist for any length of time. They are never really torturing.

I have come to the conclusion that this phenomenon contains a severe inner reproach, leveled by the unconscious conscience. The element of "senselessness", and the absence of conscious understanding, are the work of the unconscious ego, which thus keeps the conscious ego free from the need to pay penance. Instead of guilt, mild surprise—or at worst, mild annoyance—appears on the surface, in consciousness.

These "senseless" words, tunes or images also appear at the moment of awakening. A patient complained: "I woke up at four in the morning and couldn't get to sleep again. Nothing was really bothering me, except for—a protruding eye. I know how foolish it sounds, but there was the protruding eye, and it kept me faithful company until I got up to keep my appointment with you. The eye is hard to describe; I don't even know whether it belonged to me or to someone else. My own body was like a sham, or a jellyfish."

"How about a few associations?"

"I know that trick. I've tried it—no results."

"How do you know that you will still get no results when you try it now?"

"I just know."

"You shouldn't predict. Let's have it: what about protruding eyes?"

"The only thing that comes to mind is a girl-friend of my wife's. The girl really has slightly protruding eyes, perhaps because of a slight case of Graves' disease. My wife raves about her; she claims that this girl is the only nice person we know."

"What do you mean by 'nice'?"

"A friendly, kind person. Not one of those bitches."

"Your distaste for associations is quite unjustified. You have just solved the riddle."

"I don't get you."

"Let's connect a few loose ends. After long inner conflicts, you divorced your first wife because you were not sexually attracted to her. You attached yourself to your present wife, not in spite of her aggressive nature, but because of it. She satisfied your wish— your unconscious wish, to be sure—to be kicked around. We have discussed these connections again and again. You yourself have admitted that your recent divorce made you jumpy, although you shifted the blame very plausibly to guilt at having made your first wife unhappy. Yesterday you reported that your ex-wife had called you up. Your conscience picks up the thread, and in an innuendo tells you: 'You are a weakling (jelly-fish). You cannot stand real love and kindness, which were provided by your first wife.' "

Here the unconscious ego is at its work of neutralizing severe reproaches. Only a mildly disturbing image becomes conscious. The superego's reproach is "arrested" and made ineffective.

That these mechanisms, which counteract and weaken self-torture, are operative, can be proved by a microscopy of the statement made on page 294: "out of the middle of vague, half-formulated thoughts, one item is seized on for the purpose of self-torture." Mr. Q., the writer quoted on 294 and 295, reported that on one particular morning he woke up thinking—quasi-optimistically—that today, unlike yesterday and the day before yesterday, he had no disagreeable appointments; then he thought of Budd Schulberg's *The Disenchanted*, which he was reading. But his third thought was disagreeable: a malicious and derogatory review of one of his books, which had belatedly reached him the day before, came to his mind. "In any case," said the patient ironically, "for the length of two thoughts my ego was strong enough to ward off the self-torture! Of course, one could say that when the Schulberg book crept into my mind it was a foreshadowing of torture—the book describes the final deterioration of a writer. But it took the inner conscience three tries to score—one should be grateful even for a respite."

"Unpleasant thoughts" on awakening, protracted to "pre-breakfast" torture,* are a common phenomenon which testifies to the power of the cruel superego. This torture is by no means restricted to neurotics, it is merely exaggerated in them. What is euphemistically called the "normal" person is equally subject to the phenomenon.

Why is the power of the superego so clearly manifested precisely in the moment after one has awakened? It seems that the motoric helplessness of the individual who is still in a half-drowse (it is not by chance that many people escape the discomfort of painful thoughts on awakening by immediately jumping out of bed), his lack of full conscious cathexis, increase the habitual cruelty of the superego. A contributing reason may be its "irritation" at the knowledge that the conscious ego is about to regain full possession of the weapons relinquished in sleep. The unconscious ego's counter-forces are already at work, however, as can be seen from the appearance of hypnagogic hallucinations and visual pictures, as discussed above.† In any case, the "early morning blues" are

---

* Lichtenberg, in his query, lumps together *"unpleasant thoughts"* after awakening, and the typical neurotic *morning depression.* The two are not identical, although there is the same basic reason for each: *unfinished business with the superego.* Interesting, too, is the fact that breakfast frequently dissipates or lightens these *"pre-breakfast blues."* There is more to it than simple repetition of the "first reassurances" in life—oral satisfaction from a fluid (shifted to orange juice, coffee, tea). It is also an inner defense: "I don't want to be refused—I want to get." . . . After reaching an understanding of the mechanism involved, a patient expressed it this way: "In my pre-breakfast blues, I am chewing unfinished business with conscience; this *first* painful breakfast is followed by my *second*—my real—breakfast. This one is reassuring, and a solvent of fears. Don't many people say, 'Don't talk to me before breakfast'?"

† It seems possible that unconscious use of symbolism in thoughts, acts and dreams has—in addition to the two purposes already clarified by Freud: archaic language, and the circumventing of the "censor"—a third purpose, that of guarding the conscious ego against self-understanding, which spells pain.

another indication of the fact that the superego seems to be *the* power in the personality.

Our daily moods are another illustration of the superego's dominance over the total personality.

Daily moods do not begin at daybreak. They are leftovers from the torture of the night. More or less accurately, they indicate whether or not the individual has fulfilled his personal quota of self-torture, and also how successful his unconscious ego has been in warding off these reproaches stemming from the superego. If the quota was not fulfilled, or the defense was inadequate, the individual's debt of depression must be paid during his daily routine. The result is the "lousy mood."

Every neurotic is a mass-consumer of constantly changing moods. The reason is clear enough, once it is understood that the neurotic is in a much worse bargaining position vis-a-vis his inner conscience than is the normal person. The bulk of a neurotic's aggressive energy is usurped by his cruel inner conscience, which uses it to torture the victim. A relatively normal person has a good portion of this aggressive energy at his disposal; his inner conscience has been more successfully checkmated, so that it cannot attack him constantly and feverishly from within. Consequently, he can also apply this energy externally to achieve his aims in the world of reality. Furthermore, the normal individual can mobilize these aggressive forces for internal use, to ward off unwarranted accusations made by the superego whenever it chooses to renew the inner battle. With a good arsenal of weapons for use against both external and internal opponents, the normal individual can boast that his moods are relatively stable. He can seldom be caught with either his internal or external defenses *entirely* down.

On the other hand, the neurotic's chameleon-like moods reflect the fact that his inner conscience is always examining his defense mechanisms, finding them sadly wanting, and rejecting them contemptuously. The victim is on the verge of desperation. Each shoddy, wornout defense must be replaced without delay, while the victim holds his breath and fervently prays that the new dodge will hoodwink his inner judge. This rapid-fire sequence of self-defenses becomes visible—both in the neurotic's own consciousness, and to outside observers—as a parade of unstable moods.

To put it differently: *moods are surface reverberations of alibis presented to the inner conscience.* The eternal question put to the inner conscience by the frightened unconscious ego is: "Will you settle for *this?* Please!" Almost invariably the intransigent judge rejects the shabby deal, and a new proposition is hastily submitted. Each new proposition, however, is always first dramatized in the production of a specific mood.

A clinical example: A passive man is inwardly reproached by his conscience for being feminine. As a result, the man is depressed; "femininity" is a discordant note in his self-portrait, for his is a definitely masuline conception of himself. But after a few minutes of gloom, his mood "unaccountably" changes. Suddenly he feels aggressively adventurous, eager to do things, ready for anything. He proceeds to the telephone, calls up a girl, chats with smooth masculine self-assurance, and invites her to dinner. She consents. He feels "fine" for a few minutes—only to revert to his previous depressed state before even beginning to dress for his date.

What happened? The victim doesn't suspect why he felt depressed in the first place. The constructor of his moods is his unconscious ego, working frantically under constant pressure from his superego. His conscious mind is merely the passive mirror-image of the inner balance of power which rests mainly with the superego but continuously shifts from id to superego to unconscious ego. His inner lawyer, the unconscious ego, tries valiantly to defend its ineffectual client: "He isn't really passive, you see, he's quite aggressive— just look at his two-fisted masculine behavior." One split second before putting this alibi forward, the defense switches to pseudo-aggression, and the victim is impelled to call up the girl.

The defendant, of course, has no idea of the frenzied activity going on behind the scenes, and draws upon stock rationalizations to explain his behavior. He "just feels like calling up a girl." Yes, but if that were the real story, would his spirits suddenly sag as he prepares to keep the date? He himself may have been consciously taken in by the dramatized alibi, but his inner tyrant certainly wasn't. The inner bombardment reproaching his "passivity" and "femininity" continues, and the price paid by the victim is further suffering in the form of a new onslaught of depression, and taking the blame for the lesser crime of psuedo-aggression.

The astounding fact is that *each step of the alibis presented to the inner conscience is dramatized.* Theoretically, it might be imagined that the whole process takes place in the realm of unconscious thoughts. But this is never the case. Why? We can only venture a guess, with our present imperfect knowledge of unconscious mechanisms. Possibly the inner lawyer believes that a demonstration ad oculos is more effective. It acts like a man who wants to convince a reluctant seller to part with his prized possessions by dramatically flipping a big roll of bills and slapping it on the counter with a flourish. For naive people, cash is always more convincing that a certified check, even one drawn on the Chase National Bank. Perhaps, too, the dramatization of alibis hints at the general principle that the unconscious prefers to work pictorially, as it does in dreams.

It is also possible, of course, that a certain amount of irony and disparagement comes to the fore in the inner lawyer's technique. The client is put through his paces in a way calculated to make him look like quite a fool, as though he were an exhibit which would clinch the inner lawyer's argument: "You see? This man is really quite stupid and ridiculous—he couldn't possibly be guilty of all your charges. And in any case, anybody as absurd as that deserves some leniency; one shouldn't be too harsh on an utter imbecile. . . ." It's as though the inner lawyer were trying to fool the judge by this primitive form of dramatization. It should not be forgotten that the unconscious ego is not only tortured, but cunning.

This formula—specific types of moods are dramatized unconscious *multiple* alibis presented to the supergo—requires some *amplification.* Obviously, people often suffer from pure and simple depression. What kind of alibi is hidden in such a mood?

One must distinguish between simple punitive actions on the part of the superego and anticipatory-hypocritical defenses set up by the ego to prove to the superego that the "client" is experiencing not pleasure, but suffering and pain. In the former case, little or no defensive element can be discerned in the depression; the superego is merely torturing the defenseless victim. It must be assumed, therefore, that moods are not only dramatized alibis directed *against* the inner conscience, but are sometimes simply the result of punishment meted out *by* the inner conscience. The incidence of this type of depression depends primarily on the strength or weakness of the unconscious ego. If the unconscious ego can still defend the client, the individual's moods will be of the *alibi-type;* if the inner lawyer is temporarily silenced so that inner conscience can hurl its reproaches without opposition, the *penalty-type* of mood will take over.

Alibi moods and penalty moods alternate, just as do the fortunes of war in the inner battle. The superego attempts to impose a Carthaginian peace, a cruel "peace" of slavery and extermination. On the other hand, the unconscious ego fights to get its client off with as lenient a sentence as possible, when full acquittal is out of the question. The inner battlefront is always fluid.

Moods are the outward reverberation of the dynamic fight between the different parts of the unconscious personality. These episodes in the life-long inner struggle in which the inner conscience is victorious are marked by depressive, *punitive moods of the penalty-type.* Alternating episodes, in which the unconscious ego presents mitigating circumstances to the inner conscience through dramatization of the defense, produce shifting *moods of the alibi-type.* The stretches in between are *periods of stalemate.*

(The superego's predominance in the formation of moods is also visible in the narcissistic victories achieved by the ego, such as external success, acknowledgment, flattery. The ensuing conscious "elation" represents the unconscious ego's elation at having discovered a new weapon for use against the superego.)

This formula is a psychic blueprint of our daily moods. It contains, in broad outline, the secret of the emotional see-saw on which we all teeter throughout the day. It is because this up-and-down mechanism operates in all of us, to one degree or another that one must caution the exuberant man, emerging refreshed and optimistic from a good night's sleep, not to be too cocksure about what the day will bring. One cruel barb, plunged into his psychic Achilles' heel, will be enough to set the emotional see-saw in dizzy motion. Then the "optimist," his euphoria suddenly crumbling, will begin once more to rant and complain about the "injustice" and "hostility" of this "mean" world, and be seized by a transitory depressive mood.

One can sit down to breakfast in this "best of all possible worlds"

only to have discovered, by lunchtime, that "life is no picnic."
See-sawing between dramatized alibis and penalty moods, the complaints and lamentations pour out more indignantly than ever. . . .

What about well-balanced moods? Where does normality fit into
this dismal picture? Surely reasonably healthy people do not, like
neurotics, ride the emotional Ferris wheel all the days of their
lives. Surely there are some stable people who, emotionally speaking, get through the day on an even keel.

There is no reason, as previously stated, for idealizing normality.
The so-called "normal" person, it is worth repeating, is simply
one who isn't *too* neurotic. He, too, has his battles with inner conscience. His well-balanced moods are not nearly as stable as he
likes to pretend they are.

True, the normal individual is less helpless than the neurotic
in the face of a superego attack. Well-balanced moods merely denote
a situation in which no unpaid bills of staggering proportions are
presented to the ego by the inner conscience—or at least indicate
a situation in which the ego is strong enough to checkmate the
inner conscience temporarily. Clearly, such happy episodes in the
battle of moods are more often encountered in so-called normal
people than in neurotics. When they are met with in neurotics,
we find that they are produced in a very different way. The neurotic may feel happy, benign, relaxed and at ease *after* a spell of
particularly severe self-torture—torture so severe that his cruel
jailer, the rampant inner conscience, is temporarily satisfied.

In normality, the more typical technique of achieving a state
of well-being is to keep the inner conscience in its place by counter-
aggression from the strong, hard-boiled ego of the "go to hell" type.
The neurotic is distinguished by the absence of a strong, hard-
boiled ego. His inner lawyer, while sly and shifty, always avoids a
knockdown, drag-out battle. Shyster that he is, he pleads and
insinuates, offers the shadiest of deals, but lacks the guts to tell
the inner Frankenstein (inner conscience) to "go to hell." For
the inner lawyer is fully aware that all his ingenious defenses rest
on shifting sand, and that his client's case is weak.

The character of the neurotic's moods—shifting, ephemeral, "now
you see it, now you don't"—are quite in tune with the character of

the inner lawyer. The unconscious ego of the normal individual need not be quite so adept at legerdemain, nor quite so much of a quick-change artist; it is not always necessary to pull a new and spectacular rabbit out of an inexhaustible top hat. Consequently, the normal individual is not always being forced to enact an endless series of alibis. When he produces an alibi it stands a good chance of acceptance, which accounts for his apparent stability of mood. But the difference between the normal and the neurotic individual is only one of degree.

The vicious cycle of neurosis is different: stalemate—reproach—depression—dramatized alibi—rejection of alibi—new dramatized alibi—depression, and so on. The cycle is repeated interminably. Only the deathbed sees the end of the emotional merry-go-round.

The morning may be a time of boundless optimism, for those who have emerged victorious from the "dream game." The always harrowing "pre-breakfast" blues may have been bypassed. But this good start, this having "got up on the right side of the bed," is no guarantee that the happy mood will survive the batterings to be received between nine and five. The way in which most people constantly misuse reality factors for half-neurotic or three-quarters-neurotic purposes—the way in which they find hitching-posts in the outer world on which to hang their alibis against inner masochism—gives the impression that they are never satisfied until they have consumed their daily dose of "masochistic cocktails," to quote an alcoholic patient.

Normal and neurotic people alike seem to ask themselves unconsciously, "Have I had my full quota of injustice today?" The only difference is a slight variation in the size of the dose required.

To exemplify with but one instance of inexplicable "changing moods":

Mr. T. reported: "I woke up this morning feeling depressed. Don't ask me about my dream—I don't remember it. At first I was furious at my entirely innocent wife, but her martyred expression spoiled the fun of baiting her. In the subway I nearly got into a fight with a woman who looked at me reproachfully, as if expecting me to be gentlemanly and offer her my seat. As soon as I reached the office I gave my secretary hell for forgetting to have me sign some quite unimportant letters the previous afternoon.

Afterwards I reproached myself for being so nasty with the poor girl—she takes everything so tragically. I suddenly developed a flippant mood and began to joke with her, making fun of everything. The stupid girl remarked: 'Why, Mr. T., you're a cynic.' This made me furious all over again. To myself I thought, 'You can't even make a harmless joke without being misunderstood.' Then I went to lunch, and eating really put me in good spirits. Now it's two in the afternoon and I'm still in a good mood. Not even the thought of coming to see you, doctor—a thought which always depresses me—could deflate my good humor. I'm curious to hear how you will explain the whole sequence of events, but before you start explaining I must warn you: I don't know your reasons but I thoroughly disapprove of them. Whatever you believe, I'm against it." The patient laughed at his own joke.

This patient had entered analysis because of constant conflicts with his wife. He criticized her interminably, his main objection being what he called her "infantile childishness." Analysis proved that he was inwardly a passive-feminine person himself, who devoted most of his psychic energies to proving to himself what a he-man he really was. All the reproaches heaped on his poor wife's head were merely expressions of unconscious jealousy: "She can display her feminine 'childishness' and helplessness, is even considered 'cute' when she does it; but half-hearted as I am about the pose, I always have to act the tough and aggressive man."

Mr. T.'s passivity was masked with the slightly ridiculous false-face of "serious manliness." When this interpretation was suggested to the patient, he ridiculed it. Asked why, in view of his sarcasm, he continued his treatment, he replied that he was a fair-minded person, ready to give everybody a chance. Since there was "one chance in a million" that I knew what I was talking about, he had decided to reduce me to absurdity by "sticking it out."

Mr. T. produced a series of dreams in which he was invariably chased, mistreated, or at the very least unjustly treated by men. Every attempt to correlate these clear indications of inner passivity with his difficulties in life was ironically rejected as "poppycock." During one appointment he had reported such a dream, dismissing it immediately afterwards with the words: "I just dreamed it to do you a favor." I told him that he need not exert himself to be considerate of me—dreams are never motivated by such altruistic impulses—and suggested that he try to recall whether he had ever had such dreams before he entered treatment.

He promptly denied having had such dreams before analysis, but a few minutes later his inner conscience played a trick on him. He did, finally, remember "one solitary dream of that sort" dating from his pre-analytical period. This isolated memory plunged him into a deep depression, but he "saved the day," as he put it, with another wisecrack: "You see, doctor, your silly influence has even managed to reach into my past, too." He left in a flippant mood, but for the rest of the day felt gloomy. The night was a restless one. He dreamed, and then quickly repressed the contents. Then followed the morning described above, the morning of snappishness and malevolence, with women as the targets.

A reconstruction of his many-phased moods during the morning in question leads to several assumptions. Still under pressure of guilt because of his now thinly-veiled unconscious femininity, he wakes up with unsettled debts due to his conscience. Result: a penalty-type of mood. As an alibi, all his pseudo-aggression is mobilized, and he upbraids his wife. She does not fight back, however, but assumes the role of martyr, which accounts for his complaint that the "fun was spoiled." Unconsciously, of course, he means something quite different. The inner reproaches continue, because his wife has not risen to the bait in a way that would justify his belligerence. Consequently, he has to elaborate the alibi presented to the superego by his inner lawyer, and on the subway finds an opportunity to be rude to another woman. His rudeness means: "I'm really not feminine, I dislike femininity—precisely the opposite is true about me." But his inner tormenter, rejecting the reformulated alibi, says: "Nothing doing."

The next step is undertaken in the spirit of "You can't blame a guy for trying again." He had attacked his wife and the woman in the subway for no apparent reason, but now he tries a new twist. His pseudo-aggression against his secretary has a realistic base, for she had really made a mistake in not giving him his letters to sign on the previous afternoon. This time the aggression *is* justified; the defense *must* work. But he knows that the letters are really unimportant, and that he is making a mountain out of a molehill. The defense is further marred by his secretary's view of his reproach as a tragedy. His inner conscience comments: "One more martyred woman, you weakling—another female martyr, just like your wife, and just as artificially created by you." Once more, the fake aggression collapses.

In his desperation, the man now tries a "slave revolt." He makes fun of everything, including the authority of the inner conscience, only to have his defense punctured by the secretary's observation that he is a "cynic." This comment is seized upon by conscience, which argues: "Not even that stupid girl takes you seriously— you're really making a fool of yourself, with all your elaborate pretenses." To counteract the returning depression, Mr. T. reverts to an attitude of anger and hostility towards his secretary. He goes to lunch, and at this point his mood changes "for the better," remaining a cheerful one right up to the time of his appointment with the analyst.

Eating, in general, meant little to this patient—his appetite was poor, his interest in food practically non-existent. On this day, it was as if eating had given him a new lease on life. The unconscious reasoning (based on the repressed infantile megalomaniac fantasy that food is provided because the mother yields to the infant's omnipotence) is: "If I eat well, if I enjoy my lunch, it means that mother loves me, feeds me, and therefore all the threats and accusations against me are not to be taken seriously. I *don't* want to be mistreated—certainly not by a man, even though my analyst says my dreams indicate such an absurd desire. No, in reality all I want is to be loved—by a woman. Well, I am loved. I eat heartily, smacking my lips over each mouthful. My mother loves me." Eating meant, in other words, "I don't want to be refused, I want to get." *

This new alibi, which reduces all threats to his ego to absurdity by the device of simple incredulity, lasts for some time. But the patient's persistent insecurity is visible in his identification with me. The joke about "disagreeing with your arguments without knowing what they are" was sheer plagiarism, because some time before I had told him the very same joke in connection with an episode in the old Austrian House of Deputies. (A filibustering deputy had

---

* As usual, the patient's regression to the negative Oedipus covered a more deeply repressed oral substructure.

said to the secretary of state: "I am not familiar with the government's reasons, but I disapprove of them.") Mr. T. is not aware of the fact that he is plagiarizing, nor that he is in this way trying to "borrow some strength." Nor does he remember the point I made when I told him the anecdote—that the statement made by the deputy was an example of a thoroughly *senseless* objection. As usual, even his newest alibi misses fire. There's a new depression in the offing.

XI. Are Parents or Inner Conscience, To Blame for the Neuroses of Children?

POPULAR OPINION, TAKING ITS LEAD FROM STATEMENTS MADE BY MANY psychiatrists and psychologists, places the blame for the neuroses of children squarely on the shoulders of the parents. This accusation seems to me not only exaggerated, but quite unjustified. In my opinion, the influence of the parents, even during the educational process, is not sufficiently powerful, not sufficiently penetrating, to serve as the instrumentarium of neurosis. To repeat, neurosis is *not* a photographic copy of reality.

The whole problem hinges on one fact, which must be clearly understood: the four trouble-makers which are conducive to neurosis are operative in the infant and baby quite apart from parental influence. These trouble-makers are:

(a) Desperate clinging to infantile megalomania;
(b) Desperate fight with passivity;
(c) Desperate though futile attempts to express and implement aggressive "countermeasures" against this passivity;
(d) Rebounding of this unusable and inexpressible aggression against the ego, and its accumulation in the pre-stages of the superego.

If my assumption—the end result of the infantile conflict in every human being is orally based psychic masochism—is correct, then the scourge of masochism is due more to inner than to outer forces. It is of course undeniable that parent's stupid mistakes can *aggravate* the child's intra-psychic conflicts—aggravate, but not *create* them.

The acceptance of the Freudian principle of accumulation of aggression in the superego (see quote in Foreword) makes it impossible for one to go along with the naive theory that the parents are the sole culprits in cases of later neuorsis.

In *Civilization and Its Discontents* (pp. 110 ff.) Freud stated:

Experience proves that the severity of the superego, which the child develops, does by no means mirror the severity of treatment which he actually experienced, as correctly stated by Melanie Klein and other English authors.* This severity of conscience seems independent of it; even when the education was a mild one, a child can develop a very severe conscience. Nevertheless, it would be erroneous to exaggerate this independence; it is not difficult to convince oneself that the severity of education has a strong influence on the development of the infantile superego. What it amounts to is that inherited constitutional factors and influences of the real environment work together at the making of the superego and development of conscience. This is by no means surprising, but the general etiological condition of all such phenomena.

Two facts emerge from this Freudian deduction:

(a) The severity of the superego is not the direct result of the educational process.
(b) The "X" of "inherited constitutional factors" must be taken into consideration.

Personally, I believe that—to express it simply—some children "cannot take" the unavoidable hurts inherent in unavoidable infantile frustrations: hurt to megalomania, hurt via inexpressibility of aggression. Whether or not the real pivot is the "X" of inherited constitutional factors is open to question, especially since the masochistic solution is universal.

In any case, the *worst* the parent can do is to force the child to create specific defenses, while *at best* the parent cannot prevent specific infantile misconceptions. Psychically, what differentiates one child from another is whether neurotic defenses, created *ad hoc,* are temporary only, being discarded when the *ad hoc* situation changes, or whether these *ad hoc* defenses, although superfluous in later life when the *ad hoc* situation has become part of the historical past, are retained as a permanent part of the psychic structure. In both cases, the psychic masochistic solution is used— as a temporary expedient in one case, as a permanent inner institution in the other. Perhaps Freud's allusion to constitutional factors —under which heading must be classed the inborn amount of aggression and megalomania—also pertained to a certain varying

* The last part of this sentence is a footnote in the book.

elasticity of the unconscious ego, greater elasticity spelling greater ease in coping with the inner situation.

This cannot be denied: although we have already progressed to the point where the genetic and clinical pictures in psychic masochism can be stated, *and* are capable of changing the scourge analytically, we are far from able to explain why one child does, and another child does not, acquire the scourge—even under identical external influences. However, since all neurotic defenses, including the "masochistic" solution, are created by the unconscious ego as concessions to *appease the cruel* superego, it seems to me justifiable to name the superego as the culprit responsible for the ensuing consequences.

Sometimes the term, "traumatic experience," is taken too literally. Freud clarified the issue: not only real facts, but the child's fantasies also, are traumatic agents. No experience *per se* will produce a traumatic effect if the soil is not fertile. The idea, frequently met with, that some *one* experience is responsible for a neurosis is an attempt at simplification. If one examines such a supposedly "traumatic experience" through the microscope of analysis, one finds that thousands of little incidents have preceded it. Furthermore, a so-called "traumatic experience" is often only the culmination of these preceding incidents, and equally often real "experiences" have been misconstrued to suit unconscious fantasies.

Another proof that traumatic experiences are not in themselves responsible for neurosis is the fact that often siblings, exposed to the same shock, react differently. In some cases, one sibling becomes neurotic, the other does not; in some cases, the two develop different neuroses; in still other cases, the "trauma" does not register because the neurosis is already established.

Moreover, the child may himself unconsciously provoke some psychic traumata, or misinterpret so-called real facts to fit into the child's specific neurotic situation.

The decisive factor seems to be the elaboration of inner and outer facts by the unconscious ego. A neurotic mother may be equally disagreeable to each of her two sons; when they are grown, one will *correct* the experience by marrying a kind and loving woman, the other *perpetuate* the experience by choosing to marry a shrew who will soundly mistreat him.

On the other hand, some undoubtedly tragic and "traumatic" experiences in childhood leave no decisive marks.

A writer of thirty-two entered analysis because of complete stagnation in his literary work. He came from an old and aristocratic European family. The patient's father was a high dignitary in the court of the emperor of his country. The mother was described by the patient as a "gentle, kind person" whom he "lost" *at the age of seven* in a strange and dramatic way. The father, having discovered that his wife was unfaithful to him, had their marriage annulled. The two children (the patient and his brother, one year his senior) were summoned to their father's room by a servant. The father was seated at a table, his army pistol before him. (He was a reserve officer, and had just returned from army maneuvers.) He informed the children that their mother, who had been away for the last few days (presumably visiting friends in the country), would not return. They were to forget her completely. Now he was asking the children for "absolute loyalty" to him. If they did not show the degree of allegiance he expected, he said, he would kill himself with the pistol which he showed them. Needless to say, the children promised everything, despite the fact that they understood only that they were to be deprived of their mother.

Here is a "traumatic experience" of dramatic power which might well have "knocked out" any child. What happened in this specific case? *Nothing at all,* as far as the patient's neurosis was concerned. He had already developed an oral neurosis, obvious in analysis because of his writing difficulties and his specific form of potency disorder (ejaculatio praecox). His attempt at "self-cure" through writing (see #2, Chapter V) broke down after a few successes, and at the same time his potency deteriorated: he was "refusing" in that sector, too.

The patient's inability to write and his potency disturbance sprang from the same cause: the futile attempt to prove to his inner conscience that he did not want to be *masochistically refused,* but that he did the refusing. In other words, his constant feeling of inner guilt forced him to produce an inner pseudo-aggressive defense expressing itself in the form of "I refuse." This refusal in productivity and in sex resulted in creative sterility and genital impotence.

Here is a precise formulation of the difference between the productive and the sterile writer. The *unproductive,* neurotically inhibited writer exhausts his psychic energy in the creation of his pseudo-aggressive unconscious alibi ("I refuse"), while at the same time he still retains the unconscious masochistic wish *to be refused.* The *productive* writer, experiencing the same conflict, solves it by eliminating the mother intrapsychically: "*I, myself,* autarchically, *give* ideas and words (milk)." The successful writer sets a magic gesture into motion: he dramatizes, unconsciously, how he allegedly wanted to be treated—kindly and generously. (See #6, Chapter V.)

What was the psychic mechanism by means of which the patient achieved, through psychoanalysis, both productivity and genitality? After working through his masochistic attachment he identified himself with the kind, generous, "reformulated" image of the mother, and "gave" words and sex.

This case shows that even an extremely "traumatic experience"— the revolver scene with the father—can remain without consequence if it does not coincide with the child's inner conflict. At the time of the scene, the boy's neurosis had already been established. From that point on, oral regression was inevitable, with or without "traumatic experience."

Although the "revolver scene" was without consequence as far as the patient's basic conflict was concerned, it did speed up the regression from the Oedipal to the pre-Oedipal stage. There is no doubt, too, that it produced scars: the patient's tendency to hypocrisy had its affective basis here, for he lived on the basis of lip-service, which he later introjected in fighting his inner conscience.*

Man's inhumanity to *himself* means the amount of psychic masochism present in quantitatively different degrees in every human being. Can something be done about it? The basic fact—the existence of a restricting inner conscience—is unchangeable, as previously stated, because the protracted maturation time of the human child is unchangeable. In the first years of motor helplessness the

---

* For details of the mechanism of hypocrisy see "Hyprocrisy," *Journal of Criminal Psychopathology,* IV, pp. 605–628, 1943.

cornerstone is laid for the anti-libidinous dictatorship of the inner conscience. In these first formative years, too, the child acquires with unchangeable regularity the pleasure-in-displeasure pattern which is psychic masochism. And if left to himself, his immature ego's weak attempt to hit back becomes codified, stenciled, and— lifelong.

The methods and moods which characterize the educational process have little effect on the eventual results. The ready-made inner pattern merely utilizes these external factors as hitching-posts. Lenient education does not produce an easy-going superego, nor does a sadistic upbringer automatically create a severe superego.

No educator would admit to that; and of necessity parents and teachers overstimate the importance of their roles. Nothing is more tragic than the sight of parents hesitant about every move, scared to death that their actions will have lasting and disastrous effects on their child. Where once children were in awe of their parents, parents now stand in awe of their children—and the outcome is just as unsatisfactory.

Time and again parents whose educational media are love, understanding, persuasion and kindness have reported that the child is "just unmanageable" and "seems to ask for a spanking." These poor parents have a grievance against modern child-psychology; they have faithfully followed these hypermodern precepts, suppressed their anger, practised angelic patience, and as a reward are confronted with inexplicable provocations from their child.

The child's plight should not be underestimated. Modern education deprives him of previously accessible outlets for his psychic masochism. An educational system which abhors punishment and caters to adult standards leaves the child's psychic masochism— homeless.

Does that mean that one should revert to the old technique of hitting, shouting, intimidation? Not at all. It simply means that the limitations of "love, persuasion, kindness and understanding" as educational media should be understood. These limitations are an inescapable duo. A certain discipline *must* be established over the child, and a certain amount of the child's psychic masochism must be taken care of. The underestimation of the latter leads to most tragicomic consequences.

I once asked an adherent of the anti-deterrence theory: "What would you do if your three-year-old established this routine: favorite sleeping hours, eight A.M. to six P.M.; favorite eating habits, raw meat dissected with the fingers; favorite sport, setting the house on fire with matches to be provided exclusively by mother; favorite attitude towards a younger sibling, pushing a fork into the infant's eyes. Don't you agree that after the quadrangular arsenal of love, persuasion, kindness and understanding had proved ineffective, and after you had assured the child that you love him even though you disapprove of the specific action, even you would have to proceed to some kind of punishment? And who on earth can prevent the child from misconstruing your behavior as a terrible injustice? And who on earth can prevent the child from remaining unimpressed by punishment, and repeating the same routine, provocatively?"

In other words, we are dealing with *results* of inner conflicts and *not* with their cause. If a child is specialized on considerable quantities of psychic masochism, it will extract punishment even from the most benevolent of upbringers.

Another fact of the same problem is the general underestimation of the effect of facial expressions, tones of voice, and exasperated glances evoked even in the most lenient upbringers by protracted "naughtiness." The child reckons with covert as well as overt manifestations of the parent's attitude. Hence even parents who "never punish" a child are meting out what the child misconstrues as punishment.

The latest pedagogical rule seems to be: don't suppress your dispproval of the child's "impossible" actions in the child's presence, but make it clear that you love the child in *general,* though you strongly object to a *specific* deed. Not even adherents to this precept can satisfactorily explain how the child can be kept from overlooking the underlying love, and selectively concentrating on the disapproval.

The ideal solution, obviously, would be to create a psychic situation in the parents which would eliminate even indirect signs which might mean "punishment" to the child. Do such people exist? More: can they exist?

Recently I witnessed the spectacle of a professional woman who gave up her profession in order to devote herself fully to the happiness of her boy. Every feeding had to be administered by her—"to avoid frustration," she claimed. The result was terrible crying spells when mother left the child for even a moment. The poor woman was the victim of her failure to understand meaning of "frustration." She took the term verbatim, not realizing that the child can be disappointed with *too little* or *too much* indulgence, as already suspected by K. Abraham. If there is too much indulgence, the child's megalomaniacal desire becomes insatiable: he is therefore no less "frustrated" than when he gets "too little." The tragedy of the situation lies in the fact that the decisive element is the way the child accepts the *unavoidable* frustrations which are an inherent part of life in the nursery. And waiting even a few seconds for mother's attention and care may have marked effects—simply because the term "frustration" applies, not to realistic values alone, but to the child's *megalomania* as well.

I am afraid the general public views the newer psychiatric findings on child development too schematically, and too optimistically: these findings are scientific appraisals, and not cookbook recipes which, if followed precisely, assure success. In applied psychology, adding a level teaspoonful of one ingredient, a dash of a second, a touch of a third, does not guarantee that the result produced will be "good." After two or three generations, parents who discover that their children are still neurotic, in spite of strict adherence to the modern educational rules, will lose faith in the whole approach. They are much more likely to believe that the use of psychology in rearing children is "nonsense" than they are to conclude that they have misunderstood the psychological guide book, or that the book's optimism needs revision.

Today's over-optimism, shared by parents and educators, on the chances of avoiding neurosis by applying the new techniques of child-rearing is certain to lead to tragic consequences. There may even be an understandable though unwarranted reaction from the modern methods, and reversion to the outdated and old-fashioned "punishing" education. In my opinion, the children of today, and their children, will be sorely disappointed as parents if they are disciples of the cookbook idea of psychology.

There are many ways of making one's life miserable. Neurotic expectations, or ignorance of the parent's only *relative* share in the psychic development of the child, is one of them. Children *may* be a blessing for the parents; only too often they are but a source of unhappiness. There are biological reasons for the wish to have children, but in addition parenthood has a complicated unconscious superstructure. Parents are unaware of the latter, and see in children only *an investment in gratitude on approval*. Ideally, they should view their children as no more than *an investment in possible identification*. If their expectations are not modest and limited, the parents' tragedy will be that they have made *an investment in injustice collecting*.

In recent years a new form of punishment has been imposed on middle-aged and elderly parents. Their children, now in their twenties, thirties or even forties, present them with a modern grievance: "My analysis proves that *you* are responsible for my neurosis." Overawed by these authoritative statements, the poor tried parents fall easy victims to the newest variation on the scapegoat theory.

In my opinion, this senseless cruelty—which disinters educational sins which had been buried for decades, and uses them as the basis for accusations which the victims cannot answer—is unjustified. Yes, "the truth loves to be centrally located" (Melville), and few parents—since they are human—have been perfect. But granting their mistakes, they acted as *their* neurotic difficulties forced them to act. To turn the tables and declare the children not guilty because of the *impersonal* nature of their own neuroses, while at the same time the parents are *personally* blamed, is worse than illogical; it is profoundly unjust.

As I have said before, the parents are incapable of "producing" a neurosis in the child. The naivete of the "passing the buck" approach, which shifts all blame on to the parents' shoulders, is patently unfair. The parents had parents, too. How far back is one to trace the blame? In every analysis one finds that the child in the patient used certain of the parents' traits as hitching posts for his own neurotic elaborations, but it does not follow from this that the behavior of the parents is the primum movens of neurosis.

The identical grown-up children who so vociferously cry "J'ac-

cuse!" to their intimidated parents will learn from their own
progeny that all they can do is follow the formula: "Do the best
you can, the rest is out of your hands." *

The parents of today are not even given the benefit of the doubt,
the opinion that parents are *not* directly resposible for their children's neuroses is never communicated to them. Scientific differences
of opinion should not be fought out on "culprits" who may—some
day—be cleared of guilt. These parents will hardly live so long;
in the meantime I firmly believe that they are being innocently
kicked around.

I cannot abstain from recording the bitter rejoinder of an elderly
mother in exactly this situation. When her daughter, with the
backing of her therapist, violently attacked the older woman as
the "author" of her neurosis, the mother said: "Somebody should
sponsor a society for the prevention of cruelty to parents—a cruelty
executed by misusing analysis."

On the other hand, I have observed that too frequently the
parents thus accused by their children were unconsciously almost
eager to shoulder the blame, although consciously they were highly
indignant. One should not underestimate the masochism of elderly
parents, either! When informed of their guiltlessness, some said,
"This is very consoling"—and went right on living on the injustice-
collecting diet.

* A wit continued: ". . . . except that you can start to save for the child's
eventual analysis."

XII. The Tragicomedy of It All: Superego Triumphant—Man Dangling from the Shoestring of Twin Alibis

Scientific facts, as seen in a specific moment by a single observer, are stated without pessimistic or optimistic preconceived notions, or sinister purposes. Further research may confirm, invalidate or correct the facts stated by the specific microscopist. He may be wrong, in which case the research of the future will disprove his assumption, and publicize his error in capital letters. He may be right, in which case the research of the future will acknowledge his priority (if at all) in a footnote. As Sir William Osler put it, "In science, the credit goes to the man who convinces the world, not to the man to whom the idea first occurred." And the scientist's campaign to convince his contemporaries is handicapped by a small impediment: every new idea requires an incubation period of a few generations.

This question comes to mind immediately: what kind of masochistic game is embedded in scientific research? If a scientist were naive enough to expect his research to bring him rewards—monetary, social, narcissistic (acknowledgment)—he would indeed be a masochist of the worst order. His only positive—and for that matter, immediate—reward is enmity and rejection, and both of these are forthcoming in rather generous proportions. It is as though "quieta non movere" were the generally accepted rule which the poor man has broken.

The culprit's usual answer is that neither recognition nor rewards matter; scientific research is a purpose in itself. Quite true, except that clarification of this statement is in order.

Yes, scientific research is a purpose in itself, simply because it produces one of the greatest pleasures known to human beings: the ability to pierce the unknown. The dark, "forbidden" territory—the terra incognita—becomes terra inhabitata, populated at least by theories and assumptions.

This search for the unknown is unconsciously not directed by such elevated principles as the "pursuit of the elusive truth." It represents a sublimation, of which some people see only the Oedipal connotation—a symbolic expedition to explore less symbolic sexual mysteries which originally pertained to the Oedipal mother. Behind this superficial layer, deeper ones can be detected. Clinically, this can best be studied by observing protagonists far removed from science—writers and artists in general.

In *The Writer and Psychoanalysis* (and in #2, Chapter V of this book) this connection was adduced: the writer solves his dual conflict of infantile peeping and masochistic attachment to the pre-Oedipal mother by changing voyeurism (imagination) into exhibitionism (by putting his ideas on paper he exhibits before the reader), and disproves the charge of masochistic attachment by negating the very existence of the "disappointing" mother. He regresses to a pre-oral megalomaniacal autarchy by acting *giving* mother and *recipient* child at the same time: he gives *himself,* out of *himself,* and for *himself* beautiful words and ideas. The pleasure thus achieved is that of "clear conscience"—or more precisely, conscience outwitted—*plus* narcissistic-megalomaniacal-autarchic satisfaction. In short, he attains the most profound pleasure known to human beings. The victory over the superego is not absolute, of course; conscience inevitably renews its attack, making it necessary for the writer to construct new alibis. Even wealthy writers, therefore, are impelled to continue to embarrass their early followers by poor writing. If additional alibis are not supplied, the "sublimation on probation" becomes unworkable, which accounts for the typical picture of temporary or permanent "writer's block."

In the same way, the scientist is in bondage to his conscience when he persists in his unacknowledged research. There is but one decisive difference. The writer, if he is not inhibited, uses his imagination freely:

> . . . . and as imagination bodies forth
> The form of things unknown, the poet's pen
> Turns them to shapes and gives to airy nothing
> A local habitation and a name. . . .
> *(A Midsummer Night's Dream)*

The scientist, however, is limited to *observing* his material. In short, the scientist is a writer with a specific solution within the sphere of his voyeurism. He has the "right" not to invent freely but only to report existing phenomena. Basically, this amounts to a childlike excuse offered to conscience: responsibility is shifted to the object of research. This condition satisfied, imagination is permitted some latitude, and new interconnections may be *perceived*.

The proof of the deduction can be found in the juxtaposition of two cliches which I have frequently adduced to point the difference between the scientific and the creative writer. The strongest objection against a creative writer is: *"He has no imagination;"* the corresponding, and equally weighty, indictment of the scientist is: *"He does not stick to facts."*

Once this substratum has been clarified, one can subscribe to the generalization: "Scientific research is a purpose in itself."

The comedie humaine can be thus defined: the child's life starts with the *fantasy* of *absolute power;* the *reality* of the adult begins and is prepetuated by the *reality of absolute power*—of *inner conscience!* Conscience forces specific people into research, as their specific dual alibi. This does not guarantee correct results. It merely explains the tenacity of specific researchers, and the unfailing appearance of new crops of scientists, in the face of external disadvantages. There will be no scarcity of people who continue to be fascinated by their own findings:

> Delightful task! to rear the tender thought,
> To teach the young idea how to shoot.
> (James Thomson)

Whether or not those who are forced into research by the pressure of their inner defenses will also prove to have "a talent for a talent" (Goethe) is another story.

In essence, these are the results of investigations pertaining to the inner conscience: *the superego dishes it out, and the ego takes it*—takes it, and occasionally launches a counterattack, weak though cunning. Life in the shadow of the superego is life in enemy-occupied territory.

This triad seems to me characteristic for the human child:

(a) Desperate fight with passivity;
(b) Desperately weak aggressive counter-measures;
(c) Desperate clinging to infantile megalomania.

The outcome is—only too often—psychic masochism.

By using the counterdevice of psychic masochism, the unconscious ego has found a remedy which is more than fantastic. It is the philosophy of the slave who believes that he has outsmarted his master when he inwardly reduces the torturer to absurdity by making pleasure out of displeasure. Thus *he gets a kick out of being kicked.* A rather meager payment for his labors!

To repeat, the *severity of the superego*—the inner torture-machine—is *unchangeable* because no method has been, or can be, invented to shorten the maturation time of the human child. Nor is there any possibility of changing another biological factor, for human drives are present at birth. Unusable, especially in the aggressive "department," they turn inward, building the core of the anti-libidinous Daimonion.

Moreover, unconscious psychic masochism is a pattern of the utmost tenacity once it has been established. A new, though self-damaging, pleasure is discovered and clung to. Proof positive is the tenacity with which analytic patients resist the change to all-too-publicized normality.

It is quite true that the inner scourge of psychic masochism can be solved by analysis in the majority of cases if properly handled. These analytic successes are impressive. But in some cases even proper handling is ineffective.

Scrutinizing the problem of these hopeless cases, one can begin by stating the analytic banality that the patient's and the analyst's aims are always at odds. *Unconsciously,* the patient wishes to preserve as much as possible of the inner wishes and defenses embedded in his neurosis; both *consciously and unconsciously* the analyst works for the destruction of the entire neurosis. This dichotomy in aims exists despite *consciously* proclaimed "good intentions" on the part of the patient.

The analyst's dynamic "maximum program" is constantly opposed by the patient's resistance—the static element. Only too frequently the analyst is viewed as the disturber of the patient's inner idyll.

Elsewhere, I have described the patient's typical attitude as that of a man who is sinking deeper and deeper into quicksand and frantically calling for help, but when a possible rescuer appears, treats him as an intruder; the endangered man does not exactly say, "Leave me in peace," but he acts that way—he looks in the other direction, and continues to cry for help.

In such situations, looking at his medical license, which obligates him to help people in medical distress, is of some service to the analyst. The analyst can also do himself some good by reminding himself that the patient voluntarily requested medical help. These two steps, plus the practice of some medical hygiene on himself, should enable him to continue performing his thankless task without furor therapeuticus.

Resistance per se is of course not an indication of an unfavorable prognosis. Resistance is unavoidable in every analysis. Nobody is allowed to lay hands with impunity on the infantile part of the patient's personality. Resistances have to be *"solved,"* and frequently they are solved by the correct application of analysis of the transference and resistance situations.

Still, a certain—though small—proportion of our patients show resistances which, though correctly worked out time and again, are *unsolvable*. We have to exclude cases in which the analyst is on the wrong path, and misunderstands the patient's real problem. Such cases do exist: e.g., there are tragic situations in which an orally regressed patient is confused with a hysterical neurotic, or a homosexual is analyzed ad infinitum on the Oedipal basis, or the pseudo-aggression covering more deeply regressed psychic masochism is mistaken for real aggression. These and similar cases were extensively dealt with in my book, *The Basic Neurosis*.

But let us assume that the case has been correctly handled, and nevertheless no real results are visible—after a reasonable time. What about these neurotics?

Sometimes the disgusted patient takes the initiative, sometimes the analyst. The patient may decide to end the perennial "fight between the door and the couch" in favor of the door, and run away. Or he may decide to consult another physician. The analyst may voluntarily suggest that the patient continue his treatment with a colleague.

Hope springs eternal, and nobody can blame the patient for clinging to the consoling fantasy that the physician is at fault. In cases in which the deeper layers were tapped, change of physician is without effect, except for the transitory "euphoric phase" based on the patient's pseudo-aggressive "proof" that the first analyst was to blame.

Patients who run away, or have the tendency to run away, after protracted analysis, are of three types: the *"acting out"* the *"resigned,"* and the *"naive"* varieties.

1) In the transference, the *"acting out"* type projects a specific infantile situation, and cannot be brought to understand what he is repeating. I described such a case in *The Writer and Psychoanalysis* (pp. 122–123).

2) The *"resigned"* variety of patient does not necessarily blame the analyst, and hardly ever does so when—as frequently happens—there is personal acquaintanceship with cases having identical difficulties who were helped by the identical analyst. Here the patient puts the entire blame on himself, and of course masochistically misuses it. Why these patients remain in analysis for so long a time is superficially not clear: they have given themselves up. One of the possible reasons is the pseudo-aggressive pleasure they derive from reducing the introjected mother image to absurdity: "You cannot achieve anything with me." The whole procedure of the defense is unconscious; consciously they cling to "vague hopes."

3) Patients of the *"naive"* variety fool themselves extensively, constantly claiming that "so much" has already changed. It is the analyst's business to show how little has really changed.*

In analysis, some neurotics present a particular problem when an attempt is made to solve a specific sector of their personality difficulties: for an interminable period they cling to pseudo-aggressive tactics in their relations with other people. Time and again during treatment, both in the transference repetition and outside it, they are shown how senselessly they provoke their fellow men, unconsciously only in order to prove to themselves that they are not masochistic but "aggressive." At bottom, they gain little by this technique; the inner conscience, for whose benefit the show is

---

* I have described such cases in "The 'Empty Bag' Type of Neurotic," *The Psychiatric Quarterly*, 25:613–617, 1950.

produced, remains unconvinced, and the victims of their provocation retaliate, usually with interest. Nevertheless, the technique is persisted in, and is in some cases unchangeable.

In analyzing these deeply masochistic neurotics, I have found that in addition to the so obvious defense against inner passivity, another element enters the genetic picture: an ego so weak and empty that—bereft of its typical defense—it has nothing to offer, and is incapable of finding a substitute. This "empty bag" attitude reinforces the defensive technique which is typically encountered in orally regressed cases, and at times makes it insurmountable.

Here are two representative examples.

An editor in a big publishing outfit, in analysis because of impotence, constantly quarreled with the authors "under his supervision," the phrase which, in his megalomania, he devised to describe his type of mechanical and not creative editing. Most of these conflicts grew out of his technique of making objections. Money-making authors were handled with kid gloves; those whose books sold less well were not. In a rather cowardly fashion, he capitalized on the fact that the less successful the author, the less chance there was of rebellion against his tactics. He got into trouble when a younger author complained to an older friend (also the "property," but in this case highly valued, of the same publisher). The established writer was amazed. "Incredible! He is submissive to me in a rather disgusting fashion." The older writer was so indignant that he called the matter to the attention of the editor-in-chief; my patient was energetically called on the carpet. It was this, coupled with his poor potency, which pushed him into treatment. But even in analysis, his peculiar superciliousness remained static for a long time. The patient denied being overbearing and disagreeable; his claim was that he just did his "duty."

Another patient, an executive in an advertising outfit, used the identical technique with his subordinates, especially the "so-called creative bunch," as he put it, tactfully. He got himself fired from his job, and when he was later rehired under humiliating circumstances, his new assignment was deliberately chosen to keep him from any contact with "the bunch." His supervisor told him: "Your personality makes it impossible. Why can't you 'live and let live?'"

In these and similar cases a very specific and, I believe, typical genetic pattern was discernible. The childhood history of these neurotics produced the image of a disagreeable, nagging, pretentious and opinionated mother (the father being a weakling). Instead of the normal process of overcoming the childhood disappointment, these children became masochistically attached to their mothers. Later in life, these only externally grown-up children still act two types of inner defense, both pertaining to the enshrined image of the mother:

(a) Pseudo-aggression, covering up and leading to masochistically enjoyed self-damager.

(b) Unconscious execution of a "negative magic gesture": "I shall show you in my behavior how I *did not* want to be treated." In this "reversal," these patients unconsciously acted the "bad" mother, demoting the innocent (by chance) victim to an image of—themselves.

Also typical was lack of precise opinion in their specific fields of endeavor. Even the first, very supercilious, opinion could be swayed by merely listening to the opposite opinion, authoritatively expressed. This, too, was camouflaged; these neurotics called it "being able to see both sides of the problem." In short, passivity can be disguised, not eradicated, by an inner defense.

It was interesting to observe in all these cases that the humiliating treatment these neurotics regularly gave their victims was also regularly compensated for by financial advantages for the very same victims. This, too, represented an anachronistic weapon: "The only thing I got from mother was money; but even this only gift was handed out in a disagreeable way." In recreating the *dependence in reverse* ("unconscious repetition compulsion")—now seemingly actively dishing it out, whereas previously they themselves had been on the passive-receiving end—they "proved" the alleged activity, and narcissistic "restitution." The helpless fury of their victims was another "proof" of how "powerful" and active they now were, the fury of the victim being their own feeling in childhood.

Finally, why the "empty bag" attitude? One can but tentatively surmise that creation of these weak and ineffective defenses left the ego bare of aggressive and libidinous energy, despite good intelligence. This, by the way, could also be proved in the marriages of these neurotics: they were all fashioned after the principle of "injustice collecting."

In a larger context, the theoretical question arises whether or not exactly the "singlemindedness of neurotic purpose"—condensed in the "empty bag" attitude—accounts for some otherwise inexplicable therapeutic failures.

What is the key to recognition of these hopeless cases? As pointed out, it is not the resistance per se, but the *chronic and boring repetitiveness of the identical attitude—unchangeable by the analytic procedure.* Interesting differences are encountered among the three types described above.

The "acting out" type will at all costs avoid understanding what hit him.

The "resigned" type understands everything, and even believes in the interpretations; as a perceptive patient expressed it, he plays the role of "mournful attendant of himself."

The "naive" type repeats the identical feature again and again, without the slightest conscious understanding. When the motivation of the specific action or reaction is explained, he argues as he did in the beginning, and then hypocritically accepts the interpretation, only to repeat the very same procedure on the next occasion. The naivete of his complaints is also characteristic: there are always the same "mounting tensions," the same accusations of husband against wife, or wife against husband. What they really want in treatment is a wailing-companion, not an analytic debunker of their imaginary woes.

There are three indications pointing to an unfavorable prognosis in the course of analytic treatment:

(a) If the patient, despite prolonged working through, persists in taking his depressions at face value, and is unable to devaluate them as bribes offered to the superego. ("I don't enjoy my masochism—see how I am suffering.")

(b) If the patient, despite prolonged working through of transference repetitions, still falls for the ruse of "taking the blame for the lesser crime," and constantly attaches his guilt to alleged pseudo-aggressions, whereas it really pertains to his psychic masochism. These patients behave as though the "bad" analyst, identified with the "bad" mother, were trying to force something down their throats—a procedure which they resist violently.

(c) If the patient, despite prolonged working through of transference repetitions, uses all analytic understanding for the sole purpose of renewed masochistic self-flagellation, without changing his attitude. This amounts to a pseudo-identification with the analyst—in reality, an ironic reduction of him to absurdity.

No possibility exists of predicting these reactions beforehand.

What is to be done with these hopeless cases? We can dismiss them, they can dismiss us. But before retiring to this quasi-solution, another possibility should be discussed: that of the *minimum-program*.

We could tell the patient of types 2 and 3: *"Imagine a prisoner whom we want to help towards his parole. He refuses, and decides to spend his life in prison. The maximum program has been made impossible, but we can still make his life easier—within the framework of his prison. This minimum program is not much, but still it is better than nothing."*

What it practically amounts to is finding *a way for the patient to live with his unchangeable psychic masochism.* This is not easy: it is always painful to accept an unchangeable damaging fact. The alternative before the patient is less engaging: to run around till the end of his natural life with the fury-producing "conviction" that he is but the innocent victim of other people's "meanness," at the same time conveniently overlooking the unconscious self-creation (or misuse) of these "injustices." In short, the consoling fantasy is half-discarded, and some kind of understanding substituted. In effect, it is the equivalent of teaching a person who has lost a limb on the battlefield to accept his loss inwardly, and live with his limitations.

Three advantages are included in the resigned attitude of the patient who accepts the "minimum program."

First, it is possible to halt the automatic increase of the neurosis, an increase which is otherwise unavoidable. Neurosis is a progressive, not self-limiting disease; if not stopped, its growth is automatic. To prevent playing for increasingly higher stakes in the *vicious*

circle of "mounting tensions—mounting pseudo-aggressions," therefore, is a minor achievement.

Second, the narcissistic aggrandizement which results from understanding other peoples' masochism gives the patient the feeling of
being "above the situation."

Third, not everything the patient has "learned" in analysis is
lost. The typical "runaway" from analysis ejects and "forgets"
everything he acquired in treatment, and spends a good deal of
time and emotion in collecting allies against analysis (his inner
guilt needs alleviation) who will confirm his judgment that the entire science is "nonsense." The unchangeable neurotic who accepts
the "minimum program" does not do this. The small voice of conscience reminds him—sometimes—of the inner reasons for his
actions thus—sometimes—checking the extent of his self-damage.

The decision to "throw in the sponge" in a specific case is a
difficult one for the analyst. If he is not a naive beginner, he knows
only too well that the "how like a god" attitude is but a malicious
misunderstanding on the part of outsiders. He also knows that
there is a margin for error in his crystal-gazing expectations: cases
which he had considered "hopeless" were helped; cases in which he
was optimistic at the start remained unchanged. Still, even at the
risk of being wrong, the decision has to be made—sometimes. My
experience has been that the majority of so-called hopeless cases,
so designated by colleagues, were simply cases where the masochistic-
oral substructures were neglected. Many of these neurotics *can* be
helped. Some cannot (these are rather exceptions), and it is to
them that the suggested "minimum program" is applicable.

All the recent talk of poor therapeutic results of analytic therapy
notwithstanding, I believe—on the basis of experience—in the
efficacy of analysis. It is the best psychotherapeutic technique ever
devised. That analysis is not a cure-all can readily be admitted.

One of the tragedies of human life has never to my knowledge
been stressed. The *psychic apparatus seems more poorly equipped
to deal with reproaches of the superego than with id wishes.* The
infinite variety of defensive modifications of id wishes and the
equally developed ability to accept substitutes, as the case may be,
is in marked contrast with human beings' virtual inability to
neutralize the torture principle of inner conscience. The inner

lawyer, the unconscious ego, does come to the rescue, but once the half-hearted presentation of defenses has been completed this inner ally has little to offer. The inner lawyer's "ace in the hole" is always advocacy of "taking the blame for the lesser crime," a device which leads, in its end result, to the creation of pleasure in displeasure—psychic masochism. Both the defensive expedient and its eventual end result presuppose acceptance of defeat.

The tragicomedy resulting from the superego's power is even more far-reaching. At best, in so-called normality, the human "machine" operates at only fifty per cent of capacity. The other half of the individual's psychic energy is deflected from productive work and pleasure in order to ward off the constant onslaughts of the superego. What a travesty! No saboteur could even approach the superego's achievement.

An understanding of the problem centering around the inner institution of the superego is further handicapped by two rather sweeping difficulties. *Outsiders* do not even know of the superego's existence, and tend to view it as a joke. Objectively, their attitude is almost ludicrous. *An individual who speaks lightly and disparagingly of the power of conscience has gone beyond naivete. He is playing handball with an atom bomb, which he has mistaken for a plaything.*

Insiders, on the other hand, are still influenced by the early concepts behind Freud's early formulations (which he later changed and modified) concerning the genesis of conscience.* The sub-

---

* The erroneous concept that the workings of the unconscious can be directly translated (completely neglecting the *double* defense) has even been used as the basis of a game played at cocktail parties. Recently, I heard of an especially silly one: name your associations to four key words; describe a garden, a key, a container for a key, and a garden after a rain. The "brilliant" idea here is the sexual symbolic meaning in each case, which the participants in the game naively believe makes it possible to draw direct conclusions regarding the "state of sex" of the player. Assuming, e.g., that a man's association with "container" is "coffin," and he describes the garden after rain as "trampled down," the conclusion of the simpletons reads: he has "sadistic" ideas about sex, and wants to "murder" the woman in sex. What if this is but the secondary defense and the test object is a severe psychic masochist using pseudo-aggression as defense?— Cocktail party "analyses" (including dream interpretations, "explanations" of parapraxies and the above-mentioned game) are but proof positive that their promoters do not grasp even the ABC of psychoanalysis. Simplification and simpletons are synonymous.

stratum of these differences of opinion is a tricky question: is, or is not, the superego a benevolent institution? Older theories, which use the Oedipus complex as basis, draw this picture: If you, a boy of five, renounce the incestuous desires directed at your mother, and your consequent hatred of your Oedipal father as competitor, you become a good boy who is quite well-treated by the introjected paternal image, the alleged core of conscience. The paternal sword is drawn only when incest is the issue. After de-sexualizing and 'de-aggressionizing' yourself Oedipally, you can live in peace.

This idyllic precept, created at the time when the Oedipus complex was the whole of analysis, was of course given up by Freud later on. If one compares it with his theory of fusion and defusion of life and death instinct; with his later statements explaining suicide as dominance of pure death instinct in the superego, driving the ego to destruction; with his acceptance of the relation of undischarged aggression to the severity of conscience; with his famous statement on the superego's "one-sided selection," which perpetuates only the "harshness and severity" of the educators and not their loving care (quoted in the Foreword)—not a shadow of a doubt remains that the later Freud no longer believed what the earlier Freud had assumed quoad superego. Even today, however, and even in analytic circles, the tale of the benevolent conscience is not dead.

No, the superego is not a benevolent institution. In *Civilization and Its Discontents,* Freud described the reasons for ill-feeling in civilization as based on exaggerated restrictions imposed on the id: the ego cannot take it. The more decisive obstacle to human happiness is given only a cursory mention, and that is the exaggerated restrictions imposed by the superego. The restrictions of the culture are *man-made,* and therefore can be *modified.* Modifications of restrictions—in essence, progress—are achieved in democracies, which acknowledge self-choice as the highest and most inalienable right of the individual. This is in complete opposition to the concept of the dictatorship of the "left" or "right," where the human being is the slave of the megalomaniacal dictator, and where no sacrifice—of the slaves!—is too high. The spectacle of the slave-states, which are endured by most, but accepted by some of their subjects in the allegedly enlightened twentieth century, is a gauge of the degree to which masochism is a living reality, in its tragic exaggerations of serfdom.

Restrictions emanating from the *superego,* on the other hand, are *biological;* as I have emphasized before, there can be *no modification* of the maturation time required by the human child. Nobody claims that human institutions are perfect; neither are nature's institutions. People will always quarrel about both, although so far they are ignorant of the role of that inner Frankenstein, the superego. Perhaps the most intelligent statement on human life in general is that made by the elder Huxley: "This may not be the best of all possible worlds, but to say it is the worst is mere petulant nonsense."

How does the average person, forced to live under the shadow of the Frankenstein, come to terms with his many-faceted disappointments?

People indulge in many forms of self-delusion; one of the most dangerous is the mistaken belief that they can better their lot by giving up situations, positions or professions they "dislike." No doubt, *external* circumstances may be unfavorable, and change beneficial, but these *externals* hardly affect *inner* conflicts, and by and large they are used as hitching posts for alibis or provocations. A neurotically querulous person will be querulous in any occupation; a neurotically incompetent person will remain a bungler no matter how often he changes his position; a neurotic injustice collector will be "mistreated" here, there, and everywhere. Confusing reasons with results, however, people go right on changing their external settings, even when the decisive difficulty is *internal.*

This situation becomes especially tragic in the late fifties and early sixties. With a minimum of financial security, some people "retire"—from their troubles, they believe—by giving up work.* What they fail to see is that *the specific amount of masochistic self-damage* which they unconsciously crave, and which previously they deposited in the difficulties of their external occupations, *is deprived of its accustomed source by their retirement.* Of course, they believe that getting rid of the "disturbing" profession guar-

* For elaboration of this thesis, "work as punishment necessary for the psychic economy," see *Battle of the Conscience,* pp. 118 ff.

antees contentment. Once more, reasons are confounded with results, and *self-torture is but accentuated.* Instead of inner peace, the effect of retirement is increased self-torture. In short, ignorance of the existence of the inner "torture machine" does not serve as a certificate of exemption. "Coelum non animam mutant qui trans mare current."

This is undoubtedly a bitter pill to swallow. *People do not know that psychic masochism is part of their daily menu, and unchangeable without psychiatric help. Hence, they struggle against their destiny, fighting a shadow! This is the real human tragedy, and it is made even more poignant by the fact that neurosis is a progressive disease.*

The analytic definition of emotional health is frequently given as "the ability to work and to love." As suggested in *Divorce Won't Help,* this rather limited formula needs enlargement.

A simple yardstick for recognizing neurosis is the lack of ability to work (sublimation), to love (tenderly and with normal potency retained), to have normal social contacts and interests, to enjoy one's hobbies. As long as there is relative *contentment* on that quadrangular score, there is no reason to become alarmed (p. 239).

I now believe that the "quadrangular score" needs further extension. Two partes constituentes are missing: *the ability to come to terms with one's disappointments* (at bottom this means to remain within the margin of safety for masochistic injustice collecting), and *continued ability to build the illusions and fantasies* which make life tolerable. Perhaps, since not-too-extensive injustice collecting and the ability to build harmless castles in the air are closely interrelated, the two could be subsumed into one classification: *"coming to terms with disappointments without any break in the flow of illusions."*

The necessity of producing *comforting and harmless illusions* (not to be confused with the partially or fully psychotic inability to perceive reality as it is) was stressed by myself eighteen years ago in my study on Grabbe (later included in *Talleyrand-Napoleon-Stendhal-Grabbe*).

The ability to create and to hang on to changing fictions (illusions) is a mark of normality, hence a process in which a current illusion is hyper-cathexed with libido. [Today I would add, "with aggression and narcissism."] When the illusion eventually collapses, a suitable period of mourning follows. This postpones but does not permanently prevent construction of a new illusion. Like its predecessor the new illusion will in time collapse (p. 162).

In German original, I called this technique "fictionsfaehig"—the ability to build illusions ("fiction-making") is an approximate translation.*

Investigation of peoples' "illusions" proves them to be defense mechanisms of varying valency. To take the most familiar neurotic paradigm: every psychic masochist claims that he has but one wish—to be "really" loved by a kind, giving woman. This conscious fantasy covers the real dilemma: he attaches himself to a shrew, is soundly mistreated by her, consciously quarrels, complains, but *unconsciously* loves it. The pitiful fantasy of "real love" is but a defense, created by his unconscious ego for the purpose of finding some refuge in "the battle of the conscience," and to provide himself with a narcissistic face-saving mirage.

In contrast with this is the fantasy of the writer rejected by the reader's indifference and lack of understanding, by the critic's malice and lack of understanding. Rejected or not, he believes that he writes for posterity. Stendhal, it will be recalled, constantly claimed that he wrote for readers one hundred years in the future. Here, too, an illusion is built under the influence of the accusing conscience, which gloatingly points to failure. The illusion's chances of fulfillment are immaterial. In some cases—as in Stendhal's—the claim has validity. Others who have considered themselves "posthumously born" (to quote Nietzsche's apt phrase) did not make the grade. Max Beerbohm's delightful satire, *Enoch Soames,* tells of a very minor and very "advanced" poet of the 'Nineties, who retained his faith in his future even though nobody read his verse. The proof of the pudding, he was convinced, could be found in the file of the British Museum in 1997—if only he could get there. Making a convenient compact with the Devil—his soul in exchange for an hour in the Museum's Reading Room of a century ahead—Enoch Soames arrives in 1997 and finds that the only men-

---

* Fictions of the imagination, not fiction-writing, are alluded to. In German, the word "fiction" has no connection with novel-writing.

tion of his name is in a precis of a story, written by Beerbohm, describing his compact with the Devil and his search in the Museum files. After Soames finishes telling Beerbohm his story, the Devil appears to claim his due, and the poor poet vanishes in a puff of smoke. Aside from the incidental fact that Beerbohm, in his story, betrays his own assurance that he is writing for the ages, the satire is both accurate and revealing.*

Although it is admittedly a broad generalization, but we are justified in calling the masochist's fantasy, as described above, *neurotic,* and the writer's fantasy, *normal.* The distinction is not far-reaching, for both illusions are built under pressure of inner conscience.

The differentiation becomes possible if we take into consideration the other ingredient: the amount of injustice collecting present. In general, *I believe that the extent of the individual's masochistic whimpering is a reliable yardstick for judging emotional health or the lack of it.* The more submerged a person is in unconsciously creating and unconsciously enjoying his self-constructed defeats, the higher is his position in the "neurotic brackets." On the other hand, since *nobody* is free from psychic masochism, *nobody* (not even the so-called normal, meaning not-too-neurotic person) fully escapes the fate of injustice collecting. Obviously, only quantitative differences exist.

Still, the *quantitative* difference makes for a *qualitative* distinction. Psychic masochists exhaust their emotional budgets with their unceasing production of "injustices," either by unconsciously creating them, or by misusing reality factors. To repeat the simile used earlier in this book: these people are eruptive volcanoes, producing injustices instead of lava. This "lava" is used for two purposes. A part cools off and petrifies—the product can be used for a lifetime as Exhibit A of the world's injustice to "poor little me." The other part is expendable, and ever-renewed for daily use.

---

* That such fantasies of posthumous glory are counteracted by irony of the superego cannot be denied. One such unrecognized writer, a patient making his living as a teacher of psychology, caught himself thinking, "Sure, you will become a scarecrow for pupils in A.D. 2040, when some poor college boy will curse you!"—Another writer, in such a situation, thought of Friedell's satire in which Goethe fails to pass an examination because he cannot satisfactorily interpret a poem by—Goethe.

The "fantasies" of these people are mainly regurgitations of injustices or impotent pseudo-aggressive revenge pictures. Both allegedly assuage the inner conscience: "See how unjust the real world is," and "See how I will dish it out!"

The technique of the slightly less neurotic confrere (the "normal") is slightly different. The same technique is used, in dosi refracta, but something is added: "Fiktionsfaehigkeit." *Somewhere defeat is accepted, too,* for who can pride himself on achieving every ambition? But the ability to "concentrate his interest" for some period of time on ever new "trifles" is present.

Does this mean that resignation is the only aim? Not at all. It simply denotes that the technique of playacting in the inner drama is different, as far as *deposition of infantile megalomania* is concerned.

The pronounced psychic masochist exhausts his energy in unconsciously proving: "It isn't the bad mother (the outer world) who is punishing me; *I*—because of my initial provocation—am *making* her punish me!"

In his fantasies, the "not-too-neurotic" individual retires from the disappointments of reality and *playacts for his own sake.*

Basically, the neurotically-defensive fantasy and the healthily-narcissistic consoling fiction differ in one way: *the neurotic still wants to convince his conscience, while the "healthy" (having paid the price of disappointment) wants to amuse himself—inwardly.* Strangely enough, the latter resigns himself "better" and with more grace than the former.

One could ask, of course, what difference, if any, distinguishes the daydream from "the ability to build harmless fictions." The difference is in whether or not the fantasy is implemented. A daydream remains ineffective and its real contents are kept "strictly private," while the "fiction" has reverberations in reality (actions or at least verbally).

Voyeurism plays an important role in this process. "To give audience to one's own fantasies" (Heine) presupposes the absence of neurotic inhibitions from the scopophiliac "department." Otherwise, "alysosis" (boredom) results.

One can enjoy the little pleasures of "fiction-making" on an elevated or banal plane—the results are the same. Freud alluded to the elevated plane of fiction-making in *Civilization and Its Discontents*, when he included artistic and scientific endeavors in his enumeration of the techniques used in fighting mental misery ("Leidabwehr"):

> Another technique of fighting mental pain uses shifts of libido which our psychic apparatus permits, and which renders its functions much more elastic. The problem to be solved consists in shifting *aims* of drives in such a way that *these cannot be hit by the outer world.* The sublimation of drives lends its help in that endeavor. One achieves the most if one is capable of sufficiently increasing the *pleasure stemming from psychic and intellectual work.* In this case, *Fate can harm that person but little.* Contentment of this type, like the pleasure of the artist in creation, or in the personification of his fantasies, or that of the scientist in the solution of problems and finding of the truth, carries with it a specific quality which—one day—we shall surely be capable of characterizing metapsychologically. (*Gesammelte Schriften XII*, pp. 45–46; my italics.)

Freud speaks of sublimation; it is doubtful whether all results of "fiction-making" are to be classified as such. For in sublimation part of the stress is laid on the element of social usefulness, and the outer world's acknowledgment of it. All this is not required at all in the process described as "fiction-making." From the standpoint of the future, specific fantasies may be useful; at the moment, they may be considered "foolish" and "a waste of time."

Sublimations and "fiction-making" are distinct psychic entities. "Fiction-making" is a purely narcissistic endeavor. Its purpose is hedonistic and no more. Most of the time, this amelioration of one's lot is possible only after the acceptance of a good deal of disappointment—which, as usual, has been misused by the superego for purposes of torture. Again, this proves that the superego is the real boss in the personality.

The ability to produce fictions and cling to them does not mean that the superego's "misery machine" stops production. All the usual techniques—superego's torture and defensive counterattacks from the unconscious ego—are encountered, including reproach, regret, remorse, depressive moods of futility and failure, painful thoughts and recollections, dreary expectations, rage, fury, injustice collecting, etc. But *parallel* with all this a "buen retiro" is temporarily found, to last until the next attack of conscience sets in—and till death concludes the spectacle.

There is grim irony in the restricted choice of pleasurable external diversions possible for most people. In an excellent novel published a few years ago, (Walter Von Tilbourg Clark's *The Ox-Bow Incident*), a stranger to a small Western town is given a list of the diversions open to him: drinking, gambling, fighting. The fourth possibility is out, since the only local prostitute is out of town on a visit.* The stranger settles, first, for a sexy fantasy evoked by a semi-nude picture in the center of the bar. Shortly afterwards, he is involved in a severe conflict with his own conscience, trying in vain to prevent the lynching of an innocent white man, unjustly accused of rustling.

The *inner* avenues are no less restricted. You can think the thoughts dictated by conscience, but they lead only to self-torture. You can think defensive pseudo-aggressive or pseudo-libidinous thoughts (daydreams) to prove to your conscience that the indictment is without foundation. "Tell it to the Marines," tell it to anybody—conscience is not convinced. You can submerge yourself in your work or your hobbies—they, too are all manipulated by inner conscience. Finally, after paying your dues to conscience in the form of *accepted disappointments,* you can retreat to your much battered narcissism, and "build fictions."

With only minor exaggeration, one could claim that "fiction-making" is an attempt on the part of the adult to escape to the pre-superego stage—a hopeless attempt. It becomes slightly more realistic when the price of external disappointment is paid as "conscience money." An anonymous poet wrote:

> There is a mystery in human hearts,
> And though we be encircled by a host
> Of those who love us well and are beloved,
> To every one of us from time to time,
> There comes a sense of utter loneliness.
>   (A Solitary Way, 1885)

"The grave's a fine and private place" (Andrew Marvell); the transitory stage which precedes the grave, when the individual himself is alone with his own fictions, has never been characterized by so flattering an adjective as "fine."

---

* The permanent resident in that town, of course, would have had available the more lasting pleasures of tender love, satisfactory home life, etc.

The opposite of "fiction-making" is either continued bitterness from the storehouse of injustice collecting, or full masochistic resignation—like the resignation exhibited by Melville's Billy Budd (see Chapter V), who shouts "God bless Captain Vere" just before his head is placed in the noose to which the captain has unjustly sentenced him.

But people accept life under *any* conditions—even vegetable ones.

The first time a patient presented himself with the complaint that he *could no longer "fabricate fantasies,"* I admit that I found it difficult to understand what he meant. When his complaint was clarified, and it was established that he was referring to daydreams, I asked when this ability had ceased. The patient explained that this had been a gradual process; little by little he had lost his "appetite" for his familiar dreams of "glory, sexual adventure, success." He was unable (or unwilling) to describe specific external failures preceding the painful event.

Since this first encounter with the lapse of the ability to daydream, this problem has confronted me repeatedly. I am reproducing a discussion of recent date with one of these patients.

An important man in his field consulted me, describing the identical difficulty as "fading daydreams." One fact was established very quickly: the starting point of his fading ability to daydream. The man was an innovator in a specific scientific field; his publications were bitterly attacked by more "backward" confreres. He found himself, first enmeshed in a succession of scientific feuds, and later entirely isolated. He was in his late fifties, and had amassed enough money to live in semi-retirement with the help of infrequent consulting jobs. He admitted to a "degrading scene," which had pushed him into treatment. One day, he looked through his own publications, and found himself holding back *tears* of self-pity, because his work was so little appreciated. This convinced him that he "must be really sick."

This was his avowed philosophy for his "remaining years": "What's the purpose of searching further and writing another dozen studies? They are, at best, for posterity; I don't believe in working for posthumous rewards."

"What did you expect, as an innovator?" I asked. "Aren't you familiar with the fact that the incubation period for every new and important idea is measured in generations?"

"Theoretically, I know all that. Practically, I don't know how to take it. Do you believe it is easy to see mediocrity and malice triumphant?"

"That's only natural. The coalition of adherents of quieta-non-movere is predominant in every field."

Subsequently, I discovered the reason this man had consulted me, specifically. He was acquainted with many psychoanalysts, and therefore was familiar with the fact that many of my own findings had been furiously rejected by some members of my own profession. He thought that in me he would find a "fellow-sufferer." He was astonished and rather disappointed (and even indignant) to discover that the putative "fellow-sufferer" was a "cheerful" person, as he expressed it.

He especially resented what he called my "sense of humor," and the tendency not to take adversities too tragically. "What are you so contented about?" he asked. "Or, since you are probably acting out some private comedy, tell me your recipe. What's the gimmick?"

"You are mistaken. After a rather long period of typical disappointment, anger, fury, I simply accustomed myself to my fate. It isn't easy, but it can be done."

"I don't believe you. You must still cherish some hopes of acknowledgment."

"I don't." To prove my contention, I showed the gentleman a passage from my book, *Money and Emotional Conflicts,* which had just been published. The passage dealt with my "lifework," *The Basic Neurosis:*

This is not, so to speak, a book but a *time bomb* which will go off in approximately one hundred years. Pursuant to the trend of thought suggested by the tombstone question of my patient (the preceding passage reports such a question, and my reply that I would choose as my epitaph: "A quotation from *The Battle of the Conscience*—'Man's inhumanity to man is equaled only by man's inhumanity to himself'—a reference to my studies on psychic masochism), I can only express regret that I shall not be present to witness the spectacle" (p. 258).

The prospective patient was not impressed. "Fiddlesticks. That's an official pronunciamento. The old tale of people 'born posthumously'—isn't that Nietzsche's phrase? Feeble attempts at consolation! What I'm after is the *real* suffering self, not the drapings of untouchability. Come on, give!"

Nothing could convince him that "no trick" was involved. I simply told him that there are psychological reasons for the fury aroused by "not being acknowledged," that the reasons are slightly different in different individuals, and that they *can* be analyzed. Though full of skepticism, the man entered analysis.

That patient had a hard time in his transference-neurosis. He had read some of my books, and "admired" some of them, which made it difficult to play the usual game of derogatory deprecation. His choice of me as an analyst had been based on identification. In his opinion—justified or not—we were both "pioneers misunderstood by the stupid outer world." He constantly reverted to the argument that my detached attitude towards "lack of acknowledgment" constituted some kind of pose. Even so, he envied me my possession of a "trick," a "gimmick," which he wanted to acquire. I countered with the statement that one should analyze *why* external "acknowledgment" should be so vitally important.

"That's a silly question," was his retort. "Why work creatively in the first place?"

I explained that basically any creative or scientific work has but *one* intrapsychic purpose: to furnish a suitable defense to one's superego. I added:

"Isn't it true that the scientific discovery of hitherto unknown interconnections is a pleasure in itself?"

This he admitted, but immediately followed with another objection: "Why don't you write for yourself? With your plethora of published books and papers, you yourself are the living refutation of your statement."

This question came at the end of an appointment; the patient left hurriedly, giving me no chance to reply. The next day, he reported that he had finally been able to remember his first dream. In this, *someone* tried to take a printed sheet away from him; he fought desperately, and awoke deeply disturbed.

"Here you have the answer to your question. Productively used imagination means voyeurism; publishing, and being "appreciated" means the defense—exhibitionism. Obviously, being debarred from the latter, you are stripped of your defenses. This probably constitutes one of the cores of your unhappiness!"

The great man was flabbergasted. He recovered quickly, and ironically asked: "As simple as that?"

"Not so simple at all. The fact that the two parts of scopophilia are exchangeable as defenses was not even suspected before the early thirties.* Now, assuming for the moment that infantile peeping is guilt-laden, the absence of absolution (external 'acknowledgment') via publication can cause severe conflicts in a person of this type. Don't underestimate the danger of tampering with that monster, the superego."

"Do I understand you correctly? By removing the infantile guilt from peeping, one becomes, as artist, writer or scientist, more or less independent of outside rejection?"

"Intrapsychically, yes. There still remains the narcissistic wish to 'shine,' and external advantages derived from prompt acknowledgment. Still, that's something no pioneer can reasonably expect. Therefore analysis of the 'scopophiliac exchange mechanism' can lessen the conflict, to use an understatement."

"Is *that* your gimmick?"

"Better tell me why, in your dream, you projected on me the role of the preventer of exhibitionism? What are you repeating?"

The man was quick on the mental trigger; he instantaneously understood the interconnection. Now he was willing to analyze the "scopophiliac department," as he ironically called it.

Without going into the abundant material pertaining to his pre-Oedipal and Oedipal phases, the result suffices: voyeurism (imagination) was freed from remnants of the infantile forbidden, thus imparting increased stability to the shaky material used in the sublimation. Hence the inner necessity of the exhibitionistic defense, surpassing the practical advantages of any defense, was diminished.

The next problem was working through the patient's projections of his severe superego upon the analyst. In his early dreams, "someone" (associations led to the analyst) *prevented* his exhibitionistic

---

* First described in "The Mechanism of Depersonalization," by myself (in collaboration with L. Eidelberg), *Int. Zeitschrift fuer Psychoanalyse*, 1935. Later enlarged in a series of studies summarized in *The Writer and Psychoanalysis*, l.c.

defense. Moreover, though the man did not at first admit this, the external rejection of his theories by his colleagues had produced an inner doubt of his being on the right track. It took him some time to understand that the anti-hedonistic superego *misuses* the absence of "acknowledgment" as a weapon of attack.

"Do you mean to say that elimination of this hurdle is your *second* gimmick?"

"You will admit that nobody is a sterner judge of an idea than its own creator. Having passed self-criticism, external criticism is comparatively unimportant. The point is: did you convince *yourself?*"

This, too, was worked out. The patient, though much calmer, reverted to his original pessimism.

"OK, I understand the role lack of appreciation and self-doubt played in my depression. But take objective facts: the promise of acknowledgment one hundred years hence seems illusory."

"Of course. If an innovator is correct, he will be mentioned in a footnote—if at all—by his successors or plagiarists. If he is wrong, refutation of his theories will rate more space and considerably more publicity. All this, of course, comes after his death. All he will earn in his lifetime is enmity and rejection. Therefore any illusions about posthumous success are a harmless game of consolation. It is less harmless when an innovator expects success during his lifetime— here the game played is that of psychic masochism."

Once more the inevitable question—"Is relative diminution of masochism your *third* gimmick?"—was posed.

All this working through took a few months. The man became much more reconciled to his fate. His pseudo-aggression diminished, and some kind of stabilization was achieved.

He was so elated by his "return to the working and living category'" that he had to be reminded of his original complaint— running out of daydreams. This could be understood quickly. Before analytic treatment began, the man had been under attack from his inner conscience on three fronts:

(a) By holding up his *psychic masochism:* here exaggerated pseudo-aggression against his scientific detractors was used as defense;

(b) By holding up his *infantile guilt-laden peeping,* incompletely rarefied in the creative imagination: here exhibitionism was attempted as defense, but without success (misuse of lack of acknowledgment);

(c) By holding up *ironic doubts concerning his "rejected theories"*: here only unproductive and exaggerated fury against his "detractors" appeared as defense.

The helpless and beleaguered ego had tried to avoid a series of dangers by "losing" its ability to fabricate consoling daydreams. The inner reasoning read: "If I don't imagine anything, I cannot be a guilty peeper; I cannot be masochistic in failure, nor create something new." In this triple defense of the "good boy" variety, the man sacrificed one of the basic techniques of inner consolation—the creation of defensive and narcissistic daydreams, and fiction-making. Fortunately for him, this ability, too, could be restored.

The case of the man who "ran out of daydreams" is not reported because there are so many innovators, and not even because there are so many people who lost their ability to construct consoling fantasies. It is cited as another demonstration of the power of inner conscience—which is all-pervasive and all malicious.

The *metapsychology of "happiness"* was clarified by Jekels and myself in 1933 in "Transference and Love," where we defined this feeling as the reflection of the *unconscious ego's transitory and elusive checkmating of the superego.* As paradigm, we adduced the high point of requited love. At this time, the lover can "produce" (by projecting his ego ideal) an unimpeachable witness who will attest *on credit* to all the wonderful ideas of grandeur his ego ideal harbors, and which are habitually used as torture material by Daimonion when they are not—and they never can be—fully achieved. Thus the Daimonion is temporarily rendered helpless for it has been deprived of its instrument of torture, the discrepancy between ego and ego ideal. Since the ego ideal contains a great deal of infantile megalomania (attenuated to narcissism), the latter is seemingly materialized, too. *The temporary absence of inner guilt, plus the tangential "fulfillment" of infantile megalomania, spells happiness.*

Intrapsychically, contentment and happiness denote the presentation of unimpeachable credentials in the form of inner defenses which—*for the moment*—are immune from attack by the inner conscience. The immunity is shortlived; consequently happiness is but a series of exceptional and transitory victories in a sea of typical and permanent defeats.

Of course, it is a banal analytic experience to observe that simple release of libidinous or aggressive tension is by no means identical with happiness. Neurotics are quite correct in their negation of happiness in sex proper: they claim that there is nothing more to it than *"release of tension."* They cannot achieve happiness because of their *inability to love* tenderly. There is another argument pointing in the direction of infantile megalomania in happiness. In all experiences of this sort, the time element is freely disregarded. This was pointed out in 1946 by Roheim and myself in our joint paper, "Psychology of Time Perception," (*The Psychoanalytic Quarterly,* 15:190–206, 1946).

If one wishes to be technical, one could distinguish a third subdivision, making the classification read: *happiness, release of tension,* and *satisfaction (contentment).* The latter pertains to having temporarily furnished suitable defenses to the superego. This is visible, for example, in successful writers. The deep *dis*satisfaction felt by the unsuccessful writer when his work is rejected by critics or the public *unconsciously* pertains to the inability to furnish the exhibitionistic defense, *and* to the ineffectiveness of the pseudo-autarchic defense. (See #2, Chapter V.)

All attempts to explain the phenomenon of happiness *without* taking the ego ideal-Daimonion subdivision into account, or considering the superego at all (such attempts have been made) are futile from the start.

Powerful as the superego may be as *generator, promotor, distributor, and bearer* of "bad news" for the battered ego, it still must reckon with its antagonist, the unconscious ego. The latter is the *absorber, mitigator, cushion-the-blow lawyer* of a beleaguered and plagued client. It performs its function remarkably well. If it cannot prevent the succession of blows emanating from the "torture-machine," it at least keeps the client ignorant of the reasons for them and thus spares him the additional pain of self-understanding. *This artificially created ignorance of one's real motivations and punishment* is soothing—*and a limitation of "intelligence."*

This technique can be observed in numerous phenomena. Torturing thoughts and reproaches dispatched by the superego are "scrambled" in transmission and remain unintelligible to the conscious self. The afflicted person casually wonders why that remote or buried fact occurs to him. For example, a patient who prided himself on his intellectual independence could not figure out why he so frequently thought of a recently elected official who did not interest him as a person at all. The dignitary was a party-machine figure who had been cast aside when nominations were in order, and had then risen against the machine and gained the confidence of the voters, who obviously identified themselves with the spurious rebellion of the alleged underdog. Analysis of the "political thought," as the patient called it, revealed an ironic accusation: "You pride yourself on being an independent thinker, but that's a fake. If you had not been slighted by the 'machine' you would have been just as faithful as machine politician as the dignitary in question." No hint of this unflattering characterization became conscious to the patient.

The same applies to "taking the blame for the lesser crime." From the masterpieces of the neurosis, the neurotic symptom, to the banal—as, for example, little "accidents"—the same technique of concealment prevails.

In this category, also, belong the techniques in which "a senseless word, tune, mental picture creeps into my mind." These are discussed at some length, in Chapter X.

Judging from the analytic literature on the subject it must be admitted that additional clarification is needed in the problem of assessing the precise results of analytic therapy in the department of the superego. The general formula seems to be: the superego becomes milder and more "tolerant."

Personally, I doubt the direct applicability of the quality of benevolence to a monster such as the superego, whether the individual's state be that of health or neurosis. I would rather say that psychoanalytic therapy changes the technique of torture. The alleged "benevolence" of the post-analysis superego seems to me to be a mirage, made visible by the failure to differentiate between ego ideal and Daimonion.

To clarify the issue:

1. The technique of torture, meted out by Daimonion, *always* detours to *take in* the ego ideal. "By holding it up like a silent model" (see original Jekels-Bergler formulation, p. 54), the unavoidable discrepancy between the grandiose promises of childhood and the realistic achievements of the adult are mercilessly contrasted, and afterwards penance and guilt are dictated.

Since the ego ideal is *also* an unconscious structure, it is inaccessible to change by *logical* means. In analysis, *affective* living out and working through of the infantile repressed conflict, through transference and resistance, (not to forget the helpful effect of being made to understand the conflict analytically) *achieves a change in the ego ideal.* This serves to dull Daimonion's instrument of torture, for a more realistic ego ideal is one in which discrepancies are less blatant—for the ego.

2. There is agreement that analytic therapy renders the *ego* "*stronger.*" Quite true, but why? The decisive point seems to me the analytic reversability of psychic masochism—in favorable cases. Since psychic masochism is genetically misdirected aggression, which boomerangs against the ego because of guilt and is secondarily libidinized (Freud), analysis can—to some degree—reverse the process. The ego thus possesses an increased store of genuine aggression for use in fighting the superego.

3. The *neurotic corruptability* of the superego—bribed by suffering and depression—is *changed into the incorruptability* of a stern judge in so-called normality. Hence, unconscious abstention ("keeping in repression") from too obvious infantile wishes and defenses becomes more pronounced than it had been in the neurotic state.

Whether or not this really means that the superego becomes "milder," in the idyllic sense of the term, is problematical. During neurosis, the ego smuggled in many defensively cloaked innuendos of pre-Oedipal and Oedipal fantasies in exchange for giving the superego its "cut" in the form of the victim's suffering. In so-called normality, and in health artificially produced through analytic procedure, the superego means "no" when it says "no," and consequently many wishes and conflicts are nipped in the bud.

4. Sublimations are more strongly pronounced in emotional health than in neurosis. Sublimation is *the* masterpiece of health; while the neurotic symptom, according to Freud, is the masterpiece

of neurosis. Sublimation denotes a victory of the ego over the superego (see Table, p. 64 f); and it will withstand for a long period the corrosion of the anti-libidinous inner conscience. Thus the inner Frankenstein's ability to inflict damage is lessened at this point.

5. Genitality, freed from counterfeit-sex, leads to strengthening of the ego, as pointed out in *Neurotic Counterfeit-Sex*.

6. All these restrictions in power, via the instrumentality of the artificially strengthened ego, by no means render the inner torturer helpless. Quite the contrary. Torture continues, but with the restrictions of cultural "normality." Among these restrictions are work, and the thousand unpleasantnesses of reality, freely provided every day, "lousy moods," torturing dreams, "malevolence in trifles," * regrets and reproaches of infinite variety. And there is no escape from the sordid fact that each individual carries his torture machine within himself. "Each with his jealousies and feuds, and sorrows. . . ." (Siegfried Sassoon). One could enlarge on the list: each with his personal grievances, regrets, sordid expectations, imaginary injustices, missed opportunities, not missed hypochondria, worries, etc.

7. The decisive argument against the idyllic, utopian picture of the "benevolent" superego is the fact stressed again and again in this volume: at best, the individual is conceded the *defenses* against his real wishes, never his real wishes.

Human happiness is impeded by more than external obstacles. The inner barrier to happiness—the superego—is impenetrable, cannot be removed or weakened without analytic help, and must simply be accepted as a fixed fact in the human equation, like death. Unfortunately, only a negligible number of people have at their disposal the only corrective measure available—psychoanalysis. And this therapy, with all its immense possibilities, does not provide too much help to many of these people—even in favorable cases— simply because psychic masochism is by no means accepted as the crux of neurosis in scientific circles. I hope (probably without reason) that some day the situation will change. In any case, by applying the precept sketched above, one can, even today, contradict the statement made by William Ewart Gladstone in 1878:

* See *Conflict in Marriage,* Chapter I.

The disease of an evil conscience is beyond the practice of all the physicians of all the countries in the world.

The adherents of many religions have been taught, again and again, that happiness is not the aim of life, and have been told, for a variety of reasons, that a feeling of guilt is inevitable for every human being. This may have been more than a mere device for ensuring fidelity to the individual's church or temple. It may just as well have been based on intuitive understanding of the inner obstacles to happiness.

No more convincing evidence of the misery of life exists than the fact that humans have forged their internal happiness out of—suffering. Psychic masochism is, however, a poor surrogate for *external happiness,* and not exactly a solution to be recommended. On the other hand, this factor cannot be sufficiently stressed: *psychic masochism is a universal human "trait,"* which, though unconsciously synthetically produced, secondarily acquires the propelling force of a perpetuum mobile. Nobody can go through the helplessness of childhood without "acquiring" at least *some* of that poison. Since the poison is subsequently transmuted into an allure, *every human being—in quantitatively differing degrees—becomes "addicted" to psychic masochism.*

Many philosophers have deplored the shortness of life, and the small share of happiness it offers in comparison to the large doses of suffering it entails. If they had been aware of the existence of that inner ogre, the superego, their formulations of regret or pessimism would have been considerably more succinct.

Still, knowledge does help—somewhat. Confronted with *the* enemy of human happiness, one is better off knowing what it is all about than merely fumbling about for a scapegoat. Nor does this awareness necessarily lead to pessimism; knowledge, in this case, is also the potential power to accept reality factors without much ado and without whimpering of the "I feel sorry for myself" variety.

Index

Acting, 66f
  and stagefright, 71
  structural basis of, 67f
  theory of actor's talent, 68
  voyeuristic basis warded off with exhibitionistic defense, 67
Active repetition of passively endured experiences, *see* Unconscious repetition compulsion
Additional factor in oral regression, 49f
"Admission of lesser crime," 5f, 8, 61n, 62f, 68, 70, 77, 79, 83, 90f, 92, 94, 109; *see also* Group of fifty
Aggression, defined as mixture, 13
  all neurotic aggression but pseudo-aggression, 5, 65, 83, 246
  inborn, 104f; *see also* Malice
  inexpressibility of, in infants, ix, 11
  and life and death instincts, 12f
  normal and neurotic aggression, differentiation between, 247
  and pseudo-aggression, 44, 47, 51, 71, 75, 77, 83, 84, 92f, 104, 137f; *see also* Group of fifty
  and psychic masochism, *see* Psychic masochism
  recoiling against the ego, ix
  used as defense, 6, 92, 264f
Alcoholism, 185f
  conscience money in, 186
  defense against the defense, 188
  five layer structure in, 185f
  four phases in, 186f
  ironic lipservice conformity with ego ideal precepts, 186
  psychic microscopy in, 185f
Alibis, unconscious, *see* Defense mechanism
Alysosis, *see* Boredom
"Ambition," 179
Ambivalence, 36f, 165f
  in anal regression, 40f
  conscience money in, 166

Ambivalence—continued
  in cynicism, 120f
  defense against the defense, 166
  fight between "progressive" and "regressive" elements in, 42
  five layer structure in, 166
  ironic lipservice conformity with ego ideal precepts, 166
  oral substratum of, 40f
  problem of, 40f
  psychic microscopy of, 166
  three tributaries to, 42f
Anal regression
  ambivalence in, 40f
  "anal penis," fantasy of, 38, 41
  autarchic fantasies in, 37
  "castration" in, 37
  content of, 42f
  elimination pleasure in, 37
  fight against oral-anal passivity, 42f
  four mechanisms of narcissistic gratification in, 43f
  megalomaniacal fantasies in, 38
  pseudo-aggression in, 41, 51
  pseudo-aggressive countermeasures in, 37
  relation to negative oedipus complex in, 41
  rescue station from oral danger, 37, 41, 47f
  "sadism" in, 37, 51
  structure of, 41f
Analysis, basis of, 1ff
Analysis of superficial layers no substitute for analysis of "basic neurosis," 48
Analyst's prerequisites for analysis of psychic masochism, 56
Analytic "torture chamber," fantasy of, refuted, 81f
Analytic geology, 30
Anticipation tendency in neurotic guilt, 250

Pessimism—continued
   defense against the defense, 134
   five layer structure in, 133f
   ironic lipservice conformity with ego
      ideal precepts, 134
   psychic microscopy, 133
Pessimo-optimism, 130ff
   conscience money in, 134
   defense against the defense, 134
   five layer structure in, 134
   ironic lipservice conformity with ego
      ideal precepts, 134
   psychic microscopy, 133
Phallic regression
   rescue station from oral-anal dan-
      gers, 47
   confused with deeper layers, 50
   see also Oedipus complex
Pierced, fantasy of being, 34; see also
   Septet of baby fears
Pillars of analytic therapy, 2; see also
   Transference, Resistance
Pity, 221f
   conscience money in, 226
   defense against the defense, 226
   different theories, 221
   ironic lipservice conformity with ego
      ideal precepts, 226
   of outdistancing, 222
   psychic microscopy, 225
Playboys, 213f
   conscience money in, 215
   defense against defense, 215
   five layer structure, 215
   ironic lipservice conformity with
      ego ideal precepts, 215
   psychic microscopy, 215
Pleasure, unconsciously derived from
   displeasure, see Psychic masochism
   of being less and less under influ-
      ence of unconscious, acquired in
      analysis, 84
   experienced at libidinous zones, 45f
Poisoned, fear of being, 34
Poor therapeutic results, traced to neglect of psychic masochism, 48

Premature ejaculation, 6, 263, 275
   and transition to aspermia, 276
"Preventive depression," 250
Projection
   in anxiety, 77
   in baby fears, 34
   in love, 151, 193
   in transference, 84f, 87f
Provocation, unconsciously employed
   by psychic masochists, see Psychic
   masochism
Pseudo-aggression, as defense against
   oral-passive tendencies, 6, 14, 41,
      44, 47, 71, 78f, 83, 109ff
   as technique of cashing in on psychic
      masochism, 110
Pseudo-analysis, 49, 55f
Pseudo-boredom, 228f
   conscience money in, 231
   defense against the defense, 231
   five layer structure in, 231
   ironic lipservice conformity with ego
      ideal precepts, 231
   psychic microscopy, 231
Pseudo-humbugs, 20
Psychic masochism
   aggression, boomeranging because of
      guilt, and secondarily libidinized,
      as genetic basis, 47, 53f
   and anxiety, 77f
   analysis of, does not invalidate ac-
      cepted technique, 47
   analyst's prerequisities for analysis
      of, 49
   arrogance of masochist toward
      "weaker," 57
   clinical picture of, 47, 53f
   complexity of, 49f
   deepest of all dangers, 46
   defense mechanism, not id wish, 47
   emotional resistance to analysis of,
      49
   end result of infantile conflict (oral
      regression), 8, 46, 47, 164f
   first priority among unconscious de-
      fense mechanisms, 9ff